D1598687

PAIN AND SHOCK IN AMERICA

Pain and Shock in America

POLITICS, ADVOCACY, AND THE

CONTROVERSIAL TREATMENT OF

PEOPLE WITH DISABILITIES

JAN NISBET

With Contributions by Nancy R. Weiss

BRANDEIS UNIVERSITY PRESS

Waltham, Massachusetts

Brandeis University Press
© 2021 by Jane A. Nisbet
All rights reserved
Manufactured in the United States of America
Typeset in Arnhem by Passumpsic Publishing

For permission to reproduce any of the material in this book,
contact Brandeis University Press, 415 South Street, Waltham MA 02453,
or visit brandeisuniversitypress.com

Library of Congress Cataloging-in-Publication Data
NAMES: Nisbet, Jan, author.
TITLE: Pain and shock in America: politics, advocacy, and the
controversial treatment of people with disabilities / Jan Nisbet,
Nancy R. Weiss; with contributions by Nancy R. Weiss.
DESCRIPTION: Waltham, Massachusetts: Brandeis University Press,
[2021] | Includes bibliographical references and index. | Summary:
"This book is a historical case study of the Judge Rotenberg
Center. It chronicles and analyzes the events and people that
contributed to the inability of the state of Massachusetts to stop
the use of electric shock and other severe forms of punishment on
children and adults with disabilities" — Provided by publisher.
IDENTIFIERS: LCCN 2021030975 (print) | LCCN 2021030976
(ebook) | ISBN 9781684580743 (cloth) | ISBN 9781684580750 (ebook)
SUBJECTS: LCSH: Judge Rotenberg Center. | People with mental
disabilities — Abuse of — Massachusetts — Case studies. | People
with mental disabilities — Behavior modification — Massachusetts
— Case studies. | Electric shock — Government policy —
Massachusetts — Case studies. | Electroconvulsive therapy —
Government policy — Massachusetts — Case studies. | Punishment
— Government policy — Massachusetts — Case studies.
CLASSIFICATION: LCC HV3006.M42 J865 2021 (print) |
LCC HV3006.M42 (ebook) | DDC 362.2/309744—dc23
LC record available at https://lccn.loc.gov/2021030975
LC ebook record available at https://lccn.loc.gov/2021030976

5 4 3 2 1

The Publisher is grateful for the generous contributions
of The International Center for Ethics, Justice and Public Life,
and the Legal Studies Department at Brandeis University
for their support in the publication of this book.

CONTENTS

FOREWORD

Shain M. Neumeier and Lydia X. Z. Brown

"How can this still be happening? What can be done to stop it?"

These two questions, or some variation on them, are the most common reactions people have to hearing that there's a self-described school and treatment program in the United States today that punishes its disabled residents for alleged misbehavior with electric shock. Both of us have heard these questions from countless people we've talked to over the years about the Judge Rotenberg Educational Center (JRC) and its use of aversive behavioral interventions. We ourselves had these same questions when we first learned about the JRC's existence more than a decade ago, which led us to track down, read, and eventually create a public archive of hundreds of articles, investigative reports, and other sources on the subject as part of our ongoing efforts to shut it down.

As the sheer amount of available information would suggest, the answers to these questions are long and complicated. However, in *Pain and Shock in America: Politics, Advocacy, and the Controversial Treatment of People with Disabilities*, Jan Nisbet with contributions by Nancy Weiss provides a detailed account of how JRC has largely succeeded in defending its use of electric shock and other aversive interventions on multiple fronts for nearly fifty years. This book represents the first attempt to tell the full story of the JRC, including the often-forgotten fourteen-year period before it began using its most infamous form of behavior modification.

As disabled self-advocates (who also happen to be lawyers), both of us often read accounts that erase or minimize disabled people's own contributions to and leadership in both disability advocacy work generally and deinstitutionalization work specifically. While this book does focus necessarily on the work of nondisabled parents, lawyers, professionals, and researchers spanning nearly half a century, it also intentionally highlights the hard-fought battles of disabled survivors like Jennifer Msumba and disabled-led advocacy organizations like the Autistic Self Advocacy Network. It also records the pivotal April 2014 hearing where we both gave testimony alongside many other self-advocates—spending our first relationship anniversary drafting the testimony we'd ultimately give before a panel during which one expert questioned whether autistic people like us could even feel pain.

Yet we wonder how much more of our histories have been lost because they were always passed down through oral tradition, unrecorded, in small self-advocacy meet-up groups and whispered between bunks in institutional buildings. We have so much left to learn from disabled ancestors and elders who have survived abuse in the JRC—for at least the last two decades, the vast majority of whom have always been disabled Black and Latinx people—those whose histories and lives are much more readily erased and omitted from our retellings.

It would be easy for other people to wonder why JRC warrants so much study and, more generally, why many of us have focused so much effort on ending the JRC's abuses in particular. After all, it's only one institution, with fewer than three hundred total residents, and there are thousands of other institutions with tens of thousands of other disabled people also subjected to all types of abuse every day. But as you'll read in exacting detail in *Pain and Shock in America*, the rhetoric espoused by JRC's founder and his almost cult-like supporters and the approach that such rhetoric has enabled represent a particularly harmful nexus of ableist beliefs and practices. The JRC's core philosophy is based on the beliefs that our distinguishing traits are inherently incomprehensible, bad, and worth suppressing and therefore that anything people try to do to change us is okay so long as it is framed as treatment. The JRC, like all other institutions and much of the disability services industry overall, treats nondisabled parents' interests and perspectives as interchangeable with, a substitute for, and, more important, more *human* than our own. The JRC's aversive interventions, some of the most overt and extreme forms of disability-specific abuse, represent the logical conclusion of the dehumanization of neurodivergent people. The JRC symbolizes some of the worst manifestations of ableism—and that's why so many of us continue to fight so vehemently against it.

Many disabled activists, advocates, and community organizers have survived similar kinds of trauma, including coercive care, forced treatment, medical experimentation and discrimination, and emotional and psychological abuse. Our community has long forged bonds through these shared experiences of trauma, even across many differences in our identities and experiences. Thus, we feel viscerally the impact of the JRC's abuses—and what it says about how our society thinks about disabled people that those in power have repeatedly refused or failed to shut down the JRC. Stopping the shock and closing the JRC would not end all ableist violence against disabled people, but it would send a powerful message that no other disabled people should ever have to be tortured in the name of treatment again.

At the risk of spoiling the ending to the book, the story of the disability advocacy community's fight against the JRC and its use of aversive interventions is, sadly, not over yet. The JRC and its allies in the medical profession, the legislatures, the courts, and the media could very well undermine, if not undo, all the progress we've made if the past fifty years discussed in the following pages are any indication. Still, we have in fact made progress, and perhaps one day, it will lead to a further reckoning for the JRC's founder, leadership, and apologists. Meaningful accountability and reparations to the survivors will be difficult, if not impossible, to measure or obtain through the legal system that has long defended and upheld ableist violence. But we will keep fighting both inside and outside the courts, the agencies, and the legislatures until every one of us is free.

We imagine what it might be like to live in a world where not only is the JRC part of history, but its practices are completely unimaginable and inconceivable. We might one day teach young people about the unspeakable atrocities committed against disabled people both at the JRC and in other sites of institutionalization and incarceration, at school or through memorials on the grounds where they occurred. We might study how and why our societies and political structures enabled and allowed the horrors that occurred in such sites, as well as and as part of eugenics and genocide, often at deadly intersections of disability and race. And we might study not only the inner workings of the people and systems responsible for those horrors, but also the lives and work of the people who survived and witnessed them and who fought unceasingly to end them. We bear witness to their legacies, and we honor all those people, named and unnamed, who have always struggled toward freedom and who have never stopped dreaming of justice by continuing their work.

ACKNOWLEDGMENTS

Many people contributed to the publication of this book. I thank Brandeis University Press and Brandeis University for publishing this book. Gunnar Dybwad, the founder and former director of the Starr Center at Brandeis University and many Brandeis University students were key players in this narrative. Sue Ramin has been enthusiastic about the book from the beginning and kindly pushed it to the finish line. Lillian Dunaj meticulously reviewed all of the photos, figures, tables, charts, and formatting and provided advice and support throughout the process. Thank you for being great partners.

I acknowledge David Cataneo who edited the entire book, chapter by chapter, version after version. His experience as a newspaper writer and a University of New Hampshire English faculty member was invaluable. More important, he provided encouragement when the words were not flowing and reassured me that rewriting several times is simply part of the process.

Diana Post worked as my research assistant when I was director of the Institute on Disability at the University of New Hampshire. She doggedly contacted individuals and organizations, acquired and filed documents into chronological order, and provided helpful insights throughout. Each time I pull a file and find the required information, I say thank you.

All my colleagues at the Institute on Disability discussed the many features of this book with me over and over. They listened to my frustrations when people were reluctant to tell me their stories on the record. They read early versions and provided useful comments, and, most important, they supported the project with their minds and hearts.

My colleagues Doug Biklen and Wayne Sailor read early versions of the book and provided provocative questions and suggestions. They helped steer me in different directions that ended up enriching the book. Bob Williams reinforced the importance of civil rights protections and provided unending support for the historical significance of the story. Steve Eidelman and Cathy Ficker Terrill read the almost final version of the book and highlighted confusing material and prompted a rearrangement of the text to help tell a more compelling story.

Susan Amster and Brenda Ulrich provided careful legal analyses of the text, helping me to understand and follow copyright law and appropriate legal referencing, and ensure that statements were fair and well documented. Their attention to detail was always impressive. Also, thank you to David Godine and Sara Eisenman who provided me with a better understanding of the book contracting process and the publishing business and gave me sound advice.

Nancy Weiss has been a supportive colleague and writer. She is the first author of the last two chapters of this book and provided helpful comments and insights throughout. Since the first time she visited the Behavior Research Institute, she tirelessly attempted to bring an end to the use of aversives on people with disabilities through publications, establishment of national organizations, petitions and letter-writing campaigns, engagement of the media, and partnerships with self-advocacy organizations. In 2011, while working as the senior vice provost for research at the University of New Hampshire, I put the manuscript in a cardboard box underneath my desk. I simply did not have time to work on it. It sat comfortably there until I returned eight years later to the faculty in 2019. Nancy contacted me in the spring of that year, and asked, "How is the book coming?" We agreed that she would help me with the final chapter, which turned into two. I am sure it would have taken me several more years to find all the information and to understand the recent events involving the formerly Behavior Research Institute, now named the Judge Rotenberg Center.

My husband and reader, John Moeschler, has watched me work on this book for over twenty years and never asked, "When are you going to be finished?" Thank you for that, dear. And my fabulous children —Eddie, Eliot, Kate, and Emily and their spouses and children—were my cheerleaders, always understanding the importance of the task: many, many thanks to you. And thanks to my mother, Jane Colby, who introduced me to children with disabilities and their families and taught me to value our differences and cherish our relationships.

Finally, I acknowledge all the people with disabilities and their families who have struggled to find high-quality education and community services and supports. Many have had to make very difficult choices

ACKNOWLEDGMENTS

and decisions. I also recognize the advocates and self-advocates, families, professionals, administrators, journalists, lawyers, and researchers who worked tirelessly to expose the practices at the center and to push for their cessation. I hope this book tells their stories and recognizes their sacrifices. I could not have written this book without them.

PAIN AND SHOCK IN AMERICA

1 : A LONG STORY

January 2013

Dear FDA,

My name is Jennifer Msumba and I attended the Judge Rotenberg Center. I am writing to ask you to please reconsider your approval of the Graduated Electronic Decelerator (GED) for use on ANY human being. I was placed on the GED about 2 months after arriving. I started out on the GED-1, and during my last few years I was placed on the GED-4. There are so many of us that were tortured with these devices, this "treatment." I believe the reason why more ex-students haven't spoken out is because they are either non-verbal, afraid, or believe that no one cares about us or it will not make a difference. Parents and families that speak and rally in favor of the GED, are not the ones who have to experience it, the pain and anxiety, day after day for years on end.

The GED is harmful, even the GED-1. I was burned many times, and I still have scars on my stomach from being repeatedly shocked there, by the FDA approved GED-1. The electrodes had actually burned into my skin. I experienced long term loss of sensation and numbness in my lower left leg, after getting a shock there. I felt searing pain all the way down to the bottom of my foot and was left with no feeling in my skin from the knee down for about a year . . . Also, I would like you to know that the devices have a tendency to malfunction and go off all by themselves. The Judge Rotenberg Center (JRC) refers to this as a "misapplication." It happened to me and other students so many times I cannot count. Sometimes the GEDs will just start to go off and shock you by themselves. Other times the staff shocked one student but the remote can also set off someone else's device at the same time. I have also gotten accidentally shocked from staff mixing up my device with another student's device, shocking me instead.[1] Then there are the times when staff intentionally misused the GED. I have had staff who became angry with me and started pushing more than one remote at a time, shocking me several places on my body at once. I have had staff intentionally give me shocks for things I didn't do in places like the bus where there was no camera to prove it. I have had numerous staff over my years there threaten me with a GED, antagonize me to try and get me to have a behavior they can then shock me for, merely for the sport of it. Staff can and DO use the GED to scare non-verbal students into doing what they want them to by pretending they are about to shock them. Some even laugh when they do this.

Many of the things I and others get shocked for at JRC were very small things. They would often shock us for things simply because staff found them annoying and they would keep writing therapy notes until our psychologist added it to our program. I got shocked for tic like body movements, for which I have no control over, and which don't hurt me or anybody else. I would be shocked for waving my hand in front of my face for more than 5 seconds, for closing my ears with my fingers, which I do when things get too loud, because I cannot tolerate too much noise. I would be shocked for wrapping my foot around the leg of my chair, for tensing up my body or my fingers, and the list goes on and on. There was a period of time where I and many of the other students were getting shocked for having 5 verbal behaviors in an hour. A verbal *behavior* is a minor behavior like talking to yourself, noises (such as clearing your throat), or talking without permission. Every hour would start a new block. And if you were pinpointed more than 4 times in that hour, on the 5th you would get a shock, and then for EVERY minor verbal behavior after that you would be shocked. If you talked out a 6th time, shock. If you had to go to the bathroom, and you had to go really bad, but you asked more than once, that would be nagging, which is a verbal behavior. And these were the things we were getting shocked for.

. . . I was paralyzed with fear every day. No matter what I did I was doomed. I ask those who read my letter to think to themselves about how often they do some of these things while they are working. Twirl their pens, talk to yourself or think out loud, ask a question to someone nearby, hum a song that's in your head, laugh at something funny in the room. These are things humans do. And they are not harmful. Yet we were being subjected to terrible pain and fear for doing these simple things . . . People NEED to know these things happened . . .

There was a time when I was there that I was on the portion program. This is where JRC starves you as a punishment for having a behavior. For example, my first plan was that for every time I had a minor behavior, such as talking to myself, rocking, wiggling my fingers, I would lose a part of my next meal. My meals came to the classroom cut into tiny pieces and divided into portions inside of a little plastic cup. Every time I had one of these little behaviors, I was forced to stand up and throw one cup away. There were many days I would lose most of my meals. And the hungrier I got, the more frantic and restless my body became. This caused me to have more behaviors like tics and rocking, and in turn I would lose more food. My mind clouded and I could no longer concentrate. I would often become so frustrated from this I would end up hurting myself. At the end of the day, at 7pm, I was offered "LOP" (loss of privilege) food. This was made intentionally to be completely unappetizing. It was ice cold, and it was made up of chicken chunks, mash potato, spinach, and then doused with liver powder, then set to sit in the refrigerator for days. The smell alone made me sick. And I never once was able to eat it, no matter how hungry I got.

Most of us on GED's had to sleep with the devices on. That means locks and straps that get all tangled around you and make it very hard to lay down in a comfortable way. I was very anxious to close my eyes, always fearing a shock for something I might not have even known I did. My fears came true one day, and I was given a GED-4 shock while I was asleep. It was not explained to me why I got this shock. I was terrified and angry. I was crying. I kept asking why? And they kept telling me "No talking out." After a few minutes Monitoring called and told the staff to shock me again for "Loud, repetitive, disruptive talking out." The next day I asked the supervisor why I had gotten that GED. She explained that staff had found a small piece of plastic in my self-care box, which contained my shampoo bottles etc., and that they considered this a hidden weapon. I could not believe it. I did not hide anything in my self-care box. I had not done anything wrong. Yet I was shocked for it . . . That piece of plastic, which I was never shown, had probably broken off of one of the plastic containers inside the box. And I was severely punished for this. After this incident I really stopped sleeping. Every time I closed my eyes they would jump open, anticipating that jolt somewhere in my body.

I truly believe that the judges that approve us for the GED have no idea what it really is like. All they have to go on is what JRC claims. The GED does not feel like a "hard pinch" or a "bee sting." It is a horrible pain that causes your muscles to contract very hard, leaving you sore afterward. I would often have a limp for one or two days after receiving a GED. The devices JRC puts on us are not the same ones they show to the outside world when they let outsiders try the GED. Students wear a different electrode, a long one with 2 metal electrodes that radiate the electricity across a large area.

Besides the physical pain, life with GEDs is a life of constant anxiety. I experienced heart palpitations daily, had a very hard time sleeping and eating, and became paranoid, always wondering if I was about to get shocked and constantly alert in all directions. I eventually became very depressed there and contemplated suicide every night. Now, after having been gone almost 4 years, I am still having nightmares and flashbacks during the day, especially when I hear certain noises that remind me of GEDs and JRC.

I want to mention, similar to many other students, I was also tied to the 4-point restraint board and given multiple shocks for a single behavior. And if I screamed out in fear while on the board, I would be shocked for that as well. I was shocked for behaviors I had no control over, such as tensing up and tic-like body movements. We were always having to watch others getting shocked in the room. Hearing others scream, cry, beg to not be shocked. Students would scream "I'm sorry, No, Please!!" all day. I, like other students, would cringe and feel sick and helpless while watching others getting shocked. I was so anxious about getting shocked that I would many times bang my head just to get it over with. The GED often was the cause of my behavior problems. The students that get shocked the most at JRC are non-verbal. So, they cannot speak up. I feel that just because we were born different, we are not given the same rights to be protected from tortures like the GED.

We are at the mercy of guardians and judges. When I was brought to court to be approved for the GED, I was not told where we were going or why. I was brought into the courtroom wearing a helmet and restraints on my wrists and ankles. I was not questioned by the judge. All he had to go on was my appearance in those restraints, testimony from JRC officials, and charts of provoked behaviors. These behaviors came from being forced to sit in isolation with a straight upright posture, in the center of a hard restraint board, day after day, week after week, for two months. I received no real help and no socialization. For those two months I was not allowed to sit in a chair, at the classroom or residence. I was to sit on the board. Also, JRC provoked me by not allowing me to shower during those two months. Instead of showers, I was bathed tied to a restraint board, naked, while staff washed me, putting their hands all over me. All in front of cameras, where Monitoring watched, including men. Being tied on a restraint board, naked, with my private areas exposed to the staff in the bathroom and the cameras was the most horrible, vulnerable, frightening experience for me. I would scream out "rape, rape!" And these were recorded as major behaviors for me.

When I first arrived at JRC, I was immediately subjected to humiliation and provocation by them forcing me to wear a diaper. I in NO WAY needed or have ever needed a diaper as an adult. I am completely independent in all toilet and hygiene skills. And they knew that. I had NEVER worn a diaper up until that day, except of course when I was a little baby. And that is exactly how they made me feel, like a little baby. I was embarrassed and confused and angry. I took that diaper off constantly. When I would take the diaper off they would mark that down on my chart that they would later show the judge as destructive behavior. I would often get restrained on the 4-point board for taking off the diaper and fighting staff not to make me put it back on. In these ways and more, JRC provoked many behaviors in me that were shown on a chart to the judge. There is no way the judge could know what was provoking my behaviors. JRC told the judges that their program was the only thing that could help me. That theirs is the only last resort treatment.

I was considered a difficult case. I would like you to know that I am doing very well in a new program that is nothing like JRC. I don't get shocked or put in restraints, and I am given help by staff and doctors that I can talk to. I am not drugged up as JRC claims I would be if I left. JRC made no attempt to understand me. Feelings do not matter to JRC and we were specifically not allowed to express them. I felt like an animal test subject there. My new program does not punish me for my problems, that are the result of having Asperger's Syndrome. I have gotten so much better from getting real help instead of constant punishment and pain.

I ask you to please investigate carefully into the GED. The ones that are actually being used on the students, not the samples JRC provides, as I have experienced them to be extremely manipulative in all things. There are no doctors overseeing us with the GED. Every few years they would drive me to a doctor's office near Framingham and not tell me why. In his office he would literally walk in, say hi how are you, and before you can answer he has signed their papers and you are shown the door.

I hope [this] will share a new perspective for you, the perspective of the ones that should matter the most, the human beings on which these devices are being used.

Sincerely,

Jennifer Msumba[2]

THE BEGINNING

On the night of October 19, 1976, two children were playing in the parking lot of the old St. Anthony's School in Providence, Rhode Island. They happened to look in a basement window, then rushed home and told their parents that they saw a man being beaten in the church basement. The parents immediately contacted police. The Providence Police Department report stated, "The children had observed through a window in the basement in the building a white male juvenile handcuffed to a chair in gym shorts being beaten by several adults to the degree that it was leaving red marks. At this time the police went to the window and observed exactly the same treatment to apparently the same child."

The building was leased to the Behavior Research Institute. The police report continued, "At this time we gained entrance to the building by the service man and went to the basement room where the same two subjects were removing restraints from a male juvenile who appeared to be 14 or 15 years of age. We then spoke to James Nussi and Vera DeMarco,[3] who stated that they had written permission from the parents of these children to use physical restraints and slaps. They then showed us two typewritten letters signed by people they claimed were the parents of this child. The letter stated that the center has permission to use physical restraints and also to strike the child on his bare legs and also his buttocks."[4]

One of the students being restrained was William McVeigh, aged 19, who had been at the Behavioral Research Institute (BRI)[5] for less than two weeks. Matthew Israel, founder and director of the center, told police that William was getting "treatment" because he had attacked adult men without cause and pulled their hair until it came out, and the students' parents had signed a waiver that allowed the treatment. The other student being restrained was a 14-year-old Maryland girl who had been placed by the state because she had scratched off part of her nose. She wore a plastic guard to prevent her from gouging off the rest of her nose.[6] Two detectives spoke to Israel, reviewed the consent forms the parents had signed that permitted punishment and restraints, and toured the facility.

A detective concluded in the report, "I did not think it was necessary to bring anyone into the office for investigations. Dr. Israel was more than cooperative with the investigation. He called one of his workers in from home so that we could talk to her and he was open about the activities and did not deny the fact that the incident took place. He further stated that this is a relatively new concept in treating students and there are pro's and con's on the subject."[7] Walker and Ricci concluded that BRI required no further investigation. They could not have predicted the subsequent deaths, investigations, lawsuits, complaints, news stories, advocacy efforts, legislative bills, tax dollars, and state regulations that would involve the BRI over the next forty years.

Two years later, William McVeigh's mother removed him from BRI and explained why in a letter to Israel: "While we are grateful to you for the positive changes your program has made, Billy's most urgent need and primary purpose for attending BRI remains unresolved. Hopefully, someday, just as it appeared in adolescence, it will leave him as he matures. In the meantime, we will continue to seek ways to cope. We feel Billy's basic personality is a beautiful one, and we don't want to jeopardize that in the process of changing one negative behavior (dangerous, as it might be). While we feel that for Billy and others like him behavior modification is a most useful tool for habilitation, we question the inflexibility of it as it was practiced in Billy's program. We felt a 'second order change' was certainly very long overdue when the aversives had no measurable effects, even in the severity that they were practiced in this case."[8]

The incident in the church basement is just one of many involving the Behavior Research Institute, later renamed the Judge Rotenberg Center. This book is a historical case study of BRI that chronicles and analyzes events and people involved with the center for over forty years. The story involves Rhode Island, Massachusetts, New York, Michigan, New Mexico, and other states that became entangled in lawsuits and complaints about BRI's practices. The story is long, complicated, and filled with questions about society and its ability to care about, protect, and support the most vulnerable citizens. It is a story that calls into question the degree to which people who do not have disabilities can separate themselves from those who do, allowing painful interventions that they themselves would not likely tolerate.

Professionals in the fields of psychology, education, and disability studies have debated the use of aversive interventions (procedures that are painful, dehumanizing, or cause psychological or emotional harm for the purpose of controlling behaviors) such as those used at BRI. Lawyers have filed complaints and lawsuits to support the use of "aversives," and other attorneys and advocates have filed complaints and lawsuits to ban them. Legislators have passed bills outlawing the use of painful procedures to control behaviors, and legislators have passed bills permitting them. Human service agencies have restricted their use, and other human service agencies have sanctioned their use. Scientists have written hundreds of articles supporting them, and scientists have written hundreds of articles arguing against them. Bureaucrats have lost their jobs trying to limit them, and bureaucrats have lost their jobs permitting them. People with disabilities have lost their lives after being exposed to them, and others, some would say, have lived their lives because of them. There are families who believe deeply in the need to use painful procedures to control their children with dramatically harmful or dangerous behavior. There are others who believe the techniques used at BRI are torture.

Some of the decisions about the use of these procedures are informed ones; others are made without understanding the extent and nature of the punishment used. BRI welcomed all children and adults with severe behavior disorders with the assurance that students would not be drugged, and for many, this was a welcome relief from the overuse of psychotropic medications and other drugs administered to children and adults with serious behavior disorders. Many students had been repeatedly rejected from many other programs, and for some, ending up at BRI was considered to be life-saving. Parents reported that their sons and daughters were so self-injurious that they feared for their children's lives. Placement at BRI was never an easy choice. But lacking an alternative that offered affordable, humane, and evidenced-based interventions, with a lack of skilled professionals and appropriate programs, it was often the only choice available. This is the essence of this story. Most of these families have children excluded from educational and treatment programs because of the severe nature of their behaviors and have challenged or exhausted the existing systems of education and human services. For most of the families, placement at BRI was referred to as a last resort.

Approximately six states send children and young adults to JRC. In 2007, New York and the District of Columbia sent the largest numbers of students. In 2014, California, Connecticut, Delaware, Maine, Massachusetts, New York, New Hampshire, New Jersey, Pennsylvania, Rhode Island, and Virginia funded placement of children or adults at JRC.[9] In 2007, residents from New York made up 60 percent of the enrollment,[10] and New York continues to send and fund the majority of people housed at this facility. Over time, the student body of 234 has expanded to include not only those with developmental disabilities and autism but also students with emotional disabilities, some of whom have been in the juvenile justice, foster care, and mental health systems. In 2007, the annual cost of placing each student was approximately $220,000. In 2020, the cost was $277,915.[11] Reports commissioned by the New York Department of Education cite numerous problems associated with JRC treatment practices, but the state continues to send students to the center.[12] One of the perplexing questions is why they do so. Do the state of New York and the District of Columbia have a disproportionately high number of individuals with severe behavior disorders? Or is there another answer, this one related to the capacity of state and service systems to support people with challenging behaviors?

The Judge Rotenberg Center provides a lens through which we can understand the societal issues facing people with disabilities and their families. It is an extreme lens. We have laws that protect animals from cruel and unusual punishment, even if owners claim they are training their pets. But the use of pain to control humans is not forbidden if it is considered "therapy" or "treatment." Oversight by federal agencies is limited. Appeals to the U.S. Department of Justice to investigate civil rights violations of people with disabilities have failed. Although the Department of Justice announced an investigation of JRC in February 2010 in response to a letter signed by thirty-one disability organizations and the investigation was conducted, no reports or outcomes from the investigation were ever made public, and no action was taken to restrict the use of painful procedures.

DR. HERB LOVETT'S DEATH MOTIVATES A CLOSER LOOK AT THE HISTORY OF BRI

I decided to write a book about the use of aversive interventions around 1998, when there were attempts to close the Judge Rotenberg Center located in Canton, Massachusetts. The BRI had moved from Providence, Rhode Island, to Canton, it had changed its name to the Judge Rotenberg Center, honoring the judge who had permitted use of the aversive behavioral techniques for many years. In 1998 I was the director of the Institute on Disability at the University of New Hampshire. I also had just finished a term as the president of the board of directors of The Association for Persons with Severe Handicaps (TASH),[13] which developed a resolution opposing the use of all aversive procedures. My friend and colleague, Herb Lovett, the author of *Cognitive Counseling and Persons with Special Needs* (1985) and *Learning to Listen: Positive Approaches and People with Difficult Behavior* (1996), and an ardent opponent of the aversive practices used at BRI, had recently died in a car accident. He believed that "people with severe reputations[14] are our teachers if we are wise enough to learn from them. Their behavior—protests and civil disobedience if you like—are often telling us: you are not giving me the help I need; you are hurting me; your ideas may be good but your actions aren't; and you can do better."[15] A subtle, intelligent, and wickedly funny man, he wrote and gave presentations throughout the United States and the rest of the world that advised family members and practitioners that communication and respect, as well as positive behavior supports, were the foundations of successful treatment or therapy. The impact of his untimely death in March 1998 and the successful lawsuit brought by BRI against the former Massachusetts commissioner of mental retardation, Philip Campbell, prompted me to explore why the center remained open despite intense efforts by highly regarded human service professionals to close it.

I first learned about BRI in 1981 when I attended an Autism Society of America (ASA) meeting in Boston as a graduate student in the Department of Behavioral Disabilities at the University of Wisconsin–Madison. Lou Brown, a professor active in deinstitutionalization and advancing exemplary educational practices for students with the most severe disabilities, was my mentor and advised me to attend. Connie and Harvey Lapin, parents of a child with autism and active members of ASA, had traveled to Boston from California. They were furious that BRI was allowed in the exhibition area, a hall filled with vendors selling books and videos, providing information on programs, and displaying emerging technologies. Connie, attractive, articulate, and vivacious, and trained as a speech therapist, was outspoken against the treatment their son, Shawn, had received at BRI. Harvey, a dentist, energetic, fast-talking, and equally outspoken, relentlessly pursued ways to stop the use of aversive procedures in California and nationwide. It was the first time I learned that these procedures were being used.

The Lapins, in their efforts to care for Shawn, with the support of another future adversary of BRI, Anne Donnellan,[16] had recruited Matthew Israel, the director of BRI, to come to California to develop a program in which their son was later enrolled. Born in 1968, Shawn appeared to be a healthy, happy child. "He had words, he crawled early, and walked early. And then one day at 13 months, he dropped out," Connie said. "He cried, he screamed, I couldn't hold him. There was no sleeping, no information, no support, and no help. We had locks on the refrigerator because in the middle of the night, Shawn would get into everything." Like other parents of children with autism and related disabilities all over the country, the Lapins sought help and support.

A program similar to BRI in Massachusetts was started in Southern California in 1971 by Judy Weber,[17] mother of a young son with autism, Tobin. Like the Lapins, she was seeking treatment for his behaviors. Weber visited Israel's program in Providence, and with several other families, she tried to replicate the school in Northridge, California, also naming it the Behavioral Research Institute and hiring Israel as the consulting psychologist. The Lapins enrolled Shawn in this new residential behavioral program that relied on the same punishment techniques used at BRI-Providence. But Connie and Harvey Lapin quickly removed Shawn when they discovered bruises on the bottoms of his feet, the result of pinching, a form of punishment that was part of his treatment. Over the next two decades, the Lapins worked to ensure that other children would not receive the same treatment as Shawn. They advocated for nonpunitive approaches to behavioral problems, referred to as positive behavior supports (PBS), and helped to start the California-based Jay Nolan Center in 1975, a community services organization committed to positive approaches and individualized services and supports. Now in his 50s, Shawn lives and works in the community with support and services.[18]

The 1981 Boston autism conference took place at a time when a wide range of behavior modification procedures were being used in educational and residential settings for people with autism and other developmental disabilities. Many articles reported that these procedures, which involved both positive and negative reinforcement and punishment, reduced problem behaviors and provided the foundation for skills development. Universities across the country were then teaching, and continue to teach, techniques that involve a systematic approach to analyzing antecedents, behaviors, consequences, reinforcers, and punishers, often referred to as applied behavioral analysis. The idea behind these approaches was to identify the things that happened before and after the actual behavior that tended to elicit support or reinforce the difficult behavior. B. F. Skinner, a Harvard professor and founder of the approach to human behavior sometimes known as radical behaviorism, coined the term *operant conditioning* to describe conditioning in which the desired behavior or increasingly closer approximations to it are followed by a rewarding or reinforcing stimulus.[19] Skinner considered operant conditioning fundamental to behavior modification and rejected "unobservable phenomena," such as cognition or emotions, that served as the basis of psychoanalysis.

He believed that humans act in reaction to external stimuli in the environment and that these reactions over time are the basis for developing behavior. Many educators adopted his techniques to teach people with disabilities. Skinner, widely known as the inventor of the operant conditioning chamber, or the Skinner Box, which he used to train pigeons, rats, and humans, is considered to be one of the most influential psychologists of the twentieth century. Skinner was one of Israel's professors at Harvard, where he received his PhD in 1960 after completing his dissertation, "Variably Blurred Prompting in the Analysis of Paired-Associate Learning."[20]

Soon after the 1981 Boston autism conference ended, concern grew nationally about the painful aversive procedures used at BRI. Advocacy organizations such as The Association for Persons with Severe Handicaps (TASH), United Cerebral Palsy, National Association of Protection and Advocacy Services (NAPAS), the Association for Retarded Citizens (ARC),[21] state agencies, and others filed complaints and held press conferences to speak out about the practices. Newspapers and television documented treatment techniques and attempts to close the facility. Over the next decades, Oprah Winfrey, Barbara Walters, Connie Chung, and the *Boston Globe*, among others, covered BRI's use of aversive procedures. Nevertheless, some parents of children who lived at BRI were, and remain, its strongest defenders. The Reverend Deacon Ricardo Mesa, father of Nicole, a young woman who attended JRC, exemplifies this sentiment. In a 2006 editorial in the *Boston Globe* he wrote, "Nicole attended top behavioral schools and was treated with drug and behavioral therapy without success. After consultation with our neurologist and judicial approval, she began skin shock therapy at the Judge Rotenberg Center. After two days, there was a reduction of self-inflicted punches to her eyes and head from 1,400 per week to one every three to five weeks. She is improving and spends her days learning, communicating, and developing healthier behaviors. Our kids are one punch away from going blind or killing themselves, and we need effective treatments that work quickly with minimal side effects. It would be a terrible injustice to deprive a child of such an effective treatment, simply because it makes some adults feel more comfortable."[22]

I have read and heard many heartfelt statements like this from families who have placed their children at JRC. I also have letters and testimonies from families filled with pain and contempt who protest the techniques. When people in the field heard that I was writing this book, boxes smelling of mold, probably from being stored in garages and basements, arrived in my mail. Some had return addresses; others did not. The boxes were filled with files, transcripts, photographs, letters, educational reports, behavioral records, and newspaper clippings. Supplemented by newspaper and refereed journal articles, books, and Freedom of Information Request documents (which were heavily redacted in many cases) from the National Institutes of Health and the Food and Drug Administration, I tried to make sense of this story. Many people associated with BRI/JRC would not be interviewed. A lawyer who was a key player in the story told me that he had nothing to offer and an interview would violate attorney-client privilege. One mother whose daughter died while attending BRI told me she simply could not relive that period of her life. A staff member previously employed at JRC met me and told his story, but he could not bring himself to sign the permission form I had brought with me that would allow me to use his conversation with me in this book.

BRI AS THE CENTER OF CONTROVERSY

BRI/JRC is not the only place in the country that uses punishment as a means to reduce serious behavioral issues. Some schools, residential facilities, and institutions use it as well. The difference between the programs is the kind of and intensity of the punishments. By definition, an aversive is an unpleasant or painful punishment designed to reduce a behavior. The National Institutes of Health Consensus Conference on the Treatment of Destructive Behaviors (1989) described aversive sensory stimulation in this way:

> Aversive stimulation is presented immediately following occurrence of the target behavior. A disagreeable-tasting substance placed in the subject's mouth may be used as a punishment procedure. This is often used when the behavior is ruminative vomiting, pica, or biting, although bad tasting substances have been used for other behaviors as well. This approach includes mouth-washing (usually with a commercial mouthwash), oral hygiene (which could include teeth brushing or the use of commercial mouthwash), and placing a few drops of lemon juice, pepper sauce, or Tabasco sauce in the person's

mouth. Other forms include using a device that dispenses a stream of air, water mist (usually dispensed from the type of bottle that is used in misting plants), ammonia salts placed briefly under a person's nose, tickling, or a slap.[23]

NIH also described the use of faradic or nonconvulsant electric shock, overcorrection and positive practice[24] restraint and protective intervention, facial screening, time-out, response cost, verbal reprimand, satiation, extinction,[25] and pharmacological agents. Pain-inducing electric shock is another aversive procedure.

The JRC in Canton is renowned for its use of electric shock delivered through the Graduated Electronic Decelerator (GED).[26] Staff use a remote-control device to deliver an electric shock to individuals with disabilities who are acting out or otherwise acting in a manner that is not approved. Students at this school have received shocks for behaviors as innocuous as taking their eyes off their work, getting out of their seat, failing to maintain a neat appearance, or speaking without having been spoken to. In 1989, a court approved the use of an electric shock helmet for a young man for exhibiting the following behaviors: head shaking, breaking objects, applying pressure to his collarbone, getting out of his seat, getting out of bed, walking or running away from the group, blinking his eyes rapidly, holding his head to his shoulder, leg shaking, and clicking his teeth.[27]

Students carry the batteries that operate the shock device in a backpack and have electrodes attached to different parts of their bodies. Staff members use graduated levels of electric current to shock the child or adult when certain behaviors occur, such as swearing or hitting someone, or self-injury, such as biting or scratching oneself. Other forms of punishment have also been used at the center. Food deprivation, physical restraints, white noise, slapping with a spatula, and facial spraying with ammonia water are some of the techniques that have been described in interviews, court records, newspaper and magazine articles, television reports, court documents, and agency records.

Despite numerous lawsuits, no Massachusetts judge has ordered a permanent stop to these procedures.[28] Permission forms signed by parents and ethics committees have been developed to ensure disclosure and oversight of these aversive procedures. How the ethics committee members get selected and the biases they bring to the decision-making process is also the subject of debate. In February 1995, Massachusetts lawmakers heard testimony for and against this school's continued use of electric shock and other aversive procedures. Under questioning, Matthew Israel, the school's director, conceded that one student had received over 5,000 shocks from the GED in a single day.[29] In his testimony, Israel stated that over a 24-hour period, the student, a teenager who weighed 52 pounds, was subjected to an average of one shock every 16 seconds. During some periods, he was automatically shocked every second if he lifted his hand off a paddle, Israel said. Israel testified that the intent of the frequent electric shock was to "save the student's life."[30] Some families removed their children once they realized what was happening. Other families were unable or unwilling to remove their children because they believed that no other options were available to them. In truth, the physical and mental effects of long-term punitive electric shock on children has not been adequately studied.

There is substantial professional disagreement about whether these techniques are necessary. Alfred Bacotti, the retired director of the state's Glavin Regional Center in Shrewsbury, Massachusetts, believes they are not. Bacotti is an intense man who responded to questions with well-chosen words because at the time of the interview on June 12, 2008, the commonwealth of Massachusetts remained under court order discouraging criticism of JRC.[31] In his conference room overlooking the Glavin grounds, he reported, "We have had people come here after being at JRC. They have not been cured by electric shock. If anything, they have learned not to trust people. We make them feel safe, which sometimes means wearing a helmet or protective clothing and receiving positive reinforcers. It works. It takes time, and careful data collection to know what is working and what is not working. We gave up time-out and punishment years ago." Others from community-based agencies such as Delta Projects based in Dedham, Massachusetts, share Bacotti's experience that individuals with severe behavioral disabilities can be served without the use of electric shock and other aversives. Delta Projects focuses on person-centered services and supports that enable individuals with complex disabilities and life challenges to acquire skills they need to be more independent and engaged in their own lives.

Matthew Israel believes otherwise. He has written and testified repeatedly that for some individuals, no other technique will work. He is ardently opposed to the use of antipsychotic medications regardless of the psychiatric diagnoses of the residents of the facility and says of his critics, "They don't really understand, the students with whom we use the skin shock are students who can't be served anywhere else."[32] Israel, often described as a calm, quiet, and soft-spoken man, remains persistent, adamant, and unquestioning of these techniques despite all the lawsuits and negative media attention. After receiving a Ph.D. in psychology, he started two companies to manufacture "teaching machines" and established two communes. The teaching machine companies were intended to finance the communes but were not successful. It was in one of the communes that he deployed punishment with a noncompliant girl. The 3-year-old, Andrea, would "walk around with a toy broom and whack people over the head. When Andrea was good, Israel took her out for walks. When she misbehaved, he punished her by snapping his finger against her cheek . . . Instead of being an annoyance, Israel said, she became a charming addition to the house."[33] In 1971, he founded BRI in Rhode Island.

The discrepancy between the techniques used at BRI and the non-punitive approaches that Bacotti and others advocated provided the platform for state policymakers to try to stop or decrease the use of aversives at BRI. Many would lose their jobs in the effort. They include Mary Kay Leonard, Massachusetts commissioner of children and families, who was terminated from her position after trying to enforce licensing and certification requirements; and Philip Campbell, Massachusetts commissioner of mental retardation, and his deputy, Mary Cerreto, who, along with several staff members, lost their jobs while attempting the same enforcement. Soon after Leonard, an attorney by training, assumed her position in 1986 as commissioner, she learned of Vincent Milletich, who died after receiving aversives at BRI. He had been in shackles and wore a specially designed helmet that emitted static noise through earphones. The medical examiner who reviewed the case determined that Milletich died of natural causes related to his disability. In fact, all of the coroners who examined the bodies of students who died while attending BRI/JRC concluded that they died of natural causes related to their disability. With respect to Milletich, both Leonard and Campbell believed that aversive procedures at least contributed to the death. Both have expressed their view that if aversives had not been used, Milletich might be alive today. The coroner and court disagreed.

More than thirty years after police investigated the incident at St. Anthony's School in Providence, and after years of regulatory and legal battles in which JRC prevailed, a prank led to renewed scrutiny of its practices. In 2007, two JRC students, 16 and 19 years old, were awakened by staff in the middle of the night at the request of an unknown caller. The caller identified himself as a JRC quality assurance worker who claimed that he had reviewed video recordings and demanded that the students who lived in a JRC group home in Stoughton, Massachusetts, be shocked for behaviors they had allegedly exhibited five hours earlier, which none of the staff on duty had witnessed. Four of the six staff had been employed at JRC for less than three months. Both students were awoken, both insisted they had done nothing wrong and asked to know why there were being shocked. The staff members shocked one of the students twenty-nine times and the other seventy-seven times at the instruction of the caller.[34] When interviewed, the two students

> reported that they were awoken from their sleep when
> they received GED shocks that were administered by staff.
> Each reported receiving additional shocks while strapped to
> a 4-point board in the recreation room. They asked staff what
> they did wrong and were told that they were being punished
> for behaviors they had exhibited during the 9 pm hour. The
> students denied having any problem behaviors during the
> identified time period. At 4:32 am, one of the students told
> staff that he was sweaty, his mouth was dry, blood pressure was
> racing and he felt as though he was about to have a stroke."[35]
> One student was later taken to the hospital for treatment of
> two first-degree burns. Police were notified of the incident on
> August 27, 2007.[36]

Patricia Wen, a reporter for the *Boston Globe*, pieced together the story and reported that staff never checked with anyone before repeatedly shocking the young men. The caller in the middle of the night turned out to be a student who had lived at the JRC-run group home and had run away two weeks earlier. The next morning, the caller's voice was recognized in a review of the surveillance tapes, and he ad-

mitted making the calls and posing as a quality assurance officer because he had had some difficulties with the identified students. At one
point, the staff members did try to call the monitoring staff but were
unable to get service because of problems with their cell phones. The
entire incident was videotaped by automated internal security cameras. After the incident, the students who were shocked complained of
pain related to the applications received and requested that the nursing staff be called. But they were not examined by the nurse until the
following day, when photographs were taken of their injuries.[37]

The staff reported that they were not trained to use the shock devices and were not knowledgeable about reporting abuse. Two of the
staff members present had failed their basic training exams, and two
others were on probation for infractions.[38] Initially the staff misinformed investigators about their actions, but the videotape revealed
that the staff had been aware of the unusual demands to shock students in the middle of the night and communicated with each other
about these concerns throughout the evening. This story compelled
editors of the *Boston Globe*, a newspaper that had long been supporters of JRC, to question the facility's use of aversive procedures for the
first time.

The videotape of the two students receiving shocks that evening
was reviewed by Canton, Massachusetts, police and investigators. Because there was a criminal investigation, the investigating officer specifically told Israel to keep a copy of the videotape.[39] But at a legislative
hearing in January 2008 in Boston on a new version of an anti-aversive
bill, Israel reported that he had destroyed the tape because, he said,
he feared the tape would get into the media. State senator Brian Joyce,
a cosponsor of the bill being heard, said he believed the tapes were
intentionally destroyed and intimated a cover-up was underway. He
asked Attorney General Martha Coakley to investigate. A grand jury
convened, and in May 2008, state police removed an unknown number of files from the JRC. In May 2011, the grand jury indicted Matthew
Israel on charges of being an accessory after the fact and misleading
an investigator or a witness. A week later, on May 25, Israel agreed to
five years of pretrial probation for interfering with an investigation. He
had already announced that he would resign as the director of JRC on
June 1.[40] Glenda Crookes, who had worked at JRC for over twenty years,
starting as a direct care person, took over as executive director after Israel's dismissal.

JRC had bigger concerns than the commonwealth of Massachusetts. In 2010, Mental Disability Rights International issued an urgent appeal to the United Nations Special Rapporteur on Torture in a report: *Torture Not Treatment: Electric Shock and the Long-Term Restraint in the United States on Children and Adults with Disabilities at the Judge Rotenberg Center.*[41] In response to the appeal, Manfred Nowak, the UN special rapporteur, appeared on June 30, 2010, on ABC-TV's *Nightline* and characterized aversive treatment as it is practiced at JRC as torture and urged the United States to act. He said, "Frankly I was shocked when I was reading the report. What I did on the 11th of May was to send an urgent appeal to the United States government asking them to investigate."[42] Nowak had no way of knowing that the U.S. Attorney General's office was already looking into the Judge Rotenberg Center and that there would be no public reports or findings. Why not? The answers lie in the chapters that follow, beginning with the origins of behavioral analysis and founding of BRI in Providence.

2 : HOW WE GOT TO THIS PLACE

The intervention procedures used at JRC can be traced to the origins of behavior analysis. In 1957, the Society for the Experimental Analysis of Behavior was formed by a group of individuals whose research was based in the theory of operant conditioning. This was not appreciated by many research psychologists because of its applied focus, as opposed to the theoretical focus of the premier journals: *Journal of Experimental Psychology* and *Journal of Comparative and Physiological Psychology*. Charles B. Ferster, the founding editor of the new organization's *Journal of Experimental Analysis of Behavior*, had been a student of B. F. Skinner at Harvard, and the initial board of editors included some of the most prolific researchers in behavioral theory at the time: Skinner, Nathan Azrin, Ogden Lindsley, R. J. Herstein, and Murray Sidman. Published articles included research on animals with some application to humans. The purpose and objectives of the society were "to encourage, foster, and promote the advancement of the science of experimental analysis of behavior; the promotion of research in the said science and the increase and diffusion of knowledge of the said science by the conduct of a program of education by meetings, conferences and symposia, and by the publication of journals, papers, periodicals and reports."[1] Articles such as "On the Law of Effects," "Auto-Shaping of a Pigeon's Key Peck," and "Relative and Absolute Strength of Response as a Function of Frequency of Reinforcement," are some of the most frequently cited in today's literature on behavioral theory and applied analysis (Figure 1). This was the beginning of a major paradigm shift in the fields of psychology and education.

In 1967, ten years after its formation, the Society for the Experimental Analysis of Behavior established the *Journal of Applied Behavioral Analysis* (JABA) to provide a forum for articles that applied the theory of behavioral science to socially important problems. Montrose Wolf from the University of Kansas, a center for behavioral research, was the first editor. The initial board of editors of the new journal included Donald Baer, Todd Risley, and Stewart Agras, all well-published

Figure 1. B. F. Skinner in laboratory with pigeon.
Science History Images/Alamy Stock Photo.

behavioral researchers. The journal provided an important vehicle for communicating and disseminating research on how to intervene and change human behavior, including behavioral disorders such as self-injurious behavior, self-stimulation, and rumination, all commonly exhibited by institutionalized people.

Research published in JABA demonstrated that the use of systematic behavioral strategies could change the behavior of individuals. Researchers demonstrated that behaviors are learned as a way of accomplishing what people want or need, that people with autism and developmental disabilities could learn, that their behavior could be changed, and that as a society, we had underestimated their capacity to acquire skills and change challenging behaviors. This research coincided with a period of deinstitutionalization in the United States, and many of the JABA articles were used in testimony about the need for people in institutions to move to community services to emphasize the importance of teaching and systematic instruction, as well as the potential for community placements for people who had spent their lives languishing in institutions. Articles that appeared in the journal included such titles as "Manipulation of Self-Destruction in Three Retarded Children," "The Elimination of Autistic Self-Stimulatory Behavior by Overcorrection," "The Effects and Side-Effects of Punishing the Autistic Behaviors of a Deviant Child," and "A Rapid Method of Toilet Training the Institutionalized Retarded."[2]

Some researchers realized that the technology of behavioral science in itself was not enough. Societal values, the concept of the right to live in and be served in the least restrictive environment, the right to education, and positive behavioral approaches also had to be part of the professional literature. Some maintained their affiliation with JABA but joined an emerging organization, the Association for the Education and Treatment of the Severely and Profoundly Handicapped (AESEPH), founded in 1974 by another group of university professors: Norris Haring, Alice Hayden, Lou Brown, Bob York, Ed Sontag, Wayne Sailor, Diane Bricker, Mark Gold, Richard Whelan, Francis Anderson, Marilyn Cohen, Laura Dennison, and Doug Guess. AESEPH was in part a reaction to the policies of the American Association on Mental Deficiency, the Council on Exceptional Children, the Association for Retarded Citizens, and others that maintained that institutionalization was a necessary part of the continuum of services for people with disabilities. AESEPH was renamed TASH in 1983. Lou Brown, a professor of behavioral disabilities at the University of Wisconsin–Madison, wrote:

We have TASH because in the late 1960s and early 1970s it was abundantly clear to a few parents and professionals that no other organization was addressing the ideological, research, financial, and programmatic rights and needs of people with severe disabilities; the most vulnerable, segregated, abused, neglected, and denied people in our society. The people who were quarantined in horrible institution wards; who were excluded and rejected from public schools by too many of the continuum tolerators; who were confined to segregated activity centers and workshops; and who were quarantined in nursing homes and other unnatural living environments that were certified as acceptable by the ruling professionals.[3]

TASH members, who included parents and family members of people with severe disabilities, rejected institutional and segregated practices and wanted to improve educational practices for students with the most severe disabilities. Sontag, coordinator of special education services in the Madison, Wisconsin, public schools and was later the U.S. director of special education services, and Haring, a professor at the University of Washington, clarified TASH's purpose: "It was our vision in 1974 to create an organization that was unique and would make a difference in the lives of children with moderate, severe, and profound disabilities. We succeeded in establishing a professional community recognized for excellence in the education of these students. The principles under which this organization was established are as viable today as they were then."

Many TASH members were publishing in JABA, but they were also publishing through TASH's own journal, *Journal of The Association of Persons with Severe Handicaps* (JASH; later renamed *Research and Practice for Persons with Severe Disabilities*). TASH was clearly values based. It focused on advancing community inclusion and human worth, as well as sound teaching practices, and it specifically rejected the use of aversives.

This emphasis on values was distinctly different from JABA's emphasis on objective treatment or intervention, based on the science of human behavior. This distinction, at the root of the professional disagreement over the use of aversive interventions, forms the foundation on which BRI has been allowed to operate. Researchers who supported aversive approaches did so because they believed there were data to support their effectiveness, so their use was "based in science." Arguments over the importance of human values were not, it could be argued, based in science and therefore were not entirely relevant. This belief in objectivity taking precedence over human values was described in 1975 by psychologist E. M. Opton, who criticized the treatment of individuals living in psychiatric institutions:

Recent years have witnessed increasing use of the medical metaphor. The language of behavior modification is ideally suited to this defensive operation, for it is abstract enough to include, yet disguise, any exertion of institutional power through reward and punishment . . . The language is useful in distracting the public, the legislature, the judiciary, and perhaps, occasionally, the inmates. But most of all, the language of behavior modification is marvelously suited to soothe the consciences of institutional administrators.[4]

More recently, researchers such as Richard Foxx in his 2005 book chapter, "Severe Aggressive and Self-Destructive Behavior: The Myth of Nonaversive Treatment of Severe Behavior," argued that not all severe behavior problems can be treated exclusively with positive approaches.[5] This position has been used to justify many of the procedures used at BRI/JRC.

RHODE ISLAND: THE EARLY YEARS

Matthew Israel spent his undergraduate and graduate years at Harvard studying behavior modification. In his freshman year, he read B. F. Skinner's *Walden Two*, which described a utopian society based on behavior modification. Israel focused his studies on the topic and after graduation formed the Association for Social Design with the goal of establishing experimental communities committed to Walden Two principles in cities throughout the world.[6] In 1967, he formed an experimental commune in Arlington, Massachusetts, where he practiced behavioral interventions on its members. Eventually the commune disbanded, and another was established in Boston's South End. This commune and the Association for Social Design did not succeed, and Israel decided to apply Skinner's behavioral theories to children with autism and other behavioral disorders.[7]

Soon after, Israel moved to Providence, where he ran a federally funded program at the Patrick I. O'Rourke Children's Center, and in 1970, he started a behavior modification program at the Emma Pendleton Bradley Hospital. When federal dollars ran out at the O'Rourke Center, Israel formed the Behavior Research Institute in 1971 and moved the program to the Fogarty Center, a program for "disturbed children and adolescents."[8] He also established the Behavior Research Institute Camp on Prudence Island off the coast of Rhode Island in

Narragansett Bay. The first residential program began in 1972. Israel describes the history of BRI/JRC on his website:

In the late 1960s I consulted to the Rhode Island Children's Center where I developed a behavior modification program for neglected and dependent children in one of the homes at that Center. In 1970 the director of the Emma Pendleton Bradley Home for Children in Riverside, Rhode Island, invited me to establish its first unit for the treatment for autistic children.

In 1971 I started the Judge Rotenberg Educational Center (JRC) by offering behavioral treatment consultation in the homes of parents of autistic-like children. JRC's first residential program was started in the fall of 1972, within a private home in Cranston, Rhode Island. The program at that time served two adolescent students. One was the schizophrenic child of the parents who lent us a wing of their home to use as the treatment center. From 1971 to 1994, the program was known as Behavior Research Institute.[9]

Matthew Rossi was the parent who in 1972 offered his home and summer camp on Prudence Island to Israel to create a program for two adolescents, one of them Rossi's son, who had schizophrenia. In the early years, Israel did not use electric shock. In 1974 the *Providence Journal* interviewed Israel and reported, "Although a mild electric shock is considered an appropriate punishment in many behavior modification programs, Israel says he prefers not to use this. The most severe punishment allowed at BRI is a slap on the thigh, and this is administered only after parents have been consulted and given their agreement to the action."[10]

Rossi related his early experience with Israel in a letter dated September 9, 1976,[11] to Harvey Lapin, who was working to oppose a bill to provide $250,000 to a program associated with BRI in California.[12]

I first became acquainted with Dr. Matthew Israel in 1972. At that time, he was supposedly working with children with emotional problems. I made available to him in the fall of 1971 my house over my office of 5,000 sq. ft.[13] We were living here because my son — age 20 years at that time — was stricken at childhood, about age 3 years, with what you would classify as autism, later was what would become classified as schizophrenia. Dr. Israel and his staff operated both a day care treatment center from my home and a residential center for my child and one other boy age 18 yrs. During the summer of the same year he was allowed to use another property of mine on Prudence Island RI of 800 acres and several buildings. The use of my home and camp was at no cost to Dr. Israel and in return the treatment of my son was to be at no cost to me. I supplied all utilities and there was no rent on the properties to him or his group. Specific incidences: at the day treatment or residential center on the main land.

1) A parent came unexpectedly one day and found his daughter at age 15 years being held by the hair against a wall. The parent removed his daughter from day care and did not complain.

2) His staff split up because of disagreement of therapy but he would displace the ones who disagreed with others who were eager for the so-called experience and training.

At the camp:

1) A closet was padded on 3 sides and 1" holes made in the upper panel of door for ventilation. Children who did not conform were put in closet including my own. Filing cabinets were used for the same purpose. Because I did not believe this had its place in behavior modification I removed my son from the camp and took him back home with me.

2) At Camp a pigeon (bird) was also to be treated by behavior modification, however the bird was not fed and died. This was explained by the assumption that the building was damp and he died because of pneumonia.

I know that my son did not die from his treatment in any way, but I certainly know he was not helped in any way.

It is my opinion that Dr. Matthew Israel is not the right person to be treating any children in spite of his degrees. I know that his pictures are deleted of the miserable situations and show only the nice things, which nice things have no connection to his treatment. I firmly believe that those treated and particularly the parents are being used by Dr. Israel.[14]

Two years after the founding of the BRI, in February 1973, George Nazareth, head of the Human Rights Committee of the Rhode Island planning and advisory committee on developmental disabilities,[15] wrote a report on BRI.[16] Nazareth had a son with a disability and was active in the Association for Retarded Citizens (ARC). The Human Rights Committee was charged with ensuring that people with developmental disabilities were treated with the same dignity and respect that others were afforded. The planning and advisory committee was authorized in the 1970 federal Developmental Disabilities Act and was responsible for producing an annual plan for services and to provide overall oversight to state agencies providing services. It was advisory in nature and did not have a direct role in licensing and service provision. However, it could make recommendations to the governor and key state agencies, such as the Department of Mental Health and the Department of Education, both of which had separate licensing authority. The committee study lasted four or five months and included interviews and observations of individuals involved in the BRI programs. Nazareth's report noted:

> Lack of written agency program guidelines which limit the use of aversive consequences to only certain specific extreme circumstances and which also provide adequate safeguards for the individuals undergoing such programming is an open invitation for abuse. The Behavior Research Institute admittedly lacked such written guidelines ... Another area of extreme concern to this Human Rights Committee involves the total effects that a rigorous behavior modification program can have on an individual. This is especially true when the individuals are severely handicapped children who may not comprehend the reasons for their use ... On the committee's second visit to the Behavior Research Institute staff members related to this Human Rights Committee how they "successfully eradicated" the intensely destructive behavior of a teenaged boy in their program through the use of an aversive technique (squirt of water in the face). They further related that they have used this squirt of water in the face to eliminate some of this boy's more "subtle" inappropriate behaviors and that at the present time the squirt gun is being used to eliminate his occasional inappropriate laughter. The Human Rights Committee is concerned that, unless specific criteria for determining deviant behaviors are developed, an individual with behaviors of

PAIN AND SHOCK IN AMERICA

questionable deviance might be subjected to a therapy program of excessive intensity merely because his parent or teacher has a low tolerance for the particular behavior exhibited by the individual . . . It is obvious to this Human Rights Committee that the intensive use of behavior modification techniques, especially aversive consequences exert tremendous influence upon the personality of the individuals undergoing the treatment. The public has a right to expect that these powerful behavioral tools will be used only when appropriate and only to the degree of intensity that is necessary and under proper written safeguards.

While concerns were being raised by the Human Rights Committee about the lack of guidelines for behavioral interventions, Judge Michael DeCiantis of the family court ordered the town of Cumberland and the Department of Mental Health to pay the $16,000 tuition for a boy labeled severely emotionally disturbed to attend BRI. The judge was impressed with the before-and-after videos presented in court: "These films show a boy who, before treatment, displayed violent tantrums and who, within a month of the start of the treatment had become cool, calm, collected and a cooperative and enthusiastic learner . . . certainly, the cost of the program, $16,000 a year, is worthwhile if it enables a boy who might otherwise have had to live a vegetable existence in a state mental institution for the rest of his life, to have the possibility of learning to function as a normal person and to live and work in normal circumstances."[17] The use of these videos and the involvement of the family court would be paramount in future litigation in Massachusetts.

As a result of Nazareth's report and allegations by a former BRI employee, a team of experts in the field of applied behavior analysis, led by Richard B. Stuart from the University of British Columbia and the Association for the Advancement of Behavior Therapy, was asked by Rhode Island Mental Health Services for Children and Youth to conduct a site visit to BRI on April 9 and 10, 1975. Stuart and members of his team, Nathan Azrin, Todd Risley, and Ralph Schwitzgebel, were briefed on the department's concerns about possible abuse of emotionally disturbed children and young adults placed at BRI.[18] Each was considered a leader in the field of applied behavioral analysis. In contrast to Nazareth's report, the team issued praise for BRI after its visit but recommended better oversight.

The differences in opinion between these groups reflected what would be future decades of differences between those associated with applied behavioral analysis as objective intervention science (if it works, use it) and those associated with human rights (the use of pain violates basic human rights). Stuart wrote, "Our observation of the program supported your belief that the Institute does indeed offer a high level of service to a most difficult client group. We found the staff to be maximally involved in productive contacts with the youngsters all but one of whom (a child who was in an extended time out) were engaged in individually planned training programs. The programs appeared to be well conceived, the staff well motivated and the children quite content with their participation. The program seems to be succeeding with a population which no other programs have been able to benefit."[19]

Stuart's team recommended formation of a human rights committee, a standardized means of reporting progress, monitoring progress of all treatment, and finally that "alternatives be sought for all physically coercive techniques, especially the finger pinch, hair-pulling, nose-hold, blindfolds, shackles, and extensive time-outs. Where corporal punishment is deemed necessary, such commonly used punishments as spanking should be considered first in preference to the more easily misunderstood and less familiar ones listed."[20]

The Rhode Island Department of Education licensed BRI to conduct a program for emotionally disturbed children for the 1975–76 school year. But from July through September 1976, after a rate hike by BRI, all eleven children[21] who were funded by the Rhode Island Division of Mental Health to attend BRI were transferred by the state to an alternative program, the Behavioral Development Center, in Providence.[22] The founder of this center, Dr. June Groden, had worked closely with Israel in Providence, but their collaboration ended in disagreement over educational practices. Although the transfer meant that the state of Rhode Island no longer funded children at BRI, it continued to be responsible for overseeing licensing requirements for day treatment.[23] This meant the state remained involved with BRI and had to handle complaints against the facility. For example, June Ciric complained to the Rhode Island attorney general when her son, who attended BRI, required hospitalization on June 28, 1978. When she learned that no action would be taken against BRI, she wrote a letter to Governor J. Joseph Garrahy:

From a well-informed source I learned today that the Attorney General of Rhode Island is not going to pursue the maltreatment and subsequent hospitalization of my son, Michael, as a result of aversives received at the Behavior Research Institute in Providence. The reason—no criminal intent. If you remember, Michael was admitted to the Rhode Island Hospital on June 28th with acute cellulitis, blood poisoning of his right arm, a black eye, eight inch black and blue areas on both inner thighs and multiple bruises and lacerations all over his body. The wrist lacerations were caused by the continuous use of police handcuffs.[24] He had lost a great deal of weight because of food deprivation. His condition was described as life threatening and he faced possible amputation of his right arm if he did not respond to antibiotics. The Chief Surgeon, Dr. John Bowen told me this. Hospitalization revealed a large bruise on his scrotum. Mike was ten days on the surgical ward.

If this kind of abuse does not constitute criminality what does? Must one be robbed or raped in Rhode Island before child abuse or assault and battery are evident? If Michael had been admitted to a hospital in that condition from our home, make no mistake, the proper authorities would remove him and we would be charged with abuse. Rhode Island seems to have a nice refinement of the law . . .

Rhode Island Hospital has not yet sent proper medical records to New Jersey. An illegible scrawl from a Dr. MacMillan who does not wish to become involved was received. I was told that Massachusetts Licensing received this from a Dr. Goldstein — "a young male, autistic admitted with slightly irritated wrists." Innocuous to the point one would wonder why he was in the hospital much less on a surgical ward for ten days . . .

You might review the police record of Captain John Laydon, Director of the Juvenile Bureau the night of October 19, 1976. It concerns Billy McVeigh of Albany, N. Y., a student at BRI for a year and a half. His mother removed him when she discovered on an unauthorized visit that his feet had been pinched to hamburger between his toes, insteps, soles and arches . . .

Another parent told me she removed her son, when on an unauthorized visit, she came upon this scene. An eighteen-year-old white girl shackled hand and foot on the kitchen floor, naked, with two therapists beating her, one with a belt buckle and the other with a switch.

You may expect more of the same from BRI. There are two rumored deaths. Stories of physical abuse abound. No visitor or professional will ever see an aversive in action. A New Jersey social worker told me she specifically asked to see an aversive in action. She was told it would make the therapists too uncomfortable. She was escorted everywhere on her visit to BRI. Therapists require no college degree, two weeks on the job training qualifies them.

Aversives are very private affairs. Nakedness is a prerequisite. There is no torn clothing. Can anyone inflect this kind of torture on a handcuffed, tied down, naked child in a rational unimpassioned manner? I think only the psychopathic. Both Billy and Michael, who never experienced a grand mal seizure before attendance at BRI, are now on anticonvulsants for the next five years. Billy experienced his first a week after removal from BRI. Mike had five since he came home. I believe Mike was admitted to Rhode Island Hospital with a history of seizures, there were taped tongue depressors over his bed in the hospital. Rhode Island Hospital has not answered with reference to this. Does BRI have a pain index on a scale of one to ten, if five doesn't work, move it up to seven? . . . Are the children submitted to such pain and mental anguish that a grand mal seizure intervenes?

I think you have a snakepit in Providence, operating with impunity from the law. BRI is no longer an abandoned appearing old Catholic school on a back street in Providence. I have alerted every professional and agency involved. Ignorance of the situation does not exist. John Moss, Chairman, Subcommittee on Oversights and Investigations, requested all data and records from BRI on aversives and decelerating consequences from Feb. 6, 1976, to the present. This predates Mike's experience. CBS Los Angeles is active in this issue.

My husband phrased it quite succinctly $38,000 tuition per year is a lot of money for something as "unsophisticated as brute force." Even at $38,000, parents were asked on June 28th of this year to loan him [Matthew Israel] $1,000 each as he cannot provide for more than one hour of one-to-one therapy presently. A person could attend an Ivy League college for four years, have access to the finest staff in the country, and emerge with $10,000 cash for the price of one year at BRI. A million and a half dollars for 40 students' tuition per year might instead make a healthy contribution to medical research in the field of autism.

If aversives or brutality are the criteria necessary for the successful rehabilitation of the autistic, why are these procedures not on film? Why is there no professional assessment of this treatment?

Please forgive the lengthy letter, but perhaps it is definitive. I too fear reprisals, as do anonymous social workers from New Jersey who spoke of the horrors of treatment at BRI in the Newark Star Ledger article caption "Abuse Treatment of Autistic Kids" (date Feb. 6, 1978, reporter Linda Lamondolla).

I realize Rhode Island does not have any children in the program at BRI, the 20 children from your state were removed July, 1976. How can the states involved monitor their children at BRI from such distances?

Who will protect these children? I don't think Caveat Emptor on the BRI letterhead will suffice.[25]

As a result of Ciric's allegations of child abuse, Massachusetts and New Jersey conducted investigations. The New Jersey Department of Health and Human Services found that the allegations were unsubstantiated. Although the investigators did acknowledge that Michael Ciric had been hospitalized with cellulitis as the result of metal handcuffs, they wrote that "the use of aversives at BRI was reasonable and appropriate for the population."[26]

BRI located its administrative offices in Rhode Island for fourteen more years until 1987. In a 1986 letter to Governor Edward DiPrete, Nazareth,[27] then president of the board of directors of the Rhode Island Protection and Advocacy System, admonished the state for licensing BRI even though the state sent no students there:

In 1976 Rhode Island removed all of its children enrolled at BRI after the death of another student. To this day, Rhode Island will not send any Rhode Island autistic person to BRI. Yet Rhode Island continues to license BRI as a special education program serving out-of-state students. At the present time, the States of New York and Massachusetts are taking steps to remove their children from BRI's controversial program.

The Rhode Island public would be outraged if similar procedures as used at BRI were inflicted on helpless animals. How can we stand idly by as helpless children and adults are routinely and systemically inflected with such outrageous punishments within our State?[28]

Nazareth received a letter from Peter Dennehy of the Office of Mental Health Advocate, dated July 24, 1986, stating that BRI's license may not be suspended or revoked under existing Mental Health, Retardation, and Hospitals (MHRH) regulations. Dennehy wrote, "Like you and your board members, I am outraged by some of the Massachusetts findings. Behavioral therapy is an inexact science, but the line between therapy and nonconsensual corporal punishment is not a narrow one. But for our lack of jurisdiction, my office would have initiated formal legal proceedings long ago . . . I recommend that your Board seriously consider commencing formal action in state superior or federal district court. I have no doubt that advocacy agencies both within and without the state will provide assistance."[29]

Piecing together the history of BRI in Rhode Island was not easy. I relied on agency reports, letters from family members and agency officials, interviews, and articles in local newspapers. Several people who had experiences with BRI did not want to be interviewed because they worried about possible legal action against them. However, I was able to determine that the state of Rhode Island quickly understood the problems associated with aversive procedures and removed all Rhode Island residents from BRI with little fanfare. The state was able to provide an alternative program to BRI in part because June Groden was opposed to aversive procedures and opened a school that relied on positive approaches and progressive relaxation procedures. Her program continues to operate today. Parents did not appear to effectively protest the move from BRI to Groden's Behavioral Development Center because in Rhode Island, they had somewhere else to turn.[30] The state removed the children from BRI without having to file a lawsuit or decertify the facility based on licensing violations. There appeared to be little protest by Israel. His relative silence may have been because it was relatively early in the history of BRI and the legal strategies that were later used in California and Massachusetts had not been fully developed. Significantly, Roderick MacLeish, BRI's effective attorney, had not yet been retained. His skills as an aggressive litigator and excellent communicator would protect the interests of BRI for decades.

3 : ENCOURAGED TO EXPAND
TO CALIFORNIA

In 1974, two years before Rhode Island moved its students out of the Providence-based facility, California was attempting to identify successful interventions for children with autism spectrum disorders. Intrigued by the technology of behaviorism and its reported successes in treating children with autism and other behavioral disorders, parents and educators wanted their children to "get better." In order to learn more about the program, Anne Donnellan,[1] a psychologist and an administrator at Los Niños Remedial Center in San Diego, visited Matthew Israel at BRI. In a note to Israel shortly after her visit in August 1974, she wrote, "I just want to take a moment to say a very sincere and hearty thank-you to you and to all of your staff for the most enjoyable visit we had with you. I felt I really learned a lot. Your program is marvelous and I am really glad that I was able to share it with you."[2] This gracious note would become important when Walsh later became BRI's most vocal critic.[3] She later explained her letter: "I did not see any aversive procedures being used, only the typical 'chaining' (the reinforcement of successive elements of an activity involving a series of steps such as eating, dressing, tying one's shoe, etc.) and other teaching strategies."

Anne Donnellan Walsh, Connie and Harvey Lapin, and Jordan and Judy Weber were all involved early in importing BRI's technology to California. The Lapins and Webers had children with disabilities. Like many others initially attracted to BRI's practices and stories of success, Donnellan eventually rejected the approach that relied heavily on the use of aversives in favor of more positive practices. The Lapins, after withdrawing their son from BRI, committed themselves to progressive, community-based, positive behavioral practices for people with autism and other developmental disabilities. They became active supporters of the Jay Nolan Center, a community-based program for children and adults with autism. Donnellan became an international expert on nonaversive interventions and positive behavioral supports.

Judy Weber, however, remained a strong supporter of BRI; in 2005, she married Israel after her first husband died.

The story of BRI requires an understanding of the events that took place in California. As with Rhode Island, piecing together the story was difficult because of the long span of time over which events occurred and the wide variety of players, many of whom left positions and moved during the 1970s and 1980s. Initially, the California disability community seemed enthralled with BRI but soon was skeptical of its practices, with the exception of Judy Weber and her colleagues. BRI in California was eventually renamed "Tobinworld," after Judy Weber's son. After many conflicts with BRI, the state regulated the use of aversives to the point that BRI was unable to use many of them without explicit permission from the state.[4] California's experience helped teach BRI in Rhode Island many important lessons: the need for high-level and aggressive legal representation, political connections, parent advocacy, and court oversight; the importance of the media; and the need to understand the boundaries of state licensing and regulatory authority. BRI would come out of the battle with the California hardened, tactical, and with many more strategies to fight the next battle to survive. These lessons would prove useful in its struggles later in Massachusetts.

BRI GETS STARTED IN CALIFORNIA

Judy and Jordan Weber helped lead the effort to establish BRI in California. Teaming with the Webers was Robert W. Fredricks, president of the National Society for Autistic Children (NSAC) state chapter, who worked with the North Los Angeles County Regional Center (NLCRC) to secure funding for BRI.[5] On June 17, 1975, NSAC passed a resolution to provide $5,000 to help support the first three months of the school's operation and consideration for future funding.[6] Controversy immediately surrounded this model project, including unauthorized use of the NSAC logo. By May 1975, the Los Angeles County Chapter of the California Society for Autistic Children and the National Society for Autistic Children had rescinded their endorsement of BRI. They accused the Webers and other BRI advocates of sending three hundred unauthorized telegrams advocating for funding for BRI to Richard Koch, then the manager of the Community Services Division, California Department of Health.[7] This accusation became particularly contentious when Koch decided to proceed with funding despite resistance from the local NSAC chapter.[8] On November 12, the board of trustees of the NLCRC, which would have administered the contract between the state and BRI, unanimously voted to withdraw its endorsement of the BRI pilot project and directed its executive director to actively oppose its funding by the state. The chapter also urged California's attorney general, Evelle J. Younger, to investigate the unauthorized telegrams.[9] Some early adopters of BRI's methods expressed concerns about the use of aversives and began a countermovement focused on positive practices. Despite these concerns, BRI managed to open its program in Van Nuys in 1976. The program was turned over to parents, who formed a separate corporation and ran it as a cooperative. Judith Weber was the executive director, and Israel served as a consultant.[10]

BRI'S OPPONENTS LEARN FROM
EXPERIENCES IN RHODE ISLAND

Harvey Lapin was diligent in studying BRI's history in Rhode Island in order to inform the policymaking process against BRI in California.[11] In the first year of the Van Nuys program, he and his wife, Connie, removed their son, Shawn, after they discovered bruises on his feet. Over time, the LA County NSAC chapter members who were trying to close BRI and prevent it from expanding its services communicated with government officials in Rhode Island. Lapin and members of NSAC also sought information from past BRI employees in Rhode Island. Some of these employees wrote letters describing their concerns with BRI's employment and treatment practices, which were used as evidence of ongoing problems at the center. One letter stated, "Chris, a deaf boy living at the Children's Center, was punished for lighting matches. For one week, from the time he came in at 9:00 AM until he left at about 4:30 PM he was placed in a box (approximately 3 feet high by 2 feet wide). Chris wore only his underwear and was let out only to go the bathroom and to eat lunch. When the State ride came to get Chris we had to be sure that he was not allowed downstairs and did not see Chris undressed or in the box."[12]

When Weber became executive director of BRI in California in 1976, BRI's newsletter celebrated:

So happy to see the first part of their dream come true! A California Campus of BRI has actually opened, and five children are now attending the day program. The children's ages range from 5 years old to young adults. Two of the children were taken out of a State Mental Hospital and the parents are so grateful because they can now have their children live at home. This is possible because the school is open 6 days a week from 9 am to 5 p.m. The staff has had intensive training with Dr. Israel in behavioral techniques and procedures. The teachers also go into the home and train the parents, so the treatment can be continued at home as well as in the school. The teachers also give the parents training in taking their child to the Doctor or Dentist; this is so important because so many of us need help desperately in this area.

Investigations into BRI's practices began almost immediately. Neighbors of the Van Nuys center reported hearing screams and seeing children running from the residence. This prompted a state inquiry, which revealed that BRI had never applied for licensure and was out of compliance with California law. On November 29, 1976, William Bronston, the medical director for the Department of Developmental Disabilities, led an investigation team assembled by the California Department of Health. He was part of a growing group of professionals and parents in California who opposed the use of aversives. Raised in Hollywood, he was also the son of a major movie producer, Samuel Bronston, and the great nephew of socialist revolutionary Leon Trotsky. After medical school and his residency at the Menninger School of Psychiatry at Topeka State Hospital, he moved to New York, where he served as the main physician for the Black Panther Party.[13] But it was Bronston's experience as a physician at the Willowbrook Institution in New York during the famous deinstitutionalization lawsuit in the early 1970s, described in the book *Willowbrook Wars*, that gave him insight into the importance of programmatic and treatment safeguards.[14] As an investigator, he asked BRI:

> What written policy on control of aversive procedures exists for your program? How do you define aversive interventions? How do you identify behaviors that justify these procedures? What alternative interventions are required

before implementing aversive procedures? How are aversive interventions controlled and who implements these aversive interventions? What parallel procedures to accelerate adaptive or developmentally sound behaviors exist? How is data kept on the use of aversive and parallel procedures? What measures exist for informed consent and the protection and safeguarding of client rights (parent or peer review, professional review, legal screening, etc.)? How is the legal and professional concept of 'least restrictive alternative' measures built into your program design and applied?[15]

The report led to the decision by the Department of Health to deny BRI's application for a license because of the lack of treatment guidelines and protocols. Attorneys, families, experts, and policymakers in many states would ask BRI questions similar to these over and over again for the next thirty years.

BRI had been open in California for only a short time when Robert Fredericks, president of the California Society for Autistic Children and the father of two children with autism, expressed opposition to the licensing of BRI and sought to have the Department of Health deny it a license to operate. He objected to Israel's ignoring state licensing procedures, health and welfare codes, and other statutes. He also informed Katherine Lester, manager of the Los Angeles District of the Department of Health, that Israel's membership in the National Society for Autistic Children had been rescinded by the board of directors. In a letter dated December 28, 1976, to her, he wrote:

> As President of this statewide advocacy organization, I wish to express my dismay at the situation that has developed concerning the potential licensure of the Behavior Research Institute, Inc. as a provider and operator of a community care facility in California. I strenuously object to the issuance of any facility license to B.R.I., Inc. at this time. I am most profoundly concerned with certain activities of B.R.I. and its Executive Director, Matthew L. Israel, both in California and in Rhode Island.
>
> I have in my possession a letter dated October 12, 1976 and signed by Alice M. Baxter, ACSW, and a Senior Casework Supervisor in the Department of Mental Health, Retardation and Hospitals of Rhode Island. In this letter, Ms. Baxter states

that on September 5, 1976, all eleven autistic children funded by Rhode Island were withdrawn from the B.R.I. program in Providence, and transferred to an alternative program. One can draw one's own conclusions from this official action by the Rhode Island authorities, especially in view of the peculiar circumstances of the long-standing non-licensure of B.R.I. by the Department of Mental Health, Retardation and Hospitals of Rhode Island. It is a fact that although the B.R.I. operation has existed in Rhode Island since 1972, it has consistently failed to meet the DMHRH's standards for regular licensure. One can again draw the appropriate conclusion from this fact.

In addition, B.R.I. and Dr. Israel have a less than satisfactory history in California. First, the B.R.I. operation in Van Nuys opened on April 30, 1976, without applying to your office for licensure. It was not until late June 1976, when your Valley field office responded to a neighbor's complaint, and an investigator was sent to the B.R.I. facility in Van Nuys, that an application was filed. This non-compliance with the Health and Welfare Code of this State does not impress me as proper conduct for any provider of community care services.

With regard to Dr. Israel himself, I again find that serious questions arise concerning his compliance with California statutes. On October 16, 1976, Dr. Israel appeared at his own written request before the Board of Directors of the National Society for Autistic Children in New York. As Secretary of NSAC, I was present at that event. During his presentation, Dr. Israel was asked by one Director to describe his function in the B.R.I program in Van Nuys, California. Dr. Israel answered that he was "clinical director of treatment." Dr. Israel's signed Statement and Designation of Foreign Corporation No. 752341, dated August 15, 1975 on file in the Office of the Secretary of State in Sacramento clearly states the purpose of B.R.I. of applying Behavior Modification as treatment of autistic children. Section 2903 of the Business and Professions Code of California clearly defines as practice of psychology the rendering of treatment by Behavior Modification, and if this is done without possessing a valid California License as a Psychologist for salary or fee, it is a misdemeanor.

Dr. Israel, although his program opened on April 30, 1976,

in California, only applied for a license as a Psychologist on October 25, 1976, some nine days after he had been criticized for apparently practicing in California by the NSAC Board. I find this pattern of behavior, namely ignoring California's statutes governing facility and personal licensure, to be most objectionable. Because both B.R.I. and Dr. Israel have a long record of operation in Rhode Island, it is difficult for me to see that a plea of naiveté concerning such licensing requirement is valid.

As you may already know, the Board of Directors of NSAC, by a vote of nine ayes, two nays and one abstention, voted on December 27, 1976, to remove Dr. Matthew L. Israel from membership in the National Society for Autistic children. These Directors of NSAC are geographically distributed over the nation. Furthermore, they acted on the recommendation of NSAC's Professional Advisory Board, who concluded that to their satisfaction, Dr. Israel was practicing without obtaining a California license, and had admitted to operating a facility without applying for licensure in a timely manner.

Also there are additional circumstances in Rhode Island, of which you may be aware, that appear to mandate a delay in any decision to license B.R.I. in this State. Independently, however, I feel that the record here in California and the licensure difficulties of B.R.I. in Rhode Island warrant a denial of licensure at this time. As a taxpayer and father of two autistic young adults, I resent the ignorance of California Law exhibited here. I question whether any person or entity with such a past record can be trusted to obey laws in the future."[16]

Concern about BRI's clinical practices and the use of aversives was now moving beyond California. The NSAC directors had terminated Israel's membership. In a letter, Dr. Lapin, now in a leadership position of NSAC, wrote, "This is the first time such action has been taken in our history. It is the feeling of the National Society for Autistic Children that professionals that serve our children should obey the laws and codes that govern their profession."[17] Yet the California Board of Medical Quality Assurance, after conducting an investigation of allegations against Matthew Israel and BRI, concluded, "Based upon the information obtained, the Board was unable to confirm any violations of law related to the practice of Psychology."[18]

On January 17, 1977, Charlene Harrington, deputy director of the California Department of Health, Licensing and Certification Division, sent Israel a strongly worded letter informing him that the BRI program was being denied his application for license to operate a group home for Children:

> There is unsatisfactory evidence that you are "reputable and responsible" in relation to the operation of a licensed facility and/or that you have the ability to comply with applicable regulations. First, you have shown a disregard for the law by operating your program without first obtaining a license from this Department to do so. Your extensive experience with licensing agencies in other states precludes any doubt that you are aware that such program requires licensure . . . Further our correspondence with the Department of Mental Health, Retardation, and Hospitals in Rhode Island, where you operate a similar program, indicates that despite lengthy interaction, they have not been successful in securing your compliance with Rhode Island's licensing standards . . . Our own review of your program has led us to conclude that your use and controls on the use of painful aversives would be considered unsatisfactory by professionals actively engaged in and knowledgeable in the use of aversive therapy on the following grounds: a) the aversive intervenors which you use or evince a willingness to use are unjustifiably harsh; b) there is a lack of meaningful peer review of your choice of treatment; c) pain infliction and other physically coercive techniques are employed when it is not necessary to do so; d) alternatives to the use of painful aversives are not adequately explored; e) individual aversive techniques are continued in use beyond apparent effectiveness; f) painful aversives are used to teach a behavior that the child does not presently have, rather than limited to the purpose of suppressing existing behavior; g) record keeping of the administration and effect of, and the preconditions to the use of aversives are inadequate; h) again, there is inadequate supervision of treatment choice and utilization by qualified staff.[19]

LICENSING AND REGULATIONS DETERMINE
BRI'S FUTURE IN CALIFORNIA

In 1977 California assembly member Gary Hart tried to establish guidelines for the use of aversive procedures in educational settings. The California Department of Education and Board of Education did not back these regulations but did alert school districts of their potential tort liability if they did not appropriately treat their students.[20] State and local officials understood the complexity of the controversies surrounding BRI and were sharing information with one another through official memoranda and letters. In a July 14, 1978, confidential memorandum, Katherine Lester, manager of the Los Angeles Department of Health District Office, briefly summarized the history of BRI in California for Mari Goldman, chief of the Community Care Licensing Branch, Department of Social Services.[21] In her memo she provides a brief history and points out that Israel and BRI had hired former Governor Gerald "Pat" Brown Sr. to represent their appeal for recertification. Retaining a highly visible and high-powered attorney was essential to BRI's survival:

> This memorandum is to bring to your attention the above-named facility which is licensed as a Group Home for Children and Adults, six capacity, subject to Specified Program Flexibility Monitoring: which is stated on the license.
>
> This program and its antecedents are highly controversial and have been in CA since 1975. The program is an outgrowth of similar programs operated by Dr. Matthew Israel, clinical psychologist who runs similar programs in Massachusetts and Rhode Island. The introduction of the program into California was through the efforts of some professional people in the Developmental Services and the National Society for Autistic children. In the initial stages of development of the program (1975) legislation was introduced which would have provided $200,000 for a pilot program. Due in part to intensive lobbying by parents in NSAC who had become actively opposed to the program the legislation was defeated in 1976.
>
> Meanwhile, however, Doctor Israel, with active encouragement from a group of parents of autistic children, brought his program to California and opened on 3/31/76 an

unlicensed facility providing a day care program only. His funding came from Sedgwick (Department of Education) funds plus parental contributions. Doctor Israel's program is strictly behavioral and involves the use of aversive techniques including spanking, pinching, cold showers, etc. in an elaborate program of accelerating and decelerating consequences.

By November of 1976, Health's Legal Affairs determined that the only way that the program could be evaluated was by establishing a team of five experts. The Treatment Division assembled a team under the supervision of Dr. Bill Bronston and an evaluation was conducted in December, 1976. In January of 1977, Dr. Harrington denied the application (for a license) due in part to the Department's decision that guidelines were needed to control the use of aversive techniques. Despite a cease and desist order effective January 31, 1977, the program continued to provide day care for the same children. The parents of the children announced that they reorganized themselves as a cooperative and that they were providing education only (taking advantage of two exceptions in current law and regulation). Meanwhile BRI and Doctor Israel hired former Governor Pat Brown to represent them in their appeal of the denial and in negotiating with Health for both licensure and funding. A special team appointed by Doctor Harrington was asked to prepare guidelines for the use of aversive therapy in licensed programs and BRI was asked to form a new corporation which would exclude Dr. Israel and develop an appropriate program.

When the new BRI of California presented the LA office with a new application in August 1977, one of the members of the new corporation was Mark Adams, an attorney in former Governor [Jerry] Brown's office. Mr. Adams, who is still a member of the BRI Board of Directors, is currently on leave of absence from the law firm to participate in Governor Brown's re-election campaign. Since the proposed guidelines for aversive therapy were still only in draft form, both Moss Nader and Don Hauptman participated in the negotiations and decision to approve a modified program of aversive therapy. At the same time, the Treatment Division approved funding at a level of over $30,000 annually for each child. The license was issued on October 25, 1977.

This office has monitored the program regularly since it opened. I also have participated, along with John McConnell, on the task force writing the guidelines. Ralph Zeledon was chairperson.

Due to new federal and state legislation making it mandatory that Developmental Services and the Department of Education have appropriate guidelines and procedures by 7-31-78 if aversives are to be used, the task force was recently reorganized and has been functioning at an intensive pace with some persons from the Department of Education working on it full time under the leadership of Dr. Bill Bronston (John McConnell is still participating but I did not attend the most recent meeting last week since Jesse and I agree this will be a matter for the Policy Bureau to approve).

On July 11th, Dr. Bronston arranged a visit to BRI so that the Inspector of Developmental Services could personally see the program. Dr. Bronston has requested that this office provide close monitoring and he considers this a top priority matter for the Department of Developmental Services.

At the present moment this office is continuing its normal supervision procedures. A meeting is scheduled to discuss a number of pending issues. No unusual concerns exist. However, because of the great controversy surrounding the program, the high importance placed on it by Developmental Services Department, the involvement of political figures, and because there are still no official guidelines for aversive therapy, I felt you would want to have this background information.

This memo was a warning that pointed out that BRI was represented by a high-powered law firm, employed highly controversial procedures, was organized as a cooperative by supportive families, had strong opposition by other families in the state that successfully defeated legislation that would have provided funding for BRI, had been reviewed by a team of five experts, and despite a cease-and-desist order continued to provide day care for the students. The memo conveyed that despite serious concerns held by the Department of Health and Dr. Bill Bronston, as well as a lack of official guidelines for the uses of aversives, a license to operate was issued in October 1977.

Families with children at BRI were aware that the program was under significant scrutiny, and they were organizing and expressing opposition to potential closure. Jordan Weber (Judy Weber's husband at the time), an attorney in Panorama City, California, out of concern for the future of BRI, wrote to Joseph Bevilacqua, director of the Rhode Island Department of Mental Health, Retardation and Hospitals,[22] and requested that the report about Rhode Island's relationship with BRI be provided to California. Bevilacqua responded that although behavior modification is a recognized and acceptable form of treatment, "we are concerned that Dr. Israel uses such techniques exclusively . . . We do not at this time plan to issue a report on our past relationship with BRI to anyone in California. However, should such a report be required, you may be sure that it will be factual and objective and not based on opinions in any way."[23]

Despite repeated objections by the California Society for Autistic Children, a one-year license was granted to BRI effective October 25, 1977, to operate and maintain a group home for six children and adults ages 6 to 25, subject to specified program monitoring. The local NSAC chapter's resistance to the license prompted a letter-writing campaign by families supportive of BRI to celebrities who supported NSAC's Save Autistic Children Telethon, which was organized by Harvey Lapin, one of the parents who had removed their children from BRI. The supportive BRI family members who signed the letter complained that the money raised by the telethon was supporting the newly formed Jay Nolan Center[24] headed by Gary LaVigna.[25] The founding of the Jay Nolan Center in the middle of the BRI controversy provided an alternative that was focused on community-based services and positive behavioral practices. BRI was not to receive any funds from the telethon. BRI parents argued that the Jay Nolan Center excluded some people with autism, so the public was being misled that pledge money would be spent on all autistic children. On November 10, 1978, executive director Judy Weber and other parents filed a complaint with the Federal Communications Commission arguing unfair practices by WCOP, the station that sponsored the Save Autistic Telethon. The Los Angeles chapter of NSAC issued a letter countering the charges.[26] The issue was later resolved in favor of NSAC and the Jay Nolan Center.[27] The telethon was not required to provide any funding to BRI.

Amid the discussions and arguments among regulators, parents and professionals, and lawyers, BRI's use of aversive interventions was prompting abuse allegations. On November 27, 1978, the California Department of Social Services informed the NLACRC about a 12-year-old with autism, Christopher Hirsch, attending BRI whose feet were pinched for thirty minutes, causing severe bruising and blistering that rendered him incapable of walking. The chief of medical services, Robert Rafael, and Ronald Fairbanks, recommended to the regional center that funding of BRI be immediately discontinued.[28] On January 10, 1979, the center's board of directors voted to discontinue funding placement for clients placed at BRI, concluding that it was seriously jeopardizing the rights, health, safety, and welfare of children at the facility. BRI appealed the decision, and a Fair Hearing, an administration process involving trained hearing officers acting as judges external to the center, was held to review the board's decision on March 14 and 15.[29]

The Hirsch incident was reported more than three months later in the *Los Angeles Times*, March 14, 1979, the day of the hearing.[30] Kathy Corwin, a treatment worker at BRI, told the *Times* that Israel was using the feet pinching technique on Hirsch to teach the boy to stop soiling his pants. The pinching incident was reported to have left Hirsch's feet so badly blistered and swollen that he was unable to wear shoes for several days. Corwin filed a child abuse complaint again Israel with the district attorney's office. The California attorney general's office initiated an investigation, but it was dismissed based on insufficient evidence.[31] In response, Israel described Corwin as "a disgruntled employee making some complaints on television."[32]

Despite these complaints against BRI, the Fair Hearing panel, acknowledging administrative issues, decided in BRI's favor on March 29, 1979. The panel was unable to determine whether the nail pinch was a nonapproved aversive technique but did find "that in general, the programmatic and administration, including accountability, procedural effectiveness and organizational controls at BRI were not sufficiently rigorous."[33] A special permit to provide aversive behavior interventions was issued March 30, 1979, on the condition that BRI hire a full-time, behaviorally trained individual with a doctorate, comply with the program requirements contained in the February 14, 1979, draft of the California Guidelines for the Use of Behavior Interventions to Restore Personal Autonomy, and establish a national review and evaluation team.[34]

Christopher Hirsch was under a court protective order or injunction prohibiting the use of pinching. After the incident at BRI, an Orange County superior court judge awarded temporary custody to his father, Clement Hirsch, a BRI critic, and ordered that the child not be pinched when he returned to the center.[35] After the special permit was granted, the Department of Health wanted to ensure the safety of Christopher and the other children at BRI. Dr. Bronston, medical director of the California Department of Developmental Services, scheduled on-site technical assistance to BRI but was "fundamentally interrupted by a serious finding." He wrote a memorandum in April 27, 1979, to the director of developmental services, David Loberg,[36] describing the situation:

> As you are aware, Chris Hirsch, the child who had previously been under court protective order following the episode where he was heavily bruised during "treatment," was again found to have multiple bruises over his body. This was corroborated by two physicians, one of whom previously examined the boy on the occasion of his first injury.
>
> Jim Macy and Terry Huff [North LA County Regional Center] have assured . . . me that subsequent to the court order prohibiting the use of pinching and related aversive interventions, that members of regional center staff, acting as monitors of BRI, documented pinching going on with Chris in direct violation of the injunction. Yesterday, the second documented episode of bruising was found by the boy's father. The BRI staff indicated that "muscle squeezes" were the cause of the injuries administered as an alternative to pinching. Muscle squeezes were not specifically prohibited by the judge when the intervention was queried in court.
>
> It is my professional opinion (and that of Dr. Rafael) that despite the cursory distinction made by the judge that imposed the injunctive relief on BRI between pinching and muscle squeezes, that there is no essential difference in terms of pain or tissue damage. In fact, if the issue of superficial bruising and trauma to the child was the court's concern, then muscle squeezes, which ordinarily don't show superficially, that causes

bruises can only be seen as a flagrant violation of both the spirit and the intent of the protection order.

Both Pat and I were astounded at the singular lack of recognition on the part of either Matt Israel or Judy Weber of the injunction's meaning. Such lack of judgment or understanding in the unrelenting pursuit of traumatic aversive interventions represents the final demonstration of BRI's inability to be trusted with the kind of social and technical autonomy, which is an absolute prerequisite for the special permit use.

Prior to further discussion of this particular situation, I call your attention to the long history where repeated, if not continuous, efforts on the part of top state and regional leaders to urge the dominant use of positive reinforcement techniques over aversive and the relentless pressure on BRI to establish a truly independent human rights oversight body and safeguard procedures have been consistently ignored by the facility despite lip-service to the contrary.

The pattern of our relations with BRI has become monotonous: an alarm has been raised in relationship to the proceedings in BRI, followed by top level intervention by our Department and leaders in licensing. Promises and entreaties by BRI, associate[d] with their invariable claims of foul play, lack of standard, bias, conflict of interest, always pointing to the state hospital bugaboo as the only alternative available, albeit unacceptable, have become litany. In each of the regular incidences since 1976, apparent resolution and supposed correction has followed, only to be broken by the next episode of suspected or real program irregularities. Each time the same concerns regarding the lack of external accountability of the program, ineptness in providing competent educational approaches and the obsessive use of aversive interventions have been set forth, to no concrete avail. It is, in fact this obsession with using aversives to prove a point that emerges foremost in the agency's value system.

Specifically, the issue is not whether ABI [applied behavioral intervention] is valid and needed in some instances, nor that the children at BRI would not possibly benefit from appropriate individualized use of ABI. The essential issue is that there is no way to separate the child's need from the imposition of ABI by the BRI program regardless of whether alternative measures were equally valid. Further, that the use of ABI in the program's hands poses a violation of the child's rights and has been a clear and evident danger as the lack of common sense and social judgment by BRI is so grossly unreliable.

Having read, discussed and analyzed the Israel April 9 response to the draft guidelines, a clear and evident pattern exists. The insistence and pride in using aversive interventions as a mainstay in the BRI program results in the most diabolical and preposterous propositions and concerns in Israel's April 9 response. The conclusion which I draw is that the child is forced to fit the program, rather than a truly individual program being established for the child. Such a fixed preconception is wholly antagonistic from the approach where issues such as the least restrictive normalizing procedures aimed at social integration and the return of liberty and autonomy to the child govern. This is in direct violation of the philosophy and the principles of the Right to Education law and national court decisions. I am prepared to go into depth personally and with experts to corroborate this opinion.

When Pat and I arrived at BRI this morning, we intended to investigate the finding of injuries to Chris Hirsch and were concerned about the physical status of the other five children. We requested that Dr. Robert Rafael join us. Our intent was to look at each child in an effort to settle the matter regarding the violation of the court order before addressing the original purpose of our visit. Both Weber and Israel's response to Rafael, who they had never seen, was explicitly hostile; not only refusing to allow him to look at the children, but questioning his very presence at their facility. Moreover, when we requested to examine the six children, we were initially refused and each parent and the BRI lawyers contacted in an indelible display of adversary distrust. Such a closed response in the situation adds to my conviction that this program cannot be allowed to serve our clients who, powerless and undefended in BRI, are at high-risk to their safety and well being. We were finally able to examine one boy on the premises and three others, indirectly, late in the afternoon. We were absolutely prohibited from looking at the Hirsch child and the other boy.

Later in the afternoon, Pat and I returned to BRI to try and again consummate our intention to provide technical assistance. We were met with Israel, Weber, and four members of the youthful BRI staff. The usual concessions and agreement to comply were forthcoming. Yet there was not a real sense that the right to education and the real restrictiveness of the BRI program was acknowledged. It is my opinion that, despite verbal agreements, no amount of technical assistance nor formal compliance with our standards, will result in a reliable and safe program. Truly independent oversight is an alien concept to BRI and its importance wholly not understood by either Weber or Israel. Further, it is my opinion that as a result of the violation of the spirit and intent of the court order and the clear breach of discriminating judgment in the management of aversive behavioral interventions that we must immediately call for the cessation of any further sanction of aversives in their hands and pursue measures to see that support is given to contempt proceedings.

I have made contact with relevant leaders in the Department of Education, Los Angeles County School District Department of Special Education, the Director of the State Department of Social Services, the chief investigator for the Department of Social Services, the Assistant District Attorney in Los Angeles in order to inquire about the situation. Pat in turn has not only shared in these discussions but spoken to our Department's lawyer and the client rights advocate. Pat also met with the monitors who witnessed and documented the post-injunction use of pinching on the Hirsch boy. We will supply detailed reports of our empirical findings on the visit and support documents, separately, at your request.

I insist that we take action to terminate our relationship with this program, in all respects, permanently. I recommend immediate withdrawal of all state support with appropriate relocation of our clients on an emergency basis. Any further relation to the guidelines must be seen as inappropriate until this former matter is carried to conclusion.

Bronston's analysis that children had to fit into a program that lacked individualization and external accountability, was inept in providing competent educational approaches, and that obsessively used aversive interventions would be reiterated by regulators and observers from Massachusetts and New York over the next four decades, particularly with the introduction of electric shock as a "treatment." Bronston saw and warned about what was coming.

Bronston's memo and his personal contacts with state and county agency personnel had an impact. The NLACRC appealed the decision to grant BRI a special permit on April 19. David Loberg, director of the California Department of Developmental Services, upheld the regional center's decision to cease funding of BRI on May 11, 1979. The parents and BRI in turn appealed Loberg's decision to California Superior Court in and for the County of Los Angeles.[37] One week earlier, on May 3, a memorandum[38] from Loberg to Marion Woods, director of the California Department of Social Services, requested that the expanded portion of the license of BRI be suspended to stop the sanction of aversive behavior interventions as part of its therapeutic program. The memo offered seven reasons for this recommendation: absence of appropriate assessments, absence of data documenting the need for aversive interventions, blanket permission from parents to use a full array of aversive procedures, the application of aversive interventions for behaviors that were not dangerous but might be embarrassing in public, lack of administrative controls over the use of aversives, acceptance of tissue damage as inevitable, and BRI's deep commitment to the use of aversive behavior interventions.

In this and in future litigation involving BRI, the fact that licensing and program approval were conducted by different state organizations or divisions created confusion and problems. One organization would approve a license and certify that the facility met state rules and regulations, while another would disapprove the services being offered. In this case, the Department of Health, the Department of Social Services, and Los Angeles County Developmental Services were all involved. This confusion created an opportunity for BRI to argue that it was the victim and therefore being mistreated by the state. The decisions against BRI continued, followed by appeals and then more decisions, none of them able to terminate the use of aversives.

Woods agreed to Loberg's request to stop the sanction of aversive procedures, and on May 24, 1979, she informed Judy Weber[39] by letter that the special permit and accompanying letter she had received in March from Mari Goldman, deputy director for Community Care

Licensing, were issued without statutory or regulatory authority and were therefore void from the beginning. She also wrote that "any express or implied, oral or written waiver of statutes or regulations, or other authorization to use aversive therapy at BRI, including but not limited to those issued by Moss Nader of the Department of Health on October, 25, 1977, and Mari Goldman on February 23, 1979, March 22, 1979, March 25, 1979, and March 30, 1979, are hereby rescinded. The department neither has at present nor intends to adopt regulations which would allow the use of aversive therapy in community care facilities in California." With this letter, Woods was notifying BRI that it was not allowed to use aversives even though they had previously been sent letters from other state agencies allowing their use.

The California Department of Social Services continued to investigate abuse allegations reported by parents of children at BRI. One such investigation involved Andrew Carr, who testified that his son, Samuel, had marks on his buttocks from spankings and marks on his inner thighs from pinching.[40] After Carr complained to Weber, Israel allegedly demanded that Carr remove his son. In his affidavit, Carr stated he was concerned about the changes in personnel at BRI. Samuel was moved to the Ray Hammon Home in Riverside, California, where his father reported he was now able to function at "a higher level than before but he appears to be eating much better than when at BRI, he no longer appears frightened nor is he like a machine . . . During Samuel's weekend home visits [from BRI] we observed that he soon reverted to his former behavior, the effects of the treatment was not lasting."[41] While some parents of young people at BRI were opposed to the treatment, other BRI parents were staunch advocates who argued to legislators and state officials that BRI was making a positive difference in their children's lives. Having parents who objected to BRI's aversive practices and others who advocated for them made it difficult for judges to arrive at a workable resolution forbidding the use of painful procedures.

BRI'S LEGAL STRATEGY

BRI threatened litigation following California's May 1979 revocation of its license to use aversives. The law firm of Ball, Hunt, Hart, Brown,[42] and Baerwitz represented BRI and laid the groundwork for successful strategies that would be used in future litigation. BRI's attorney, Albert H. Ebright, wrote a letter on May 31, 1979,[43] to Woods questioning her motives for revoking the special permit:

> The big question is why is this being done. It is not being done for the good of the children at BRI which should be your paramount interest. A brief conversation with any one of the parents of the children there would convince you of that fact. We do not know the motives of you or of your department. However, we contend, and if necessary, we will prove in court, that your conduct and that of your department on this matter is arbitrary, capricious and lacking in due process. Moreover, to the extent permitted by law we will seek attorney's fees and damages should such unlawful conduct continue.

Edmund "Pat" Brown, senior partner at Ball, Hunt, followed with a letter on June 5, 1979, to future Governor Gray Davis, then the executive assistant in Governor Jerry Brown's office. Brown remarked in the letter that Woods's attacks on BRI were "vicious and inexcusable" and recommended "an independent, objective inquiry as to the best thing to do with the six children and the desires of their intelligent parents."[44] Clearly, political and familial connections were being leveraged to support BRI.

On August 6, 1979, the parties agreed that the decision to discontinue the use of aversive procedures would be vacated and the matter of whether aversives would be allowed or disallowed would be revisited.[45] The parties agreed to submit separate legal briefs. The State of California continued to collect statements from personnel knowledgeable about BRI. On August 9,[46] Benjamin N. Calderon, a senior special agent for the Client Protection Services branch of the Department of Social Services, filed an affidavit. He reported witnessing numerous uses of water squirts to the faces of three clients at BRI. As a result of this affidavit, Woods, the director of the California Department of Social Services, again sent a letter to Weber informing BRI that the use of water squirts violated California Administrative Code and any further use of "water squirts, or any other technique involving corporal or unusual punishment, infliction of bodily pain, deprivation of essentials, or any type of degrading or humiliating punishment will result in immediate disciplinary action against the license of BRI, Inc. to operate a community care facility."[47] A return letter from BRI attorney Ebright immediately followed, citing a California decision in the case of *Kate School v. Department of Health*, which set precedent and supported the use of aversives as a therapeutic technique as long as adequate professional supervision and adequate human rights protections were in place.[48] He recommended that the parties sit down and "iron these problems out."[49] With BRI's organized resistance including high-powered attorneys and families arguing for aversives to be permitted, anti-aversive advocates were delivered a harsh blow.

On August 16, 1979, Anne Bersinger, chief of the Community Care Licensing Division in the Department of Social Services, recommended that California once again initiate procedures to revoke BRI's license. Pat Brown, BRI's attorney, made a personal phone call to Woods and requested a nonadversarial meeting to discuss the problems between the Department of Social Services and BRI. Woods rejected that request in a letter to Ebright, Brown's law partner. She believed that the use of aversives violated the licensing regulations[50] that prohibited the use of aversive behavioral interventions.[51] BRI and the State of California were at an impasse.

BRI and its attorneys urged the legislature to get involved. On December 3, 1979, Woods received a letter informing her of a State Assembly Health Committee hearing on the "Use of Aversive Behavior Interventions in Community Care Facilities" scheduled for December 17. Committee chairman Art Torres requested that the Department of Social Services testify as to whether aversive behavior interventions should be used in facilities licensed by the department and, if so, under what conditions.[52] The hearing originated with the earlier Assembly Bill 1919, sponsored by Assemblyman Robert Cline on behalf of BRI in order to allow it to continue to use aversive procedures.[53] The bill was a "highly unusual 'urgency' statute that sought to correct the problems caused by the administrative actions of the state by allowing BRI to continue to use aversive therapy."[54] After testimony by parents, advocates, and agency officials, the bill was sent to an interim committee. One neighbor who lived three doors down from BRI's facility in Northridge said, "The bureaucrats, and professionals don't go to sleep with what we sleep with. They don't know any part of this nightmare . . . They tell us it's a state affair and we should keep out of it . . . We've been told from the beginning to drop it, to forget about it, and we'd be sued if we complained. The state licensing people told us they [BRI] had very powerful attorneys and we didn't have any right to interfere with these kids' rights."[55] The neighbors were referring to the wild and hysterical screams of children. Torres, chairman of the Assembly Health Committee, said it was not a wake or the end of the bill and that there was a need to schedule a hearing "with the hope of developing regulations governing their use."[56]

Consultants who were hired by BRI prepared a background paper that recommended consistent guidelines across departments and argued that "the most effective safeguard against abuse is insistence upon trained staff members who have demonstrated an ability to perform the techniques in an unemotional, objective, and client-oriented manner."[57] It was clear that there would be no unified professional position on whether the use of aversives should be allowed. One group of experts supported the use of aversives as an effective means of controlling behavior. The other group supported positive approaches that did not rely on the affliction of pain. Uninformed legislators did not know who to believe.

The issue before the committee at the December 17 meeting was whether "aversive behavior interventions should be used in community care facilities; whether or not guidelines should regulate aversive programs in all settings, and where within state government the responsibility for regulation should be placed."[58] Reed Martin, a nationally known special education attorney, supported guidelines for aversive interventions. Gary LaVigna, then the executive director of the Jay Nolan Center, and Ole Ivar Lovaas, who was considered one of the fathers of applied behavior analysis and an early user of punishment, also testified to the need for guidelines for aversive procedures. Lovaas's practices had been documented in a *Life* magazine article, "Screams, Slaps and Love: A Surprising, Shocking Treatment Helps Far-Gone Mental Cripples."[59] It was only Adam Maurer, a child and school psychologist and member of the Task Force of Children's Rights, the American Psychological Association (APA), and the Committee to End Violence against the Next Generation, who testified that physically painful aversive techniques were unnecessary and unwise even as a last resort with "special populations of handicapped children." At the end of the hearing, Assemblyman Cline concluded, "There is very little disagreement among the experts as to the efficacy of the use of aversives . . . the problem comes down to licensing and under what conditions." It was clear that aversives and BRI's practices were not going to be banned. Rather, a promulgation of regulations to control and standardize their use proceeded through state approval processes.

Additional allegations of physical abuse of children attending BRI would soon again be reported. On May 1, 1980, Barbara and Gene Ross, Josh and Foumiko Greenfeld,[60] and two witnesses appeared at the Devonshire Division of the Los Angeles Police Department and stated that their respective sons had been physically abused while patients at BRI. The Rosses reported that their son, Daniel, had been a patient at BRI from November 18, 1978, through July 18, 1980:

> On May 8, 1980, Mrs. Ross visited her son at BRI and observed severe bruises on the back of his legs between his buttocks and knees. Mrs. Ross reviewed the record of her son's aversion therapy and noted the record reflected that on April 24, 1980, 174 spanks had been administered. Mrs. Ross expressed her dismay to Judy Weber and was informed that the matter would be looked into. BRI issued a memo explaining that the amount of spanks administered was an error in recording procedures. The memo further explained that the symbol indicating spanks administered actually indicated the number of "adverse" behavioral incidents attributed to their son, rather than the number of spanks.[61]

The Greenfields reported to the police that their son, Noah, was placed at BRI on January 4, 1980:

> During the first week of May 1, 1980, they had occasion to pick up Noah and take him home. At their residence, it was observed that Noah's buttocks bore red lines, bruises, and abrasions (a photo was presented to the officer). The Greenfields stated they complained about the condition to Mrs. Weber who responded that it was unusual, but she would look into the matter. Mrs. Greenfield requested to view the records which indicated the number of times Noah was had been spanked. Mrs. Greenfield's request was denied. The Greenfields withdrew their permission to permit spanking of Noah who was then punished for "adverse" behavior by being placed out in the yard in 100 degree temperature for two to three hour periods.[62]

On June 11, 1980, David Loberg, director of Developmental Disability Services, reversed the decision of the Fair Hearing panel dated

March 29, 1979, and upheld the NLACRC decision to discontinue the purchase of client services from BRI.[63] Soon after, BRI and supportive parents filed an instant amended petition for writ of mandate (a request of the superior or appellate court to direct an administrative body to do something) to vacate Loberg's decision and prevent removal of BRI clients. They were successful. But the Department of Social Services was another significant player and responsible for issuing or denying a license to operate a community care facility and continued to have oversight authority for BRI.

The state continued to conduct unscheduled site visits to ensure that regulations were being followed. A report from the Department of Social Services Community Care Licensing Branch in Los Angeles, dated March 20, 1981, described the findings from an unannounced site visit by evaluators Janice Smith and Patrick Wolberd, who filed a complaint alleging "that one of the residents had received damages from the use of aversives. Further concerns that this particular resident should not have been subjected to some aversives because of a physical condition that required an operation on 2/20/80. Complainant further alleges that resident's medical exam had been delayed in order that the swelling on the back could go down." When they arrived, Smith and Wolberd found two residents in restraints. The restraints were removed from one resident after approximately five minutes; the other resident remained in restraints.[64] BRI was cited for using restraints and reminded that their use at the facility had not been approved and continued to be in violation of Title 22 of the California Administrative Code. Civil penalties of $750 were assessed on April 3, 1981.

Another unannounced site visit took place on April 13, 1981. Three individuals were observed being restrained despite the fact that BRI was not approved for use of restraints.[65] BRI submitted a request to the state for an exception. On May 20, 1981, the Department of Social Services filed a complaint in the Small Claims Division of Los Angeles Judicial District Court for BRI's lack of payment of the civil penalty of $750.[66] Another unannounced site visit by the Department of Social Services occurred on June 5.[67] Again, individuals were in restraints. BRI was cited for this violation and for the lack of a qualified administrator with a doctorate in behavioral sciences, specifically aversive therapy. The facility was given until June 15 to correct this deficiency. The site visits, penalties, and contingencies were adding up. And then there was a death.

Despite oversight and these efforts by the Department of Social Services and amid the unannounced site visits, a 14-year-old student at BRI died. Danny Aswad's death, the first of several involving BRI, brought media coverage that highlighted BRI's practices to the general public. The *Los Angeles Times* reported that on July 18, 1981, Aswad was found dead in his bed in the Northridge group home across from the California State University campus. He was found face down; his legs and left arm were strapped to the bed with plastic cuffs, and his right hand was covered with a sock and tied to the bedpost with a belt-like strap. The staff reported that the straps were used to prevent him from injuring himself and gouging his eyes.[68]

Aswad had been referred for residential placement on April 4, 1979. His parents were born in Lebanon and moved to California before Danny was born. He was diagnosed with "profound mental retardation" and lived with his family until March 1974. His father allegedly left Danny and his two siblings because he could not deal with the situation.[69] School records indicated that Danny was aggressive, hyperactive, and abusive. His mother, Rachael, said that he did not demonstrate these behaviors at home. Perplexed by his behaviors, she had taken him to Czechoslovakia to find a cure in the mud baths and Lebanon to seek religious healing. She removed him from a school after he severely injured himself, then placed him at Pacific State Hospital when she could no longer care for him. Staff there reported that Danny "would give attendants no warning and run head bound into a wall suffering head injuries, throw himself sidewise across objects and injure himself . . . He had continuous screaming and yelling spells most of the day. This boy was found to be the most happy when under medical restraints and became very agitated when not restrained. His mother removed him after a visit when she discovered that he was black and blue, underweight and dressed in oversized clothes. He also had placements at two other facilities. Mother reports none of these behaviors were reported at home."[70]

Deputy district attorney George Oakes, head of the prosecutor's medical-legal section, requested an inquest into Aswad's death. The state investigator said that restraints were not approved for use at BRI and that BRI had broken the law. But the coroner's deputy medical examiner who performed the autopsy told the jury that "it was possible that a child could die from a combination of restraints and aversive therapy but that I don't think I could prove it."[71] John Arterberry, a physician attached to Northridge Hospital who had treated Danny, testified that "Danny fought like a tiger and was a wild kid; and that it was laughable that Oakes could suggest that the Institute's therapy may have contributed to the death."[72] In a unanimous decision, the jury voted that Aswad died of natural causes. Judith Weber, BRI president said, "The truth won out."[73] The coroner's report was not conclusive but "noted that the boy's mental retardation and brain malformation were factors."[74] A coroner's finding of death by natural causes would be repeated in subsequent deaths involving BRI.

CALIFORNIA ATTEMPTS TO REVOKE BRI'S LICENSE

Prompted by Aswad's death, the California Department of Social Services filed a sixty-four-page complaint containing multiple allegations involving numerous clients against BRI.[75] In a settlement with the state, BRI agreed to stop using physical punishments, but the settlement did not end California's monitoring and oversight and investigation responsibilities.

BRI was now operating programs in Massachusetts and California. Both states had regulatory and licensing concerns and were involved in litigation against BRI operating as two separate organizations with two different executive directors, Israel and Weber, respectively. In 1985, four years after Danny Aswad's death, Vincent Milletich, a student at the Massachusetts BRI facility, died while being restrained, and the Massachusetts Office for Children was involved in a contentious battle with BRI. As part of an overall litigation strategy, Kim Murdock, an attorney in the Massachusetts Office of the Attorney General, was seeking information from the California Department of Social Services about its experiences with BRI. Marsha Jacobson, California Department of Social Services staff attorney, summarized BRI's interactions with the department between 1981 and 1986 in a letter to Murdock:

> The Department took action to revoke BRI's license in 1981. On July 26, 1982, the day the administrative hearing was to have started, BRI stipulated to a revocation of their license and DSS

agreed to allow BRI to continue to operate with a probationary license. The probation severely limited BRI's use of its aversive program. The probationary period was successfully completed and after extensive negotiations DSS agreed to issue "waivers and exceptions" to BRI to allow a modified behavior modification program.[76]

In December 1985 BRI applied to operate two additional homes for six children near San Francisco. (At this time BRI was licensed to operate a home for six children in Northridge, CA). The requested licenses were granted in January 1986 subject to the waivers and exceptions issued to these two new facilities and that for the Northridge facility was that Matthew Israel was prohibited from being involved with the clients or their programs. The waivers and exceptions issued to the Northridge facility were modified this year to include the same exclusion.

On April 6, 1986 there was a fire at BRI's Northridge facility. There were numerous problems with BRI's handling of the situation after the fire. Therefore, BRI was issued a provisional license for its replacement facility in Southern California.[77]

BRI's Northridge facility, which housed six residents was burglarized, and then a disgruntled employee set a fire. No one was injured. BRI not only survived but acquired three additional homes and a day school near Oakland in northern California. During 1987 and 1988, a series of incidents reported by the Regional Center of the East Bay, under contract with the Department of Developmental Services to provide services, advocacy, and oversight, involved physical abuse by a BRI staff member.[78] "BRI had hired a man with a history of arrests for attempted murder and burglary convictions. The man struck and injured three clients, two with a belt."[79]

In 1989, California again requested that BRI's license be revoked and renewal denied. Allegations against BRI included (1) its failure to retain an administrator who had knowledge of and the ability to comply with applicable law and regulation; (2) an inability to meet client needs evidenced by several instances of self-injury and aggression toward staff; (3) failure to obtain necessary medical treatment and failure to provide care; (4) failure to provide health-related services; (5) lack of care and supervision; (6) failure to maintain for each client a record of centrally stored medications for one year; (7) failure to report behavioral incidences; (8) failure to present personnel records for review; and (9) other allegations involving food and safety at the facility.

During this period of time, Paul Smith served as a consultant to the state's Attorney General Office to assist in gathering and analyzing information on BRI. He summarized his findings gathered through interviews and record reviews:

> The most generous interpretation of these ratings would result in an overall evaluation that the Behavior Research Institute is not meeting the standards for care, supervision and treatment of its clients, and needs to improve. A generous interpretation of these ratings may not be justified, however. Two of the reasons that a generous interpretation of these ratings may not be justified are: 1) the operational problems signified by these poor ratings have been a source of concern for years, and have resulted in the Department's refusal to renew the facility's license, and 2) facility managers have not demonstrated either the willingness or ability to meet the standards imposed by statute and regulation.[80]

In 1989 there was a four-month administrative hearing in Los Angeles and San Francisco. During this period, the regional centers were not placing individuals at BRI, and parents were withdrawing their sons and daughters who were already there. The decision, which centered on regulations and licensing, helped end BRI's California saga and the use of aversive interventions. Before another scheduled hearing and after a magistrate had ruled that TV cameras would be allowed at the hearing, BRI and the state reached an agreement that "virtually banned all physical aversives, restraints, and meals as rewards or punishments."[81] According to Matthew Israel, the center ultimately agreed to stop using aversives because they could not fight the battle legally.[82] The agreement was made before the hearing was scheduled to take place, in part because of concerns that the presence of a TV camera in the courtroom would have brought BRI's practices into public view. The practices eventually were brought into public view in October 2012, over thirty years later, when a Massachusetts judge ruled that tapes of Andre McCollins being shocked at Israel's center could be shown in court.[83]

Throughout the tumultuous period of the 1970s and 1980s in California, those opposed to the use of aversive interventions were organizing for legislation that would end their use on children with disabilities. In 1990, the California Advisory Commission on Special Education developed policy language that led to legislation, known as the Hughes bill,[84] that was signed into law by Governor Pete Wilson in 1990. The final version of the bill was adopted by the California Board of Education in September 1992 and implemented in May 1993.[85] It required that a student with a serious behavior problem undergo a functional behavior analysis by a behavior intervention case manager, who was required to have training and experience in positive behavior intervention.[86] The interventions could not involve the inflection of pain or trauma.[87] The regulations[88] specified that even in emergencies, interventions may not include release of toxic or unpleasant sprays near the student's face; denying adequate sleep, food, water, shelter, bedding, comfort, or access to bathroom facilities; subjecting the student to verbal abuse, ridicule, or humiliation or cause emotional trauma; use of locked seclusion; impeding adequate supervision of the student; depriving the student of one or more of his or her senses; or employing any device, material, or object that simultaneously immobilized all four extremities (except for emergency prone containment).[89]

This law changed the landscape in California for students with severe behavior disorders. BRI then became known as Tobinworld,[90] a school in northern Glendale, California, that claimed not to employ aversive procedures.[91] The law ensured that children with disabilities in California would not be exposed to the kind of procedures that continued to be used on children with disabilities in Massachusetts. Other states since then have passed similar legislation outlawing aversive interventions. But in Massachusetts, often thought to be a bastion of liberal policies, aversive interventions continue to be used today despite many efforts to outlaw them. BRI learned important lessons from its challenges and controversies in California and used these lessons to make Massachusetts efforts to regulate BRI difficult. Clear battle lines were being drawn by lawyers, judges, the media, legislators, parents, and advocates about the use of aversives.

4 : PUSHING BACK

While California struggled with BRI's practices, Massachusetts was deciding whether it should regulate the use of aversives or outlaw them altogether. The withdrawal of Rhode Island students in 1976 and the licensing battles of BRI in California prompted researchers in the field of applied behavioral analysis to line up and take sides over the use of aversives. Compromise was not on the table: professionals and parents were either for them or against them. A showdown between the two sides was about to take place in the commonwealth of Massachusetts.

Experts in behavioral sciences were lending their analyses to the issue. On the pro-aversive side was Bernard Rimland, a renowned behaviorist with expertise working with children with autism, the director of the San Diego–based Autism Research Institute, the founder of the Autism Society of America, and the father of Mark, a son with autism (Figure 2). In a March 1978 paper, "Risks and Benefits in the Treatment of Autistic Children," he argued that using aversive treatments is similar to surgery in that some pain is necessary to cure an illness or to repair an injured limb.[1] In essence, the ends justify the means. Rimland was specifically referring to Ivar Lovaas, a UCLA faculty member and one of the early founders of applied behavioral analysis who used aversive methods. He wrote:

> They [referring to professionals and parents arguing against the use of aversive interventions] were perfectly willing to have the child "gassed and cut with sharp knives" in the operating room, where severe pain and long-lasting discomfort would be inflicted and the risk of death would be run, when they believed that it was all being done for the child's welfare. How strange it was, then, that they should get upset at the use of far milder, far less dangerous, and far less physically damaging methods by Lovaas and his group, when again it was all being done for the child's best interests.[2]

Figure 2. Bernard Rimland with Carl Peter Lewis, a child with autism.
Photo by Duane Howell/Denver Post via Getty Images.

In the paper, Rimland described how the use of a "hand-held in-ductorium" (known also as a shock stick, zapper, cattle prod, or, more euphemistically, a "tingle stick") helped reduce the aggressive and self-destructive behaviors of two teenagers with disabilities. He also outlined the objections to aversives: ideological opposition, fear of overuse or abuse of them, the belief that they are not helpful, confu-sion between aversive stimuli and punishment, and dread of electric shock. He wrote:

> The point is obvious—no decision, major or minor, whether
> a decision to act or to refrain from acting—is free of risk. The
> risk of harming the child either physically or psychologically
> through the use of aversives should not be taken lightly. On the
> other hand, neither should the risk be taken lightly of hurting
> the child through not using aversives when their use may
> be appropriate—especially when it is recognized that harm
> from the former decision is hypothetical and speculative, as
> compared to the often demonstrable harm from the decision
> not to use aversives . . . Anyone who thinks he is being humane
> or playing it safe by generically prescribing aversives has
> obviously failed to think the matter through clearly. It is not
> that simple.[3]

Rimland's argument that aversives should be cautiously considered and used when appropriate would be used to counter future litigation and attempts by governmental agencies and advocates to intervene, pass regulations or legislation outlawing the use of aversives, or decer-tify BRI and force its closure.

MASSACHUSETTS: FLASHPOINT FOR THE BATTLE

Rhode Island had removed all of its students from BRI in 1976, but Massachusetts students were attending the school in Providence, and thus the commonwealth of Massachusetts was responsible for certifi-cation and approval. Additionally, BRI group homes that housed the children were located in Massachusetts, so students were transported from their homes in Massachusetts to Rhode Island every day. In 1977, the Massachusetts Department of Education began to scrutinize BRI's aversive procedures. Susan Leary, chairwoman of the Massachusetts State Review Board in the Division of Special Education, inquired into

BRI's compliance with state laws and regulations. In response to these inquiries, Israel wrote that the center was in compliance:

Children at BRI are not subjected to cruel, hazardous, abusive treatment, humiliation, or verbal abuse. No child is subjected to corporal punishment. A behavior therapy program is used that does involve certain physical contact consequences to decelerate the bizarre and inappropriate behaviors of severely autistic children. A hierarchy of consequences is used to decelerate self-injurious, other injurious, bizarre, and inappropriate behaviors, in which measures such as a firm "No!" together with regard for appropriate behaviors are used first. Data is scientifically collected and evaluated as to the effectiveness of each step in the hierarchy, and the treatment advances to pre-specified and parent-approved physical-contact consequences only if this data shows that the earlier steps in the hierarchy are not succeeding. The hierarchy is basically as follows:

1) Firm "No ____!" name of behavior and reward for opposite behavior.
2) Token fine and reward for opposite behavior.
3) Spank on buttocks and reward for opposite behavior.
4) Muscle squeeze on shoulder and reward for opposite behavior.
5) Finger squeeze and reward for opposite behavior.
6) Standing time out and reward for opposite behavior.
7) Cool shower and reward for opposite behavior.

We do not regard this behavior therapy procedure as constituting a form of corporal punishment. Food is never denied as a form of punishment.

Children are never secluded in any kind of room or booth, locked or unlocked.[4]

At about the same time that the Massachusetts Department of Education was inquiring into BRI's practices (1977–1979), California denied Israel's application for a license to operate the BRI in Van Nuys. State officials in California, Rhode Island, and Massachusetts were communicating with one another. Jessica Weld of the Massachusetts Division of Special Education received a letter about BRI from Katherine S. Lester of the California Department of Social Services.[5] The carefully worded letter outlined concerns about BRI and documented that the center had been denied a license to operate a Van Nuys facility. Lester wrote that although there was no written report available of the California program review, Weld could contact William Bronston, who conducted the review, to inquire further into its details.

Despite knowledge of BRI's California experience, numerous inquiries, and two site visits, the Massachusetts Department of Education State Review Board granted full approval to BRI effective for one year starting June 1, 1977. Based on the Guidelines for Use of Behavioral Procedures published by the National Association for Retarded Citizens (NARC), the state review board established a committee of five members to report to it on an ongoing basis on the accuracy of BRI's record keeping, implementation of the treatment plan as written, and interpretation of data for the purpose of developing or modifying treatment approaches.[6]

Before BRI's one-year approval lapsed, the Massachusetts Department of Education (DOE) made an unscheduled visit to the center on March 10, 1978. On the whole, the state review board was impressed with the "degree of learning that was in process"[7] but also found major areas of concern and requested a response to these concerns within fifteen working days. The problems centered on the fact that BRI had not applied for a group care license from the Office for Children (OFC), which had licensing authority in the state.[8] The group homes had to be licensed by OFC. The state review board cited the fact that the school was approved by DOE, but that it was not possible under Chapter 766 for the Department of Education to place students in a house that did not meet the OFC group care standards. These standards would be the subject of an intense lawsuit that ensued after a BRI student, Vincent Milletich, died in July 1985.

The Massachusetts State Review Board also was concerned that Israel was at the California program during its unscheduled site visit to the Providence facility. At the site visit on April 26, 1977, the review board asked for assurances that Israel would always be present at BRI in Providence, and he would always approve final decisions regarding changes in a student's program. Israel responded to these criticisms in writing and stated he had withdrawn from the directorship of BRI-California and would be present full time in Providence.[9] The fact that Israel was at the California program for two weeks that year confused the reviewers, and they requested copies of the incorporation papers of the California program, the names of the director and all consultants, and a written statement outlining Israel's specific work schedule as it related to BRI in Providence. Concerns about the techniques used also appeared in a letter to Israel:

> In March of 1977, you submitted a document to the Board entitled, "Treatment System at BRI." Exhibit 13 on page 119 lists 8 steps of decelerating consequences currently approved for use at BRI. It was the understanding of the Board that only one consequence per behavior is to be used at any given time. However, during our review of your program, it was observed that consequences, a spank and a water squirt, were used interchangeably to avert one behavior? Has this practice been approved by the Human Rights Committee? Who makes the determination as to which aversive technique is to be used?[10]

Reviewers were honing in on the types of aversives being used, as well as how they were being used. In a typical behavioral plan, the behavior is identified, and then a specific consequence is chosen. Reviewers expressed concerns about whether the consequences, in this case aversives, were being appropriately selected and used discriminately.

NEIGHBORS' CONCERNS

Students attending BRI in Providence were living just over the border in southern Massachusetts. A month after the Massachusetts State Review Board raised concerns, the Massachusetts Department of Education received a complaint from neighbors of a BRI group home in Attleboro. On April 10, 1978, two neighbors, Shirley Slattery and Mary Cull, who allegedly were not happy about the group home being in their neighborhood, reported to the police an incident they said took place at 6:05 p.m.:

> I, Shirley Slattery, was standing out in the street in front of the Behavior Research Institute group care facility located at 26 Lorusso Drive, Attleboro, Massachusetts and Mary Cull was standing in the door way of her home across the street at the time this incident took place. Also a few of the children in the neighborhood were playing out in the front of the house. A station wagon was returning to the group home to bring the children back from the Behavior Research Institute. The car

stopped in front of the house and the children were getting out of the car. Suddenly, a girl, about five feet five inches tall, went running up the street yelling "help! help! help!" As she was running, her pants, both under and outer, fell down below her knees. They were very stretched out at the waist. Her buttocks was red with marks on it. The attendant grabbed her by the pants and brought her to the house, still pulling her by the pants. The next day, this girl did not return to the house on Lorusso Drive.[11]

The letter from these neighbors was followed by a phone call from Susan Leary to Israel. He responded to the incident:

   The children were unloaded from the car when the car arrived at the Lorusso House, and it was after Jane [a pseudonym] had stepped out of the car, in the normal course of the unloading process, that she bolted about 40–50 yards from the car. As she ran she did yell something, although the therapist does not recall what she said. She also pulled her pants down while running. This behavior of undressing in public is one of the inappropriate behaviors that she had when she entered our program, and it is one that we have been working to decrease. The therapist immediately ran after her, and when he caught up with her the first thing he did was to pull up her pants. She then returned to the house on her own power, but as a precaution against any further undressing the therapist held onto her pants while Jane walked back into the house. The incident occurred on Monday, April 10, 1978 . . . It is important to recognize the political nature of this complaint. The neighbors in the Moberg/Lorusso houses have sworn to harass us until we leave their neighborhood. They have blocked the roadway with their cars against us, have set their dogs after our staff members, have punctured our tires with nails, have made threatening telephone calls to me, and sent scurrilous misinformation to the Office for Children and now to your office in an attempt to get either or both of these agencies to deny us a license to operate . . . I am hopeful that your office—and the Office for Children as well—will show some understanding to our side in this controversy with the Lorusso/Moberg neighbors. If these people are successful in preventing us from having group homes on Lorusso Drive and Moberg circle, what is the real future for deinstitutionalization in Massachusetts?[12]

There were now two Massachusetts state agencies involved: the Department of Education, responsible for certifying and regulating the educational programs, and the Office for Children, responsible for licensing and regulating the residences. After the Attleboro incident, the OFC stated that the licensing of the five group homes in Massachusetts remained uncertain because of two issues: the fact that some or all of the children in each residence could not pass a "self-preservation" test as required by the group residence building code and concerns that some of the aversive techniques employed as part of BRI's therapeutic program violated regulations prohibiting the use of corporal punishment.[13] None of the five group homes in Attleboro, Rehoboth, and Seekonk were licensed because they failed to meet state building requirements[14] and because the children did not meet the requirement for self-preservation, thereby requiring a more intense staffing pattern. BRI had to hire additional staff.

THE PARENTS WEIGH IN

OFC's concerns about the safety of the children residing at BRI were expressed at the same time the Department of Education and the Massachusetts legislature were conducting their own reviews. In March 1979, Matthew King and Lewis Williams from the Audit Division of the Massachusetts Department of Education wrote a position paper on BRI, which was formally approved by the State Review Board.[15] BRI's Providence school had eight Massachusetts residents among its thirty-five students. This paper summarized observations of and interviews with students, staff, and parents. It recommended continual state and parental oversight and a joint planning process with other agencies to improve the Massachusetts capacity to offer programs to students with autism, severe autism, and behavioral disorders. The report contained comments from parents, such as, "This is the best program our son has ever been in, although we haven't found many programs that can work with him."[16] "I don't mind at all. I'd rather aversives than animal behavior." "All they have done works and I will sue if they try to take my child out of the program." "People who don't have children like these don't understand. No one should confuse aversives with abuse." The authors of the report included a case study submitted by a parent as grounds for recommending that BRI continue operating:

Steven [a pseudonym] lived at home and attended the Spear Education Center until he was 17 when he becomes too difficult for them to handle. While waiting for a placement at BRI, Steven spent five months at Medfield State Hospital, the "worst five months" of his and his parents' lives. Constantly sedated, indeed over sedated at first which caused him to tremble, he was in a ward with a group of 60 adults, alcoholics and retarded patients and only six attendants. When he entered BRI and came off drugs he and those who worked with him needed to wear a helmet for three months to deal with his aggressive and self-abusive behavior. Over the past five months, however, his progress has been impressive; his tantrums have decreased, he has moved beyond echolalic speech, and he is a good deal less aggressive. While he has not gotten to the point where his parents feel that they can replicate the procedures at home, they are optimistic given what they have seen. Steven's parents have signed permission for the full range of aversives and renew their permission every three weeks. Endorsing aversives has not been a problem for them because they found that when he's in a rage nothing else works.[17]

Seen in this context, using physical punishments within a program after having exhausted less aversive alternatives is justified when the program effectively eliminates or reduces bizarre, dysfunctional behaviors and replaces them with more adaptive normal behaviors.

The report also included a section that cited professional critics who expressed fear that children over time would develop an increased tolerance to aversives, withdraw, or react by "counter-aggression." Their fears rested in the knowledge that individuals accommodate to punishment over time, thereby requiring increased intensity. For example, someone receiving electric shock as punishment for hitting could over time require increased voltage to suppress the same behavior. The influential *Boston Globe* commended the King and Williams report because it considered "at length the morality of using aversives," citing Israel's argument that the use of such alternatives as psychotropic drugs or restraints resulted in lowered educational expectations.[18]

Despite the *Globe*'s endorsement, the issues raised in the King and Williams report worried state Senator Jack Backman, a Brookline Democrat and chair of the legislature's Joint Committee on Human Services.[19] Backman sought additional information. He was well known for representing the interests of those who had no voice in government and "represented not just his constituents in liberal Newton and Brookline, but an entire population of otherwise disenfranchised citizens: prisoners, mental patients, street people, drug addicts."[20] He helped to create the first Office for Children, and through legislation, he helped fund implementation of consent decrees that U.S. District Judge Joseph Tauro ordered to improve conditions at state facilities for individuals with disabilities. He believed it was his role to "push the envelope of social justice."[21] In this role, Backman received a letter from a "big brother/lay advocate" of a man who was profoundly deaf and attended BRI. The big brother wanted to provide information to support Backman's concerns about the procedures being used at BRI. The letter read:

> Dave [a pseudonym] had been institutionalized, routinely sedated with Thorazine and in the wake of an investigation into excessive use of drugs at state facilities, Dave and a number of other youth were sent to BRI during the day. In 1974 RI School for the Deaf developed a day program for disturbed deaf children. Dave attended these classes erratically in the mornings, while continuing to attend BRI in the afternoons. He continued to sleep at the state shelter . . . Conflicts developed among the Rhode Island Child Welfare Services, the School for the Deaf, and BRI following accusations of child abuse (strippings, physical and mental punishments) leveled by myself against BRI. In response, the State instructed BRI to discontinue physical punishment. BRI then removed Dave from the School for the Deaf, despite resistance from the school. In spring 1975, upon the instigation of Congressman Ed Beard, the RI Attorney General's office interviewed a number of witnesses whose names had been furnished. Dave was removed from BRI. The results of the AG's informal investigation were never made

public. Later Dave received formal sign language training and became fluent in American Sign Language.[22]

The Massachusetts Department of Education wanted to remove the eleven children from Massachusetts at BRI, citing the high cost of the program: $35,000 per year for each student. The families of children placed there were anxious about this development. In the middle of what appeared to be a basic disagreement between the Massachusetts legislature and the Department of Education about BRI's procedures, Backman announced in November 1980 that his special committee on seclusion, restraint, and deaths in state facilities would investigate the October 30 death of 25-year-old Robert Cooper of Lowell at BRI.[23] Backman said, "I don't know much about it. I don't know what transpired. I am just exploring it. I don't know if it was akin to negligence or not."[24]

Cooper had become sick and was driven to the hospital by a BRI staff member. Joel Zirkin, associate Rhode Island state medical examiner, said Cooper died of a hemorrhagic bowel infarct, a disease that usually arises from a twisting of the bowel or a tumor.[25] Cooper, who had autism, was born at Lowell General Hospital on March 10, 1955. When he was 5, a pediatrician at Floating Hospital in Boston told his parents, "Your son is a zero . . . I think you can consider him the closest thing to a vegetable." Bobby always seemed to be in pain. He never weighed more than 90 pounds, and as he grew older, he had tantrums, banged his head, and became more difficult to control.[26] Cooper was enrolled at BRI for two years and received spanks, muscle squeezes, pinches, cool showers, and water sprays to the face. BRI was the only school that would accept him, and he made substantial progress in activities of daily living while he was there. Cooper's father reported that it was "difficult for myself and my wife to allow Bobby to be pinched or spanked. But there were no alternatives. Every other alternative was really no alternative. In a state institution he would have become a vegetable." Cooper's father also said that it was unfortunate that Backman was rallying around the case because of a philosophical difference with BRI. Parents of other children at the center said they would be willing to bring a lawsuit to keep their children there. Cooper's parents visited him two days before his death. His father said, "It was probably the best visit we ever had. He was totally verbal to the point where he could make me understand that someone had taken his radio. We had given him a tape recorder and he showed me how he worked it. He knew what all the buttons could do. He could count to 15 and was putting together some nuts and bolts. He was very proud of that. He walked up and down stairs. The progress was unbelievable."[27]

Cooper's death was determined by the coroner to be from natural causes and not related to aversive procedures. Zirkin said he died of a hemorrhagic bowel infarct.[28] But Backman still wanted to review the state's monitoring of BRI, stating, "There is a lot of trauma here. Some experts approve it and others are horrified by it. I oppose it very strongly." When asked to comment, Israel said he believed that Backman had a philosophical objection and "we are a controversial program."[29]

After Cooper's death, several articles appeared in the *Boston Globe* and *Providence Journal* about the fact that Massachusetts was considering removing eleven Massachusetts children with autism from BRI. This prompted a *Globe* editorial supporting BRI:[30]

> As much as anyone might be put off at the spectacle of severely handicapped children being pinched or squirted because of behavior they cannot control, the atmosphere of BRI is itself so compassionate—and so serious about helping its children (many of whom have not been helped by less-controversial programs) to achieve control over their self-abusive behavior—that it tempers the initial distaste for aversive techniques . . . Meanwhile it seems hard to justify removing the 11 children from BRI and forcing them to take their chances in a state not completely equipped to care for their needs.

On December 10, 1980, Backman sent a letter to Gerald Koocher, president of the Massachusetts Psychological Association, stating that "it is my personal conclusion after study of this matter and after consultation with very able psychiatrists and psychologists that this line of education or therapy should not be utilized.[31] However, it would appear incumbent upon your profession to come to grips with the controversy. There should be dialogue, recommendations and a position by your Association. Hopefully, you will come to the conclusion that other forms of professional care should be used for our children with these special problems. However, regardless of the outcome for the study it is important that it begin."[32]

Letters sent to members of the special committee, Senators Joseph Timilty, Gerard D'Amico, and Jack Backman, by parents, advocates, and educators concerning problems at BRI and other facilities in Massachusetts contained frustrations about the grievous lack of options in private residential schools and other alternatives for autistic and emotionally disturbed children in the commonwealth. In truth, families had few options. Children with disabilities did not have a federal right to education until the 1975 passage of Public Law 94-142: The Education of All Handicapped Children's Act. The Massachusetts special education law, Chapter 766, had been passed just a year earlier. Before this, children with disabilities were routinely excluded from public school, and those with significant disabilities were institutionalized. Families who chose to keep their children at home were often left on their own with no appropriate educational programs and no formal systems of family support. Few programs had professionals specifically trained to teach children with severe behavior disorders, and there were only a few specialized university professional preparation programs.

The families of the eleven children from Massachusetts who were at BRI were successful in preventing their removal. As a result, the Developmental Disabilities Law Center, the state's protection and advocacy agency,[33] established and supported an autism task force to oversee state policies and practices and advocate for positive practices for children and adults with autism. Once again, despite the ongoing issues being raised about BRI's use of aversive practices, the Massachusetts OFC recommended that BRI receive a regular group care license to operate six residences in southeastern Massachusetts in July 1982.

STATE OF NEW YORK ATTEMPTS
TO REMOVE STUDENTS FROM BRI

Meanwhile, New York State was conducting program audits and threatening to remove BRI from its list of approved programs. The *Los Angeles Times* report on the alleged abuse of Christopher Hirsch was being widely circulated, and advocates against the use of aversive interventions were pressuring New York to develop alternative programs and requesting close monitoring of BRI.

During 1978 and 1979, the New York Department of Education and the New York Office of Mental Retardation and Developmental

Disabilities compiled several site reviews of BRI.[34] Both agencies provided funding for students from New York who were attending BRI and were therefore responsible for oversight. A site review conducted in fall 1978 by a New York State interagency group documented serious concerns about BRI's practices and recommended that it employ a certified teacher of the deaf, a full-time speech therapist, a certified full-time dietician, a full-time nurse, and full-time staff in psychology and social work. The state reviewers observed the physical condition of the twenty-seven students at the school and reported "numerous red marks observed on shoulders and upper arms, high number of cuts noted on feet, heavy marks and open cuts noted on right foot and heavy marks and cuts from spanks on upper legs and thighs."[35] The report concluded, "Your program currently does not reflect minimal educational standards for services to handicapped children." The reviewers wanted to ensure that students were receiving appropriate services to support their education and their health.[36] Additional site visits would be scheduled in February and March 1979.[37]

The press was covering the New York controversy, and during the final months of 1978, the *Knickerbocker News* of Albany reported on BRI events as they developed.[38] One mother of a BRI student, Sheila McVeigh of Albany, reported that she had removed her 21-year-old son, William, from BRI after he "lost 50 pounds, was hospitalized three times and came home for a visit covered with bruises and scars . . . including broken skin on the soles of his feet." William had been approved for placement at the Rhode Island BRI facility in 1976 and was one of its first students. McVeigh described the move to bring the children back to New York as "a blessing in disguise that those parents haven't recognized yet."[39] Israel said McVeigh "has been on a vendetta against the program for some time." He admitted, though, that "some of these procedures do cause some bruise marks" and said that McVeigh was always unhappy about anything that would cause a bruise.[40] The *Knickerbocker News* also reported after interviewing Israel twice that he acknowledged that his program was controversial but denied the allegations of cruel punishment at BRI, including the program in California.

Of course, Sheila McVeigh did not represent all the New York parents with children at BRI. Other parents were concerned that removal would have a negative impact on their children. Another New York official, Cora Hoffman , a special assistant to the state Office of Mental

Retardation commissioner Thomas Coughlin told the *Knickerbocker News* that some parents "were very very happy" with the program but also acknowledged that professionals in the field "do not look on aversive therapy as the most appropriate thing."

On December 21, 1978, the *New York Times* reported that Louis Grumet, New York assistant commissioner for Children with Handicapping Conditions, would remove the children from New York who were at BRI in sixty days based on a November site visit. Grumet, an attorney with a master's degree in public administration and international affairs, was the youngest person to serve in this role and was a special assistant to Mario Cuomo, then secretary of state under Governor Hugh Carey. In the meantime, BRI had permission from the State of New York to continue the use of physical punishment. Grumet acknowledged there was no suitable facility in New York but said he would remove the students as fast as possible. Although the state wanted BRI to agree to use physical punishments only in cases where a child's behavior was self-injurious or injurious to others, Israel insisted that he "be allowed to keep the option of physical punishment to break the children of such bizarre habits as rocking, mumbling, grinding teeth, spitting, inappropriate touching of others, public masturbation, taking clothes off in public, screaming, and such property destructive behaviors as breaking windows, breaking teaching machines, breaking TV sets, tearing apart books, tearing clothes."[41] The *New York Times* also reported that "Dr. Israel said the bizarre behaviors must be eliminated because if any of these things happen you could not take the child to a public restaurant. And he said property damage must be included among punishable actions because you can't allow that to go on forever or your program can go broke."[42] Another *New York Times* article stated that when Israel was asked about studies showing that habits eliminated through punishment sometimes return when the punishments are discontinued, he responded that his methods "would not result in a patient being cured in the absolute sense."[43] He said "it was more like insulin, you do have to maintain it," and he said he envisioned a long-term behavioral society based on his methods to care for the children in the future. In the article, Israel also compared the fear of his methods to the fear of surgery several hundred years ago. "Now, when a surgeon puts a knife into you, you don't call it assault," he said. When B. F. Skinner was interviewed for the same article about BRI's methods, he said, "This is not the Matthew Israel I remember. I always regarded him as a very humane person with high ideals" and "bitterly opposed to any kind of punitive action," and he called the reports about BRI "very disturbing."[44]

In January, New York announced its intention to develop a program at the O. D. Heck Development Center in Schenectady. The first twenty-four places at the center, which was designed to have higher staffing levels than BRI, were available to students currently at BRI. However, many of parents wanted their children to remain at BRI and resisted moving them. Grumet told the parents, "We cannot force you to put your children" there.[45] Israel responded to the new program saying, "You can put 10 staff in front of these kids and they won't necessarily learn." He called the state's plan "just another mental hospital, which is a real step backward in this day and age."

OVERSIGHT REVEALS MORE PROBLEMS

To follow-up on Grumet's decision to remove the New York children from BRI, continue to gather evidence supporting the decision in the wake of parental resistance, and ensure the safety of the students, the New York Department of Education with the New York Office of Mental Retardation and Developmental Disabilities made an unannounced site visit to BRI in January 1979 to determine if their recommendations were being followed. At the time, New York had sixteen students placed there. In the final section of the report, the review team summarized its disapproval of BRI:

> Over the course of the three-day visitation, the January team found BRI to be a professionally conceived, well documented, and rigidly implemented behavior modification program. Its effects on the students was the singular most depressing experience that team members have had in numerous visitations to human service programs.
>
> Rather than being a program of neglect which harms children by not assisting them in growth, the BRI program utilizes current professional ideology to deny children the opportunity to grow; to deny them any choices; to deny them developmental experiences in decision making; to deny them normal experiences in leisure-time pursuits; to deny them any opportunities for fun; to deny them an opportunity to demonstrate anything other than a few pre-selected responses.

Superficially, and on a brief tour of the school, the program is very impressive. Children, who are obviously handicapped, are engaged in activities and are seldom exhibiting inappropriate behaviors or mannerisms. On longer term observation, however, it becomes evident that the children are controlled, rather than in control of their behaviors. The activities which they are provided for the vast majority of the day, 365 days each year are meaningless.[46]

In response to this report, New York state officials were again threatening to withdraw tuition support for these students if the aversive conditioning that included spanking, pinching, and "some alleged harsher punishments" was not discontinued. The state restricted BRI's use of physical punishment. Aversives were to be used only if the child was likely to cause serious physical danger and only after positive reinforcement had been tried.[47] In making this decision, Grumet cited as support for his position the forty-one-page program review criticizing both the use of aversive conditioning and the use of food as a reward for good behavior.[48] Grumet noted that "the school makes an active attempt to discourage any direct contact between the child and parents; classes are conducted in basement rooms with the windows covered; five of the six classrooms are supervised by uncertified teachers; and food is used as a reward for good behavior and is withheld if students do not meet goals, with the result that no student is fed on a regular mealtime basis."[49] But despite Grumet's concerns, on February 15, 1979, the U.S. District Court of New York temporarily restrained the State Education Department from withdrawing funding for the New York children at BRI.[50] However, this did not stop the department from continuing to conduct rigorous oversight.

On March 7, the New York Department of Education issued a summary of the reviews conducted of BRI's education program. The DOE listed nine professional concerns in addition to other findings and concluded in a letter to Israel, "When the compliance issues and professional concerns remaining are combined, we believe they reflect a program that does not meet the minimal standards necessary for the New York State Education Department to consider your facility for future approval as a school for contracting purposes under the provision of the New York State Education law."[51] The report in the form of a letter to Israel also stated:

Although your facility has made some efforts to modify its aversive techniques used in your behavior modification program, the facility's basic philosophy for the education of these students has not been substantially changed particularly in the area of the use of aversives for behaviors which are not self-injurious or injurious to others . . . The alterations that you have made in your program have been duly acknowledged in our report when supporting documentation was provided to us. On the other hand, our original report questioned the continued approval of your program if you adhered to the basic philosophy of the use of aversive techniques, coupled with the use of them in an unacceptable fashion, we see no reason to modify our position.

The letter ended with this paragraph:

We regret our repeated severe criticisms of your program, but believe that we must continue to bring them to your attention in the best interests of each handicapped child residing at your facility as well as promote their common welfare.[52]

Because of serious concerns over the students' health and safety, the New York Department of Education conducted another site review by in March.[53] The report from that visit included a list of observations of the physical status of the New York students. The team conducted a physical exam of each student and asked a nurse to explain the marks and discolorations. The team noted that marks were observed on all the students, although their age and origin could not be verified. Some of the marks were attributed to pinches administered four days earlier. The report stated, "It was also noted by the observers that during the examination of the students one child became frightened when the nurse started to take off his shoes and socks, as if expecting to be hurt on the bottom of his feet, and another child repeated the words 'Take me home, I want to go home' throughout the examination period."[54] The report acknowledged that a reward area had been established in each room but concluded, "It is believed that the Behavior Research Institute has made some progress in meeting the requirements of New York State since the time of the original site visit, but that the school is still not an appropriate educational facility."[55]

The program reviews prompted the New York Department of Education to remove BRI from its list of approved schools for the education of students with disabilities. This meant that the state would no longer fund BRI placements and would send students to approved programs elsewhere. Some parents were unhappy with this action and pursued legal remedies to keep their children at BRI. The *New York Times* reported on the decision to remove the children and the reviews conducted by state officials and documented other comments by the state investigators, who had observed the physical condition of the students at the school.[56] The investigators reported "numerous red marks observed on shoulders and upper arms, high number of cuts noted on feet, heavy marks and open cuts noted on right foot and heavy marks and cuts from spanks on upper legs and thighs. Israel was offered a chance to respond, but instead he telephoned and sent registered letters to the parents of the 14 youngsters telling them to pick-up their children." The parents who received the letters contacted state officials and pleaded that their children not be removed because, they said, there were no appropriate placements in New York.

One family took legal action to keep their child at BRI. Melanie Stanger contested the New York Department of Education's decision in a federal lawsuit, *Stanger v. Ambach* (1980).[57] The suit resulted in an injunction that "restrained all defendants, including local school districts and BRI, from removing the children until the parents have had the opportunity to exhaust their due process remedies under PL 94-142 and Article 89 of the State Education Law."[58] BRI's attorneys also filed a complaint in the New York Supreme Court related to the reimbursement rates set by the Department of Education, arguing that they were too low. BRI threatened to immediately discharge all the New York students, thereby agitating the New York families who were supportive of BRI to push back against the Department of Education. The parents and BRI's tactics and arguments were successful, and BRI was put back on the list of approved schools in 1981.[59] The Stanger family's resistance to the state's action, the court decision, and BRI's success in the courts foreshadowed future legal strategies and decisions.

5 : THE DEATH OF VINCENT

On July 23, 1985, Vincent Milletich died at age 22 after being restrained at BRI.[1] His death followed those of Robert Cooper in 1980 and Danny Aswad in 1981. Vincent's death precipitated the first major lawsuit against BRI in Massachusetts, while the states of California and Rhode Island looked on. Advocates who opposed the use of aversives believed this was their opportunity to close BRI. And BRI, with the assistance of legal counsel, Roderick (Eric) MacLeish, was prepared to fight back to ensure that aversives, which they described as the most effective type of intervention for people with severe behavior disorders, would continue to be used.

Vincent was born in Queens, New York, on October 30, 1963. When he was 2, he was diagnosed with phenylketonuria (PKU), a failure of the body to oxidize phenylalanine, an amino acid. When PKU is untreated, phenylalanine builds up in the body and causes tremors, spasticity, hyperactivity, and intellectual disabilities. If a child with PKU is placed on a phenylalanine-free diet at infancy, the prognosis is excellent. But by the time Milletich was diagnosed,[2] he had already suffered brain damage. Now, all babies in the U.S. are screened for PKU so early treatment can be started and brain damage prevented.

Milletich was also diagnosed with Tourette syndrome, which involves motor tics and sometimes vocalizations. In 1977, in early adolescence, Milletich began to have grand mal seizures. He was prescribed antiseizure medication as well as the antipsychotic drugs Haldol and Mellaril. Both have common side effects that include drowsiness, vision problems, and, with prolonged use, tremors and other involuntary movements. When Milletich reached puberty, he become assaultive and destructive and was refused placement in numerous residential programs in New York. His family was desperate for a placement, and he was admitted to BRI on January 18, 1982. He was taken off antipsychotic medications, and medical staff concluded that he did not have Tourette syndrome; rather, they said, his symptoms were related to untreated PKU. He resided at BRI for a little more than three years before he died.

An inquest into Milletich's death began on September 10, 1986, pursuant to a request from the Bristol County district attorney, dated February 14, 1986, under Chapter 38 of the General Laws, Section 12: Medical Examiners and Inquests to identify any person whose unlawful act or negligence contributed to the death. Barbara Cutler, a parent of a son with autism and a vocal anti-aversive activist, had brought Milletich's death to the attention of the Disability Law Center, the Massachusetts protection and advocacy agency. (The center requested an inquest into Milletich's death, which the coroner had ruled as related to his disability. This explains the six-month lag between his death and the inquest.)

THE EVENTS OF JULY 23, 1985

The inquest into the death of Milletich provided the following details:[3]

On the day in question, Vincent left for the BRI school from the house as usual. Vincent did not remain at the school and was to take part in a planned field trip. Vincent, along with staff and other students, traveled to a local McDonald's restaurant and purchased their lunch. The staff members accompanying the students were Peter Smith, a teacher; Michael S. Douglas, a behavior therapist; Jeffery F. Ryder, an instructional aide; and Mary B. Caffersion, a behavior therapist. When they were finished, the group then proceeded to the Seekonk group home located on 5 Back Street.

On their arrival, the students were brought into the house and were seated in the living room area. The Video Recording Cameras were not activated at that time, since they were primarily used in the nighttime hours.

At approximately 4:00 pm, Vincent while seated on the living room couch, exhibited an inappropriate noise. Peter Smith pinpointed the noise and immediately began the restraining procedure. He was aided by Michael Douglas, who came into the living room to assist. His hands were placed behind his back and cuffed, and his legs were also cuffed together. The White

Noise Visual Screen Helmet [essentially a football helmet with an opaque screen that delivered white noise as a punishment] was then placed on his head . . . Vincent acted aggressively while the helmet was being applied, and continued to thrash about. Vincent was then taken from the couch and laid on the floor face down. Peter Smith held down Vincent's legs and Michael Douglas interlocked his fingers with Vincent's (to prevent him from pinching). Douglas also applied minimal pressure to Vincent's back to prevent Vincent from raising up and striking his head on the floor. Vincent's head was placed on its side. While on the floor, Vincent continued to move about violently and continue to mimic repeatedly the last words he heard before being placed in the helmet ("no noise").

After approximately 15 minutes in the helmet, Vincent suddenly became quiet and went completely limp. Michael Douglas, realizing that something was wrong, immediately removed the helmet. Douglas had first thought that Vincent was suffering from a seizure, but it became apparent that Vincent's condition was much more serious. He was pale, his eyes were dilated and his lips were discolored. He was not breathing and there was not a sign of a heart beat or a pulse. Douglas called the school nurse, Doris Barron, who told Douglas to begin CPR and call the police, which he did. Douglas began mouth-to-mouth resuscitation, since a slight pulse had been detected shortly after the phone call to Nurse Barron. Soon after, a member of the Seekonk Police, Officer Thomas Piquette, arrived. On his arrival at the scene, he radioed for assistance and initiated CPR procedure. He was assisted in this by Michael Douglas. Another Seekonk Police Officer, Raymond Blackledge, arrived, and took over for Mr. Douglas in assisting Officer Piquette. Both officers continued the chest compressions and mouth-to-mouth resuscitation until the Rescue Unit from the East Providence Fire Department arrived. The paramedics then took over the efforts to save Vincent's life. The paramedics detected a slight heartbeat, approximately 12 beats per minute. In an attempt to speed up the heart beat an Atropine IV was started. This failed to stimulate the heart. The paramedics also made several attempts to insert an airway through Vincent's esophagus into the lungs. Each attempt to intubate Vincent proved unsuccessful. At no time did it appear to the paramedics that Vincent had vomited. The paramedics tried to stimulate Vincent's heart by using electric shock, but this proved unsuccessful. Vincent was then placed in an ambulance and rushed to Rhode Island Hospital in Providence.

At the Hospital, the Emergency Room Staff continued the lifesaving procedures initiated by the police officer and paramedics. Another attempt was made to intubate Vincent. Air was forced into the stomach, causing it to expand. This tube was removed and another attempt to intubate proved to be unsuccessful, and, at approximately 5:30 p.m., Vincent was pronounced dead.

Vincent's aunt and godmother, Mary Agnes Milletich, said that her nephew was "very happy and doing well" at the facility.[4] She told the press that despite his death, the family was "completely satisfied with everything—happy with the treatments, the people who worked there and anything else that took place."[5]

Opponents of aversives, however, were deeply concerned. Two activists stood out. Martha Zeigler was a vocal opponent of BRI, a parent of a daughter with autism, and executive director of the Federation for Children, a Boston-based advocacy organization. Barbara Cutler, a parent of a son with a disability and an author of several books on special education, had sounded an alarm earlier about BRI's practices. Both women, who were involved with the Massachusetts Society for Autism in their Campaign Against Violence asked Massachusetts officials to withdraw all students from BRI. Zeigler said, "That program is nothing more than state-subsidized cruelty to children . . . There would be many alternatives, programs which do not rely on punishment as treatment, if others were given the funding to provide the high level of staffing there."[6] She argued, "You can't do these things to prison inmates or prisoners of war: There's no reason to do them to people with autism."[7] Zeigler and Cutler both remained resolved to help ban the use of aversive interventions and to remove students from BRI.[8] Milletich's death was the beginning of their organized opposition to BRI.

The Massachusetts Office for Children (OFC) was created by legislation introduced by Senator Jack Backman and was now headed by Mary Kay Leonard, an experienced state human services attorney with a law degree from Northeastern University.[9] The OFC licensed BRI in 1982 after being convinced that the controversial techniques were appropriate for some cases.[10] Leonard's appointment as commissioner in 1985 coincided with Vincent's death. In 1986, BRI requested a renewal of its license to operate group homes, but the decision was delayed pending an autopsy report on Milletich. Lewis P. Williams, who cowrote a mixed 1979 report on BRI with Dr. Matthew King, investigated the death for the Massachusetts Department of Education. He learned from nurses at BRI that Milletich had developed grand mal seizures within the previous year and had suffered twenty seizures between April and his death in July. The *Boston Globe* reported Williams's account of the events at BRI: "They told me they used the white noise because he was making inappropriate noises. I wonder if the seizures could have led to an increase in the noise behavior. They put his head between his legs, cuff his hands behind his back, put the helmet on and drop the mask so he can't see . . . They put him on a couch, but he flipped around so much, they put him on the floor. A behavior therapist trying to quiet him felt his hands go limp. They took off the helmet and found his lips were blue. He had no pulse."[11]

After Williams's investigation, the Massachusetts Department of Education ordered BRI to halt using white noise and other aversives until the autopsy report was completed. Both the Department of Education and OFC were responsible for overseeing BRI—the Department of Education for certifying that the educational program met state standards and the OFC for ensuring that the residential programs met state standards. Mary Kay Leonard reported that the renewal of BRI's Massachusetts license was delayed pending an autopsy report on Milletich.[12]

Milletich's death seeded arguments for and against the use of aversive interventions. Some advocates of the program described it as "a last resort," while opponents described it as "a well-organized program of punishment for symptoms of autism."[13] On September 26, 1985, the OFC, under Leonard's leadership, issued an emergency order in a well-publicized news conference suspending BRI's license in fourteen days.[14] The action also included an emergency order to correct deficiencies and an order to show cause why the license should not be revoked. This order followed an inspection on September 15 that showed "that clients were clearly in danger from repeated use of punishments to control behavior. It wasn't a question of a few spanks or pinches. For example, the records showed that one student received 173 spanks to the thighs, 50 spanks to the buttocks, 98 muscle squeezes and 527 finger pinches to the feet among the aversives administered on a single evening."[15] Leonard believed that the BRI clients were in jeopardy and also ordered BRI to immediately halt all physical aversive treatment in the automatic vapor spray station (AVS). "While restrained in the AVS, the clients most often receives ammonia vapor in each nostril and a bucket of chilled water is dumped on him or her."[16] Leonard also ordered that no more students be admitted to BRI.

ORDERS TO CLOSE BRI RESIDENCES

Based on numerous OFC site visits, Leonard ordered that BRI's license to operate seven group homes in Massachusetts be suspended and announced that a permanent revocation would be sought.[17] Michael Avery, a licensing specialist for OFC, had visited BRI for a total of 250 hours during March and April 1985 and made additional visits the following August and September after Milletich's death.[18] During his visits, Avery underwent all of the aversives, except spanking and the cold-water bucket, to try to understand the impact these treatments were having on the children. He had reservations about their use, but others in OFC expressed support for the facility. Avery also had concerns about a food program being used at BRI:[19] food was contingent on a student's behavior. Students who did not receive basic nutritional requirements were given a food supplement. Betty McClure, director of the substitute care licensing program for the OFC, described the food deprivation regimen:

> On March 27, 1985, without notice to the Office, BRI again altered its contingent food program from supplementing solid food three times a day to a mixture of water, desiccated liver powder and sustagen (hereafter supplement) to be given at

9:00 p.m. only. The amount of the supplement to be given each student was measured in correlation to the amount of solid food not earned.[20]

Not everyone shared Leonard's and McClure's concerns. The *Boston Herald* reported that Michael Coughlin, an OFC licensing official, argued that this "form of treatment and restraint is normal in autistic children who are the most severely disturbed you can imagine. At the time we are satisfied with the process and the procedures they used. We are investigating the circumstances around the death. We are awaiting the autopsy report. There is no indication of inappropriate action."[21]

BRI protested Leonard's decision to close the residences and an administrative hearing was held, as required by law. Avery testified before the magistrate, Joan Fink, that his understanding of BRI policy concerning the limitations on the use of aversives was that no more than ten physical aversives could be administered in a five-minute period and no more than forty physical aversives could be administered in an eight-hour shift. However, upon reviewing the student records, Avery learned that many students received aversives vastly in excess of the limitations. Child H received almost 1,000 physical aversives on July 16, 1985, including 173 spanks to the thighs, 50 spanks to the buttocks, 98 muscle squeezes to the thighs, shoulders and triceps, 88 finger pinches to the buttocks, 47 finger pinches to the thighs, approximately 527 finger pinches to the feet, and 78 finger pinches to the hand. In addition, child I had received 133 spanks in a two-hour period.[22] He testified that he was concerned about the lack of staff training and about an unapproved contingent food program in which at least one student was receiving only one full noncontingent meal every three days. Paul Hardy, a behavioral neurologist at Tufts–New England Medical School and the medical director of the Fernald State School and the Eunice Kennedy Shriver Institute, testified to the medical contradictions in the use of aversives, particularly with seizure-prone children. BRI presented eight witnesses. Parents in support of BRI presented five witnesses. The BRI-friendly witnesses testified to extensive record keeping, medical oversight of the aversives, and the overall health of the children, including improvement in behavior. Different attorneys represented BRI, parents, and children residing at BRI.[23] Over the next twenty years in different legal battles, this strategy of using multiple attorneys ultimately proved effective for BRI and the families who supported its programs.

Immediately after the hearing, BRI submitted a posttrial brief and argued that there were problems with the language of the OFC regulations and "there is no reasonable cause to believe that an emergency situation exists at BRI which endangers the health, life or safety of BRI clients."[24] Parents of students at BRI represented by attorney Robert Sherman[25] issued a response to the closure: "The parents are prepared to do whatever they have to do to keep the school open. We hope it will be possible to solve the problem by negotiations with the Office for Children and prevent a lawsuit."[26] Parents argued that their children's behavior had improved at BRI. A Connecticut parent said, "State officials making rules about aversives can't comprehend the problems of these children . . . [my] son felt tormented in other places, seems to be happy there. Do you think a kid who pulls out his own teeth without a whimper could be bothered by a slap on the backside?"[27] Israel issued a statement: "We vigorously deny allegations that we have abused any of the children or that the techniques which are the subject of the Office for Children action have been inappropriate or used without appropriate medical supervision."[28]

Despite the protests by Israel and parents, Leonard suspended the licenses of the seven group homes in Massachusetts in an emergency order, citing numerous examples of unauthorized use of aversives, including food deprivation. BRI's school itself, however, was located in Providence, out of Leonard's jurisdiction, and therefore it remained open. But now the students had nowhere to live. OFC needed to place children residing in the BRI group homes elsewhere, and as Leonard met with providers around the state, it was clear that placement would not be easy. Vincent Strully, executive director of the Efficacy Research Institute, said, "It would be safe to say, only a few of the 19 children could be accommodated at existing programs. I would argue that the overwhelming majority of those children can't be accommodated."[29] The lack of placement options and the overall lack of planning by Massachusetts to develop alternatives to BRI made it difficult to move students from the group homes. Programs such as the Delta Project, founded in 1976 to provide community supports and nonaversive interventions, were able to support some with severe behavior problems, but they were unable to accommodate the number of residential placements needed to accommodate all the Massachusetts students who were being served at BRI group homes. This inability to provide effective alternative programs for the students at BRI created an ongoing impediment to attempts to decertify aversives or close BRI homes. Martha Ziegler articulated this impediment saying, "Parents protesting the state action have watched their children being shunted from program to program with little services for years . . . we must respond to their real and immediate concerns with programs that are stable, capable and positive."[30]

Strully had identified the issue that would plague those who argued to close BRI and cease aversives. Many of the students placed at BRI had been in other programs that had expelled them. Families were desperate for a program that would "take their child." Many believed that BRI was better than placement in a state institution. In fact, many state institutions were then under investigation for inhumane treatment. So the dilemma continued. Where could the students be placed, if not at BRI? The lack of alternative educational programs that employed nonaversive practices may have been one of the reasons that BRI was able to convince a court that these students needed aversive interventions.

BRI appealed the OFC's emergency order on October 2, 1985, and filed a class action suit in U.S. District Court in Boston charging that the OFC's order violated federal law. Parents supporting BRI held a news conference and offered testimony. "My daughter Caroline came here on a stretcher covered with bandages," said Pat Bogner, a parent from Trenton, New Jersey. "She could not talk. She was virtually a vegetable. She would have died if she didn't come here. Today she is well-behaved and works on a computer. This is where they start to live."[31] Mary Flanagan, president of the Queens chapter of the National Society of Autistic Children and Adults, had her 28-year-old son at the facility despite opposition from the National Autism Society. Flanagan wanted the facility to stay open. She said, "My son was like a wild man before he went to the institute. Now he's ready for a group home if we can find one to take him. We do not recognize the right of well-meaning outsiders to step in and interfere."[32] Meanwhile, the Massachusetts Civil Liberties Union, the Massachusetts Federation for Children, and the Developmental Disabilities Law Center supported the closure order.

Roderick (Eric) MacLeish Jr. was one of the key players in the story of BRI's survival. His aggressive legal representation and extensive and powerful Boston connections were instrumental in the successful lawsuits against the commonwealth of Massachusetts and its executives, including Mary Kay Leonard and Philip Campbell. MacLeish was named one of the top trial lawyers by the *National Law Journal* and has been described as an attorney who relishes representing outsiders.[33] He was described as "a tenacious trial lawyer with political aspirations who is said to be happiest when snarling at the heels of tough adversaries while representing the disenfranchised—contends that the most effective way to advance his clients' cause is to thrust them into the spotlight, as long as they are willing."[34] He is a graduate of Boston University School of Law and attained national attention when he represented the sexual assault victims of Reverend James Porter. He is "not afraid of a lawsuit. And his propensity to sue opponents of the center—or at least threaten to—has created fear among former employees and residents."[35]

MacLeish is a member of a well-known family. His grand uncle was the famous poet Archibald MacLeish. His father, Roderick MacLeish, was a novelist, journalist, and news director at WBZ radio in Boston in the early 1950s who also worked for CBS News in Washington and as a well-known National Public Radio commentator. No wonder Eric was considered masterful with the media. Throughout his representation of BRI, he was a legal commentator with several media outlets in the Boston area. In another high-profile case, he represented a resident of Bridgewater State Hospital in 1982 and fought for the next ten years to improve conditions for the other 425 patients at the mental health facility. MacLeish understood the problems associated with institutional care and appeared sympathetic to the viewpoint that children were better off at BRI than in the state institutional system. Initially, he was not sure that he wanted to represent the school, but after viewing before-and-after videotapes, he "was convinced that there was another side to the story."[36]

MacLeish later went on to successfully represent victims of clergy sex abuse, only to realize that he too had been sexually abused as a child while attending private school in England. His law partner,

Figure 3. Eric MacLeish, BRI/JRC attorney.
AP Photo/Cheryl Senter.

Robert Sherman, who attended law school at Boston University with MacLeish, said, "Once Eric puts his mind to something, he's like a bulldog grabbing on to a pant leg. He shakes and won't let go."[37] MacLeish's primary strategy was to show how aversive therapy had a positive effect on children. He also realized that parents were key to combating negative publicity.[38] In 2004, according to a report in the *Boston Globe*, he developed symptoms of posttraumatic stress disorder, left his law practice at the prestigious Boston law firm Greenberg Traurig, divorced, and moved to New Hampshire.[39]

I contacted MacLeish and requested an interview, but in a cordial email he wrote that he didn't think he could add any insights to this book and reminded me of his involvement in the Catholic church sexual abuse case: "You are free to write anything about me that you choose to and to rely on anyone's perspectives. You are correct that there is a volume of material about the issue and the court cases which includes a lot of quotes from me, some of which are accurate, and some which are not. I applaud that you are writing a book about this important issue; it certainly merits public discussion. I obviously had my own views on the subject, but I was an advocate, not a clinician . . . I think Judges Rotenberg, LaStaiti and the SJC [Supreme Judicial Court] looked at the evidence, applied the law and decided the cases accordingly. It certainly is unusual to have a state agency put into partial receivership. But that was the proper remedy given the evidence of government misconduct before the court."

I tried a couple of more times to interview him, but many of the questions that I had were legal ones and subject to attorney-client privilege. It is clear that MacLeish fiercely represented his clients. He has never revealed whether he personally believed in the use of aversives. Regardless, he is an accomplished attorney and well respected in his field. On one occasion, an opposing attorney told me that he wished he had MacLeish's skills and said MacLeish is the reason that BRI remains open today.

COURTS GET INVOLVED
WITH PLACEMENT DECISIONS

Despite parents' testimony, on October 9, 1985, U.S. District Court Judge Joseph L. Tauro[40] "upheld OFC's decision to close the group homes as long as other administrative procedures were available to parents protesting suspension of BRI's license."[41] MacLeish argued that behavior modification procedures were "highly effective." Assistant Attorney General Leonard Learner, representing the OFC, told Judge Tauro that "what's going on behind the wall at the Behavior Research Institute is little more than child abuse."[42] Just three days later, on October 12, magistrate Joan Fink of the Division of Administrative Law Appeals ordered the homes to stay open until October 25 or until she heard all testimony, stating, "There is no immediate danger to any of the clients by allowing it to remain open for 10 more days."[43] At this point B. F. Skinner weighed in on behalf of Israel and BRI:[44]

> I don't like the use of punishment. I am opposed to it. But there are people who are out of reach of positive reinforcement. Whether or not they ever can become normal is another issue. Israel is a very human man. Much concerned about injustice. It takes a brave man to take these cases on. Most people run as far as possible . . . Israel's methods are not comparable to torture. Whether he needs so many aversives I'm not prepared to say. It's a question of intent. I have talked with some who claim that person to person contact can bring out autistic people. I have not seen this. The alternatives in our times are heavy drugs and straight-jackets . . . Learning through punishment has been recognized for centuries by governments and by religions which threaten hell fire. All use punishment to teach control. Schools punish children every day by ignoring students and leaving them to lead wasted lives.[45]

Over the seven-day hearing, additional testimony was offered by a Providence pediatrician, Alfred Toselli, who said none of the students showed signs of physical abuse, and by John Daignault from the McLean Psychiatric Hospital in Belmont, Massachusetts, who said placing BRI residents in state institutions would cause them harm.[46] The disagreement among professionals and organizations may have been confusing to those paying attention to the hearing, particularly since the father of a radical behavioral psychology and a noted psychiatrist from an esteemed hospital testified in favor of punishment and aversive procedures.

Parental testimony supporting BRI was also compelling. A single mother, Kettee Boling relayed her son's story. She had placed him at BRI, which had a zero exclusion policy, after he repeatedly ran away and stole cars. Once at BRI, he ran away, this time taking another student with autism with him. During his escape, he drove a car into a gully. When he returned to BRI, he was placed in shackles, made to wear the same clothes for a month, and wear a white noise helmet. This football helmet, which had a visual screen to prevent him from seeing, emitted white noise and a vapor spray (a mix of compressed air and water) that every fifteen minutes was administered on his face and the back of his neck for two minutes. Ammonia was also sprayed near his nose at the same rate.

After several months, Boling's son was given more freedom, but again he ran away. He was struck by a car on Interstate 95 and was hospitalized for ten days. Seven months later, he escaped again from BRI, stole a garbage truck, and tried to run over several police officers. Rather than having him jailed, BRI received permission from the judge and his mother to put him in mechanical leg restraints, which violated OFC regulations. For approximately a year, he was in shackles, despite OFC investigator Avery's warnings. But after hearing the story, Judge Fink sided with BRI, deciding that the shackling did not violate BRI's current waiver, which allowed them to use mechanical restraints to protect both the student and property from harm. Fink ruled that there was no time limit on how long the restraints could be used. Boling summarized her view of BRI: "I would characterize it as very good care and very caring people."[47]

On October 23, 1985, Fink issued a nonbinding order that the BRI homes remain open temporarily.[48] Advocates for closure believed the decision that BRI remain open temporarily would give the state time to find alternative placements. The attorney for BRI parents, Richard Landau, issued a statement that articulated the foundation for future actions against Mary Kay Leonard and other Massachusetts administrators. He accused the OFC of "engaging in a heartless crusade without any concern for the parents' legitimate concerns for their children."[49]

The day after Fink's decision, October 24, 1985, Arthur Burns, Rhode Island deputy chief medical examiner, said that asphyxiation caused the death of Vincent Milletich but was unwilling to conclude "whether that treatment, administered while the client's arms and legs were in restraints caused or contributed to the death."[50] Immediately after reading the coroner's finding, Bristol County prosecutor Ronald Pina launched a criminal investigation into the death. He wanted more conclusive findings and announced that he would "hire three neurologists to review Burns' autopsy report to see if they can determine whether treatment at the BRI facility killed Milletich."[51] This was a high-profile opportunity for the elected prosecutor.

Mary Kay Leonard disagreed with Dr. Burns's conclusion that BRI's actions had not contributed to Milletich's death and announced that all Massachusetts clients at BRI would be removed as soon as possible.[52] The next day, a *Boston Globe* editorial argued that the OFC had overreacted to the complaints of advocates for closure and urged the state's human services officials "to work with Israel and his staff to modify some aspects of the treatment program. Changing, rather than closing, the institute would be in the best interest of the young people whose troubling affliction places them at BRI."[53] A Globe editorial argued that "the program has drawn the ire of a group of advocates who describe BRI's treatment as inhumane . . . Unfortunately, the state's Office for Children has overreacted to the complaints of these advocates and sought to close the Institute."[54] Globe editorials such as this one appeared regularly during litigation and legislation that involved BRI. Not until a student was mistakenly shocked seventy-seven times in 2007 as the result of a prank phone call did the *Globe* seriously question BRI's ability to provide high-quality treatment.

Other media outlets were also reporting on the trial and the use of aversives. Tom Brokaw and *NBC Evening News* aired a story on October 30, 1985, on BRI that included student Brendan Sussi's mother defending the program, while another mother, who had withdrawn her son, Paul Yamen, from BRI, accused Israel of treating people like animals. NBC reporter Lisa Meyer interviewed Dr. Anne Donnellan from the University of Wisconsin, Dr. Donald Cohen from Yale University, and Betty McClure, an investigator for the state of Massachusetts, who all decried the use of aversives. The major television networks would continue to follow the BRI story for two more decades.

RESEARCH ON THE USE OF AVERSIVES

The technology of positive behavioral supports was just beginning to emerge in the 1980s. Prior to this, a series of articles had been published that supported the use of punishment as a means to decrease problematic behavior. In 1966 John Watson, an early founder of behaviorism, used punishment and shock as a last resort when positive approaches appeared not to work. One of the most famous studies that used electric shock was conducted by Bradley Bucher and Ivaar Lovaas, who in the early 1960s at UCLA used punishment on four children with autism, at the time referred to as childhood schizophrenia. In the study, described in 1965 by *Life Magazine* in an article, "Screams, Slaps and Love: A Surprising, Shocking Treatment Helps Far-Gone Mental Cripples," researchers used a combination of interventions to teach children to read, dress themselves, communicate, and decrease stereotypic and aggressive behavior. *Life* described one intervention with a young girl named Pamela:

> The most drastic innovation in Lovaas' technique is punishment—instantly, immutably dished out to break down the habits of madness. His rarely used last resort is the shock room. At one point Pamela had been making progress, learning to read a little, speak a few words sensibly. But then she came to a blank wall, drifting off during lessons into her wild expressions and gesticulations. Scoldings and stern shakings did nothing. Like many autistic children, Pamela simply did not have enough anxiety to be frightened.
>
> To give her something to be anxious about, she was taken to the shock room, where the floor is laced with metallic strips. Two electrodes were put on her bare back, and her shoes removed. When she resumed her habit of staring at her hand, Lovaas sent a mild jolt of current through the floor into her bare feet. It was harmless but uncomfortable. With instinctive cunning, Pamela sought to mollify Lovaas with hugs. But he insisted she go on with her reading lesson. She read for a while, then lapsed into a screaming fit. Lovaas yelling "No!" turned on the current. Pamela learned a new respect for "No."
>
> Even more than punishment, patience and tenderness are lavished on the children by the staff. Every hour of lesson time has a 10-minute break for affectionate play. The key to the program is a painstaking system of rewarding the children first with food and later with approval whenever they do something correctly. These four were picked because they are avid eaters to whom food is very important. In the first months they got no regular meals. Spoonfuls of food were doled out only for right answers.[55]

The study by Lovaas and his colleagues proved that children considered uncontrollable and unteachable could learn and inspired a generation of research on the use of punishment, often in conjunction with the use of positive reinforcement, including food, tokens, and praise. Much of it was based on the fundamental assumption that punishment and the use of aversives were necessary to decrease problematic behaviors and maintain behavioral control. However, Donnellan and others, including her colleagues Dr. Gary LaVigna and Dr. Luanna Meyer,[56] were arguing that positive approaches, if used appropriately in the least restrictive environment—those that offered the most integration with nondisabled peers and community life—were as effective as the use of punishment and did not have the side effects, such as anxiety and fear or the ethical problems, associated with the use of aversives.[57]

WERE INTIMIDATING TACTICS EMPLOYED?

Antiaversive advocates and professionals were voicing strong opinions about the need to close the facility. Donnellan, a professor in behavioral disabilities and autism, moved from California to Madison, Wisconsin, in the late 1970s, where she started a pilot program for children with autism in the Madison Public Schools to demonstrate the use of positive practices in the least restrictive environment.[58] She was one of the most vocal opponents of aversives and argued that the techniques used at BRI were violent and unnecessary. Raised in New York City, articulate and brash, Donnellan did not shy away from controversy. She had been a key figure in bringing BRI to California in the early 1970s but became an ardent opponent when she learned the extent of the aversive procedures. She was the editor of *Classic Readings in Autism*, a collection of research studies on autism, and the author of numerous journal articles and textbook chapters.[59]

Israel was reporting that as a result of the order to stop the aversives, the students had become dangerous and staff injuries had increased.[60] Donnellan responded, "When you suppress behavior using these kinds of methods, and when you take these methods away, the behavior comes back. After six years, the treatment hasn't held for one month, that's not successful treatment. Keeping people incredibly hungry, spanking or pinching them, are primitive techniques. They may suppress behavior if they are done hard and long enough, but when you take them away, they come right back."[61] Donnellan was well aware of the research on aversives, having worked in California during the period that Lovaas, a professor at UCLA, was using punishment on children with autism.

Many parents, determined to prevent closure of BRI and termination of the aversive treatments, hired the Boston law firm, Topkins, Gaffin & Krattenmaker to represent them and their children (MacLeish represented BRI and Robert Sherman represented the parents). Richard Landau from this law firm contacted Donnellan to discuss her opposition to BRI.[62] She perceived the conversation as threatening and voiced her complaint in a letter to the Massachusetts Board of Bar Overseers:

> Mr. Landau said he was trained as a clinical psychologist at Stony Brook (sic) and then went into law. He read some of my comments in the newspapers and radio and wanted me to know that these comments bordered on violations of ethical standards of the American Psychological Association. His premise seemed to be that I was confusing a confusing situation by commenting on the treatment of individual clients whose history you had not seen in a program you had not seen, and that there was a serious question of the ethics of such behavior. Moreover, that I ought only be making such comments on the witness stand where I would be subject to cross-examination as to my bias, past deals, etc. He reiterated the questionable ethics of suggesting publicly that clinicians be restrained from using procedures, which are not supported by literature.[63]

Landau's supervisor at the law firm, Robert Sherman,[64] assured the bar that Donnellan had only been contacted for the purpose of inviting her to visit BRI.[65] She responded with a letter dated February 3, 1986, and continued to accuse the law firm of threatening tactics:

> I do not believe it is the proper role of a member of a licensed profession to call individuals who have been critical of their clients and suggest professional discipline or other sanctions if they continue to speak out on a public issue. There is no polite word for such implied threats and a great many impolite ones. Mr. Landau's sworn statement that his call was intended to "assist" me strains credulity. I am, however, willing to accept it

Figure 4. Matthew Israel with two students. Richard Howard Photography. People Magazine, *14 April 1986, 63.*

as an indirect apology. This is in spite of the fact that he refuses to refer to me by my professional titles of Doctor or Professor.[66]

There were no sanctions against Landau as a result of Donnellan's accusations.

BRI parents had this to say:

> Anne Donnellan and other critics were hysterics. "We're not horrible and sadistic," says Robert Flanagan of Port Washington, NY, former chairman of Western Union, whose severely autistic son Chris, 29, had been at BRI for eight years. "Any parent who's ever punished his child has worried about whether it's the right thing to do. We thought BRI's program might work when we sent Chris there, and were right. Chris has been doing marvelously. We knew the only alternative to BRI was the state institutions, where Chris would be sodomized, beaten and—if he were lucky—held in a straightjacket. They're torture palaces. Dr. Israel's program is a blessing. The progress the children have made is all that counts."[67]

On November 18, 1985, Israel (Figure 4) appeared at a press conference and publicly acknowledged his need for assistance with clients in his care who were regressing after OFC ordered cessation of physical aversives.[68]

Using the media to send messages during litigation was a signature strategy of Israel's attorney, MacLeish. Israel was making the point to the public that without the use of aversives, he could not control the students.

During his press conference, he said there was no easy remedy to the situation and that a new program of positive interventions and supports was required to stop the regression. This would be difficult to implement at BRI because staff were not trained to use these techniques and the environment was not conducive to success. Israel, it seemed, was implying that no one could stop the problem behaviors in the time required to satisfy the judge and parents.

After Donnellan was criticized by Landau, she received a letter from Matthew Israel requesting her assistance:

We are eager to benefit from any insights you may have developed in this area. At the outset, however, we would also appreciate your answers to the following questions:

What is your position on the use of drugs to control behavior?

Have you had any operation responsibility for a day or residential program for severe behaviorally-disordered young adults of the age and strength of our students? Have your only experiences been the pre-school program that you ran in San Diego, and the program for autistic children that you ran in Sacramento during the 1976–1977 year? What was the average age of the children in the latter program?

If the Sacramento public school project was your last experience in operating an ongoing program for person with behavior disorders, did you attempt to apply the methods you now espouse in that program? If so, why was it necessary for you to have used various aversive procedures in that project?

In a recent newspaper article, you apparently mentioned the Behavioral Development Center (BDC) [June Groden's program] as a place where autistic students can learn to communicate, to make some sense of the world. Is it true that you are on the Professional Advisory Board of that school? Incidentally, your remarks in the *Providence Journal* article of a few Sundays ago made it seem that you thought our National

Peer Review members are paid a consulting fee for their services. Please allow me to correct this misconception—they are only reimbursed for their travel expenses. Is the same true of your relation to the Behavioral Development Center, if in fact you are indeed on its Professional Advisory Board? Also concerning BDC, I would like to benefit from any insights that the school can provide and I am writing today to June Groden, its co-director.

Would you be kind enough to send me a bibliography of papers by yourself or others that deal with the topic of alternatives to the use of "aversives" in the treatment of severe behavior disorders? Please [missing word] unpublished monographs you may have written.

Donnellan declined, believing that the request for assistance was a legal ploy and lacked sincerity or a true desire to phase out the use of aversives. "Asked if she planned to visit the institute in response to his request, Donnellan said she did not. Instead she said, "I sent him a bibliography of 200 references."[69] She also was aware that Gary LaVigna, her close colleague and the clinical director of the Institute for Applied Behavior Analysis in Los Angeles, had already been similarly asked by the commonwealth of Massachusetts to provide assistance to BRI. June Groden, another critic of the program and the director of the Behavior Development Center in Providence, had also received a letter requesting assistance. Collectively, they believed the requests were insincere.

Some members of the media were paying close attention. One in particular, reporter Ric Kahn,[70] had conducted extensive research on the operations of BRI in California, Rhode Island, and New York[71] and consulted with Anne Donnellan.[72] On November 26, 1985, the *Boston Phoenix*, Boston's largest weekly paper, published his article: "Doctor Hurt: The Aversive Therapist and His Painful Record." Kahn also chronicled the deaths of the three students who were associated with the program. He ended the article with a paragraph on Israel:

The miracle man has escaped other scrapes, and he's already plotting how to get out of this one. If Massachusetts shuts down BRI, he says, he may open group homes in Rhode Island. Israel thinks the current crackdown may lead to a greater understanding of his philosophy and allow him a greater array of behavior-modification tools. "I've never used electric shock," he says in his calm, soft voice. "I wouldn't rule it out. Particularly if we were deprived of other procedures. It has a lot of advantages. It's more effective, and wouldn't bruise or cut the skin."[73]

Many of the people and organizations charged with overseeing and protecting the rights of Massachusetts citizens and people with disabilities were actively supporting OFC's attempt to close BRI and severely limit the use of aversives. John Roberts, executive director of the Massachusetts Civil Liberties Union, wrote a letter to Governor Michael Dukakis and expressed the sentiments of many in the advocacy community: "We recognize that parents do agree to the treatment program when children are placed at BRI, but many do so out of desperation knowing that there is no other placement available. However, even parents are prohibited from abusing their children."[74] The Massachusetts Psychological Association gave "unequivocal support" to OFC's intervention and the emergency suspension of BRI's license in September but made clear that the association did not want a ban on the use of aversives or restrictive procedures on severely disturbed clients.[75] National associations such as The Association for Persons with Severe Handicaps (TASH), The National Society for Children and Adults with Autism, and the Association for Retarded Citizens took a strong stand against BRI. All three organizations passed resolutions calling for a moratorium on the use of aversive procedures. Dr. Luanna Meyer, a TASH member and a professor at Syracuse University, said, "The procedures used at BRI are no longer considered the best practices and are unnecessary to remediate behavior problems . . . These are not bizarre and random behaviors of individuals who we hear have been described as animalistic. They are using their behaviors to accomplish some purpose—may it be trying to communicate or trying to let you know they have a need. In order to remediate a behavior, one has to identify that behavior and teach an alternative skill."[76]

Nationally, a great deal of attention focused on BRI. Senator Lowell Weicker of Connecticut, chairman of the Subcommittee on the Handicapped, Committee on Labor and Human Resources and the parent of a son with Down syndrome, asked the assistant attorney general of the Civil Rights Division in the U.S. Department of Justice in January 1986 to "undertake a full scale investigation of the BRI programs."[77]

The same request would be made twenty-four years later by a group of advocates and organizations outraged by BRI's use of electric shock devices.

A CASE FOR "BIASED" EXPERTS IS MADE

The Massachusetts Department of Mental Health hired Gary LaVigna to spend a week going over records, examine the students at BRI, and make recommendations about appropriate treatment. He served on the professional advisory board of the National Society for Children and Adults with Autism, an organization opposed to the use of physical punishment and abuse, which also sought a congressional investigation of programs using aversive techniques. Strategically, hiring LaVigna may not have been the best decision: he was involved in California's attempt to close BRI. Israel's attorney argued that LaVigna was biased and was not capable of conducting fair and objective reviews of the students.[78]

When LaVigna arrived at BRI in December 1985, he was refused entrance. The state sought an injunction against BRI, and Massachusetts Superior Court Judge Herbert Abrams ordered LaVigna be admitted to examine the students. MacLeish immediately sought to appeal the decision based on the contention that LaVigna was "biased"[79] because he was an outspoken critic of aversive treatments and had "feuded" for years with Israel.[80] MacLeish argued that "LaVigna has no right to come to the program without consent from parents of clients. It would be a breach of the right to privacy and confidentiality for clients and their parents alike."[81] BRI's attorneys seemed to be arguing that the commonwealth did not have the regulatory authority to conduct assessments on individual students without parental consent. If this argument was accepted, it would mean that parents could object to external review of their children's treatment plans, thereby weakening commonwealth regulatory and oversight role. Because he was denied entry to BRI, LaVigna spent the week consulting with the Delta Project on two former BRI clients, as well as providing advice about interventions for other individuals with autism before returning to California.[82] On January 28, 1986 the Massachusetts Appeals Court ruled that despite LaVigna, "being a professional adversary and severe critic of Matthew Israel, the director of BRI," and claiming that "it appears to be like hiring Ralph Nader to evaluate how General Motors makes cars" that the lower court's December 23 decision to allow him to inspect student records should stand.[83] But LaVigna had already returned to California.

JUDGE ROTENBERG BECOMES
A CENTRAL FIGURE

In fall 1985, when experts were being proposed to provide recommendations and oversight, MacLeish filed a petition on behalf of BRI seeking an exception to the state's ban on physical aversives for a BRI resident named Janine Casoria. MacLeish reported that "since the ban on aversives, the girl can no longer do academic tasks, needs two aides present to even count buttons and must wear a helmet at all times to prevent her from injuring herself."[84] On December 2, Janine's parents petitioned the probate court in Attleboro, Massachusetts, to become temporary guardians of their child and to issue a "substitute judgment" order.[85] "After finding the person unable to competently decide whether to accept or refuse the proposed treatment or procedure, the court must determine what the person would decide if he or she were competent to do so. That is, the court must substitute its judgment for that of the incompetent person."[86] The parents' attorney, Robert Sherman, requested that Judge Ernest Rotenberg authorize that treatments be resumed for Janine, saying that "her parents were heartsick and that with the treatments she was now able to go home with her parents and go out to a restaurant. Now Janine was banging her head against objects and ripping her hair out."[87] The petition to authorize the use of aversives was submitted in the county probate court that had jurisdiction over towns where BRI's group homes were located. This was a turning point for BRI. Probate courts typically deal with wills, trusts, adoptions, divorce, and other family-related issues. It is also the court where substituted judgment proceedings take place.

Judge Ernest Rotenberg was appointed to the Probate and Family Court of Bristol County in 1973 by Republican governor Francis Sargent.[88] Before serving on the bench, he had practiced law in Massachusetts as an assistant district attorney and special assistant attorney general. People referred to Rotenberg as a judge who advocated for children. He was serious, relatively tall, and wore large black-framed glasses. He was known to be compassionate, but in court, he could also be impatient and firm with lawyers and their clients.

THE DEATH OF VINCENT   107

Judge Rotenberg visited the school and watched a videotape of Janine when she was admitted four years earlier. The film showed Janine pulling out her hair, groaning, and banging her head on the floor. He also saw a videotape of Janine after treatment at BRI. In several news articles, Judge Rotenberg described Janine and her behavior, noting, "This is one of the most violent scenes I have seen in my life. Why is there a controversy? I have viewed the school. I have seen Janine. I can't understand any reason in the world why this is a controversial procedure."[89] The use of the before-and-after videotapes was a technique that Israel often used to illustrate BRI's practices. He did acknowledge that they were not scientific and were selected to represent the worst and often the best behavior.

Joseph Shapiro, in his 1995 book *No Pity*, described Janine at the time the aversive interventions were reintroduced:

> She had regressed. The helmet was strapped on again. There were fresh, oozing scabs on her scalp. Flanked by two staffers, she sat at her bench sorting colored rings. One staffer gave Janine frequent pinches on the palm—each one counted out and recorded—to try to correct her nearly constant moaning. A second staffer sat by in case Janine acted out. A small television camera, only a few feet away, broadcast Janine's behavior to the monitor in the locked video room upstairs. During the fifteen minute breaks between tasks, Janine would dive into a beanbag chair in the middle of the classroom, wrap herself tightly in a blanket, curl up into a fetal position, and moan softly to herself. She seemed to have become inured to the frequent hand pinches and other punishments. Israel said he was considering employing his harshest punishment, an electrical shock device known as the Self-Injurious Behavior Inhibiting System, or SIBIS, that would require a court's permission to use.[90]

Janine's regression seemed to support the argument that aversives were ineffective because the behavior changes were not maintained once the painful procedures were discontinued.[91] But there was a counterargument: aversives needed to be intensified to achieve the desired result.[92]

The settlement gave Judge Rotenberg the authority to decide on a case-by-case basis whether aversive interventions should be allowed, and he pushed back on OFC's ban. Robert Sherman, who represented Janine and her parents, said that aversive treatments would be resumed immediately, and he would return to Bristol Probate Court to ask Judge Rotenberg to reinstitute aversive interventions for the other children. Sherman said, "We're hoping to deal directly with the Office for Children. We don't see why the other children should be treated any differently from Janine . . . but going back to Judge Rotenberg is an option."[93]

Leonard said, "This will allow BRI one more chance to present to the office exactly what aversive procedures it wishes to use, and to demonstrate that BRI now has the needed safeguards in place." Under the accord, she also appointed a panel of experts "to advise the agency on the conditions, if any, under which aversive therapy should be authorized in Massachusetts as a treatment for autistic children."[94] BRI and the parents were concerned that the panel members were biased due to their affiliations with national organizations that actively opposed aversive interventions and made their objections known to OFC. The report was due in thirty days. In order to use an aversive, the school was required to submit requests by January 13, 1986. In the meantime, Judge Rotenberg said that he was pleased with Janine's progress; he believed that the aversive therapy was working and soon would approve aversives for five additional students.[95]

EXCEPTIONS TO THE ORDER
TO CEASE THE USE OF AVERSIVES

Many moves and countermoves were underway. Magistrate Fink had scheduled another hearing for January 6, 1986, to determine whether BRI should cease the use of physical aversive treatments. In demanding that aversive interventions be stopped, OFC should have anticipated that the children's behaviors were likely to deteriorate immediately, causing families to rebel against the order. Because of the overwhelming complaints by parents that their children's behavior was getting worse when the aversives were terminated and because of the lack of alternative placements, an interim agreement was reached between OFC and BRI on December 30, 1985, supporting Judge Roten-berg's decision to reinstate aversives for Janine Casoria.[96] Under the agreement, BRI had until January 13, 1986, to request variances to use unusual and extraordinary treatments such as spankings, pinches, vapor sprays, and other disciplinary techniques only through a formal waiver approval process that would be reviewed by a team of experts selected by OFC. BRI agreed to submit an application for license re-newal under the OFC's new group care regulations and to apply for a variance to use unusual or extraordinary treatment. The agreement also provided for the appointment of a five-member independent panel to evaluate the variance requests. Administrative law appeals magistrate Fink said she was going to postpone the hearing until Jan-uary 23 when the parties would appear before her and report on the status of the case.[97] Israel responded to the postponement saying, "I hope this means that the Office for Children will take into account the needs of students to have their programs put back together."[98]

A FIGHT OVER JURISDICTION: OFC VERSUS PROBATE COURT

BRI submitted a variance request to OFC on January 17, 1986, that would have allowed the program to use aversives. Brenda Beaton, OFC's general counsel, said they were unable to make a determina-tion due to deficiencies present in the student-specific variance re-quests and sent them to members of the panel with a request to review them as soon as possible.[99] A week later, OFC responded with a series of questions and concerns about both the general variance request and student-specific variance requests.[100] MacLeish responded to the request and argued that OFC's regulations were contradictory:

> The OFC regulations concerning "unusual or extraordinary
> treatment" clearly contemplate "aversive treatment" as
> constituting a treatment for which a variance request can be
> filed. See 102.C.M.R. Section 3/04 (14)(a)(3). Moreover, the Office
> for Children has repeatedly stated that the type of treatment
> which was utilized at BRI prior to the Office's Emergency Order
> to Correct Deficiencies of September 26, 1985 was, indeed, the
> type of treatment which qualified for a variance under Section
> 3.04 (14) of the regulations. How can the Office therefore take

the position the "aversive treatment" can be used by a school if a variance is granted, yet at the same time rely upon regulations contained in Section 3.05 which would appear to prohibit aversive treatment under any circumstances?[101]

BRI's requests for waivers were not approved. As Sherman had promised, on January 22, 1986, BRI and five parents of students returned to Rotenberg's court and filed five petitions for the appointment of temporary guardians and substituted judgment and the reinstatement of physical punishment, including the controversial automatic vapor spray helmet. The petitions were approved on January 31, after Rotenberg was convinced that the five students had regressed without the use of aversives.[102] He appointed the parents of the five students as their temporary guardians and gave BRI authority to use punishments subject to parental approval. He also noted that "not one scintilla of affirmative evidence was offered at these guardianship hearings by the OFC, even though the agency was requested by the Court to produce any reasonable available alternative or less intrusive treatment that might be adopted."[103] This essentially bypassed the regulatory authority of OFC. BRI's overall strategy was to move the treatment authority from OFC to the probate court and parents, thereby bypassing the commonwealth's regulatory and oversight responsibilities. It was working.

On February 7, the attorney general, on behalf of OFC, responded to Rotenberg's order to resume aversives and sought a stay, arguing that OFC, not the probate court, had the authority to determine the appropriateness of treatment.[104] BRI had already filed an appeal of OFC's order in superior court, but that appeal could take up to six months. The state, represented by the assistant attorney general, Leonard Lerner, believed that Judge Rotenberg did not have the authority to override the OFC, claiming that the probate court could not overturn a decision by the regulatory agency. Judge Rotenberg denied the request for a stay on guardianship and substituted judgment orders on February 24, and the OFC appealed the denial of the motion to the Massachusetts Appeals Court. On March 5, a single justice of the appeals court denied OFC's appeal and urged the parties to return to the lower court and work things out. They returned to probate court on March 7.[105] The attorney general's strategy to treat this issue as regulatory rather than one based on educational and civil rights was one of the most critical decisions in BRI history and its relationship with the commonwealth of Massachusetts. Because aversive interventions were treated as a state regulatory issue rather than a federal civil rights or constitutional issue, it was difficult to appeal to the federal courts.

Judge Rotenberg responded by saying that BRI's appeal could take up to six months and that his order was based on concern for the safety of the students because their treatment had been interrupted. Sherman argued that "the law in Massachusetts is clear that handicapped individuals have the right to maximum possible development. What the court is doing today is giving them the opportunity for maximum possible development. What this court has done is to allow these children to escape from the regression that the OFC put into effect by the stroke of a pen."[106]

These arguments over jurisdiction of treatment decisions were occurring at about the same time that Bristol County's district attorney, Ronald Pina, was conducting an inquest into the death of Vincent Milletich.[107] Pina asked Andrew J. Dooley, presiding judge of the district court in Taunton, for a closed hearing. Milletich's brother, Eric, responded to the inquest by saying that the family did not want BRI to close and believed the school had helped Vincent. "We don't blame the school," he said. "The school did him more good than we could do after years of trying. My brother was sick. He was autistic. He couldn't speak well. He had epilepsy, took a seizure and died."[108] Vincent Milletich nevertheless was still on the mind of Leonard and the OFC staff as they pursued the ban on aversives.

Rotenberg refused to stay the order that prohibited aversive therapy for an additional five students and was visibly upset when the OFC refused to respond to parents' requests that aversives be used with an additional sixteen students. On February 24, 1986, Rotenberg ordered Leonard to appear at a hearing on March 7 to determine whether aversives could be used with the additional students. She was to appear in court to explain the rationale behind banning the use of aversives that the parents had requested. Rotenberg said, "I can't devote my entire life to this case. I want the director here, and, if she's not here, I'm going to subpoena her."[109] It was increasingly clear that Rotenberg favored the use of aversives and supported BRI's practices to the point that some opponents of BRI argued that he was so biased that he should remove himself from the case.

During the last week of February 1986, BRI filed a complaint in the Bristol Probate Court, Rotenberg's court, against Mary Kay Leonard.[110] The class action suit, filed on behalf of the sixty-two students who resided in group homes in Massachusetts, sought a temporary restraining order and preliminary injunction that would allow the use of aversive therapy, thus overruling the OFC's ban. MacLeish believed that OFC's enabling statutory language stated that parents have a role in the care and upbringing of their children and that OFC had ignored this statutory obligation;[111] therefore, OFC could not override the parents' desire to have aversives reinstated. The complaint also asked that the state agency be put into receivership "to end the whole nightmare . . . and put an end to the excessive hoops they are making us jump through."[112] It specifically named Leo Soucy of Danvers and Peter Biscardi of Burlington, who had children at BRI, as plaintiffs and accused Leonard's office of engaging in

> a pattern of activity which has substantially and irreparably injured both BRI and the plaintiff class. The Massachusetts Office for Children has abused its authority and directly caused regression in the behaviors and quality of life of some of the most severely handicapped residents . . . OFC has demonstrated through its actions that it is completely incapable of fairly and impartially exercising the monitoring, regulatory and licensing function or acting in the best interests of BRI clients. The victims of OFC's wholesale failure to comply with its statutory obligations are BRI's clients.[113] The parents believe that at BRI their children have learned more, had made greater progress toward rehabilitation than would be possible at any other school.[114]

Leonard stated, "Well I think it is ludicrous. We have been serving the students at BRI quite well. At best, we have a disagreement over what is in the best interests of the students. A disagreement over best interests is not something for which you seek receivership."[115] Putting the state in receivership required that Judge Rotenberg appoint someone other than OFC to oversee state regulations. Robert Sherman, representing the group of parents, argued that receivership was appropriate when a state agency has ignored its statutory obligations

Figure 5. Mary Kay Leonard, commissioner of the Massachusetts Office for Children (1985–1990). Richard Howard Photography. People Magazine, *14 April 1986, 64.*

and cited the Boston Housing Authority, which recently had been put into receivership.

On March 7, Leonard (Figure 5) appeared before Rotenberg and agreed to form a team to determine whether physical punishment should be restored in the treatment of the sixteen students. The class action suit requesting receivership probably forced the agency to agree to the formation of a team to make these determinations. The team would include the chief probation officer of the Bristol County Probate Court, parents of the five students, and representatives from the Departments of Social Services, Education, Mental Health, and the OFC. Rotenberg threatened to appoint a master, an outside party who oversees the implementation of a court order, if the panel's activities took too much time. This panel would review individual treatment requests and recommend treatment programs, and it was to remain in place until OFC made its decision on BRI's variance request for the sixteen students.[118]

Leonard's position was significantly weakened by the insertion of the outside team into the oversight process and the loss of OFC's appeal on March 5 to the Massachusetts Appeals Court.[116] The appeal was based on OFC's belief that the probate court did not have regulatory authority to restore the use of aversive procedures to the six stu-

PAIN AND SHOCK IN AMERICA

dents. The *Providence Journal* reported that "Leonard was adamant and insisted that she retained the authority to either approve or deny the panel's recommendations. As she protested what she believed was Rotenberg's activist intervention into state regulator authority, she awaited the recommendations of a group of experts appointed to review requests the school submitted to reinstate physical punishment for most of its students."[117] She was not about to give up this battle.

NATIONAL EXPERTS REVIEW BRI'S REQUEST
FOR VARIANCES OF OFC REGULATIONS

Leonard enlisted prominent outside experts to review BRI's variance request to use aversives. The group met on March 3 in Boston to conduct the review, and their report was submitted on March 28. The group members were Judith E. Favell, director of psychology at Western Carolina Center in Morgantown, North Carolina, a nationally recognized researcher and clinician in the treatment of aggressive and self-injurious behavior, and editor of the journal *Analysis and Intervention in Developmental Disabilities*; Frank Laski, a prominent disability and human rights attorney; Ole Ivar Lovaas, a professor of psychology at UCLA and an internationally recognized researcher on the use of behavior modification techniques in the treatment of autism, who had published numerous articles on his use of punishment in treatment; Luanna Meyer, an expert in positive behavior supports from Syracuse University and the editor of the *Journal of The Association of Persons with Severe Handicaps*; and John Ratey, a clinical psychiatrist and assistant director of residency at Massachusetts Mental Health Center, a partnership between the Commonwealth of Massachusetts and Harvard Medical School.

These researchers and professionals had extensive research and clinical histories and were considered leaders in their fields. The Massachusetts Psychological Association congratulated Leonard on her choice of panel members, but MacLeish complained to OFC "that the agency has reached a predetermined result with regard to the facility's program."[119] He argued that the panel members were biased against BRI. According to MacLeish, Favell was retained by the state of California in an attempt to revoke the license of a California school that Israel had started. Laski and Meyer were executive board members of TASH, which sought to close BRI; Lovaas had a series of public disagreements with Israel; and Ratey was a psychiatrist, not a behavioral psychologist.[120]

Throughout March, as the experts were preparing their report, there were several disagreements between MacLeish and the state's legal counselors in the attorney general's office. In one instance, MacLeish complained about statements made about BRI by Lorraine Wright of the state Office of Handicapped Affairs, who was urging the state Board of Education to "cease its funding of BRI regardless of the licensing action to be taken by the Office for Children" and not "allow a facility to abuse and torture a child as a means to an end."[121] In a letter to the Executive Office of Human Services, MacLeish argued that "it is inconceivable to me that BRI can be expected to engage in meaningful negotiations with one agency of the Commonwealth while at the same time a sister agency is making defamatory accusations of abuse, torture and other violations of human rights. The Administration must speak with one voice with respect to its intent concerning BRI and its clients if the current discussions are to be productive."[122] Since both OFC and the Office of Handicapped Affairs reported to Secretary of Health and Human Services Philip W. Johnston, the implication was that Health and Human Services was not acting consistently and speaking in a single voice. OFC was ordered to comply with the parents' desire to have aversives reinstated. Its sister agency, the Office of Handicapped Affairs, was working in the background to terminate its funding for students at the facility. MacLeish began to raise issues of defamation:

> Many things have been said about my client since this controversy commenced. There have been many statements and allegations which have been untrue, defamatory and which have injured BRI. Thus far, BRI has decided to act with restraint and has devoted its litigation efforts to protecting the interests of the program and the clients rather than seeking redress in the defamation. It is obviously very difficult for me to continue to advocate that my client act with restraint when confronted with allegations that are as outrageous as those which appear in the State Office of Handicapped Affairs statement to the Massachusetts Board of Education. BRI is now in the process of assessing how it should react to these comments.[123]

It appeared that MacLeish was also directly contacting the experts who were participating on the review panel about the potential legal impact of negative statements and remarks about BRI. He was reprimanded by OFC's general counsel, Brenda Beaton, for contacting an expert panel member who was reviewing the variance requests: "As you are aware, I have been informed that you and Dr. Israel have spoken with a panel member on at least two separate occasions during the past few days. I was told that during these telephone conversations, it was impressed upon this panel member that the entire panel would be held accountable for any statements made by or actions taken by state agencies along with the contents of the report if they were negative towards BRI. If these statements are accurate, I find them to be totally unacceptable having no legitimate basis for their being made."[124]

In its final report the group of experts clearly supported the OFC and came down against BRI. It cited problems with the educational and treatment decision-making process, the peer-review human rights processes, behavioral prescriptions, and intervention procedures. It noted serious concerns about the automatic vapor station.[125] The report concluded, "This procedure is virtually without precedent in usual clinical practice and does not resemble or clearly derive from procedures researched and substantiated in scientific literature."[126] The panel cited OFC regulations that forbade the use of many of the interventions, recommended a "prohibition of the AVS and all procedures which result in physical harm," and concluded that "the procedures in question were not fully supported by current scientific literature, deviate significantly from usual and accepted clinical practice, and clearly expose clients to extreme psychological and physical stress and pain."[127]

PLANNING TO REMOVE STUDENTS FROM BRI

The OFC controversy prompted removal and defunding strategies by other state agencies in Massachusetts and New York, which had decided to transfer thirty of sixty students to other placements. The Office for Children had the authority to license and regulate the group homes but was not responsible for funding the placements. That was the responsibility of the Department of Mental Health. The total value of tuition for all students in 1986 was approximately $2.6 million. Agency officials in the Massachusetts Department of Mental Health were quietly signing contracts with the Delta Project in Waltham, Massachusetts, the Behavioral Development Center in Providence, Rhode Island,

and the Institute of Professional Practice in Montpelier, Vermont, to serve the ten students from Massachusetts who were attending BRI.[128] These programs agreed to use positive behavioral interventions and would be paid the same amount as BRI: $82,000 per year per student. According to MacLeish, the loss of tuition would put BRI out of business, which he claimed had been OFC's plan all along. He reiterated, "I think this is an appalling example of a state agency out of control."[129]

The Massachusetts Department of Mental Health denied that it was trying to close BRI. New York officials also denied that they were removing their twenty school-aged students and nine adults because of the OFC lawsuit. Phyllis Silver, deputy director of the New York Council on Children and Families, argued that "it is the governor's policy and the policy of the education department to try to serve New York students with special needs as much as possible in New York."[130] MacLeish responded to New York's attempt to remove its students by pointing out that officials had tried to do the same in 1979 but lost in U.S. District Court when families objected. He said, "They tried it in 1979 and they failed and they will fail now . . . There is some parochialism to spending New York dollars on New York programs and that is not appropriate. The kids should be served in the programs that serve them best."[131]

OFC DENIES BRI'S VARIANCE REQUESTS TO USE AVERSIVES

On April 24, 1986, in a ninety-eight-page report, the OFC denied a series of requests for variances submitted by BRI. These included fifty individual treatment program requests to use unusual or extraordinary procedures, such as physical aversives, for the treatment of autistic students; a request to use a contingent food program as a treatment for students; a request to allow open intake, that is, permission for BRI to accept new students into its programs; and a request to use corporal punishment as a treatment for students with autism. OFC ordered BRI to stop using all aversive procedures at the program within forty-five days, with the exception of verbal consequences such as saying "no," ignoring the behavior, and administering token fines. The decision also made it clear that no program in Massachusetts that was licensed by OFC was to use corporal punishment, even if it was labeled "treatment."[132]

BRI was free to reapply for licensure under these conditions and was given thirty days to develop alternative behavior plans for the students. This created a major power struggle between Leonard and Rotenberg. Rotenberg supported the parents and believed that the aversive techniques were necessary, particularly after seeing Janine. Leonard believed that the students had the right to be free from harm and that other positive interventions were more appropriate. MacLeish responded to the order by saying, "They've [OFC] essentially said BRI can exist if you go along with a radically different treatment program that they don't describe . . . No question we will go to probate court. It's our legal position that what's in the best interest of our clients has always rested with the probate court."[133]

BRI SEEKS A PRELIMINARY INJUNCTION

OFC was under attack by multiple parties. BRI filed a preliminary injunction in Judge Rotenberg's Bristol Probate Court to prevent OFC's decision from moving forward and to allow the use of aversives. This was in addition to the class action suit filed by BRI parents and BRI's request that OFC be placed in receivership and an independent monitor be appointed to enforce agency regulations. On May 2, Rotenberg issued a restraining order preventing OFC from further action. At the hearing of the case on May 13, Johnny L. Matson, a psychologist and a researcher from Louisiana State University, testified on behalf of BRI.[134] Matson, well published and recognized for his behavioral research, testified that "the OFC is playing Russian roulette"[135] with the lives of sixty individuals and that BRI was more effective than other programs he had visited in the United States, Canada, and Sweden. He testified that stopping the use of aversives "could be very deleterious and create very serious problems for the persons in the program."[136] He praised BRI's record keeping and its level of staff training. BRI presented additional witnesses who supported their practices. OFC continued to argue the case based on issues of jurisdiction and did not call researchers or other professionals who were critical of BRI. The OFC also did not raise issues of civil rights, appropriate education, least restrictive environment, or constitutional issues, such as the right to equal protection or freedom from cruel and unusual punishment. As a result, the factual evidence presented weighed heavily in favor of BRI.

Outside the Bristol County courtroom, Philip Travis, a Democrat who represented the communities of Seekonk and Rehoboth as state representative, where the four BRI group homes were located, told reporters that "the welfare of the students at BRI is not being addressed by the Commonwealth of Massachusetts. Until there is an alternative solution, what do we have available in Massachusetts for these people? Are we going to have them go someplace and sit in a corner or put them in a cage like they once did at the Paul Dever School?[137] While the agency heads are fighting these battles, the welfare of the students is being pushed aside."[138] Travis also argued that the state was forcing parents to hire attorneys, which drained their financial resources.[139] Rotenberg appeared to share a similar concern in court when he asked Robert Sherman, the attorney representing the parents, about the impact of the litigation on the families. Sherman replied, "The state has pitted all of its financial resources against these parents. It is a tremendous financial drain." Claudia Soucy, a parent of a boy who attended BRI and a plaintiff in the class action suit against OFC, said the families' legal bills had reached $110,000. MacLeish echoed the financial concerns, saying, "We can't afford to keep this up. I am not getting paid at this point. We are down to bare bones."[140]

The hearing continued throughout May. On May 21, Assistant Attorney General Leonard Lerner asked Rotenberg to step down from hearing the case on the temporary injunction.[141] He argued that Rotenberg's "conduct . . . justifies the conclusion that his impartiality might reasonably be questioned." Lerner was particularly concerned with a remark that Rotenberg had made that the OFC "comes into this court under a cloud of bad faith," which Lerner thought suggested that the judge had become a material witness for BRI. Rotenberg denied the request and said, "I don't have the slightest hesitation to do my duty, and I am mindful of my obligations."[142]

Leonard testified for six hours at a hearing on the temporary injunction request, to maintain the status quo and prevent irreparable damage or change before the legal questions are determined, and defended her decision to ban aversives.[143] She said that she was "outraged" that BRI accused her of bad faith in the execution of her duties. Leonard testified that she had worked closely with the licensing agent, Michael Avery, and found an alternative placement for the students in an unused ward at the Middlesex County Hospital in Waltham. She had also hired five experts in behavior modification to review BRI's

PAIN AND SHOCK IN AMERICA

variance request. Represented by Kim Murdock, an assistant attorney general, Leonard testified that she had been thoughtful about her decision to ban the use of aversives and had consulted two psychiatrists prior to making the decision. However, in an attempt to damage Leonard's credibility, Sherman pointed out that these consultations were not included in the interrogatory filed with the state magistrate in the fall.[144] Additional concerns were raised about a report filed by Betty McClure, OFC's director of the substitute care of the licensing program, who, after a nine-month study of BRI, filed a laudatory report in August 1985, twenty-six days before Leonard's order terminating aversives at BRI. Judge Rotenberg noted that OFC attorneys marked each page of the report DRAFT on October 2 after a Freedom of Information Act request by the plaintiffs and after it had been widely disseminated within the agency. This reinforced Rotenberg's concern that the OFC was acting in bad faith.

MARY KAY LEONARD UNDER FIRE

On June 4, 1986, Rotenberg granted a preliminary injunction,[145] overruling Leonard and the Office for Children and reinstating the use of aversives at BRI. He maintained the ban on spankings, pinching, and muscle squeezes but added that parents could ask for these procedures. The state responded immediately with a plan to appeal the ruling.

Leonard was not surprised by the decision. She said, "My job is to exercise my best judgment and rely on the best experts I can find to protect children."[146] Judge Rotenberg accused Leonard of acting in bad faith and playing "Russian roulette with the lives and safety of students" and said that her "unsubstantiated orders" were "based on no medical foundation." He called her actions "arbitrary, capricious, and beyond the scope of her authority."[147] Furthermore, he said that Leonard had "not visited the school" and "was wrong to characterize its treatment program as punishments" because the alternatives used in other institutions, such as "drugs and physical restraints, were far worse.[148]

Leo Soucy, a parent whose son attended BRI, and Israel called for Leonard's resignation, citing three of Rotenberg's findings: that Leonard's assistant stamped DRAFT on a relicensing study of BRI prepared in August after BRI's lawyers requested it, which Israel called a deliberate attempt to alter documents; the expert panel that Leonard appointed was chosen deliberately to be biased against the school and that any report made by the panel was of little value because students were not interviewed; and that the OFC acted in bad faith when a representative appointed to the review panel approved the use of two aversives when she already knew that OFC was about to implement a ban.[149]

IN DEFENSE OF MARY KAY LEONARD

Parents of BRI students also called on Governor Michael Dukakis to fire Leonard and reiterated that their legal expenses were the result of her efforts to shut down BRI. Dukakis's office responded, saying, "Mary Kay Leonard is responsible for the protection of the rights of children in Massachusetts. She has done an outstanding job. It is difficult to understand how her aggressive advocacy to protect children following a mysterious and terrible tragedy involving the death of a child at the institute could be construed as endangering children."[150]

Rotenberg apparently visited BRI several times after the aversives were reinstated for the six students, including Janine. He described being "greeted and hugged by this formerly desperate child (who had reverted to uncontrollable head banging after the ban) . . . an experience this judge will carry with him for the rest of his life."[151] Despite the court's decision, no new students were allowed to enter BRI since the OFC had suspended its license. Another hearing before Rotenberg was to be scheduled in an attempt to restore intake procedures and allow additional students to attend.

On June 5, Dukakis and parents of children with disabilities who were opposed to the use of aversives publicly supported Leonard and the Office for Children. At a news conference, Gerald Kramer, a father of two teenagers with autism and the past president of the National Society for Children and Adults with Autism, said, "The judge unfortunately doesn't know what he is talking about. Ninety nine percent of programs around the country use positive reinforcement."[152] State senator Jack Backman, Democrat of Brookline, said that "the Office for Children had made an unequivocal landmark decision to protect our disabled children from physical and emotional abuse and punishment in the guise of education and treatment,"[153] then read a draft of a bill that would outlaw aversives, which he said he planned to file immediately.

Letters to newspaper editors also supported Leonard. One of them published in the *Boston Globe* pointed out, "What the Globe did not mention is that the OFC and its director, Mary Kay Leonard, are making a valiant effort to eliminate some of the most severe and intrusive punishment procedures inflicted on our disabled citizens. OFC's actions are based on months of investigation and an exhaustive report by a panel of nationally recognized experts. The unanimous conclusion of the expert panel is that the BRI program violates applicable clinical, legal and human rights standards for treatment of severely disabled persons, and that BRI's punishment procedures result in a clear probability of harm."[154]

Federally funded organizations advocating for and advancing the rights of people with disabilities also supported Leonard and expressed concerns about Judge Rotenberg. On June 6, William Crane, the executive director of the Developmental Disabilities Law Center, the Massachusetts Protection and Advocacy Center, wrote a memo to the anti-aversive advocacy community regarding Rotenberg's temporary injunction against OFC.[155] Crane reported that Rotenberg asked to be appointed as a superior court judge for the purposes of hearing the appeal on the licensing issues. Crane stated in the memo that Rotenberg was too biased in favor of BRI and could not fairly decide OFC's appeal.[156] A letter was sent to Massachusetts court justices John Mason, Alfred Podolski, and Thomas Morse, asking that Rotenberg not be appointed as a superior court judge because of "numerous and serious reservations . . . about the objectivity of Judge Rotenberg's decisions."[157] The judges did not reply to the letter, and Rotenberg was later seated on the superior court bench for this case.[158]

Despite strong support for Leonard from the governor's office, the anti-aversive and positive behavioral support advocacy community, and some members of the legislature, the *Boston Globe* endorsed BRI and Rotenberg's decision. In a June 13 editorial, "Severely Afflicted Children's Care," the *Globe* asserted:

> In ruling that autistic youths at the Behavior Research Institute may receive physical punishment therapy, the Bristol County Probate Court has made a difficult decision, but one that is in the best interests of the severely disturbed young people and their anguished families. The ruling by Judge Ernest Rotenberg overrules actions taken by the Massachusetts Office for Children.

Governor Dukakis should now come forward and advise agency director Mary Kay Leonard to drop any further legal maneuvering in this case. If Leonard is still unwilling to cooperate with the Behavior Research staff and with young people's parents, she should be replaced . . . Like others Rotenberg would like to see alternative programs for treating the behavior of severely autistic youths. Time and again, during the months of hearing and conferences on the case, Rotenberg asked Leonard to come forward with alternative programs. Sadly, she has not been able to offer anything more than vague promises.[159]

Approximately two weeks later, on July 30, the Massachusetts appellate court upheld Rotenberg's ruling that dismissed OFC's ban on the use of aversives at BRI. Chief Justice John Greany, in a single-justice opinion, denied OFC's appeal and upheld the decision that Leonard was acting in bad faith. He said Rotenberg's "decision leaves no doubt in my mind that BRI and the affected students and their parents would have suffered irreparable harm if preliminary injunctive relief had not been granted."[160] "Put simply, the director has been enjoined from doing anything without the probate court's approval which would affect or impede BRI's operations."[161] As expected, OFC expressed disappointment in the ruling: "We had hoped to be able to go forward on our hearing on the appropriateness of our licensing decision but we plan to continue to put together our findings and experts to present an affirmative case for the probate court."[162] The *Providence Journal* reported that MacLeish responded to the ruling by saying that "he hoped yesterday's action would compel Leonard to work with us to provide the best care possible for this special class of students."[163]

ANTI-AVERSIVE EFFORTS

Rotenberg's and Greany's decisions affirming the use of aversives in Massachusetts worried anti-aversive advocates, and they met to discuss what to do next. Letting this decision stand was untenable to some. During the second week of July 1986, the Massachusetts Office of Handicapped Affairs (OHA), the state advocacy agency for people with disabilities of all ages, met with David Ferleger, a well-known disability rights attorney from Philadelphia, to seek his assistance on legal strategy in the BRI matter. (Ferleger would be retained ten years later in another attempt by the Massachusetts Department of Mental Retardation to decertify BRI.) Ferleger's parents were Holocaust survivors, and he attributed his fierce sense of justice to his mother, who was one of the last to leave the Warsaw ghetto for concentration camps, including Auschwitz, and to his father, who lived in a hole underneath a stable to escape the Nazis. Outspoken, energetic, and committed to ensuring that people with disabilities had the same opportunities afforded citizens without disabilities, he urged the OHA to raise therapeutic, moral, and social issues in as broad a context as possible. He also advised OHA to address some immediate factual concerns, including BRI's budget, Israel's résumé and history, BRI's tax status and IRS applications, liability, professional licensure, title searches, employees' criminal records, and corporate charters.

Ferleger provided OHA with several options to respond to Rotenberg's decision: initiate federal court action against state agencies responsible for allowing improper BRI actions; intervene in and activate an existing Massachusetts federal lawsuit before Federal District Court Judge Tauro [MacLeish had clerked for him]; file a taxpayers' lawsuit in state court against local school committees for improper spending of funds for BRI; criminally prosecute both for deaths of residents and for assaults on current residents; conduct congressional investigations into BRI practices; initiate legal action under international law; and challenge nonprofit status or corporate status depending on the results of the factual investigation.[164] OHA considered some of these options, and some of these legal and advocacy strategies were used in later efforts to regulate the use of aversives in Massachusetts.

ANTI-AVERSIVE LEGISLATION FAILS IN THE MASSACHUSETTS LEGISLATURE

On July 22, 1986, a hearing on Senator Jack Backman's anti-aversive bill was held in the Massachusetts legislature. Legislators, parents, professionals, and state officials backed Leonard and the bill at the hearing. Gunnar Dybwad, a professor of human development at the Heller School at Brandeis University, testified that BRI's treatments were unique and unacceptable: "During the years I have worked in prisons, including maximum security institutions, reformatories and juvenile correctional facilities, I have never encountered as vicious, as methodical, and as persistent a punishment regime as has been revealed at BRI."[165]

Israel and several parents with children at BRI were present and urged legislators to oppose the bill. Leonard testified in favor of the legislation, saying, "While we do not doubt our authority, we welcome this legislation."[166] The legislation did not pass, and despite being presented in slightly different versions over the next twenty years, it still has not. In December 1986, Backman retired after sixteen years as senate chairman of the Joint Committee on Human Services and Elderly Affairs. With his retirement, advocates opposed to the use of aversives lost an important legislator who supported their cause.

BRI STRIKES BACK WITH A CIVIL LAWSUIT

On August 7, two weeks after the hearing on Backman's bill, BRI, still represented by MacLeish, and parents of students residing at BRI filed a $15.4 million civil suit in Superior Court in Attleboro against the Massachusetts Office for Children. The suit accused Leonard of violating the civil rights of students and of making a "very arbitrary and irrational" decision when she tried to close the school. The suit sought $13.4 million for the parents and $2 million for BRI. "These kids really have been harmed by her. They've suffered in their educational skills. You just can't, by the stroke of a pen, eliminate treatment for kids like these," argued MacLeish. As expected, the OFC expressed disappointment that the families decided to move forward with the suit and hoped for a resolution that was in the best interests of the students at BRI.[167] OFC spokeswoman Helen Pelzman said, "One of the criticisms that has been central has been that . . . the only choice other than BRI was institutionalization or drug therapy, for example. Our point is that no longer do parents have to think their only option is BRI or institutionalization."[168]

On the evening of the day the civil suit was filed, ABC aired a *20/20* segment on BRI, which many have criticized as being one-sided in support of the use of aversives. Jim Mintz, professor in the Department of Psychiatry at UCLA, wrote a letter of protest to ABC News president Roone Arledge and argued against the use of aversives:

> Dear Mr. Arledge,
> I am writing to express my disappointment and outrage at the report on the Behavior Research Institute that I just watched on 20/20. Considering that 20/20 is intended as "news" and not commentary, this was a disgracefully slanted and one-sided

presentation of a most complex and emotionally wrenching issue on which responsible and concerned professionals honestly and strongly disagree. As such, it was a horribly wasted opportunity to educate your viewers about a complicated issue ... The impression presented by 20/20 — that a somewhat pious young State bureaucrat is attempting virtually single-handed to impose her ill-informed moral values on sick youngsters and their tortured and obviously honestly concerned families — just does not ring true. Responsible alternative professional opinions exist, although one would not guess so from the 20/20 presentation.[169]

Barbara Cutler, Martha Zeigler, and other anti-aversive activists believed that the timing of the lawsuit and the airing of the 20/20 segment were not coincidental and that MacLeish and BRI had effectively used the media to assist them in keeping the program open. Managing the media would continue to be an important strategy for both sides.

THE INQUEST INTO VINCENT'S DEATH

It had been a little over one year since Vincent Milletich died on July 23, 1985. In recognition of his death, a vigil was held in Taunton, where Rotenberg's court was located. The vigil was organized by Cutler, who had refused to place her son at BRI six years earlier. Buttons were passed out that read, "Vincent Milletich, July 23, 1985; Why?"; "Parents Campaign Against Violence"; and "Make Massachusetts a Torture-Free Zone" (Figure 6). MacLeish called the buttons "the epitome of bad taste" and said that BRI welcomed the inquest: "We look forward to it so we can get it over with."[170] Asked why she was holding the vigil, Barbara Cutler responded, "Vincent is a person in his own right, but somehow he has been forgotten. When I read the first articles about his death I thought that could have been my own son.[171] As long as society tolerates extremes, he [her son, Rob] is still at risk. I won't be around forever."[172]

After the vigil, Vincent's mother, Mary Ann Milletich, thanked those who attended. In a note to Lorraine Greiff of the Office of Handicapped Affairs, she wrote, "I wish to thank you and your husband very much for your participation in the prayer vigil for my son Vincent. When I learned about the vigil I [was] so elated, this past year has been very trying and at times I felt like no one cared about Vincent's death

"*Recognize and respect differences in others because differences make us individuals. Then, treat them as you want them to treat you.*"

Debate escalates on school inclusion, continued from p. 1

their disabilities, their ability to behave and function appropriately in the classroom or the education benefits they ~

The ~ for le~ plac~ the ~

to ~ cl~ th~ 20~ res~

In~ King ~ AFT Pre~ Paul March~ Arc's Governmental Affairs Office in Washington. Immediate Past President Jim Gardner also joined the nationwide radio debate to press The Arc's view that it is not only right but desirable for all children, disabled or not, to be educated together.

A copy of the broadcast on ~sette tape was distributed to all ~ chapters.

~ now the debate moves on to ~ where it really counts.

~ coming months, the ~ss will be debating inclusion ~er aspects of special ~ as they consider the ~ization of the Individuals ~sabilities Education Act.

###

ou want them to treat you."
The Peeks' audience expanded to ~illions recently when ABC-TV's ~20/20" traveled to Utah to meet ~em. The segment was aired Jan. 7 ~nd the Peeks were besieged with ~alls all over again ~ ~mply sent tw~ ~ckets to th~ ~is show. ~ But Fr~ ~vitatio~ ~ows. ~ddress ~ducati~ They ~pense ~0 E. T~ ~urray, U~ ~84.

Figure 6. Protest buttons after Vincent Milletich's death.
Courtesy Barbara Cutler.

and that I was fighting a very lonely battle to clear up how he was taken from me."[173]

The inquest into Milletich's death took place in district court in Taunton from September 10 to October 16, 1986. Approximately thirty witnesses testified, and eighty-one exhibits were entered into evidence. Special Judge Paul Ryan of the Barnstable District Court, who was appointed by District Court Judge Andrew Dooley, visited the group home where Vincent had lived in Seekonk and reviewed video-tapes of students receiving aversive interventions. County prosecutor Ronald Pina, witnesses to the death, behavioral experts, Israel, and MacLeish were present during the closed hearing. MacLeish was al-lowed to question for purposes of clarification but not formally cross-examine witnesses. Israel disputed one element of the published account of Milletich's death. He said that Milletich's head was not pushed between his legs; he said it was pushed between the legs of the staff member, who then handcuffed Milletich's hands behind his back.[174] A decision about the cause of his death would not be rendered until December 9.

ROTENBERG ORDERS THE COMMONWEALTH TO PAY LEGAL FEES

BRI parents and attorneys were arguing that they did not have suffi-cient resources to continue the necessary legal representation. On No-vember 6, Rotenberg ordered the state to pay $580,605 in legal fees to the eleven plaintiff attorneys involved in the lawsuit against the Office for Children, saying, "Financial bludgeons cannot be permit-ted to extinguish the rights and interests at stake in this case. Rather than adopt a conciliatory attitude, the omnipotent power of the state is now being utilized to continue the fight with a trial in the case due to begin in December."[175] The very large award was unusual because it was granted during rather than after the legal fight. BRI was now able to pay the $376,936 bill submitted by the Boston law firm Fine & Am-brogne for MacLeish's services.[176] MacLeish said, "I'm glad the court has recognized that litigation can't be used by the state as a bludgeon. The state felt if it made life miserable enough and expensive enough for the parents and BRI, the case would go away. This decision helps equalize what has always been a disparity between the resources of a private litigant and the resources of the state. The state has endless funds and armies of lawyers, and they can litigate until the cows come home. This decision balances that disparity, and it will have implications beyond this case. We want the money tomorrow. I intend to call the attorney general's office tomorrow after they have had a chance to read the decision. If they don't follow the court order, we'll be in court to file a motion for contempt of court."[177]

BRI parents could now also pay $203,668 for Robert Sherman's services with the law firm of Topkins, Gaffin and Krattenmaker.[178] Sherman commented on the decision: "I think it sends a message to state officials that they are personally accountable for their actions in their official capacities . . . This is an interim attorney fees award. What this shows is if we are to prevail in future proceeding, I'm confident the judge will award further fees.[179] This may be the tip of a very big iceberg. I think it is time that the state reassesses its position before this costs the taxpayers any more money." Israel, pleased with the decision, said he thought it a "ridiculous waste of taxpayers' money to have it spent on attorneys' fees. I hope this decision will provide an impetus for some reasonable discussion of a settlement."[180]

The attorney general's office immediately appealed, saying that the award was unfair and unwarranted, placed an unfair burden on taxpayers, and seemed "premature in that the case was not over and there has been no final judgment or determination that the plaintiffs are right." Rotenberg said that "the award was the plaintiff's 'key to courthouse' and without it 'a protracted, forcefully contested litigation . . . could well bankrupt them' before the case ends."[181] At this point it was very clear to many observers that the state was not likely to prevail in Rotenberg's court.

OFC CONCEDES SEEING
THE WRITING ON THE WALL

Rotenberg's award for BRI's legal fees prompted the two parties to meet prior to the class action trial in an attempt to avoid a trial expected to last two months. Attorneys from both sides met and tried to resolve several difficult issues, including the use of aversives and OFC's licensing authority. Unable to resolve the issues, the two sides met once again before Rotenberg on December 11 and 12, 1986.[182] On December 13, in a fourteen-page settlement agreement, the state agreed to allow BRI to use spankings, pinches, vapor sprays, and other disciplinary techniques subject to review by the Department of Mental Health and approval by Rotenberg. Monitors were to be appointed to review treatment plans, and the Department of Mental Health would take over the licensing responsibilities from the OFC. No damages were awarded to BRI, but the state had to pay the $580,000 award in legal fees and issue an apology to the parents of students at the center. In the event that the state did not pay the attorney fees, Leonard would be personally liable for the costs.

Under the agreement, John Daignault, a psychologist, would serve as the court-appointed monitor. An advisory committee was also formed to oversee the BRI program. John Matson, who had testified on behalf of BRI in the licensing proceeding, was named chair of the advisory committee in the settlement agreement. Three physicians, including Shervert Frazier, the chief of psychiatry at McLean Hospital and the former director of the National Institute of Mental Health, were also members of the committee. None of the members were outspoken critics of aversive interventions.

Rotenberg was scheduled to approve the settlement on January 7, 1987. In a last-ditch effort to nullify the agreement prior to the approval date, an amici curiae brief was filed by the Massachusetts chapter of the National Society for Adults and Children with Autism; New England Chapter of The Association for Persons with Severe Handicaps; Association for Retarded Citizens/Massachusetts; Coalition for the Legal Rights of the Disabled; and the Civil Liberties Union of Massachusetts. The brief urged Rotenberg to not approve the settlement. In fact, this was the second amici curiae brief he had received from the group. The first argued that "the probate court did not have jurisdiction to abort OFC's licensing proceeding by enjoining that proceeding in advance of a final agency decision and before a full factual record had been developed upon which any final decision would be made."[183] The second argued that "the probate court may not approve a settlement that requires or permits what is prohibited by law or that involves a dispute over which the court has no jurisdiction, corporal punishment was prohibited in programs serving disabled children in Massachusetts, substitute judgment proceedings may not be used to authorize corporal punishment, and disabled persons have the right to be treated using the least restrictive treatment techniques available." The legal brief restated that the probate court does not have jurisdiction over licensing matters and therefore may not approve a settlement agreement, which in effect is a resolution of a licensing dispute. Furthermore, the brief argued that substitute judgment decisions and a licensing appeal are incompatible and should not be decided by the same court.

Rotenberg was not persuaded and approved the settlement. Israel said he "was very pleased and could get back to the serious business of giving quality treatment" but emphasized that it would take time to recover from the losses of forty-five students over the course of the past year.[184] Leonard reluctantly said of the settlement, "This has gone on for a long time, and it is no good for the Commonwealth, the parents and the students for it to continue, so I am pleased with this proposed agreement. It assures the use of aversives will be much more controlled."[185]

The *Boston Globe* again weighed in with an editorial:

> The Massachusetts Office for Children's 15-month-long vendetta against a school for autistic children has ended in a victory for the school — and for the autistic children and their parents . . . Even after the students' parents came to the school's defense, and after initial court rulings in the school's favor, Leonard persisted. The reaching of an agreement in the case should now prompt human services officials to reconsider the agency's future, with a view to whether its functions would be better administered by the Executive Office of Human Services.[186]

The *Providence Journal* editorial page echoed the *Globe*:

> The outcome is a credit to the diligence of Probate Judge Ernest I. Rotenberg whose thoroughness and even-handed approach in this case set a high judicial standard . . . BRI provides a valuable service for those afflicted with autism who otherwise might be condemned to a life of custodial care in an institution. Legally and at least to some extent psychologically, BRI appears to have made its point. It has survived a bureaucratic and political assault that should not have happened. Its victory becomes a victory for the students and parents whose problems were needlessly compounded by imprudent state officials lacking the necessary evidence to justify their actions.[187]

SUBSTITUTED JUDGMENT:
WHO SPEAKS FOR ME?

One of the most important and long-lasting elements of the settlement was substituted judgment: that another person is appointed to act in the best interest of the client because he or she is unable to do so. The person who is making the substituted judgment is supposed to be independent and acting in the best interest of the client. In the case of people with disabilities, the court assumes that they are unable to speak for themselves or to express an opinion as to the treatment they desire or choose not to accept. Taking the right to refuse treatment away from an individual is a serious act reflecting a belief that an individual is incompetent.

The probate court, Rotenberg in this particular case, was in a position to offer substituted judgment. The court had to assign an independent attorney to represent the client and provide funding for an expert who could evaluate the individual's treatment plan. Factors to be considered to include the individual's expressed treatment preferences, religious convictions, the impact of the decision on parents or guardians, adverse side effects, and the prognosis with and without treatment. William Crane, director of the Disability Law Center, voiced his concerns that substituted judgment could be used to justify ill-conceived treatments by those in positions of power over people who are deemed incompetent and do not have a voice or adequate representation. He argued that no competent person would give consent to the kind of procedures used at BRI.

A REPORT FROM THE INQUEST

On December 9, 1986, over a year and half after Vincent Milletich died, the report from the inquest into his death was delivered to the county prosecutor, Ronald Pina, with the following conclusion:[188]

> From the evidence available to the court, it is impossible to conclude, with any degree of certainty, that any one person is either criminally or tortuously liable for the death of Vincent Milletich. There does not appear to be any evidence that Vincent's death was a result of deliberate, premeditated malice aforethought. Nor was Vincent's death the result of an assault and battery upon Vincent's person. The use of the White Noise

Visual Screen, as well as the other aversive treatment methods, had been consented to by Vincent's parents. Had any member of the staff present at Seekonk Home on that day taken some action that went beyond the therapy consented to by Vincent's parents, then an assault and battery would have occurred. This does not appear to be the case. The court finds that the four employees present at the group home acted appropriately, according to BRI procedures, in pinpointing Vincent's unacceptable behavior, restraining him and placing him in the White Noise Visual Screen. The four employees followed BRI policy, and did not go beyond the procedures consented to by Vincent's parents.

While it appears that no intentional act was involved in Vincent's death, it must be determined whether it was the result of an unintentional act which rises to the level of a criminal act. Involuntary manslaughter has been defined as "an unlawful homicide unintentionally caused by an act which constitutes such a disregard of probable, harmful consequences to another as to amount to wanton or reckless conduct[189] . . . What distinguishes wanton and reckless conduct from mere negligence is the grave danger to another must be apparent and the individual chose to act rather than alter his conduct to avoid the harm.[190]

Israel was found negligent for "authorizing the use of this helmet without having an expert in helmet construction design the helmet or subject it to a safety inspection prior to its implementation" but not in the death itself.[191] Judge Paul E. Ryan presided over the hearing and said that Edward Sassaman was also negligent in approving the design and use of the white noise visual screen helmet. Although she had expressed satisfaction with BRI at the time of her son's death, Mary Ann Milletich filed a $10 million civil lawsuit against BRI in New York.[192] She said she did not want to see another autistic person die the way her son did. She said, "I never wanted anybody sent to prison or criminally charged. No one got up that morning to kill Vinnie. Something tragic happened that morning to Vinnie. I am fighting to make sure that this doesn't happen again, because it never should have happened then. We don't want to address what happened criminally. We want to settle this in a civil court, because that is where we think it belongs."[193] Mary Ann Milletich and BRI reached an undisclosed out-of-court settlement and the case did not go to trial.

ROTENBERG OVERSEES SETTLEMENT DECREE

On June 22, 1987, at the six-month court review of the agreement, Judge Rotenberg ruled that he would indefinitely oversee the settlement agreement, although he had been expected to end his involvement in January 1988. He said that he would withdraw from the case when "there is no longer any possibility of harm to these children by the discontinuance of their treatment imposed by a state authority."[194] "For me not to extend my authority at this point, just when the school is finally starting to get back on its feet would be to abdicate to the wolves that are willing to kill them."[195]

The Massachusetts Office for Children was unable to overcome the successful combination of parents pleading for their children to remain at BRI, powerful and aggressive attorneys, professional disagreements, and a sympathetic judge. OFC's reliance on the legal argument that it had the regulatory authority to justify withdrawing the students and ending the aversive treatments proved to be ineffective. Perhaps if Leonard and her attorneys had raised legal issues related to appropriate education, discrimination, effective treatment, equal protection, and freedom from cruel and unusual punishment, further legal appeals to Rotenberg's decisions might have been made. Massachusetts had to live with the precedent established by Rotenberg's decisions and could not have anticipated that these would provide a foundation that would lead to the future use of painful electric shock on BRI students.

6 : THE FOOD AND DRUG ADMINISTRATION PERMITS THE USE OF ELECTRIC SHOCK ON PEOPLE WITH DISABILITIES

From the 1960s through the 1980s, during the years of controversy involving BRI, efforts were underway elsewhere to develop an electric shock behavior device for use on humans. These electric shock delivery systems would find their way into the treatment regimens at BRI, during which some children would be shocked for misbehavior many times a day. Some described the procedure as torture, others as "life-saving."[1] The use of electric shock at BRI would trigger a U.S. Department of Justice investigation in 2010, but the Food and Drug Administration (FDA) maintained a distance until recently when it held hearings on electric shock devices including the graduated electrical decelerator (GED) that evolved from the self injurious behavior inhibiting system (SIBIS). In 2020, the FDA issued a final rule that banned the use of "electrical stimulation devices" used for aggressive and self-injurious behaviors.[2] The center challenged the decision, and the ban was put on hold during the COVID-19 epidemic.

The scientists involved in the development of electric shock devices were associated with the prestigious Johns Hopkins Medical Center and the Applied Physics Laboratory in Baltimore, known for its work in translational research. Many believed that decreasing problem and self-injurious behaviors through the use of electric shock was a necessary and potentially transformative intervention. Some scientists believed electric shock was more efficient and exacting (easier to count, track, and control) compared to other punishers, such as spanking, pinching, and food deprivation.

The use of electric shock for behavioral control on humans was not new. In 1962, for example, Anthony Burgess, in his book *A Clockwork Orange*, depicted its use in aversion therapy. But the use of painful shock for the purpose of controlling behavior is sometimes mistaken for electroconvulsive therapy (ECT), which is used for treating individuals with depression or acute mania who are unresponsive to less invasive methods, such as medication combined with psychiatric therapy. In fact, the two treatments (electroconvulsive therapy and electric shock used as a punishment for unwanted behavior) are totally different. While the two methods are often confused, the only similarity between them is that both use electricity. The use of ECT as depicted in *One Flew over the Cuckoo's Nest*, both the book and the 1975 movie, remains in the minds of a generation. ECT today is vastly different from the way it was used in the 1950s, when it was applied without anesthesia. Still, its use remains controversial. ECT induces a seizure; contingent electric shock (shock delivered contingently in response to behaviors that are judged inappropriate) is used purely for the purpose of inducing pain. The American Psychological Association (APA) clearly distinguishes between ECT as an intervention for psychiatric conditions and electric shock used to control behavior. However, the APA has not called for an all-out ban on behavior modification using electric shock. It is one of the few national organizations that has not.

One of the earliest studies that used electric shock as punishment was conducted by O. Ivar Lovaas and reported in a 1965 article, "Building Social Behavior in Autistic Children by Use of Electric Shock."[3] Lovaas used shock to teach identical five-year-old twins with autism to approach adults to avoid being shocked. When the children associated adults with shock reduction, affectionate behavior increased.[4] Lovaas, in presenting the study, supported the argument that the objection to the use of pain was on a moral basis rather than a scientific basis and that "punishment can be a very useful tool for affecting behavior change." He later changed his opinion on the use of electric shock as an appropriate treatment to control behavior and "eventually abandoned these methods, telling CBS in 1993 that shock was 'only a temporary suppression' because patients become inured to the pain. These people are so used to pain that they can adapt to almost any kind of aversive you give them, he said."[5]

Although electric shock in the form of aversion therapy appeared in the behavioral literature for decades, the marketing of a device designed specifically to deliver electric shock to humans began in the 1960s. California researchers Kenneth Lichstein and Laura Schreibman, who later opposed BRI's practices in California, reviewed twelve articles on the use of electric shock with autistic children and concluded that the side effects "do not appear sufficient to rule out the use of this method of treatment" and that "we have strong evidence indicating that response-contingent shock is a powerful, effective technique for suppressing undesirable behaviors and that the side effects of shock in these situations tend to be of a clinically desirable nature."[6]

These authors did note that "many people find it difficult or impossible to use shock because of their own adverse philosophies" and cited another researcher, Todd Risley, who in 1968 reported, "Observers of the sessions in which shock was applied reported that, on the basis of observable autonomic responses such as flushing, trembling, etc., the subject recovered from the shock episodes much faster than the experimenter."[7] Former BRI employees report similar emotions, affirming that the deliverer of the shock could suffer emotional consequences as well as the person receiving the shock. One teacher I interviewed told me that he felt horrible that he had shocked the students and said that he hoped "God will forgive me."[8] Finally, Lichstein and Schreibman acknowledged, "No matter how effective shock may be for suppressing undesirable behavior in autistic children, it is useless in situations where people refuse to use it." The endorsement of electric shock by Lichstein, Schreibman, and Lovaas was used to help support the creation of a newly developed shock delivery device that became known as the SIBIS.

THE MARKETING OF SHOCK THERAPY

Between 1985 and 1987, as BRI squared off with the Massachusetts Office for Children and the California Department of Social Welfare, the Applied Physics Laboratory (APL), affiliated with Johns Hopkins University, was designing a device that would deliver contingent shock to people with disabilities engaged in self-injurious behavior such as head banging. The APL was established in 1942 during World War II to advance engineering and science. Best known as a defense contractor and for developing advanced missile systems, it is also well known for its work with sensors and signal devices, which were used in the design of the SIBIS. Considered novel and technologically efficient, the SIBIS provided the prototype for other devices that BRI would develop that delivered more intense electric shock.

Barbara Cutler, parent of a son with autism, a woman some describe as the unofficial ombudsman for disability services in Massa-

Figure 7. Gunnar Dybwad, founding director of the Starr Center for Mental Retardation at the Heller School for Social Policy and Management, Brandeis University. Courtesy of the American Association for Intellectual and Developmental Disabilities.

chusetts, sounded the alarm about this new electric shock device.[9] In May 1987 toward the end of the BRI/OFC dispute, she sent a letter expressing her fears about the new device to Gunnar Dybwad, professor emeritus at the Heller School at Brandeis University (Figure 7). Born in Leipzig, Germany, he moved to the United States in 1935. Dybwad and his wife, Rosemary Dybwad, were leaders in their fields for their work on deinstitutionalization and the international disabilities rights movement. At different points in his career, Gunnar served as the supervisor of the child welfare program of the Michigan State Department of Social Welfare, the executive director of the Child Study Association of America, and the executive director of the Association for Retarded Citizens. While at Brandeis, he was the lead expert in the famous *Pennhurst State School and Hospital v. Halderman* deinstitutionalization lawsuit, which focused on ensuring that people with disabilities at a state-operated institution in Pennsylvania had opportunities for community living.[10] He also served on the Massachusetts Department of Mental Retardation Human Rights Committee. Gunnar and Rosemary helped to form the International League of Societies for Persons with Mental Handicap, which later became Inclusion International. He viewed disability as a civil rights issue, not a medical one. Some have referred to him as the grandfather of self-advocacy. He was opposed to the use of pain as a component of treatment or therapy and was outspoken in his opposition to BRI.

Cutler wrote to him:

> I am writing this letter to alert you to a serious and dangerous development in the area of "treatment" of person with disabilities: — computerized electro-shock headbands being readied for sale in the near future.
>
> On May 8, Brian Iwata, Ph.D. of the University of Florida and formerly of the Johns Hopkins School of Medicine, presented a workshop on Self-Injurious Behavior in Framingham, Massachusetts, to an audience of 50–60 people from both institutional and various community programs . . .[11] During the last hour of the workshop (after some very heavy viewing of people who were injuring themselves), Dr. Iwata presented a new procedure which he called "electrical stimulation." He described an electronic head band which could deliver different schedules of shock in 0.5 second 9 volt bursts and be programmed both to respond with shock to certain movements and to collect data. He said that this device would meet the criteria of effective punishment because it would be (a) intense, (b) immediate, (c) inescapable and (d) discriminable (his ordering of the criteria). Furthermore, it would eliminate the slippage caused by staff using aversives because it was a mechanical device and therefore more reliable.
>
> Dr. Iwata went on to tell us that this device, which is being perfected at the Johns Hopkins Applied Physics Laboratory, is not experimental, that it has been approved for use, and that it is being prepared for marketing. He added that the firm that

will market this technological "marvel" (my word) is such a responsible company that it will sell these items only when they have been prescribed by physicians and other professionals. Of course the device can be developed for any part of the person's body, and it is even now being developed at two levels of voltage. The device is activated by movement within a circumscribed electron field.

Dr. Iwata regretted that we in the field have been insensitive in our use of terms and products: i.e., we have used cattle prods and dog shockers. Now we have a device that is designed for people. The commercial name was not disclosed.[12]

The last hour was the most chilling presentation I have ever heard. The ramifications of this device are devastating; and Dr. Iwata seemed either ignorant of those ramifications or indifferent to them. Is there anything we can do to prevent the distribution and use of this dangerous device?[13]

In my interview with Dybwad in 2000 in preparation for writing this book, he told me, "SIBIS is one of the most terrifying devices ever invented! It is not only harmful to people, it is harmful to society."

THE SELF INJURIOUS
BEHAVIOR INHIBITING SYSTEM

In 1981 the American Foundation for Autistic Children and the APL submitted a proposal to the Public Welfare Foundation to develop SIBIS. There was a great deal of institutional support for it. Phillip Calcagno, the chair of the Department of Pediatrics at Georgetown University Hospital, and Hugo W. Moser, director of the Kennedy Institute and professor of neurology and pediatrics at John Hopkins University, were enthusiastic supporters of Mooza Grant, who had held the patent for this device since 1974.[14] Grant, mother of two daughters with autism and president of the National Society for Autistic Children in 1977, developed the system as a means of reducing the self-injurious behavior of her daughter Linda. The technology worked simply: when the child slapped her head, an electric shock would be delivered to one of her limbs as a punishment.

Grant detailed the use of aversive stimulation to inhibit self-injurious behavior in U.S. patent number 3,834,379, issued September 10, 1974 (Figure 8). She described an apparatus that contained a

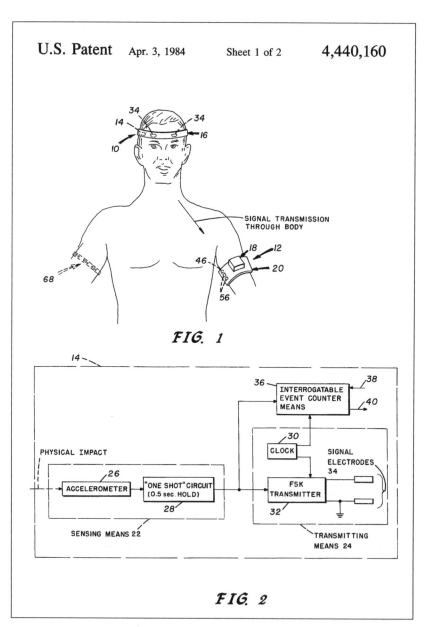

Figure 8. SIBIS patent illustration.

helmet to absorb self-injurious blows through incidents of head banging. The helmet also contained a metallic cylinder and a movable pin. When a person struck the helmet or when the helmet struck an object or surface, the pin contacted a cylinder and established an electrical contact, which activated an electronic package (described as being stored within a jacket in the person's clothing). An electric pulse generated in the electronic package was sent to the electrodes contained in an armband and provided an aversive electric shock (85 volts for 200 milliseconds) to the patient's arm. The helmet, electronic package, and stimulation electrodes were all connected by electrical wires. On the recommendation of National Aeronautics and Space Administration (NASA), Grant asked the APL to develop a wireless device that could administer the shock and count the number of head-banging attempts. APL developed this device using miniaturization techniques that were originally designed for earth satellites.[15]

Grant described her daughter's behavior in a marketing brochure produced by the SIBIS technology development company Human Technologies.:

> Our daughter, Linda was only about two years old when she started to strike her head with her fists, first sporadically and then over time almost constantly. This continued for over 15 years. The blows, sharp and smashing, could and did inflect grievous wounds on her head and hands. She would cry in pain at her bleeding cuts and bruises, or sit on her hands to restrain them, and nevertheless jerk them out to strike her head again. Her first act while still coming out of sleep was an automatic blow to the head. Nothing deterred her, although everything was tried—hospitalizations for weeks at a time, heavy doses of psychotropic medicines, sustained programs of behavior modification—all to no avail. To protect her from injury, we swathed her arms and head in thick sponge rubber shields and then for years held her arms night and day, awake or asleep; with my husband and I taking turns. For us it was ages of endless fatigue and helpless, hopeless heartbreak.
>
> We then conceived the idea that a device which would automatically deliver a harmless but unpleasant electric stimulus to Linda's arm whenever she struck her head might succeed in inhibiting her self-injurious hitting. Years of work

followed with various people, various approaches, and various models—with my husband as the principal experimental guinea pig. When the final model, contained in a headpiece, was placed on Linda, success was instantaneous. Two successive blows by her to her unprotected head each followed by an automatic adverse stimulus and she stopped hitting herself. Success was immediate and decisive. If the headpiece was removed, Linda would resume her head-hitting and struggle to have the headpiece put back on her. When the head piece was put on, her hitting would stop and she would radiate with happiness.[16]

The American Foundation for Autistic Children, which supported development of SIBIS, had an impressive board of directors. It included George Benson, former assistant secretary of defense and former research director of the U.S. Commission on Intergovernmental Relations; Paul Gibson, president of Envirotech Corporation; Leslie Grant (Mooza's husband), former deputy general counsel of AID for the U.S. State Department; Robert Scanlon, professor of pediatrics at Georgetown University Medical Center; and Edward Sheckman, M.D., vice president of J. B. Williams Co. Funding to support its design was procured from the Public Welfare Foundation, the C. R. Bard Company, Raytheon, and the Oxford Instrument Company. Robert E. Fischell, chief of technology transfer at the APL, led the development with Arnold Newman and reported that "the new technology of SIBIS makes possible a therapeutic regimen that can suppress self-injurious behavior and facilitate normal learning and social activity."[17]

Brian Iwata, who was referenced in Cutler's letter to Dybwad, and Thomas Linscheid served as primary and unpaid behavioral psychology consultants during the development phase and also conducted clinical trials. The team that developed SIBIS acknowledged the pain associated with the device but argued that "the brief discomfort is insignificant compared to the pain of repeated blows which clients with severe self-injurious behavior inflict upon themselves and which can lead to permanent mutilation, blindness, and death."[18] This justification for inducing pain was used repeatedly over the next twenty-five years in future litigation involving BRI.

Once the device was designed, Oxford Medilog of Clearwater, Florida, was licensed by the APL to develop prototype production units for use in clinical testing. The design was based "on the space technology of telemetry, the wireless relay of coded symbols used for accurate communication between Earth and orbit."[19] As required, the device was submitted to the FDA for premarket notification in July 1985:

> Section 510(k) of the Food, Drug and Cosmetic Act requires device manufacturers who must register, to notify FDA of their intent to market a medical device at least 90 days in advance. This is known as Premarket Notification—also called PMN or 510(k). This allows FDA to determine whether the device is equivalent to a device already placed into one of the three classification categories. Thus, "new" devices (not in commercial distribution prior to May 28, 1976) that have not been classified can be properly identified.[20]

In the event that a device is entirely new, it must submit a premarket approval (PMA) application. This process requires a rigorous review of safety and efficacy data obtained from scientific studies, including randomized clinical trials, risk analyses, and basic engineering and chemical studies. Oxford Medilog chose a process that would avoid this longer and more rigorous process by demonstrating that SIBIS was substantially equivalent to another device, the Whistle Stop Aversive Stimulator, already approved and in the marketplace. In order to provide additional data to support its application, Medilog sent the FDA a 1983 article by Carr and Lovaas that argued for the effectiveness of contingent electrical shock.[21]

In October 1985, the Center for Devices and Radiological Health at the FDA requested additional data on the device related to the frequency of false shocks; the leakage current; the maximum deliverable current and its impact on dry skin; the use of conduction gel; undesired muscle contractions; false signals; adverse side effects; and the possibility of a transthoracic current that could affect cardiac functioning.[22] In February 1986, after addressing its concerns about safety and compliance, the FDA notified Oxford Medilog that it deemed SIBIS "substantially equivalent" to the Whistle Stop Device and thus approved for marketing with the following caveat by Kshitij Hohan, director of the Office of Device Evaluation: "This letter does not in any way denote official FDA approval of your device or its labeling. Any representation that creates an impression of official approval of this device because of compliance with the premarket notification regulations is misleading and constitutes misbranding."[23]

The Whistle Stop Aversive Stimulator, developed in the 1970s by Farrell Instrument of Grand Island, Nebraska, had been approved by the FDA. It was approved and was in commercial distribution prior to May 28, 1976, the enactment date of the Medical Device Amendments, which established three regulatory classes of devices requiring different degrees of regulation, so Whistle Stop was not required to undergo the more rigorous testing and approval processes as devices developed after 1976. Oxford Medilog would not have to undergo an FDA-approved clinical trial if it could prove that SIBIS was substantially equivalent to the Whistle Stop device, which allowed a therapist to pair a tone with electric shock to the arm or leg. The purpose was to have the tone become secondarily aversive. Personnel at Oxford Medilog wanted to avoid conducting clinical trials and seeking approval from a human subjects review board. They argued that SIBIS was similar but had a distinct advantage over Whistle Stop, which was subject to interfering environmental stimuli such as telephones ringing and background noise that could inadvertently activate the device. The SIBIS communications link was coded and therefore had "greater noise immunity." The FDA agreed and decided its clinical trials were not required for premarket approval[24] because it judged the SIBIS to be "substantially equivalent"[25] to devices that were "state of the art" or in keeping with recognized science of the time[26] that used aversive stimulation to reduce vomiting, aggressive behavior, self-destructive behavior, snoring, and cigarette smoking. SIBIS was classified as a Class II device and had "the advantage of not requiring a therapist to administer the punisher; and had less sound interference." If the device was not deemed "substantially equivalent," then a longer and more rigorous approval process would be required, which would slow marketing and use of the device. The existing rules "created a daisy system of regulation, in which new devices simply piggy-back on earlier ones, without any examination of their safety or their value to patients."[27]

Oxford Medilog licensed the technology to Human Technologies. The FDA gave Human Technologies permission to market SIBIS in 1987, even though the device was preexperimental with no clinical trial evidence available to support its efficacy and safety for use with persons with disabilities: "This letter immediately will allow you to begin marketing your device as described. An FDA finding of substantial equivalence of your device to a pre-amendments device result in a classification of your device and permits your device to proceed to the market, but does not mean that FDA approves your device. Therefore, you may not promote or in any way represent your device or its labeling as being approved by FDA."[28]

University researchers involved in the development of the device were interested in studying its effectiveness. This was not required by the FDA. Clinical evaluation of the SIBIS device began in 1987 under the guidance of Thomas Linscheid, director of psychology at Columbus, Ohio, Children's Hospital. The device was also tested with Iwata's assistance at two Texas state institutions, the Richmond State School and the Abilene State School. Data reported in 1989 by both researchers showed a reduction of self-injurious behavior.[29] Between November 11, 1988, and January 31, 1990, BRI purchased thirteen SIBIS units from Human Technologies to use on twenty-nine students.[30]

MORAL, ETHICAL, AND LEGAL CONCERNS

Disability advocates arguing against the use of aversives and in favor of positive approaches opposed the SIBIS device. The process of device approval was confusing.[31] They asked: If the device was not FDA approved, then how could it be marketed? Why would the FDA classify this device in Class II rather than Class III, which required a higher level of scrutiny? Why would an electric shock device be classified in the same class as, for example, a pregnancy test? They feared that SIBIS would become readily available as a quick solution and would be widely adopted at the expense of alternative nonaversive approaches requiring individually designed, systematic, and potentially long intervention periods. After SIBIS was approved for marketing by the FDA, a Western Union mailgram was sent on April 8, 1988, to FDA commissioner Frank E. Young. The message was signed by the American Association on Mental Retardation, the American Foundation for the Blind, the Association for Retarded Citizens, the Autism Society of America, the Council for Children with Behavior Disorders, the Mental Health Law Project, the American Association for University Affiliated Programs, and several other national organizations. It read:

> It is our understanding that the self-injurious behavior
> inhibiting device (SIBIS) has been registered by FDA with
> no written and/or unpublished clinical trial reports and no
> standard peer review procedures. We call for an immediate halt
> to the SIBIS registration and an explanation as to why this device

designed to alter human behavior was registered without this professional validation. we request an immediate response.[32]

Six days after the mailgram was sent, Paul Marchand, head of government affairs for the Association for Retarded Citizens, conducted a press conference and demanded that the FDA withdraw registration of SIBIS and asked that Congress and the FDA develop standards for the registration of Class II medical devices.

These concerns were mirrored in a letter to the *Washington Post* by Madeleine Will, assistant secretary for special education and rehabilitative services in the U.S. Department of Education, and William Bradford Reynolds, the assistant attorney general. Will, parent of a son with Down syndrome and then wife of syndicated columnist George Will, had a long history of advocating for progressive educational reforms for children with disabilities. She and Reynolds wrote:

> The *Post* recently published two articles concerning the use of an electric-shock device to stop self-injurious behavior in people with autism and mental retardation (Metro, Aug. 27; Health, Sept. 1). We wish to state that there are serious moral and legal concerns about the use of this type of aversive treatment, as well as a body of evidence that calls into question the relative effectiveness of such treatment.
>
> The use of electroshock therapy to stop self-injurious behavior is a form of punishment. Under this treatment regime, an attempt is made to link a painful stimulus with a particular inappropriate behavior in order to eliminate that behavior.
>
> We ask, as a number of behavioral psychologists have asked us, whether society can sanction for use with disabled citizens forms of punishment, such as electroshock, that would never be tolerated for use with non-handicapped children and adults. Additionally, under both the 14th Amendment and the Civil Rights for Institutionalized Persons Act, Congress has charged the federal government with guaranteeing the rights of these vulnerable populations. As representatives of federal agencies serving these populations, we have a duty to consider whether the use of aversive punishment as treatment violates these protected rights.[33]

Some research shows that non-punishing interventions are at least as effective as and usually more effective than punishment in producing changes in behavior that are durable, widespread and without negative side effects. B. F. Skinner, the father of behavioral psychology, recently expressed his views regarding the use of aversive punishments in an interview in the New York Times:

"What's wrong with punishments is that they work immediately, but give no long-term results." He added: "The responses to punishment are either to escape, to counterattack, or a stubborn apathy."[34]

It is time that public attention focuses on the central question of whether the use of aversive treatments has any place in the behavior management of vulnerable populations. To ask this question is certainly not to signal any obvious answers, but rather to energize a responsible debate on the issue.[35]

The focus of Will and Reynolds's concerns was the 1976 amendment to the Food, Drug, and Cosmetics Act,[36] which required that medical devices be regulated. The failure of the Dalkon Shield, an intrauterine contraceptive device that caused internal injuries, and several types of pacemakers in the early 1970s drove the need for medical device legislation. Professional and advocacy groups complained about the absence of written professional standards for the review and registration of Class II medical devices. Many believed that SIBIS and the later versions of devices that delivered contingent shocks such as the graduated electrical decelerator (GED) should be classified as Class III medical devices, which required a higher level of scrutiny because of the potential to cause injury.[37]

The 1976 medical device amendments to the Federal Food, Drug and Cosmetic Act established three regulatory classes for medical devices, based on the degree of control necessary to ensure the various types of devices are safe and effective:

Class I. These devices present minimal potential for harm to the user and are often simpler in design than Class II or Class III devices. Examples include enema kits and elastic bandages. Forty-seven percent of medical devices fall under this category, and 95 percent of these are exempt from the regulatory process.

Class II. Most medical devices are considered Class II devices. Examples include powered wheelchairs and some pregnancy test kits. Forty-three percent of medical devices fall under this category.

Class III. These devices usually sustain or support life, are implanted, or present potential unreasonable risk of illness or injury. Examples include implantable pacemakers and breast implants. Ten percent of medical devices fall under this category.

Exempt. If a device falls into a generic category of exempt Class I devices, a premarket notification application and FDA clearance are not required before marketing the device in the United States. However, the manufacturer is required to register its establishment and list a generic product with the FDA. Examples of exempt devices are manual stethoscopes, mercury thermometers, and bedpans.

While those who opposed the SIBIS device continued to argue that it should be prohibited, the device was being used on individuals with behavioral disabilities. Over time, some practitioners using the device were concerned that the shocks delivered were not strong enough and people with disabilities were acclimating or getting use to the pain and not responding as predicted. They believed that new devices that delivered stronger shocks would have to be developed.

After five years of SIBIS use on twenty-nine students, Matthew Israel at BRI, with assistance from Human Technologies, designed the graduated electrical decelerator (GED) to deliver stronger electrical shocks. Between December 1990 and August 1992, BRI manufactured seventy-one GEDs and used them on fifty-three students.[38] The GED was classified as a Class II device by the FDA because it was deemed substantially xequivalent to SIBIS. Later, Israel developed an even stronger device, the GED-4, because the first GED, like SIBIS, was considered not strong enough and in some cases failed to decrease targeted behaviors. (See Tables 1 and 2.) As Lovaas noted in his 1993 CBS interview, people acclimated to the level of shock and it was no longer effective. The GED-4, like its predecessor, was classified as a Class II device by the FDA because it was deemed substantially equivalent to the first GED. In essence, the GED-4 was registered as being substantially equivalent to the original GED, which was registered as substantially equivalent to the SIBIS helmet, which was registered as substantially equivalent to the Whistle Stop device—which was never

TABLE 1: COMPARISON OF THE SBIS, GED, AND GED-IV

Features	SIBIS	GED	GED-4
Intensity	2.06 mA (rms) milliamperes (root mean square, or average); peak 4.1 milliamperes	15.5 mA (rms) milliamperes (root mean square, or average); peak 30 milliamperes	45.0 mA (rms) milliamperes (root mean square, or average); peak 90 milliamperes
Duration	0.2 second	2.0 seconds	2.0 seconds
Stimulation indicator	Indicates only that transmitter signal was received	Indicates actual skin stimulation	Indicates actual skin stimulation
Receiver	AM; sensitive to noise interference	FM; less sensitive to noise interference	FM; less sensitive to noise interference
Electrode placement	Fixed stimulator housing; can be placed only on relatively flat areas of arms, legs, or torso	Separated from stimulator (carried in belt pouch) by conducting wires; can be placed anywhere on body.	Separated from stimulator (carried in belt pouch) by conducting wires; can be placed anywhere on body.
Electrode configuration	Concentric (button inside ring)	Concentric (button inside ring) or spread (two buttons separated by up to 6 inches)	Concentric (button within) or spread (two buttons separated by up to 6 inches)
Battery	One rechargeable 12v lead-acid battery per year	Two rechargeable 12v lead-acid batteries per year	730 9v disposable batteries per year.

Note: A milliampere is a unit of electric current equal to one thousandth of an ampere. Root mean square (rms) is determined by sampling the current at intervals of time and averaging these. To determine the actual power, the rms values of current and voltage are multiplied. See https://spark.iop.org/explaining-rms-voltage-and-current#gref.

Current Levels	Probable Effect on the Human Body
1 mA	Slight tingling sensation. Still dangerous under some conditions.
5 mA	Slight shock felt. Disturbing but not painful. Average person can let go.
6 mA–16 mA	Painful shock causing some loss of muscle control. Commonly termed "let-go" range or freezing current
17 mA–99mA	Extreme pain, respiratory arrest, severe muscle contractions, individual cannot let go. Death is possible.
100 mA–2000 mA	Ventricular fibrillation, muscular contraction, and nerve damage. Death is likely.
Over 2000 mA	Cardiac arrest. Internal organ damage and several burns. Death is probable.

tested or approved by the FDA because it preceded the requirement for such approval. The GED-4 can deliver 60 volts and 15 milliamps in two-second bursts when a student misbehaves. For perspective, a Taser delivers nineteen short pulses of electricity per second with an average current of 2 milliamps of voltage.

There is no peer-reviewed research in the United States on the GED or the GED-4. Each is registered with the FDA, requires oversight, and cannot be marketed because of lack of clinical data. But according to the FDA, these devices can be used to inflict pain on people with disabilities.

7 : HERE COMES THE
NATIONAL INSTITUTES OF HEALTH
A NATIONAL OUTCRY AFTER THE OFFICE
FOR CHILDREN'S AND MARY KAY
LEONARD'S LOSS TO BRI

Judge Ernest Rotenberg's decision against Mary Kay Leonard and the Office for Children stunned anti-aversive advocates, who struggled to understand the rationale for the decision favoring BRI and its potential impact. Judge Rotenberg dismissed the $15 million in damages requested by BRI's attorneys, but that did not blunt the ramifications of his decision. He ordered the state to pay BRI's and the parents' attorneys' fees. If the state refused, Mary Kay Leonard would be held personally responsible.[1]

Rud Turnbull, a professor of special education at the University of Kansas, the father of a man with autism and challenging behavior, and the attorney who would later plead with the National Institutes of Health to convene a consensus conference on the use of punishment analyzed the court settlement for Madeline Will, assistant secretary of special education and rehabilitation in the U.S. Department of Education.[2] Will was preparing for a meeting with William Bradford Reynolds, assistant attorney general. Turnbull was a graduate of Harvard Law School and the recipient of numerous awards for his work in special education and disability policy. He also served as a Joseph P. Kennedy Jr. Foundation Public Policy Fellow, where he worked on the Senate Subcommittee on the Handicapped in 1987 and 1988. Considered one of the most distinguished and influential people in the field of disability policy, he cofounded the Beach Center on Disability at the University of Kansas with his wife, Ann P. Turnbull. He believed the Massachusetts Office for Children decision would have a "chilling effect" on efforts to ban aversives and advocated for a defense fund for policymakers trying to ban them.[3] He provided the following analysis for Madeleine Will:

What it does not decide is as important as what it does decide. It does not give blanket approval to use of aversive interventions; does not establish low procedural safeguard obstacles; and does not declare that the use of aversives is illegal under state statutes, or most importantly, under constitutional doctrines. The case turned on the application of state regulations; it did not involve state statutes (apparently they were not at issue). Or constitutional doctrines (apparently they were not even raised). It cannot be cited as precedent because it is a settlement agreement, not even a consent decree. More, it is certainly not a decision that is the result of a fully litigated case, one where the parties were not agreeable to settlement and where they took the case to the appeals court.

Clearly [this is] not as good a result as we wanted, but still not a disaster; media (The Boston Globe and 20/20, for example) portrayed it as a BRI victory; in part, and maybe in large part, it was because it will have a financial effect on [the] state and on [the] individual defendant and probably will have a chilling effect on state and any other individual's willingness to take on BRI. If Massachusetts fails to do so, Mary Kay Leonard would be held personally responsible. The main power of the settlement agreement is political. Its legal power is not so great. The open opportunities are at the point when the court must decide on a case by case basis whether the settlement agreement terms about the Least Restrictive Alternative and aversives and consent have been met. But who, after all this fight and in light of a counsel-fee bill of $580,000, will be willing to fight? Al Abeson, Executive Director of ARC-USA and I have discussed this plan. The professional and parent associations, funded by internal resources and with [a] big outside grant, would create a national legal defense fund for the purpose of defending such people as Mary Kay Leonard as they go about the business of doing their job and protecting people with mental retardation. Such a fund, if it had been in existence, might have been a more vigorous and more politically and legally successful advocate then apparently was available for Ms. Leonard.[4]

The year after the OFC settlement decree and his meeting with Madeleine Will, William Bradford Reynolds delivered a speech to the second Symposium for the Advancement of Non-Aversive Behavioral Technology on September 22, 1987, in Rockville, Maryland.[5] In his speech, Reynolds, who had been appointed by President Ronald Reagan in 1981, addressed questions related to the constitutionality of aversives under the equal protection clause of the Constitution, the presumptive validity of professional judgment, and the need to establish clear professional guidelines, guardianship, consent, and substitute judgment. At the conclusion of his speech, he said:

> The basic question in this area is not merely whether aversive techniques pass constitutional muster. At a more basic level the issue is whether aversive techniques, particularly at their most extreme, pass a more fundamental test: whether they are so cruel, so dehumanizing and abusive, so shocking to the conscience of a civilized society, that they are unacceptable as a treatment mode, even if, contrary to conventional wisdom, they should someday prove to be efficacious . . . We in the Civil Rights Division still have serious misgiving about the validity of such procedures, no matter how benevolently devised, when these procedures are designed to inflict pain and discomfort on persons with severe handicaps in institutionalized setting. We intend to examine vigorously the use of these techniques in our reviews under the Civil Rights of Institutionalized Persons Act (CRIPA)[6] and to act swiftly when we find violations of the law.[7]

PROFESSIONALS DISAGREE

Others saw the decision against the Office for Children as a victory. At its annual meeting in 1987, the Association for Behavior Analysis (ABA) presented its humanitarian award to two parents who were named plaintiffs in the case against Leonard and the OFC, Leo and Claudia Soucy, and to their attorney, Robert Sherman. The award recognized what the ABA considered their pursuit of the right to effective treatment. The decision to make the award to the Soucys and Sherman was not universally applauded, even within the ABA. Edward Morris, editor of the ABA journal and council member, disavowed any connection between the awards and support for the BRI program, and that "the matter was one of principle"[8] and "it is ABA's position that it honors parents in pursuit of the right to effective treatment and is not an endorsement of BRI or BRI's director, Matthew Israel; or aversive practices."[9]

Luanna Meyer, a professor at Syracuse University and a nationally recognized researcher on positive behavioral supports, served as a member of the OFC's expert panel convened by Leonard to review BRI's general and individual waiver requests. Meyer, known to be outspoken, resigned from the ABA over the award, arguing, "In order for the award to be interpretable as support for the family and individuals' right to effective treatment, at least two assumptions must be met: First, there must be evidence that the treatment sought is effective. Highly qualified [professionals] in behavioral programming . . . have challenged this assumption . . . Second, the program [must] be a good one in general. Again, this has been significantly challenged by responsible and highly qualified professionals."[10]

Meyer was not alone in her criticism. Gabrielle du Verglas, executive director of the Autism Training Center at Marshall University in West Virginia, also shared her strong disapproval. "Despite strong criticism of aversive procedures and physical punishment of developmentally disabled children, ABA elected to adhere to its narrow focus of "technology rather than consideration of human rights. The issue, in my estimation, is not the right to effective treatment, but the right to human dignity and protection of children's rights."[11] The division within ABA between those who supported the use of aversives as effective treatment and those who supported only positive approaches continues. Some believe that if aversives work and are used with strict guidelines and protocols, they are acceptable. Others (some who have left the ABA) argue that positive-supports intervention renders the use of aversives unnecessary under any condition. This disagreement within a major professional organization made up of well-published researchers made it difficult to argue in court that aversives are ineffective or that they are universally rejected by professionals. Because of this difficulty, many states turned from the legal process to the legislative process in an effort to restrict the use of aversives.

ADVOCATES PURSUE LEGISLATION TO BAN AVERSIVES

A major counteroffensive was being organized by attorneys, parent groups, researchers, and professionals to develop legislative safeguards that would prevent the use of aversives. Because the OFC decision was based on Massachusetts laws and regulations, anti-aversive advocates organized to change the law. Players in this effort included Gunnar Dybwad, professor emeritus at Brandeis University; James Gleich of the Massachusetts Office of Handicapped Affairs, an outspoken opponent of aversives; Herbert Lovett, a Boston psychologist and author of *Learning to Listen*, a book on positive approaches; Ann Donnellan of the University of Wisconsin; attorney Frank Laski from the Public Interest Law Center of Philadelphia, an experienced disability rights attorney known for his success in winning deinstitutionalization and desegregation lawsuits and a panel member for Leonard in the OFC case; attorneys Steven Schwartz and Kathy Costanza from the Massachusetts Center for Public Representation, a group dedicated to advocating for the rights of people with disabilities; attorney David Ferleger of Pennsylvania, an experienced disability rights attorney; Massachusetts senator Jack Backman, a vocal opponent of BRI; and Thomas Nerney, a nationally recognized disability policy expert focused on anti-aversive communications and legislation.[12] They all supported Leonard and the OFC lawsuit as an adviser, litigator, professional, or advocate. The group members were referred to as anti-aversive advocates. Attorneys for BRI were not happy about the involvement of Gleich of the Massachusetts Office of Handicapped Affairs (later named the Office on Disability)[13] at a time when the Massachusetts Department of Mental Health and the Department of Mental Retardation were promulgating regulations related to the use of aversives.[14] BRI attorneys believed that it was inappropriate for state employees to take sides. Gleich maintained that under state statute, his office had the responsibility to protect people with disabilities from harm and to support access to the most appropriate education and treatment.

MASSACHUSETTS PERMITS AND REGULATES AVERSIVES

Despite the national and state-level activities that focused on stopping the use of aversives, BRI described the period between 1987 and 1993 as one of peace, calm, and growth.[15] BRI had a supportive settlement agreement with Judge Rotenberg overseeing the state's actions. The BRI student population had increased to sixty-five by 1993 after a low

of thirty-nine after the OFC controversy.[16] Because of the contentious-
ness between OFC and BRI, responsibility for developing policies and
rules to regulate the use of aversives in the licensing process was given
to the Department of Mental Health. But soon a different agency, the
Department of Mental Retardation, was designated to oversee the settlement agreement. State agencies involved in the development of
the regulations were also supportive of anti-aversive legislation that
was being developed. As legislation was being written by advocates
in early 1987, the Department of Mental Health developed draft regulations regarding behavior management and behavior modification.
These were intended to regulate interventions that involved four procedures, including the most intrusive techniques referred to as Class
III Aversives.

The advocacy community remained skeptical about the new regulations because all interventions were allowed provided there was some
form of consent, which was accomplished through a substituted judgment proceeding in Rotenberg's court. This provided BRI with a certain level of protection. Although substituted judgment required that
a client's views and choices be considered, the use of extreme forms
of punishment was permitted. Class III aversives, such as spanking,
sprays, ammonia, and seclusion, were permitted in the regulations
but required some oversight. The anti-aversive advocacy community
strongly believed that Class III aversives should be banned altogether,
but parents with children at BRI and some psychologists resisted an
outright ban. Advocates argued that if Class III aversives were not allowed in schools or in the state's correctional facilities, then why
should they be allowed for use on people with disabilities?

Aversive interventions continued to be supported by the *Boston
Globe*, which published an editorial on April 21, 1987, against proposed anti-aversive legislation: "Opponents of the program for autistic children at Behavior Research Institute, blocked by the courts from
pursuing a 15-month-long administrative vendetta, have now turned
to the Massachusetts Legislature in a misguided effort to close it down
. . . Passage of the bill would be a victory only for bureaucrats and emotional opponents of Behavior Research Institute. It would be a setback
for the autistic children at the school."[17] Senate Bill 550: An Act Regulating the Use of Aversive Procedures, sponsored by Senator Salvatore
Albano of Somerville and Representative David Cohen, was heard by
the Human Services and Elderly Affairs Committee on March 26. The

bill proposed the establishment of human rights committees in the Executive Office of Human Services and the Department of Education to ensure that aversives described in the bill would not be used without protections and approvals. The Massachusetts commissioner of education, Harold Raynolds Jr., supported the bill, as did Philip Johnston, secretary of health and human services. The bill moved out of committee and was passed by the House of Representatives. But because Governor Michael Dukakis was running for the Democratic nomination for president, the legislative session was shorter than usual, and the senate was not able to consider the bill.[18] The anti-aversive advocates' work was essentially negated, and they would have to start over again with a new house and senate the following year. In 1988, an Act to Protect Disabled Persons was refiled.

On July 2, 1987, new behavior regulations were promulgated by DMH. They included definitions and descriptions of behavior management, behavior modification, and time-out. Additionally, the interventions were classified as either restrictive, such as the use of restraint and physical punishment, or nonrestrictive, which did not involve physical contact.[19] Bill Crane, the deputy director of the Massachusetts Disability Law Center who had previously underscored problems associated with substituted judgment and aversives, summarized the regulatory environment after meeting with Secretary Johnston:

> EOHS Secretary Johnston . . . clearly expressed to us his
> view and the Governor's [Dukakis] view that the painful
> aversives should be prohibited. In a meeting on February 11,
> 1987, Secretary Johnston strongly and clearly expressed his
> and the Governor's support of the principles contained in the
> proposed legislation and their support of OFC Director Mary
> Kay Leonard's effort to ban painful aversives. At that meeting
> disability advocates brought to Johnston's attention the
> proposed DMH/DMR regulations, which would permit precisely
> what the proposed legislation would prohibit. Advocates asked
> that the regulations conform to the principles in the legislation
> unless DMH/DMR was strictly prohibited from making them
> consistent. Although, DMH/DMR was not so prohibited,
> Executive Office of Human Services (EOHS) was becoming
> increasingly nervous about the inevitable confrontation
> with Judge Rotenberg if EOHS and DMH/DMR were to adopt

regulations consistent with the bill . . . DMR/DMH did, however, agree to language that no Class III aversive could be used in any program unless they had used them prior to the promulgation of the regulations.[20]

Crane summarized the new regulations, which would prevail for the next twenty years:

> The final regulations are an improvement over previous drafts, they include some good language regarding the standard of review and they require probate court approval of Class III aversives. However, the regulations offer no real deterrent or limitation on programs such as BRI, and indeed may serve to sanction wide use of aversives in many other public and private facilities not utilizing aversives. In fact, the Director of BRI enthusiastically commended DMH on its previous draft. It is ironic that even the OFC-BRI Settlement Agreement appears to offer more substantive protections to clients than these newly promulgated regulations.[21]

Crane was correct in his summary. These regulations allowed the continued use of physical restraint and electric shock and paved the way for the development and use of the GED, which would be used on students at BRI five years later. Not only did Massachusetts have no law banning aversives, it had a state agency and regulations that permitted and regulated them.

On December 15, 1987, Eric MacLeish, attorney for BRI, requested, pursuant to the State Public Record Statute, "copies of any and all letters or documents regarding legislation to regulate the use of aversive procedures including, without limitation, Senate Bill No. 1709. The request covers letters for and against such legislations, notes of any meetings or telephone conversation with individuals expressing opinion on legislation or any other material which refers, relates or pertains in any way to proposed legislation to regulate the use of aversive procedures."[22] MacLeish knew that the Office of Handicapped Affairs and Secretary Johnston supported the ban on aversives and publicly endorsed the new anti-aversive legislation. Advocates viewed the public records request as a form of intimidation and part of MacLeish's strategy to ensure that the state was not undermining the OFC settlement agreement by promoting and devising legislation that would have a negative impact on BRI. State officials recognized MacLeish's abilities and had watched him organize successful legal arguments and a campaign against Mary Kay Leonard, including seeking $15 million in damages from her personally. They wondered what his next move would be if legislation was passed.

ANOTHER DEATH AT BRI

On June 25, 1987, two years after the death of Vincent Milletich, another BRI resident, 29-year-old Abigail Gibson, died at Sturdy Memorial Hospital in Providence, two days after a coronary arrest. Hers was the fourth death associated with BRI. She was described as mentally retarded and prone to seizures with autistic tendencies.[23] John Daignault, staff psychologist at McLean Hospital in Belmont and the Harvard Medical School, was the court-appointed monitor designated through the settlement agreement and ruled out any connection between Gibson's death and her treatment plan, which included aversives. He completed his preliminary inquiry and found no evidence linking Gibson's treatment to the seizure that led to the coronary arrest.[24] "Her treatment plan of spanking, pinching, and cold-water showers was approved only three days prior to her death."[25] Robert Sherman, the attorney representing the families of BRI clients, hoped that Gibson's death would not create another controversy. "The findings of the court-appointed monitor right now should put that issue to rest," he said. "The fact is that these are medically involved kids and because they are so medically involved it is not unexpected that some of them will die. That should not be the cause for launching new investigations into the school."[26] The coroner supported Daignault's findings.[27]

NIH CONSENSUS CONFERENCE ON PUNISHMENT
(BE CAREFUL WHAT YOU ASK FOR)

Robert Cooper, Danny Aswad, Vincent Milletich, and Abigail Gibson were dead. Legal battles against BRI in California had been somewhat successful and resulted in prohibitive state regulation and legislation, but efforts to stop the use of aversives had clearly failed in Massachusetts. The SIBIS was now approved by the FDA. Frustrated with Rotenberg's approval of the use of punishment and the outcome of the case against Leonard in 1987, disability advocates turned to the National

Institutes of Health (NIH), believing that its consensus process could help them argue that the use of aversives was harmful and possibly deadly and that positive interventions were effective in reducing serious behaviors. NIH is the primary federal agency responsible for conducting and supporting medical research. Each year it spends billions of dollars to advance understanding of the causes and outcomes of disease and other health-related conditions. Because research results can sometimes be competing and cause confusion and disagreement in a field, NIH convenes what is referred to as a consensus conference: a series of meetings involving experts in the field who review studies, prepare chapters on topics of relevance, and hear testimony from leaders in the field. During 1987, Madeline Will, assistant secretary for the U.S. Department of Special Education and Rehabilitation and the parent of a son with Down syndrome, helped to convince NIH that a consensus conference on the use of aversives was needed. Anti-aversive advocates believed that if NIH determined that aversives were unnecessary because more positive interventions were effective, then the use of painful punishers would be ended. They believed a statement from NIH would finally resolve the issues of using punishment as a treatment modality.

Consensus conferences have been called on such topics as breast cancer, cerebral palsy, cystic fibrosis, and other medical conditions. The evidence-based conference focuses on problematic questions and intervention concerns. The subsequent statement released by the consensus panel "is an independent report of the panel and is not a policy statement of the NIH or the Federal Government."[28] The NIH describes the process in this way: "In order to resolve controversial and difficult treatment issues, all available information on the subject in question must be presented. Because the consensus panel must be an independent, broad-based group assembled for each conference to give balanced, objective and knowledgeable attention to the topic, panel members are carefully screened to ensure that they are not professionally identified with advocacy or promotional positions with respect to the consensus topic. This screening includes searches of the biomedical literature database to ensure that they have not published recently on the topic in question."[29] Screening was done particularly carefully for this consensus conference because aversive interventions were extremely controversial and the panel had to be exceptionally free from bias.

The request for a consensus conference was originally made during the OFC lawsuit. In 1986, David Coulter, a professor at the Boston University School of Medicine and president of the American Association of Mental Deficiency, wrote to Itzhak Jacoby, acting director of the Office of Medical Applications in Research at NIH, calling for a consensus conference. Coulter cited the aversives procedures used at BRI and argued that the process would "help us to resolve our differences, evaluate the available research data, and generate a consensus statement which will represent valid management guidelines and directions for further research."[30] The request was supported by the Accreditation Council, a group that advocated for appropriate standards of care for people with disabilities. The council included in its membership the Association for Retarded Citizens, the American Association on Mental Retardation, the American Psychological Association, the American Occupational Therapy Association, the Council for Exceptional Children, United Cerebral Palsy, the National Society for Children and Adults with Autism, and the National Association of Social Workers. Mary Cerreto,[31] then the CEO of the Accreditation Council, supported this request and argued that "a Consensus Conference would assist the field to determine the current state of the art, enhance the current provision of services of quality to persons with developmental disabilities, and stimulate research in the search for treatment methods that are alternatives to aversive techniques."[32] Jacoby responded to these requests expressing his concern that there might be an insufficient empirical basis to hold a conference.[33] Cerreto responded saying, "I was surprised that the question arose as to whether there are sufficient empirical data available to support a debate on this topic. Most of my colleagues and I approach the clinical debate from an empirical base, recognizing of course the tempering influences of values . . . we believe there are abundant empirical data."[34]

In 1988, after OFC's loss to BRI, Jacoby was repeatedly reassured by Mary Cerreto and Rud Turnbull that there was sufficient and compelling evidence for a conference. In his letter to Jacoby, Turnbull argued that there were "massive amounts of research [that] have been published in leading journals in mental retardation, both about the efficacy of aversive programs (found to be ineffective by most measures) and non-aversive programs (found to be effective)." Regarding the controversy, he added, "The clinical controversy, by the way, is not about efficacy; it is about the propriety of using aversives. That is in part a scientific matter, a national conference on non-aversives would certainly address that matter at its root, namely whether science justifies the technique. If NIH were to sponsor such a conference, it would go a long way to helping put a more effective science (that of non-aversives) into practice."[35]

Anti-aversive advocates arguing for a conference did not fully appreciate the extent to which the consensus process valued and relied on large studies that examined the use of punishment using randomized designs. At that time, these studies involving behavioral interventions were primarily conducted in institutional settings rather than in the community. Many advocates of positive behavioral supports believed that the institution itself was part of the reason that people with disabilities engaged in self-injurious and other dangerous or destructive behavior, thereby making large scale studies invalid. Institutions were large, impersonal, and devoid of stimulation and individual choice. At that time, recently published research that supported nonaversive or positive behavioral supports involved fewer individuals, was not randomized, often used single-subject methods, took place in less controlled community settings, and for many at NIH did not meet the necessary scientific scrutiny. Herb Lovett, a psychologist who specialized in working with people with severe behavior disorders, voiced the concerns of many who opposed the use of punishment and aversives in institutional environments. He warned against accepting "highly authoritarian" or institution-based research as sound clinical evidence:

> One of the most important lessons of behavioral thinking is the power of environments to teach. Hurting people to control their behavior necessarily takes place in highly authoritarian settings. How often do our human services ask the simple human question: How can we help this person live where she is loved and have access to the people and things she herself loves? Instead, we generally demand that people demonstrate ordinary behavior as a prerequisite, not for a life that looks to their satisfaction and happiness, but for the simple absence of pain. This irrationality defies all logic, and an error of logic and rationality is fatal to behaviorism, which has been aggressively anti-emotional and overly dependent on empiricism. The use of pain betrays its own bedrock perception: If environment is the great teacher and people are given violent environments, how

in the world can they be expected not to be aggressive and self-injurious? The use of pain to control people has become both morally and intellectually bankrupt.[36]

The Right to Effective Treatment Becomes the Rationale

As the NIH consensus panel process unfolded, other actions and battles were brewing in Massachusetts and across the rest of the country. Professionals and families supportive of aversives were aware that anti-aversive legislation had almost passed in Massachusetts and that national sentiment against their use was growing. Before the NIH consensus conference, aversive supporters formed a group that countered the arguments being made by TASH, AAMR, the Association for Retarded Children, and the National Autism Society. By 1989, the International Association for the Right to Effective Treatment (IARET), chaired by John Matson of Louisiana State University,[37] had more than sixty charter members, many of them well-known behaviorists. They now organized to defeat the Massachusetts legislation, An Act to Protect Disabled Persons, which would have prohibited aversives. In a letter to the Massachusetts Association for Retarded Citizens, IARET wrote, "As an organization, we certainly support positive programming, if such programming has been proven to be effective. If, after sufficient trials, this programming has been ineffective, we believe that after consultation with competent and experienced professionals, aversive interventions should not be ruled out."[38] Despite the attempts to pass anti-aversive legislation, the Massachusetts Department of Mental Retardation on April 20, 1989, approved BRI's application for certification to use a Class III aversive intervention (SIBIS and electric shock).[39]

Other States Attempt to Stop Aversives

Activities in Massachusetts were being discussed by disability professionals and families across the United States. There was growing concern about the use of electric shock. In 1989, a school district in Michigan barred the use of SIBIS in its schools because it violated "local policy against corporal punishment,"[40] which prompted a lawsuit in federal district court. The Michigan State Protection and Advocacy agency argued against the use of SIBIS. The Van Duser family from Flint, with the support of the International Association for the

Right to Effective Treatment, wanted SIBIS reinstated. Attorney Richard Landau, who had worked with BRI attorney Robert Sherman, represented the family. When their daughter, Amber, wore a SIBIS device and hit herself, she would hear a high-pitched beep, and a signal would be sent to an electrode attached to her leg that administered an 85 volt shock. The Van Dusers claimed that the policy barring the use of SIBIS violated Amber's constitutional rights as defined by the Education for All Handicapped Children's Act and the Fourteenth Amendment to the Constitution. They prevailed in court, and the Genesee Intermediate School District changed its position, now claiming that the school had no authority to prevent a student from using a medical device prescribed by a doctor.[41] The power of the medical profession and its ability to prescribe aversive treatments would become apparent throughout the NIH conference.

National disability organizations across the country were acting on their opposition to the use of aversives. This was no longer an issue that involved only Massachusetts. In 1989, the American Association on Mental Retardation (AAMR), the largest and oldest professional organization dedicated to people with intellectual disabilities, denied exhibit space during a convention in Washington, DC, to Human Technologies, the company that had FDA approval to market SIBIS. This angered aversive supporters. Thomas Linscheid, director of the Department of Psychology at Children's Hospital of Ohio State University and a member of IARET, was involved in the development of SIBIS and supervised the use of the device with seven individuals during its clinical review. He accused AMMR of denying individuals scientifically documented interventions and overrelying on nonaversive approaches: "I hope that AAMR is not becoming an organization willing to suppress the free exchange of information based on a scientifically yet-unproven belief or wish or to bend science to fit an ideological perspective."[42] The use of electric shock on people with disabilities was mobilizing the anti-aversive advocates. There was a great deal of growing pressure on the Commonwealth of Massachusetts to do something about BRI.

Preparation for the Consensus Conference

Anti-aversive advocates finally got their wish when efforts to have NIH sponsor a consensus conference worked. In February 1988, the NIH announced that the National Institute for Child Health and Human Development (NICHD) and the Office of Medical Applications would cosponsor the Consensus Conference on the Control of Destructive Behaviors by Developmentally Disabled Individuals. A planning meeting was convened in June. Dr. Rodney Howell, professor of pediatrics at the University of Miami, was the chair. The conference itself typically lasts two-and-a-half days. The first day and a half includes a plenary session, where experts present research and hold open discussions with an audience. The final afternoon is spent in closed session, and a consensus statement is drafted.[43] Four groups were involved with the conference: the planning committee, which set the agenda; the consensus panel itself, which involved a group of scientists representing different points of view; the presenters; and outside advocates and other interested parties. The participants included a long list of well-published individuals in the field of developmental disabilities.[44]

The planning committee had four responsibilities: identifying the disciplines and individuals who would present at the conference, preparing the consensus questions, selecting the topics for the background papers and the individuals qualified to write them, and selecting the experts who would attend the conferences.[45] The planning committee and the consensus panel were different groups. Papers on the use of punishment were commissioned for presentation to the panel. Several who were commissioned to write papers were conducting research on the use of aversives and had organizational or personal affiliations with SIBIS. The inclusion of Michael Cataldo,[46] director of the Department of Psychology at the Kennedy Institute at John Hopkins University, and Brian Iwata, from the University of Florida, prompted scrutiny and letters of complaints from anti-aversive advocates.[47] These advocates believed there was a conflict of interest and that both scientists were biased, particularly given NIH guidelines that the panel "be objective in reaching consensus without pre-judgment and promotional position with respect to the consensus topic."[48]

The consensus conference was set for September 12, 1989, two and half years after David Coulter's first request for such a conference. Dissension over process and over who was included and who was not began almost immediately. Tom Nerney, executive director of the National Autism Society, and Luanna Meyer, professor at Syracuse University, were fierce critics of the use of aversives and paid close attention to the entire process. Professional and advocacy organizations were invited to the conference to make brief presentations. Some researchers lobbied for an opportunity to present their findings and research, and some lobbied against invitations to certain groups and individuals. Panel members were David Braddock, director of the University Affiliated Program at the University of Illinois; Joseph Brady, professor of behavioral biology and neuroscience at Johns Hopkins School of Medicine; Robert Cooke, parent of a child with a disability and professor emeritus of pediatrics from SUNY-Buffalo; Jo Ann Derr, Department of Mental Retardation, Massachusetts and parent of a son with Down syndrome; Joseph French, clinical professor of neurology and pediatrics, SUNY Health Center; Leonard Krasner, clinical professor, Department of Psychiatry and Behavioral Science, Stanford University School of Medicine; Marty Wyngaarden Krauss, director of social research, Eunice Kennedy Shriver Center, Waltham, Massachusetts; Victor Laties, professor of toxicology, pharmacology, and psychology, University of Rochester School of Medicine and Dentistry; Gerald Nord, Department of Human Services, Minnesota; Joseph Noshpitz, clinical professor of psychiatry and behavioral science, George Washington University; Gene Sackett, associate director, Child Development and Mental Retardation Center, University of Washington; Sara Sparrow, professor and chief psychology, the Child Study Center of Yale University School of Medicine; and Naomi Zigmond, Special Education Program, University of Pittsburgh School of Education.[49]

In December 1988, eight months before the conference itself, the panel convened and members "were presented an extensive and preliminary bibliographic search on treatment of destructive behaviors that explored six data bases. Plans for the development of background papers were presented and discussed. In four subsequent panel meetings, background papers were presented by their authors and revisions were suggested."[50] A draft report served as the basis of the public conference, and the public and interested parties were notified through the Federal Register and thirteen thousand mail announcements.

In addition to the panel, a group of national experts was selected to speak at the conference. Each had published extensively on the topic of behavioral disabilities and included Alfred Baumeister, Madga Campbell, Judith Favell, Richard Foxx, Barbara Herman, Robert Horner, Brian Iwata, Thomas Linschied, William Nyhan, Raymond Romanczyk, Murray Sidman, Robert Sprague, Paul Touchette, and David Wacker. Gary Lavigna, who opposed BRI in California, was added at the last minute because of concerns by anti-aversive advocates that the panel was heavily weighted with individuals in favor of aversives.[51]

A Moral Argument against the Use of Pain

John O'Brien, a prominent consultant focused on people with disabilities and person-centered planning, did not believe that aversive interventions should be the subject of a consensus conference or that science could answer the question of whether they should be used. He argued that there was a more fundamental and moral question at hand. O'Brien was internationally known for his work on person-centered planning and his deep commitment to people with disabilities. Often wearing suspenders and a flannel shirt to complement his bushy beard, he knew how to listen and take a genuine interest in ideas and opposing arguments. Originally his plan was to become a priest, and he spent many years in seminary. His ideas focused on the importance of establishing positive relationships with people who are served and on the power differential between professionals and people with disabilities. In response to the consensus panel process, O'Brien, under contract with the Syracuse University Center on Human Policy,[52] wrote a widely distributed monograph in 1988, "Against Pain as a Tool in Professional Work on People with Severe Disabilities." O'Brien, widely known as a thoughtful man, consulted with national and international human service organizations and groups. In the article, he expressed ethical arguments against the use of pain, many of which were adopted by the anti-aversive advocates:

> Those with professional power over people with severe disabilities face moral and ethical questions: is it good to use pain as a tool in their work? My answer is no. Pain as a tool increases the power professionals have over vulnerable people while it decreases the chances of a positive human relationship between those who choose pain and those who are hurt. People who wish to build positive relationships and less violent social settings will follow two simple rules: if in doubt, do not cause pain; and, act positively to create conditions that decrease the occurrence of pain. Right living lies in the long-term struggle to apply these two rules in the creation of fitting responses to the difficult situations arising from engagement with people with severe disabilities who injure themselves and others . . . "Aversive treatment" and "intrusive procedure" seem to me unhelpful euphemisms which cloak the use of pain beneath a long white lab coat. The terms confuse because they are

sometimes defined to include both activities that intentionally inflict pain (such as electric shock, unpleasant noises or odors, humiliation designed to cause pain, taking away thing impoverished people value most, hair pulling, and pinching) and activities that might seem odd or even offensive but may not be intended to inflict pain (such as some procedures based on the principle of satiation[53] and some forms of time-out[54]). Activities that deprive or offend against a common sense of decency deserve scrutiny and should be avoided. But because professionals in control of people with severe disabilities lack agreement on whether it is right to inflict pain, focus on the narrower question of purposeful use of pain comes first ... The use of pain as a tool with those over whom they have power connects therapists with teachers who administer corporal punishment (Mancuso, 1972), some inquisitors, some jailers, and professional torturers. The important similarity is not in the choice of methods for delivering pain, or in the pain's intensity, duration, or immediate purpose, but in the deliberate selection of pain as a tool and the social context of inequality within which they choose to use pain. Some reports of the use of pain as therapy rival accounts of torture, but these abominations can confuse the issue. When practitioners of less harsh or less bizarre hurt distance themselves from extremists, they deny their fundamental links to other professional users of pain. The denial distracts from the necessary ethical argument: why choose to hurt someone you hold power over?

Advocates against the use of pain review the evidence. They argue from inefficiency: the use of pain is costly and inefficient, other methods are more efficient. They argue from ineffectiveness: pain has not been proven effective, especially in the long term; it should be rejected in favor of other methods.

Advocates for the use of pain review the facts about "non-aversive interventions" and argue that they are themselves uncertain, inefficient, and ineffective. Advocates opposed to pain counterattack. Both sides agree that more study is needed to settle the question, though they disagree about the research agenda.

Perhaps one day this professional argument will lead to

agreement on the facts. Perhaps this is how science progresses. But for now people with severe disabilities live with the consequences of the polarization among those who control their lives . . .

Pain will remain a legally-sanctioned tool until a consensus forms against it. For now at least, professional debate is unlikely to shape that consensus with facts. Adding professional procedures and due process protections to the delivery of pain may make those who administer pain more careful and rule out some extreme measures, but they beg the fundamental questions: is it good to use pain as a tool? Those convinced that the answer is "no" have to move beyond professionalism and due process. Even when pain is finally outlawed as a professional tool, some people with severe disabilities will inflict pain on their self or other people. If they are to live in dignity with the rest of us, we must learn how to create the conditions that decrease the occurrence of pain among us.[55]

THE CONSENSUS DEVELOPMENT CONFERENCE ON CONTROL OF DESTRUCTIVE BEHAVIORS BY DEVELOPMENTALLY DISABLED INDIVIDUALS

Anti-aversive advocates were following the entire consensus development process. They knew who would be attending, the subjects of the background papers, and who would be presenting. They concluded that aversive interventions would be scrutinized but supported by the NIH. At this point all they could do was try to stop the conference. Marsha Datlow Smith, executive director of Community Services for Autistic Adults and Children in Maryland, articulated the opponents' concerns about the consensus development conference. She criticized the membership of the consensus development planning group as well as the consensus development panel members:

> The planning group had a distinct bias towards the use of aversive procedures (that is punishment procedures such as shock, noxious smells, noxious tastes, forced exercise) with persons with developmental disabilities.
> The panel is composed of individuals closely connected with people having such biases; the presenters also are

heavily weighted toward one side of the issue. There is not equal representation on the panel. Outspoken advocates of punishment are included on the panel and planning committee. Nationally recognized experts on the use of treatment without punishment have not been included in planning, presentations, or as panel members. Relevant experts, advocacy groups and national organizations concerned with treatment and rights of person with developmental disabilities were not even notified of this conference until early to mid-August. Attempts to provide substantive input at the time were rebuffed by NIH staff. Many key researchers, clinicians and advocacy groups received no notification.

NIH did not allow sufficient planning time to adequately explore the issues and to include nationally recognized experts in the process who hold views different from those of the planning committee.

The structure of the preliminary report reveals the bias of the planning committee, and demonstrates a lack of knowledge of scientifically demonstrated treatment procedures. The federal government itself had funded model demonstration projects and field initiated research over the past decade which bear direct relevance to the topic, and the results of this body of work has been excluded. The report is shamefully unbalanced in its bias.

I am suggesting that a Congressional inquiry be done into the planning of this consensus panel, as it appears to constitute a misuse of public funds, due to its bias.[56] I would also like to request that the September meeting be cancelled due to its bias and the failure to include nationally recognized experts and organizations whose views were separate from those of the planners.[57]

Datlow Smith was a pioneer and expert on the employment of adults with autism in community settings.[58] Her organization, Community Services for Autistic Adults and Children (CSAAC), was nationally recognized for its innovative practices and success in employing autistic adults with severe behavior disorders in typical businesses. CSAAC's training and support methods did not include aversives of any kind. Smith's conclusions were in part supported by research conducted by

P. M. Wortman, A. Vinokur, and L. Sechrest, who evaluated the entire NIH consensus development program and concluded that there had been previous selection bias in how questions and panelists were chosen, which she believed was a significant threat to the credibility of the consensus process.[59]

Several weeks before the September consensus development conference was to begin, NIH received a letter from the Public Citizen Litigation Group,[60] which argued that the conference violated the Federal Advisory Committee Act since a private executive session was planned. The group's attorneys argued that "all meetings must remain public unless the meetings fall under one of the narrow exemptions of the Government in the Sunshine Act that have been incorporated by reference in FACA."[61] William Raub, NIH's acting director, almost immediately denied the Public Citizen Litigation Group's request for public meetings and argued that "the closed executive sessions are necessary for the panel to weigh the scientific evidence and draft a statement addressing key issues . . . it would be impractical and counterproductive to open the closed drafting sessions to the public. Panel members would be less likely to express their opinions and the drafting probably could not be completed within the time allotted, thus making it impossible to meet the schedule for completion of the conference. Such a change in the procedures would affect adversely the effectiveness of the conference."[62]

The consensus development conference proceeded as planned. In August 1989, a draft report that included papers on the selected topics was distributed prior to the meeting. At the conference, many people for and against the use of aversives made public statements. No one was denied an opportunity to speak. Experts and family members also sent comments that were acknowledged in the final report, written after the conference. Predictably, opposing points of view were presented. Some organizations representing people with disabilities and their families were highly critical of the preliminary report.

Families of children with serious behavior disorders who were using the SIBIS were also heard. In support of the use of aversive interventions, Leslie Grant, the husband of Mooza Grant, who held the patent for SIBIS, testified about their daughter, who had a dangerous behavior of banging her head. His testimony was summarized in the consensus conference report:

At first they tried to change her environment to see if her behavior would change. They placed her in a good hospital, but after one night there, she severely injured herself. To prevent her self-injurious behavior, her arms had to be held around the clock. The hospital could not provide around the clock staffing and discharged her. Subsequent to her hospitalization, their daughter was seen by many psychiatrists, given heavy doses of psychotropic drugs, and participated in behavior modification programs, but nothing succeeded in stopping her self-injurious behavior. The family heard about SIBIS and decided to try it. SIBIS extinguished their daughter's self-injurious behavior and she has been free of harm for 13 years now. Mr. Grant said that their daughter and family have had a different life due to SIBIS. That SIBIS liberated their daughter as well as themselves. Mr. Grant concluded by saying that he was appalled to see that some whom he would think would support the device are opposed to SIBIS. He pleaded with them to open their eyes to the evidence that SIBIS works.[63]

RESULTS OF THE NIH CONSENSUS CONFERENCE

The conference report reached nine conclusions (Figure 9):

1. Destructive behavior among persons with developmental disabilities presents a unique therapeutic and human challenge. The estimated cost of treatment of these persons exceeds $3 billion annually.
2. All forms of destructive behavior have serious consequences for people with developmental disabilities and for their families, which can seriously limit their life opportunities.
3. Most successful approaches to treatment are likely to involve multiple elements of therapy (behavioral and psychopharmacologic), environmental change, and education. Treatment methods may require techniques for enhancing desired behavior; for producing changes in the social, physical, and educational environment; and for reducing or eliminating destructive behaviors.
4. Treatments should be based on an analysis of medical and psychiatric conditions, environmental situations, consequences and skill deficits. In the application of any of these treatments,

Treatment of Destructive Behaviors in Persons With Developmental Disabilities
National Institutes of Health
Consensus Development Conference Statement
September 11-13, 1989

Figure 9. NIH Consensus statement on the use of punishment.

an essential step involves a functional analysis of existing behavioral patterns.

5. The prevalence of drug treatment in persons with developmental disabilities is disturbingly high and lacks robust scientific validation. The use of pharmacologic agents should be restricted to persons with identified psychiatric syndromes or be designed to facilitate the establishment of behavioral, interpersonal, or educational therapies.

6. Behavior reduction procedures should be selected for their rapid effectiveness only if the exigencies of the clinical situation require short-term use of such restrictive interventions and only after appropriate review and informed consent are obtained. These interventions should only be used in the context of a comprehensive individualized behavior enhancement treatment package.

7. New resources must be allocated for future research on all treatment modalities, particularly behavior enhancement procedures and educational (skills acquisition) and ecological approaches.
8. Newer pharmacologic approaches merit intensive investigation. Through basic and clinical research, the potential exists to develop drugs that could operate directly and specifically on eliminating self-injurious behavior.
9. Research is needed on the origin, natural history, and ecology of destructive behaviors among persons with developmental disabilities.[64]

The sixth conclusion cautiously permitted the use of aversives.[65] National groups such as the Association for Retarded Citizens (ARC) registered "extreme dissatisfaction" with it.[66] Barbara Sackett, president of the ARC board of directors, wrote a letter to Louis Sullivan, secretary of health and human services, on behalf of the ARC, as well as the some of the major disability advocacy organizations in the United States: American Association on Mental Retardation, Autism Society of America, Community Services for Autistic Adults and Children, Mental Health law Project, National Association of Developmental Disabilities Councils, National Association of Protection and Advocacy Systems, National Association of Rehabilitation Facilities, National Parents Disability Network, The Association for Persons with Severe Handicaps, and United Cerebral Palsy Associations. In the letter, she complained about the process and the outcomes of the consensus conference:

> Contrary to the opinions stated in the consensus statement, there is *no* consensus on the use of what are euphemistically referred to as "behavior reduction" methods. Clearly and simply, the majority of these methods, which are mentioned in the drafts of both the consensus statement and the final report, are aversive procedures which have the very strong potential to cause both physical and psychological pain to the individuals who are subjected to them. Unfortunately, those most often subjected to these methods are those least able to defend their own rights. We do not believe that a consensus statement or report can be published endorsing the use of aversives when a major portion of the disability field considers these approaches

unacceptable and their use is unsupported by scientifically valid data.

It is our opinion that from the very beginning the consensus conference process was flawed. The conference planning committee had no representatives from any major advocacy organizations who work with and for the persons who were the subject of the conference. The bibliography which was the basis for the draft of the consensus report was incomplete and over-represented studies carried out utilizing aversive procedures and pharmacological procedures. Clearly, a true consensus cannot be reached when the consensus development process fails to take into account strongly held views in opposition to a particular procedure.

The Department and NIH are preparing to disseminate products on a highly controversial topic. These products are both flawed and lacking in any in depth discussion of legal and ethical issues which surround this topic. It is totally inappropriate that such products, without these critically important legal and ethical considerations, would be widely disseminated for use. The potential for continued and increased abuse of persons with mental retardation and other developmental disabilities is heightened by the irresponsible publication of these materials.[67]

The ARC conducted ongoing conversations with other federal officials at the Administration on Developmental Disabilities; the National Institute for Child Health and Development (NICHD), a branch of NIH; and the President's Committee on Mental Retardation. Their third letter in January to Secretary Louis Sullivan accused a central figure at the NICHD, Duane Alexander, of being biased and promoting the use of SIBIS.[68] They claimed that Alexander

> attempts to intervene in a school-based SIBIS issue in Michigan and "pleads for [the child involved] to be allowed to wear the SIBIS device in school, under proper professional supervision." In attempting to plead his case, Dr. Alexander, in the body of his letter to the Northville Public Schools, cites the controversial conference and states that "At the conference there was substantial evidence presented, both from rigorous experimental studies and testimony of personal experience,

that the SIBIS device was effective in eliminating self-injurious behavior . . . in a very short time . . . Although some persons at the conference spoke against the use of the device, largely for philosophical reasons, the Consensus Panel was convinced that the SIBIS device held great purpose, that its use was appropriate when clinically indicated and under proper supervision, and that studies of its effectiveness should continue. The final consensus statement is now under preparation and will reflect this concept . . . given its [SIBIS] apparent effectiveness on a trial basis at home and in school, it would certainly be consistent with the recommendations of the NIH Consensus Development Panel to permit its use in the school setting."[69]

Holding Up the Report

The ARC letters continued to argue that the report should not be published and that the NICHD director was already using the conference proceedings to support the use of aversives. The ARC and other advocacy organizations were ready to contact the press and pursue a congressional investigation to stop the report from being published. Secretary Sullivan responded in July, eight months after the original letter was sent by the ARC, and refused to intervene in the publication of the report, declaring that the report was not the opinion of the federal government and it would be inappropriate to represent the findings as such.[70] He referred accusations related to alleged civil rights violations of people with disabilities to Martin H. Gerry, assistant secretary for planning and evaluation at the U.S. Department of Health and Human Services. Gerry, a civil rights attorney, had a long history of working on issues facing people with disabilities and was a professional colleague of members of the groups protesting the consensus statement. Anti-aversive advocates hoped that the government would take steps to prevent the widespread use of the report. But by the time Sullivan had sent his response letter to the ARC, a draft of the report was already being disseminated nationally.

Discussion of the civil rights of people with disabilities was not part of the consensus conference process or the report, but scientific articles were. Many argued that NIH should not separate civil rights and the right to be free from painful and dehumanizing interventions, but others argued that outlawing aversives would violate an individual's right to effective treatment.

Correspondence from anti-aversive advocates to legislative and administration leaders continued. In September 1989, Steny Hoyer, congressman for the Fifth District of Maryland and chair of the Democratic Caucus, asked the NIH for an explanation of how the consensus conference ensured an appropriate balance of opinion on nonaversive interventions. Senator Barbara Mikulski of Maryland sent a similar letter.[71] In November 1989, Senator Dennis DeConcini of Arizona asked that NIH to respond to a member of the Autism National Society who claimed that the consensus conference excluded experts knowledgeable about positive behavior supports. DeConcini asked for a congressional investigation, as did Senator Sam Nunn of Georgia. The responses from NICHD were essentially the same: procedures had been followed and there was balance. The issue of particular concern to critics was the selection of presenters. Four of the presenters were associated with supporting aversive approaches. The participation of Linscheid, who was involved in the development of and had recently promoted the use of SIBIS, was of particular concern.

Science magazine published an article in August 1990 entitled, "What's Holding Up 'Aversives' Report?"[72] The final report was supposed to be published in March 1990. Bernard Rimland, founder of the Autism Society of America and director of the San Diego–based Institute for Child Behavior Research, a proponent of the use of aversives interventions and the father of a son with autism, urged Sullivan to release the report and took issue with the civil rights arguments made by Barbara Sackett of the ARC and other national organizations. He argued:

> The conference was organized by NIH precisely to assure the civil rights of the developmentally disabled. Is there a civil right that is more fundamental than the right to be protected from severe and disabling injury, including injury that a handicapped person might inflict upon him- or herself? . . . I do hope that the conference report, which reflects the best thinking of highly qualified and highly intelligent people, will be published in the near future, even though its publication is vigorously resisted by poorly-informed people within and without the government whose ideological commitment to their beliefs is totally impervious to the scientific evidence presented so well by the experts at the conference.[73]

NIH finally issued the consensus report in July 1991. Following its release, an Associated Press article appeared in publications under various headlines: "Experts Back Use of Pain in Treatment of Retarded," "NIH Panel Endorses Some Use of Pain to Control Behavior," "Pain Endorsed as Means to Stop Self-Destructive Behavior," "Panel Backs Punishment Therapy and Pain Treatments for Head-Bangers," "Experts OK Pain to Help Protect the Retarded," "Panel Accepts Pain to Treat Disturbed," "Pain Called Good Therapy," and "Pain Backed as Control Method."[74]

These headlines and stories represented a major setback for advocates arguing against the use of aversives and a clear victory for those who supported them. The use of aversives on people with disabilities was now nationally sanctioned. Electric shock devices were approved by the FDA and were being distributed across the country. According to much of the press, the camps were divided into scientists and advocates. Scientists were knowledgeable and anti-aversive advocates were misinformed ideologues. To many in the pro-aversive camp, it was impossible to be both scientist and advocate. The argument that people with disabilities had the right to effective treatment, even if it involved pain, became an argument used in court cases related to the use of punishment. The next lawsuit, in 1995 in Massachusetts, would use all of the arguments and findings featured in the NIH consensus report to support the use of aversives. For those arguing for the cessation of the use of pain to treat severe behavior disorders, the NIH consensus conference had made matters far worse.

8 : STAGING THE NEXT BATTLEGROUND

During the NIH consensus process, Massachusetts was responding to Judge Rotenberg's decision to permit the use of aversives and fine Commissioner Mary Kay Leonard for acting in bad faith. The coroner's inquest had determined that Vincent Milletich died of natural causes. There was some chaos because of changing state agency roles in oversight of BRI and personnel were adapting to a less-than-desirable situation. As required by the Office for Children settlement agreement,[1] in 1988 Massachusetts wrote and adopted new regulations with input from BRI on the use of aversives. Mary McCarthy, assistant commissioner of mental health and later commissioner of mental retardation, who succeeded Leonard in overseeing BRI, was ordered by Judge Rotenberg to participate in the determination of a treatment plan that included developing regulations for aversives.[2] Leonard and McCarthy were close friends and became business partners after Mary McCarthy retired. It was not easy for McCarthy to implement Rotenberg's settlement agreement. Kim Murdock, who was OFC's attorney in the first unsuccessful case against BRI, moved to the Division of Mental Retardation and resumed her role as counsel to a state agency. She would later attempt to litigate the second case brought by BRI against a future commissioner, Philip Campbell. Her legal and litigation skills again would be challenged by BRI's attorney, Eric MacLeish.

For the first time, DMR was now required to certify and license not only children's services but also the use of Class III aversives. There were several drafts of the proposed regulations. On June 12, 1987, "A parade of witnesses urged the state Department of Mental Health to revise proposed regulations to disallow the continued use of painful 'aversive' therapy on mental patients."[3] They wanted aversives prohibited. Implicit in these new regulations, however, was that aversives, including electric shock, were necessary and could be administered in Massachusetts, the most extreme being the SIBIS and eventually the GED, which could only be used through a substituted judgment proceeding in the probate court. The regulations stated, "It is the department's strong policy that behavior modification procedures which pose a significant risk of physical and psychological harm to the clients or which are intrusive or restrictive should only be used as a last resort."[4] There were ongoing efforts to pass legislation in Massachusetts to ban aversives, but these efforts always failed to win support of both chambers.[5]

Over the next several years, other states did not idly stand by as Massachusetts developed and oversaw regulations that permitted the use of aversives. The decision against OFC and Leonard and the new Massachusetts regulations that included Class III aversives activated people across the country. Instead of new regulations, anti-aversive and anti–electric shock legislation was introduced in New Jersey, Rhode Island, Massachusetts, South Dakota, Washington, Nevada, and Connecticut, the only state in New England that passed legislation. Resistance by advocates of aversive interventions in the other states prevented the bills from moving forward.

After several years of advocacy, Connecticut governor Lowell Weicker signed a bill on June 28, 1993, banning the use of electric shock to control the behavior of people with disabilities. The state's house approved the bill with a 133–5 vote, and the senate approved it 36–0.[6] Weicker was the parent of a son with Down syndrome and championed the rights of people with disabilities. Connecticut's ability to pass legislation outlawing electric shock inspired advocates in Massachusetts, and they continued to promote legislation that would do the same. But as advocates prepared legislation, another battle was brewing.

On July 17, 1991, Massachusetts governor William Weld named Philip Campbell, executive director of the Association of Retarded Citizens of Waltham, Massachusetts, since 1986, to serve as commissioner of the newly formed Department of Mental Retardation (DMR).[7] Campbell replaced Mary McCarthy, who had overseen the interactions with BRI after authority was transferred from the Office for Children to the Department of Mental Health and then to DMR. Campbell's appointment concerned some pro-institution family groups because he had been a vocal opponent of state institutions and supported their closure. He was immediately approached by the anti-aversive community who proposed that his department develop a quality assurance strategy that would render aversives extinct. As history will tell, this strategy was unsuccessful in Massachusetts.

There were other signs that the DMR might be gaining authority over BRI. In 1990, the Massachusetts Supreme Judicial Court in a 4-to-1 decision overturned a preliminary injunction that Rotenberg had issued.[8] (A preliminary injunction may be granted before or during trial with the goal of preserving the status quo before final judgment.)[9] The court ruled that Judge Rotenberg did not have the authority to issue a preliminary injunction directing a specific placement at BRI because in so doing, he would be interfering with the DMR's obligation to provide treatment and habilitation. Justice Herbert Wilkins wrote, "The placement of individuals and the coordination of the provision of services financed by the department are executive functions. Individually focused mandates impinging on those functions are not generally warranted and would be disruptive of attempts to carry out broad department policies."[10] The case, involving Christopher David McKnight, was remanded back to probate court where additional proceedings could take place. The DMR had assumed care of him after his father relocated to Massachusetts from Wyoming and proposed placing him in Samoset House, a program that did not use aversive procedures. Samoset House cost $75,000 per year while BRI cost $126,000 per year.

Between 1977 and 1979, McKnight was placed at BRI where he "improved" and then attended a school in Arizona where he "got worse."[11] McKnight exhibited destructive behavior and running away. He lived at home for a brief period afterward and in 1982 was once again placed at BRI. Since 1982, the Natrona County School District in Wyoming which David attended, had been paying for McKnight's BRI placement because his father, Arthur Duncan McKnight, wanted him there. The placement was in spite of two reports written by district educators, including a behavioral specialist, Geoff Colvin, who had visited the facility, arguing that the punishments and consequences were inhumane "to the level of abuse" and recommended that David be immediately removed.[12] One local citizen from Casper, Wyoming, wrote, "I am horrified at the amount of money spent on this autistic boy at Behavior Research Institute. Why are we spending $86,000 to have this boy tortured? I don't know anything about autistic children, but it seems to me that if he has to be tortured somewhere, we can torture him right here in Wyoming for less money."[13] Local *Casper Tribune Star* political cartoonist Gregory Kearney also weighed in (Figure 10).

"In February, 1989, BRI informed David's father, who was also his

Figure 10. Gregory Kearney political cartoon. Casper Star Tribune, 1985.
Courtesy American Heritage Center, University of Wyoming

Massachusetts-appointed guardian, that BRI would terminate David
due to the lack of funding for his enrollment. David was over the age
of 21 and the school district was no longer responsible for the cost of
care. On February 27, 1989, David, through his attorney, his father, his
guardian ad litem, and BRI, moved in the Bristol County Probate and
Family Court for a preliminary injunction against the Department of
Mental Retardation (department) that would require it to 'provide [a]
safe and adequate treatment and habilitation program' for David."[14]
Rotenberg issued a preliminary injunction requiring the state to place
David McKnight, aged 23, at BRI.

The state appealed to the Massachusetts Supreme Judicial Court,
which ruled in the state's favor:

> The record does not support the conclusion that on
> a permanent basis BRI, and only BRI, can furnish the
> appropriate care for David. The injunction should have left
> the determination of where David is to be treated in the
> discretion of the department without requiring it to return
> to the court for approval of some other provider before David
> could be moved from BRI. The placement of individuals and
> the coordination of the provision of services financed by the

PAIN AND SHOCK IN AMERICA

department are executive functions. Individually focused judicial mandates impinging on those functions are not generally warranted and would be disruptive of attempts to carry out broad departmental policies. Such a mandate can be justified, as we noted earlier in this opinion, only if there is but one way in which a governmental agency can carry out its lawful duties. See Attorney Gen. v. Sheriff of Suffolk County, 394 Mass. 624, 630 (1985). That unique situation is not shown to exist in this case on a permanent basis.[15]

The court endorsed the view that state agencies can make placement decisions based on department policy and that a judge could not require DMR to place an individual in a specific facility. Mary Kay Leonard had also made this argument in the OFC lawsuit, but Rotenberg had dismissed it. The *McKnight* ruling, particularly the dissent by Justice C. J. Liacos, provided insight into the interactions between the DMR and Judge Rotenberg. "In the present case, the Probate Court judge's findings that the department acted in bad faith, knowingly misled the court, considered improper political motivations in making its decision and failed to provide any competent clinical evidence to support its proposal . . . warranted a conclusion that the department had abandoned its proper role in this case," wrote Liacos.[16]

In 1991, the Massachusetts Supreme Judicial Court (SJC) ruled on two other cases in a decision involving BRI that supported the state's contention that it did not have to pay the annual rate of $153,351 for two students, Joseph A. Ferrara and Timothy Green, even though tuition payment was part of the OFC settlement agreement. The SJC decided that the students were not entitled to it: "We see nothing in the relevant Federal and State statues that requires a particular provider of services to be paid a particular rate. The plaintiffs do not attempt to show that there is no facility available that can provide Ferrera with the education to which he is entitled at a rate below $153,351, but argue only that BRI cannot do so."[17] The SJC decisions were seen by anti-aversive advocates as a positive sign: a weakening of the authority of Judge Rotenberg's probate court and an increase in the state's authority to oversee and regulate BRI.

The court refused to hear another case, declaring it moot because the plaintiff, Marc Sturtz, was deemed competent, and it concluded, "His placement by his parents in BRI under a treatment plan

authorizing restraint of liberty and aversive procedures was tanta-
mount to involuntary commitment to a mental institution. The Sturtz
decision held that courts can authorize involuntary commitment only
upon a finding that a failure to hospitalize the person would result in a
likelihood of serious harm to himself or to others."[18] This decision created a higher standard for placement and use of aversives, which, with
the other contemporaneous decisions by the SJC, weakened Judge
Rotenberg's authority.

The Massachusetts attorney general and the Massachusetts Center
for Public Representation lawyers representing Sturtz attempted to
appeal the May 25, 1990, decision of the SJC not to hear the case "because it was moot." Raising constitutional questions, the appellants
wanted the decision to be applied more broadly, thereby affecting others at BRI or at risk of placement at BRI. The case was granted direct
appellate review but again, the SJC concluded that the case was moot
and the constitutional issues raised in Sturtz's appeal could not be addressed.[19] Although the original decision created a higher standard for
placement and the use of aversives, the failed appeal prevented important constitutional protections from being considered.

THE DEATH OF JUDGE ROTENBERG

On July 7, 1992, Judge Ernest Rotenberg died at the age of 67 at his vacation home on Cape Cod. His various obituaries acknowledged his
extraordinary service to his community. He was described as "a super
judge; hardworking, firm and fair, a very able person who had been
considered for chief justice of the probate court system. He loved his
work and he had tremendous energy. Anyone who appeared before
him knew he could be a difficult taskmaster and at times seemed iras-
cible."[20] Rotenberg was the first Massachusetts judge to receive the
Franklin N. Flaschner Award, given for outstanding performance in a
court with limited and special jurisdiction.[21] Eric MacLeish, BRI's attorney, delivered a eulogy at Rotenberg's funeral. Opponents of BRI
saw this as evidence of a long-standing close relationship between
MacLeish and Rotenberg. MacLeish responded to the accusations:
"The family asked me to do it because the judge cared deeply about
his work and I was some connection to that . . . I had no personal relationship with him."[22]

Opponents of BRI hoped that Rotenberg's death might give them the opportunity to try to close BRI. Stan Goldman, an attorney who supervised state-funded attorneys representing students at BRI, said, "It seems to me it is time to look anew at the underlying issue: What would [the students] choose if they were competent given their experience over the last six or seven years and the fact they are exposed to ever-increasing levels of aversive therapy?"[23] A month later, in August 1992, BRI requested approval from the FDA for a new device that would deliver a shock three times more powerful than the existing SIBIS device for use on students who had adapted to the current levels of shock. Ogden Lindsley,[24] chairman of BRI's senior peer review board, advised BRI to reconsider its technique of gradually increasing shock levels, claiming that "administering low-level shocks to students then increasing the shock level when needed is an approach doomed to failure. There is nothing more dangerous than under-punishment . . . I advise tougher punishment."[25] In response, Matthew Israel helped develop the graduated electronic decelerator—the GED.

The atmosphere was charged due to the death of Judge Rotenberg and the appointment of a new commissioner of mental retardation, legal decisions that appeared to support executive agency decisions, the introduction of the GED, ongoing attempts at anti-aversive legislation, and national attention to the issue of the use of aversives. Even Oprah Winfrey became involved.

THE GED IS DEVELOPED

In 1990, BRI formed an external working group to discuss the efficacy of continuing to treat high-frequency, life-threatening behaviors with relatively low levels of shock generated by the SIBIS. The group concluded that increasing the voltage was appropriate and that an upper limit should not be set.[26] The rationale for developing the GED was that the students adapted to the voltage and amperage (6.1 milliampere) emitted by SIBIS. Humans can feel 1 milliampere and are electrocuted when they are administered 100 milliamperes. Israel and his colleagues reported, "We employed SIBIS with 29 students. For two of these (7%) SIBIS was effective throughout its period of use. For 15 students (52%) SIBIS was effective during an initial period lasting from a few days to a few months; however, it lost its effectiveness thereafter. With one of these students there were indications that SIBIS even reversed its function, changing from an aversive stimulus into a

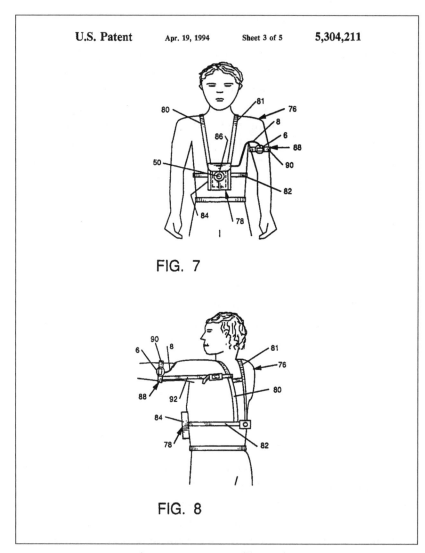

Figure 11. GED patent illustration.

positively reinforcing stimulus. For 12 (41%) SIBIS showed little or no effectiveness at any time. In order to remedy the problems described above and have ready access to repair capability and new units, we decided to design our own remote-controlled device, called the Graduated Electronic Decelerator (GED)" (Figure 11).[27]

Clearly there were two ways to interpret the data. Anti-aversive advocates argued that Israel's data supported their contention that aversive interventions are ineffective and students adapt over time.[28] Israel, however, interpreted the data and argued for the need for more intense electric shock.

From December 1990 to 1992, BRI manufactured seventy-one GEDs and used them with fifty-three students.[29] "The student wears a modified belt pack (a zippered pouch worn around the waist) or, later, a battery pack and stimulator. The electrode cord exits from a small hole in the back of the belt pack. The electrode cord and electrode are normally covered by the student's clothing. If the electrode is attached to an arm or leg, a limb belt made of cotton elastic blend is threaded though the two slots in the electrode mounting disc and secured around the arm with a suspended buckle. The electrode can also be attached to the torso using a longer belt" (Figure 12).[30]

The Center for Public Representation, a Massachusetts legal advocacy organization that was active in the Office for Children lawsuit and opposed the use of aversives, became increasingly concerned about the use of the GED on students at BRI and on December 15, 1992, petitioned the court for writs of habeas corpus.[31] "The petitioners claimed that they were being "illegally and unlawfully restrained of [their] liberty at BRI. Each petitioner asserts that his confinement at BRI against his will was without due process of law."[32] The petitions on behalf of BRI students John Kaufman and Mark Laurenz, were dismissed by the Massachusetts Supreme Judicial Court because not all administrative remedies had been exhausted. The court ruled that "each has been the subject of a guardianship proceeding and each is currently under a substituted judgment treatment plan, which the Probate Court supervises. Neither petitioner appealed from the guardianship proceedings or the proceedings determining the treatment plan."[33] Both petitioners had approved plans for aversives including the GED. Neither petitioner sought immediate release; rather both wanted alternative placements."[34] The ruling sent the petitioners back to the Bristol County Probate Court to Rotenberg's replacement, Judge Elizabeth LaStaiti.

On March 26, 1992, advocates made another unsuccessful attempt to pass legislation in Massachusetts outlawing aversives, and a hearing was held by the legislature's Human Services Committee. As was typical, there were parents for and against the use of aversives. Polyxane Cobb of Cambridge "pleaded with the committee to pass the legislation. 'If you let these horrors continue, you are endangering every child

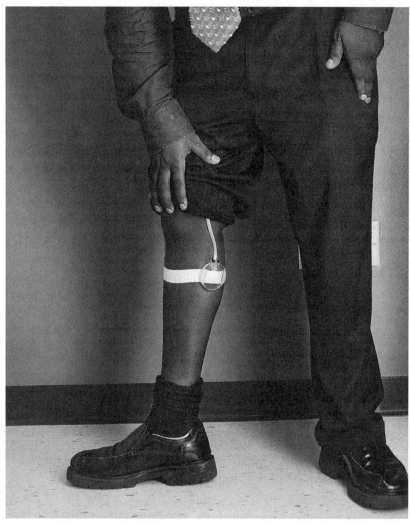

Figure 12. GED on resident's leg. Larry Sultan, Mother Jones *magazine. Courtesy of the Estate of Larry Sultan.*

who is like what my child once was. You have the power to stop this sadistic evil."[35] Another parent, Mary Duggins, traveled from Mississippi to testify against the bill: "She said that Jennifer, who used to repeatedly bang her head, bite herself, pick at her open wounds and give herself black eyes, now functions more normally as a result of shock therapy."[36] On May 3, 1992, the *Boston Globe* reported that the former house minority leader, Stephen Pierce, who had lost to Bill Weld in

PAIN AND SHOCK IN AMERICA

the gubernatorial primary in 1990, would be lobbying for BRI at the state capitol.[37] This worried anti-aversive advocates, and they turned to the media to expose the public to the techniques that BRI used. The Committee for Legislation to Protect People with Disabilities (the Anti-Aversive Group) scheduled a meeting with Commissioner Campbell on the status of Senate Bill 557 and to address steps the department could take to provide greater protections for people with disabilities.[38]

Anti-aversive advocates were reaching out to the media hoping to shine a light on BRI's use of aversives. In August 1992, Nancy Weiss, director of the Department of Community Services at the Kennedy Krieger Institute at Johns Hopkins University, sent a letter to Oprah Winfrey urging her to "consider doing a show about aversive (painful or dehumanizing) techniques that are used to change the behavior of children and adults with mental retardation and other developmental disabilities. This may be a good follow-up to the very powerful show you did on 8/10/92 on the torture of political prisoners. I think the public should be shocked to learn what goes on in our own country to the most vulnerable of our children."[39]

Weiss's letter was positively received, and in December 1993, Winfrey aired a show on the use of electric shock, which devolved into a shouting match between parents supportive of SIBIS and the GED and parents and professionals opposed to it.[40] The issue was confused by a discussion of electroconvulsant therapy (ECT), which has proven effective in treating serious depression. One exchange between Anne Donnellan, who had been active in California efforts to close BRI as well as the OFC lawsuit, and Matthew Israel characterized the tone and the arguments.

> Donnellan: The fact that shocking someone stops their bad behaviors proves that they can be taught, can learn to behave properly, and now you have to figure out a way to teach them without causing them pain. A girl named Amber died as a result of shock therapy.

> Israel stands up and Winfrey gives him the microphone for a moment.

> Israel: Dr. Donnellan, you would have us believe that because a procedure might have to be continued throughout a person's life that there was something wrong with it. Now the average

student at BRI receives less than one treatment per day. There are a lot of treatments like eye glasses which you need for the rest of your life. Artificial limbs which you need for the rest of your life. If you have diabetes you might need insulin treatment for the rest of your life. Unfortunately, there are certain treatments that are not cut and dry and all over but they are prosthetic and you have to be continued for the rest of your life. With them you can have a decent quality of life without them you can blind yourself or kill yourself through brain injury.

Donnellan: What minority will we do this to next? . . . There are no children that need cattle prods.

ANOTHER CONFRONTATION IS BREWING

Philip Campbell, former director of the Massachusetts Association for Retarded Citizens, a strong advocate of deinstitutionalization and community-based services, had served as commissioner of mental retardation since 1991. He had close ties to Gunnar Dybwad, professor emeritus at the Heller School, Brandeis University, and an outspoken opponent of BRI who encouraged Campbell to use his office to restrict the use of aversives. BRI was informed by DMR in May 1992 that its recertification would be approved. On June 10, 1992, the commissioner's office reviewed BRI's application for recertification for use of Level III interventions and, citing deficiencies, asked for four modifications to its Human Rights Committee policies and practices.[41] Israel responded that all of the deficiencies had been or were being addressed.[42] However, on August 6, 1993, DMR granted BRI "interim certification" with several conditions and findings. This signaled a renewed interest in BRI.

Matthew Israel responded to Campbell's interim certification letter with a lengthy letter voicing his concern about DMR's dealings with BRI:

> Ms. Murdock (general counsel for DMR) has informed us that the reason for the renewed interest in BRI results, in large part, from the passing of former Chief Justice Ernest Rotenberg. According to Ms. Murdock, DMR believes that your agency will now receive a fair audience from the court. DMR clinicians had apparently reported to DMR in the past that their opinions had not been listened to by Judge Rotenberg. Regardless of

the merits of this assertion, we are disturbed that regulatory interest in BRI has apparently been triggered by the passing of Judge Rotenberg. We also are concerned that since DMR's recent renewed interest in the BRI program, there has been an effort to evade one of the key elements of the Settlement Agreement between BRI and the Office for Children. As you know, this Settlement Agreement was executed in January of 1987. A key provision of the Agreement (as I am sure it can be verified by all the attorneys, the guardian ad litem and the court monitor) was to provide BRI with insulation from the state agency and some of its officials who had been found by the Court to have engaged in bad faith.[43]

The ongoing dispute in the professional community about the use of aversives was also highlighted in Israel's letter to Campbell complaining about interim certification:

> Many experts testified in these proceedings, including Dr. Bruce Wedlock of the Massachusetts Institute of Technology, Dr. Ogden Lindsley of the University of Kansas, and the wards' expert, Dr. Paul Jansen.[44] In addition, the Probate Court made exhaustive findings, determining, for example, that there was a "notable unanimity of professional opinion held that the GED was an effective and medically safe behavioral treatment technology." The Court also found that the GED device remained a highly effective behavioral treatment procedure "that can substantially benefit this small percentage of handicapped individuals who engage in debilitating and life threatening behavior disorders." The Court even cited the testimony of Dr. Jansen, who testified in favor of its use.[45]

Campbell immediately responded to Israel in a letter refuting many of Israel's assertions and offering reasons for DMR's renewed interest in BRI: "Your allegation that the Department's 'interest' in ensuring BRI's compliance with the law is new or renewed, or is prompted by extraneous factors, is incorrect. The 1989 conditions regarding initial certification, licensure deficiencies found in the May 3–4, 1992 survey, and the continuous work of our service coordinators and licensors, have all demonstrated our continuing concerns."[46] Campbell's primary concern was the effectiveness of the treatment plans being implemented at BRI, particularly those that required the use of the GED.

The parents of students at BRI continued to play an important role in influencing legislators and the court. In the same lengthy letter that accused DMR of inappropriate renewed interest in BRI, Israel informed Campbell of his concern that parents were not involved in the recertification decision:

In addition your agency (DMR) has failed, thus far, to speak with the parents and guardians of these students concerning "your concerns" regarding the safety, effectiveness and professional acceptability of BRI's treatment program and some of the aversive procedures. We sincerely hope that you or Deputy Commissioner Misilo will take the opportunity to speak to those who have witnessed first-hand some of the remarkable progress which their children have made in the BRI treatment program, particularly since the introduction of the GED. These parents are uniquely capable of assessing the effectiveness of the BRI treatment program and the dramatic, sometimes even life-saving improvement which has occurred with their children. We were pleased to learn that Deputy Commissioner Misilo has decided to meet with these parents, but we are also disappointed that they were apparently not consulted prior to your letter of August 6, 1993.[47]

There was no doubt that the parents of the students at BRI would play a role in the ongoing dispute. Fearing a lack of alternative placements for their children and a history of ineffective services, they remained supportive, some more than others, of BRI and the methods employed to control behavior.[48] Their support for BRI was reflected in the motions soon to be filed by BRI accusing the state of interfering with the settlement decree.

COMPLAINT FOR CONTEMPT

On September 2, 1993, soon after the exchange of letters between Israel and Campbell, BRI's attorney, Eric MacLeish, filed a motion for contempt,[49] declaring that DMR was violating the settlement decree. In the first OFC settlement agreement on January 7, 1987, the probate court appointed John Daignault, a psychiatrist,[50] to "undertake the general monitoring of BRI's treatment and education programs as described in the Settlement Agreement, part B."[51] MacLeish argued that the agreement specifically stated that "Dr. Daignault shall arbitrate any disputes between the parties, and in the event that any party disagrees with any decision or recommendation of Dr. Daignault, the matters shall be submitted to the Court for resolution."[52] In essence, Daignault was appointed to ensure that the state was complying with Rotenberg's orders and served as the eyes and ears of the court. He was also responsible for making sure that the treatment plans were implemented. However, it was never stated explicitly in the agreement that he would take over the regulatory authority of DMR, which had statewide quality assurance procedures to which all programs, including BRI, had to conform.

Other issues were raised in the contempt motion that related to DMR's "taking a hard line" with BRI and allegedly refusing to grant reasonable extensions to meet agency requirements.[53] The motion for injunctive relief, a court order for the defendant (DMR) to stop a specified act or behavior, also questioned the department's interference in treatment plans, requirements for emergency plans, the requirement that BRI retain and label its routinely made videotapes of its practices in group homes, and requirements for how and when mechanical restraints were utilized. DMR's jurisdiction to certify and monitor remained in question. MacLeish accused DMR and Campbell of acting in bad faith and in violation of the rights of BRI and its residents.[54] These accusations mirrored those against Leonard and the Office for Children. Now DMR waited to see whether Rotenberg's replacement, Elizabeth LaStaiti, would be as sympathetic to BRI as he had been.

WHO HAS REGULATORY AUTHORITY?

One issue facing DMR was the fact that licensing and certification were being conducted by different staff members in different agencies. For example, BRI submitted an application for recertification to DMR in July 1991. After two DMR certification specialists visited the program in May 1992, BRI was told that its certification would be granted. However, DMR received information related to licensing that led it to grant only interim certification on August 6, 1993. Adding to the confusion, DMR certified and licensed the main facility where BRI residents spent their days, and the Department of Education oversaw the educational programs. During this period of licensing and certification confusion and just prior to the motions filed by MacLeish, BRI requested a meeting with DMR and asked that Daignault be included. The general counsel to DMR, Kim Murdock, and special assistant attorney general David Ferleger of Philadelphia, who had been brought in to work with DMR on the BRI licensing case, refused to hold the meeting with Daignault present.[55] DMR was suspicious of Daignault because he received compensation from BRI's attorney's firm and the firm's clients for services as an expert witness. These matters were disclosed to the probate court.[56]

A meeting without Daignault took place on August 19 despite BRI's contention that he should be present. Hiring David Ferleger signaled that Campbell was intending to take action against BRI. Ferleger, a well-known disability rights attorney, had extensive experience in deinstitutionalization cases, including *Halderman v. Pennhurst State School and Hospital*, which the U.S. Supreme Court decided in 1984.[57] He had assisted OFC legal counsel in developing a legal and public relations strategy during the OFC lawsuit. Some people questioned the wisdom of DMR's securing the services of an outside attorney, particularly one who could easily be associated with the advocacy community, which Rotenberg had essentially dismissed as biased against the use of aversives. Frank Laski, also a successful disability rights attorney and a member of the expert panel convened by Leonard in the initial law suit against OFC, suggested that it might have been wiser to employ a more familiar Boston law firm with experience with Massachusetts courts and judges.[58] Eventually Ferleger was dismissed by DMR prior to the court hearing after concerns were raised about his high legal fees.[59]

On September 22, 1993, the DMR submitted a BRI status report to the probate court. Judge Elizabeth O'Neil LaStaiti was now responsible for overseeing the ongoing disputes between BRI and DMR. Like Judge Ernest Rotenberg, Eric MacLeish, and Robert Sherman, Judge LaStaiti attended Boston University Law School, where she graduated first in her class. Like Rotenberg, LaStaiti had a history as a family law attorney. DMR hoped that she would prove to be less favorable toward BRI than Rotenberg. The report DMR submitted about BRI was filled with many negative findings: "The Report to the Court is to set forth the current status of BRI with regard to compliance with state law and regulations. These matters are relevant to the pending motion, and they demonstrate the profound negative effect on the treatment and rights of BRI clients that would result if DMR is not permitted to ensure that BRI complies with the law."[60]

DMR was aware that arguing about the appropriateness of aversives was unlikely to be an effective strategy given the professional disagreement in the scientific literature and the outcome of the NIH consensus conference. Instead, it based its case on what it perceived to be BRI's ongoing failure to comply with existing DMR rules:

> The issues which are being addressed through the licensure and certification process include BRI's willingness and capacity to comply with existing applicable DMR rules, and to protect its clients from physical and other abuse, while providing effective interventions in compliance with the regulations; also addressed is the efficacy of the techniques utilized at BRI. Within this process, BRI has full rights to appeal and to a hearing before the Division of Administrative Law Appeals. The sustained efforts by DMR for the past four years to elicit compliance by BRI resulted in an August 6, 1993, decision to grant interim certification to BRI, effective twenty-five days later, contingent on BRI's providing certain information to DMR and appointing two people to its Human Rights Committee. BRI provided the information and appointed the individuals [Gunnar Dybwad and Carol Upshur] to its committee.
>
> On August 31, 1993, the date of the beginning of the interim certification, DMR permitted that certification to go into effect and imposed certain conditions, each of which is directly related to non-compliance by BRI with DMR regulations, or to ensuring the safety of BRI's clients. No condition interferes in any way with any court-approved behavior plan.
>
> During the period between August 6 and 31 (1993), DMR received new information from licensors (misfiring of the GED device and food deprivation) and from BRI itself which demonstrated that the degree of non-compliance by BRI with state regulations was pervasive and systemic in certain respects. During that period, BRI refused to permit inspection of its group homes which were necessary for DMR to document compliance and to process applications by BRI for waiver of the requirements of regulations.
>
> Despite the information demonstrating serious and systemic non-compliance, DMR on August 31 permitted BRI to continue

its program. The Department imposed conditions to ensure access by DMR to inspect the program and to protect the rights of the clients from abuse and neglect, and to document conditions in the facilities in response to identified problems. DMR expressed its concern about "the ability of BRI to comply with DMR regulations . . .

DMR was informed by BRI's attorney that BRI reported to state agencies that its Director, Matthew Israel, Ph.D., has been accused by former BRI staff of personally abusing a BRI client. Other abuse of BRI clients has also been alleged by these former staff. Also, other abuse investigations are pending. Investigation of one abuse complaint against BRI initiated by a BRI resident was recently completed, and it substantiated abuse upon the client. Whether other abuse is eventually substantiated or not, DMR is obligated to maintain vigilance and to enforce its regulations. The pendency of the investigation into those allegations, together with the confirmation of abuse in a recent case, support the steps taken by DMR with regard to increased monitoring of BRI and consideration of appropriate conditions for certification of the BRI program."[61]

A CALL TO ACTION

National groups were paying close attention to the events surrounding BRI. Nancy Weiss, the staff member at the Kennedy Krieger Institute at Johns Hopkins University who had alerted Oprah Winfrey, was playing a leadership role. She visited BRI in 1992 as a consultant for the state of Delaware, which was evaluating all of its students in out-of-state residential placements. During her two-day visit, she observed two Delaware students and reported that one young man received water squirts to the face after glancing at her, and a young girl ended up in restraints and a helmet for making sounds under her breath:

> The young man made a low grunting noise under his breath as he sat at his work carrel sorting objects. His attendant was behind him almost immediately. "No inappropriate noises!" the attendant shouted. At the same time he grasped the young man's head, tipping it back so that he could insert into his nose the pointed tip of a plastic squeeze bottle into which he had just broken an ammonia capsule. Several hours later this same

man stole a glance at the visitors who were there to observe him. "Eyes on work!" came the shout. The young man raised his arms, eyes blinking, as if in surrender, as the attendant grabbed the pressurized water hose. He was sprayed in the face for several minutes until he was sputtering and his shirt was soaked. With the helpless look of one resigned to the bleakness of his situation, he returned to the task in front of him, not even pausing to wipe the water from his eyes.[62]

When Weiss returned from her visit to BRI, she felt compelled to take personal action in response to what she had observed at BRI. She believed that what she saw there was no less torture than were the techniques used on political prisoners and felt that Amnesty International would be the appropriate organization to take action. Weiss ran a community support program at the Kennedy Institute (now the Kennedy Krieger Institute) that used only positive approaches. The institute also ran an inpatient behavioral unit that used some aversive and punishment procedures though none as extreme as those used at BRI. Weiss wrote a paper that became an organizing tool for professionals who were opposed to the use of aversives: "A Call to Action: Toward the Elimination of Aversives to Control People with Disabilities."[63] Recognizing the potential conflict of interest with the practices of her own employer, the Kennedy Institute, Weiss researched this issue and wrote "A Call to Action" on her own time, and when she sent copies of the paper to people who requested it, she made it clear that she had conducted this advocacy work in her personal capacity. The paper documented what she had observed at BRI and discussed the use of aversive procedures in other settings. In the form of a petition, "A Call to Action" was signed by individuals and organizations across the country.[64]

Lucy Gwin, the founder and editor of *Mouth*, a disability advocacy magazine, requested a copy of Weiss's "A Call to Action." She later called Weiss and said, "I just finished reading your paper and I'm sitting here weeping. You and I are going to close this place down." Gwin had the idea of placing a small ad in the *Providence Journal*: "Journalist wishes to talk with current and former employees of the Behavior Research Institute."[65] The paper wouldn't let her name the facility, so she described it in a way that made clear the facility in which she had interest.

Gwin received forty-four phone calls after she placed the ad in the *Providence Journal* and other papers in the Canton area, and she and Nancy Weiss conducted fourteen lengthy interviews. Some were recorded with the permission of the caller, and for others they took copious notes. They then sent a few pages of quotes from their interviews with current and former BRI employees to *Sixty Minutes*. Within days, CBS contacted Weiss and decided to give the story to a new show, *Eye to Eye with Connie Chung*. The story was assigned to Judy Rybak, a producer at *Eye to Eye*. CBS News representatives were hoping to identify someone who could get a job at JRC without falsifying his or her résumé and wear a hidden camera.[66] They asked Weiss if she would consider applying for a job there, but she was unwilling to do what would be required. Weiss and Gwin helped to identify a BRI worker, one of the people they had interviewed whom they felt would be willing to wear a concealed camera, knowing that he would have to quit his job before the show aired or he would likely be fired for it.[67]

Over the course of a year, *Eye to Eye* collected information for what turned out to be a highly controversial story. In response to the network interest in BRI, Israel wrote another letter to Philip Campbell: "We find it disturbingly coincidental that your agency's renewed interest in the BRI program is occurring at or about the same time that CBS is preparing its report. Indeed, your licensors were scheduled to make a visit to BRI at the exact same time that CBS was planning to do its filming. (CBS has since put off the filming for a week). We and the parents feel strongly that the interest and needs of these students should be unaffected by a television program whose principal agenda may have nothing to do with the welfare of the clients."[68] Campbell responded to these assertions: "We reject your assertion that our activity, which began in 1989, is caused by what you (not we) describe as possibly negative attention from a CBS television program, which, based on your letter, is a very recent development."[69]

Other media were paying attention to the ongoing BRI controversy as well. In 1993, Joseph Shapiro, a reporter for *U.S. News and World Report*, wrote the book *No Pity: People with Disabilities Forging a New Civil Rights Movement*, which documented the disability rights movement. He devoted a chapter to the use of aversives and the controversy at BRI:

> On my visit to Providence, BRI struck me as a human-sized
> Skinner Box or a scene from some fictionalized Orwellian

future. In the basement of BRI's nondescript building, "students" were lined up at workbenches, doing mundane tasks in several classrooms, as young, fresh-faced staffers, many newly armed with college psychology degrees, carefully patrolled the rooms and watched over shoulders. Upstairs, in a locked room with banks of television screens, staff monitors watched each classroom through closed-circuit hookups. Not only were the clients constantly watched and guarded but the classroom workers were, too, who could also win rewards such as extra pay or vacation based on their performance. In the first classroom I visited, one young man tired of his exercise of picking out matching shapes on a computer screen. He indicated he wanted to stop by removing his hands from the computer screen. But his teacher demanded that he continue and pinched him on the palm for disobeying. The young man, wearing a protective white helmet, made a guttural noise of protest and tried to get up. In a second, two staffers had thrown him face down on the floor. This only made him more agitated. Then came a squirt in the face with the ammonia water. The man spent a minute on the floor, trying to move and protest, but was restrained by one staffer's knee in his back and another's grip on his arms. When he gave up his struggle, the man was returned to the workbench.[70]

Despite the effectiveness of existing programs using nonaversive interventions and as moving as these media stories and descriptions were, parents continued to argue that aversive procedures were necessary to control their children's behavior. Having made the decision to allow their sons and daughters to be at BRI, often feeling that it was a last resort after other unsuccessful placements, they continued to believe and outspokenly assert that BRI was the only place that was sufficiently equipped to manage these individuals and their behaviors.

EYE TO EYE

Chung's CBS *Eye to Eye* story was in sharp contrast to one that had aired on ABC's *20/20* several years earlier by television journalists Barbara Walters and Lynn Sherr who reported on BRI in a pro-aversive piece entitled, "When All Else Fails." The Walters and Sherr segment showed before-and-after video of students at BRI and included testi-monials of parents saying that BRI saved their children's lives.

The *Boston Globe* reported on the Chung interview: "The 33 minute video tape included excerpts of his [Israel] four-hour interview with Chung, which was taped in front of angry BRI parents who consistently interrupted her and berated her for negativity and bias. In the video-tape approximately two dozen parents or guardians are sitting behind Connie Chung as she interviews Matthew Israel. In the tape they are shouting, 'you are insulting us' and 'You came in here so badly versed on what was going on, it was ridiculous.'[71] It is inconceivable that CBS allowed BRI to make its own taped record of the often chaotic scene."[72] The segment, which was highly critical of BRI's practices, was sched-uled to be aired during the fall of 1993 before the licensing ruling, but the piece was bumped when Chung interviewed skater Tonya Hard-ing, who had arranged an attack on her competitor, Nancy Kerrigan.

In anticipation of *Eye to Eye*'s negative story on BRI, Israel sent out a preemptive letter and a video entitled *Eye to Eye at BRI* to major media outlets suggesting that Chung had misrepresented and sensational-ized the program at BRI. Israel felt that the story, if aired without com-ment, could have a negative influence on the recertification process. He said, "One bad story about BRI on national television while await-ing recertification could close us down."[73] He accused the producers of altering the sound of the shock device from "a flat, shrill tone to a low whirling noise." CBS responded that when the picture was slowed, the sound was altered and blamed it on the fact that BRI would not allow them to tape enough footage. MacLeish wrote a letter to CBS complaining about the alteration: "The noise which appeared when the GED device was displayed was an undulating eerie sound reminis-cent of what one might hear in a science-fiction or 'B' horror movies when massive amounts of electricity are generated upon unsuspect-ing victims by a mad scientist. It is decidedly not the sound which the GED makes when it is activated."[74] Chung later called the BRI feature one of the most difficult and disturbing stories she had ever reported on. "In fact, a lot of people didn't want us to do this story," she said.[75] The producer of Chung's report, Judy Rybak, said, "Nobody at CBS has ever had an experience like this, not even *60 Minutes*."[76]

On March 20, 1994, Walter Goodman, a television critic for the *New York Times*, responded to BRI's criticism that Chung had altered the soundtrack and accused CBS of using "shabby tricks of the trade" to undermine BRI. Andrew Heyward, executive producer of *Eye to Eye*, responded to the criticism in a *New York Times* editorial on April 10.

> Ironically, it was the institute, not CBS News, that used editing techniques in a biased and sensational manner, which even Mr. Goodman concedes is "no model of fairness." How can he presume to judge the reporting process without any independent knowledge of the underlying facts—facts obtained in the many other interviews we did with experts, former employees, parents of former students and state investigators and in hundreds of pages of documents that *Eye to Eye* examined in our six-month investigation?
>
> Mr. Goodman barely alludes to the fact that the Massachusetts Department of Mental Retardation, the state agency that regulates the Behavior Research Institute, conducted its own separate investigation that corroborated many allegations raised in our report. Instead, he concludes that viewers were "possibly misled" by our report—surely one of the lamest phrases in a critic's arsenal.
>
> Had he bothered to pick up the phone and call me, Mr. Goodman would have learned of the respected experts on aversives who are cited by Mr. Israel in his lobbying efforts but who question his methods; he would have found out that a parent whom he portrays as a supporter of Mr. Israel is in fact a vocal critic; most important, he would have given me the chance to respond to Mr. Israel's false and unchallenged assertion of bias.[77]

The arguments, competing perspectives, and accusations in the scientific literature and the media on the acceptability of aversives once again highlighted the difficulties faced by the judiciary and legislature in deciding what was in the best interest of the child.

ANOTHER ATTEMPT TO PASS ANTI-AVERSIVE LEGISLATION

The year 1993 was busy for those involved in this controversy: BRI had filed contempt charges against DMR, the media were scrutinizing BRI's practices, and former employees of BRI testified at a hearing on anti-aversive legislation that was pending in the Massachusetts

House. "I have seen clients shocked, pinched, spanked . . . for not raising their hand before speaking,"[78] reported Anne Marie Millard, who was employed as a supervisor at BRI from 1987 to 1992. Her testimony went into great detail on the aversives she regularly encountered during her employment at BRI.

I had worked at the Behavioral Research Institute mostly in supervisory positions for five and half years, between 1987 and 1992. I left the program for a seven month period in July of 1992 and was recruited back, working four additional months training staff before quitting for good. In one of the positions that I held I was responsible for running the school on the weekends.

I was excited when I first went to work for the program. It was something new and I thought I could help the students. At first I had an adrenaline that flowed from the new experience. I have to say in the beginning I really loved it, but I was only there a short time when I began to see things. I used to almost convince myself, and say, that the director knows what he is doing. And I was sure that if we just stuck with the program with consistency and dedication, it was going to work. I would see certain things go on which I now know are abuse.

The program has been effective in letting the outside world see only what they want you to see. The bizarre, off the wall type of things that I saw I can only call experimentation. And only the people who work within the program's doors know what went on. I wish to share some of the things that I have seen.

I have seen a student who was so badly bruised from head to toe from being spanked with a spatula that she was bed ridden for three days. She had bruises even on her breasts. And that was a client who had been held out previously as one of the program's successes.

I had to apply ice to the welts on the body of a student on the orders of a program nurse. Then I circled them with a Magic Marker so we would be able to find the few remaining non-bruised areas to hit with the spatula.

While the program says that only the most dangerous and self-injurious behaviors are punished with the infliction of pain, I have seen clients shocked, pinched, spanked with spatulas and have ammonia sprayed in their face not only for dangerous or self-abusive behaviors, but for such offenses as speaking too softly, speaking without raising their hands or for stopping the tedious work that they were doing.

I have seen a senior staff member go haywire on multiple occasions and repeatedly hit clients with a spatula in areas that were not court approved for behaviors that they were not allowed to punish with painful aversives, such as speaking out.

Students were bound by the wrist and ankle for hours and hours in awkward positions, blindfolded with a very few inches of mobility in their hands. Then they were made to move bolts from one box to another box for hour after hour all day and into the evening. If they stopped they would be hit with a spatula.

I have seen students burned from receiving electric shocks and know of the shock devices malfunctioning and shocking students who had done nothing wrong.

The program has been unwilling to admit its failures. One client was restrained 24 hours a day for two years. With that client we tried shock, click, click, click, with the remote control for the shock device and over 100 shocks would be administered and wouldn't faze him. Another client received over 4000 shocks in a day before being put into restraint until they could devise a more painful aversive.

Hunger is used as an aversive. Many of the students are on a special food program where they are guaranteed to receive only 20% of the food calories per day they require to maintain 87% of their ideal body weight. Not 87% of their current weight but 87% of their ideal weight.

The program has a number of ways of manipulating the information that reaches people outside of the programs walls. Video tapes had been made when clients had been taken off their program and go off the wall. Then they use that tape to justify the use of even more painful aversives. When visitors come into school, clients in crisis are hidden from the visitors, sometimes even taken into the shower. We were instructed to dress clients in long sleeve shirts and long pants during visits to cover their bruises. Parents told me they were bullied into accepting aversives that they were not comfortable with and that they were threatened that if they didn't approve them that they could find another placement.

So why did I stay for 5½ years and come forward now. My hope in coming forward now is that by exposing the abusive practices that I witnessed, the state will act to ensure that the program's clients will finally receive the care and education that they desperately need in an environment that is free of the abuse that I witnessed at BRI.

I left the program by my own decision. It has taken me a long time to come to grips with the fact that the program does more harm than good. I have nothing to gain by coming forward and much to lose. I have been threatened by the program with legal action as have other staff that has come forward. I know many other staff that have witnessed similar events but are too frightened and intimidated to speak publicly. I hope by coming forward I will encourage more staff to speak out.[79]

Also present at the legislative hearing was Representative David Cohen from Newton, who for several years had sponsored legislation banning aversives. He accused BRI of passing off "torture as treatment" and urged that the bill be passed.[80] Testimony from former employees had been collected by the Center for Public Representation in Cohen's presence.[81] All of the testifying employees provided vivid detail of the use of aversives at the center. Israel responded by saying that they were "in cahoots"[82] with Cohen and were disgruntled, discontent, and seeking revenge. The anti-aversive legislation did not pass, in part due to the continued advocacy by the parents who had children at BRI. Legislators were reluctant to act against the wishes of families, particularly those with impressive academic credentials. David Peterson, a distinguished professor of government at Harvard at the Kennedy School and the father of a child at BRI, spoke out repeatedly when anti-aversive legislation was introduced:

> Aversive therapy has made all the difference in the world to David. He speaks a lot better, he helps in the kitchen, he feeds himself and he dresses himself . . . He seems completely recovered. He's a mentally handicapped person, so he's not going to be a university professor, but he can do repetitive tasks that he seems to get satisfaction from. David is very happy where he is . . . The shocks will always be necessary to keep him in check. If you take it away he would revert to self-injurious behavior . . . Opponents say it violates fundamental human

decency. They're just nuts . . . They're either blind or insane. It's like wearing eyeglasses, I can't get away from eyeglasses. Nonetheless I can see.[83]

THE DEATH OF LINDA

Linda Cornelison, a 19-year-old student at BRI, died on December 12, 1990, after being transported to a Providence hospital with a perforated stomach and sepsis. Her death, as did Vincent Milletich's, spiked more concerns about the safety of students at BRI. DMR did not learn of her death until almost three years after it occurred because it was reported to the regional DMR office, not to the commissioner of mental retardation or his designee, as required by state regulations. During the recertification process in 1993, Richard Cohen, director of investigations at DMR, discovered the death. Cohen was a seasoned disability rights attorney who served as the lead attorney in the closing of Laconia State School in New Hampshire, a court monitor for a Minnesota deinstitutionalization order, and the court monitor for a special education lawsuit order in Boston. DMR investigator Donna Cabral was appointed on November 1, 1993, to review the case. Her investigation interviewed seventy-two witnesses and reviewed hundreds of documents. Four outside experts also reviewed the documents and findings. The report was not completed until January 3, 1995, a little over a year after the state DMR became aware of her death. Cornelison's mother filed a suit against BRI and its director for "failing to respond to the woman's complaints of illness, an allegation that MacLeish denied."[84] The case was settled out of court.

9 : BAD FAITH OR
RESPONSIBLE GOVERNMENT?

ANOTHER ATTEMPT TO LIMIT
THE USE OF AVERSIVES

THE TUESDAY MORNING GROUP

Commissioner Philip Campbell established a group to support his efforts to ensure quality programs for people with disabilities, particularly those at BRI. Members of the group, which came to be known as the Tuesday Morning Group,[1] were Jean Tuller, special assistant to the commissioner; Mary Cerreto, assistant commissioner in the office for quality enhancement in DMR; Richard Cohen, a lawyer who was the director of investigations; Kim Murdock, general counsel; Michael Kendrick, assistant commissioner of programs; Fred Misilo, deputy commissioner; and others involved in licensing and certification. The group was organized to coordinate the activities surrounding the licensing and regulation of BRI and its provisional status and had regularly scheduled meetings on Tuesdays. When the members began to meet, they asked Murdock whether they should take notes. She replied that taking notes was fine and that the information was privileged (not discoverable in a legal proceeding and could not be inspected by another party) and would not be admissible in court. This advice proved to be incorrect and provided BRI's attorneys with the information needed to argue that the state Department of Mental Retardation had a conspiracy to shut down the center.

While the Department of Mental Retardation investigated the death of Linda Cornelison, Mary Cerreto submitted a confidential report, "Review of Psychiatric Evaluation: Behavior Research Institute," to Campbell on December 5, 1993.[2] The report resulted from concerns expressed by Dr. Paul Jansen, who had been actively involved in cases at BRI since the summer of 1988 regarding medication and medical treatment issues. Israel vigorously contested the use of psychotropic medication even when there was a clear diagnosis of a major psychiatric condition for which the prescription of medication was routine.[3] It was clear to those in DMR that Campbell was not satisfied with the status quo and was seeking to create a review process for all DMR programs that required rigorous oversight and acknowledgment of the rights of people with disabilities.

The request for the report that Cerreto provided had been made on September 10, 1993, by Kevin Layden, DMR deputy director of licensing, before DMR learned that Linda Cornelison had died. Cerreto was an experienced licensed psychologist. Prior to working at the DMR, she had served as chief of pediatric psychology at the University of Texas Medical Branch, chief psychologist for primary care at Vanderbilt University, and director of psychology at Franciscan Children's Hospital in Boston.[4] Her job was to make sure that programs funded by DMR were providing people with disabilities with high-quality services that met standards and reflected national practices required by organizations that were responsible for certifying facilities and programs. Under Cerreto's leadership, licensing, certification, and quality assurance were a unitary enterprise. This coordinated approach to reviewing Massachusetts programs serving children and adults with disabilities was considered a national model due to its rigor and attention to professionally adopted standards. The quality assurance process, referred to as QUEST (quality enhancement survey tool), replaced the old licensing system in 1994 and served as the basis of the report. The survey was divided into six categories: respect and dignity, individual control, community membership, relationships, personal growth and accomplishments, and personal well-being.[5] It was used consistently in all Massachusetts programs that served clients with mental retardation[6] and involved observations, record reviews, and interviews with staff and administrators.[7]

In her report, Cerreto identified serious programmatic and administrative problems at BRI that needed to be addressed in order to comply with DMR regulations and quality assurance standards.[8] The confidential report on BRI contained numerous negative findings that included the lack of formulation of individualized treatment plans, evaluation of use of medication for behavior modification, contraindications to aversive interventions because of health, the lack of systematic evaluation of programs and interventions, and potential side effects of a predominantly aversive environment.[9]

Campbell and his team decided that an external review of BRI's practices was necessary, particularly since BRI had filed suit for contempt.[10] The department's internal findings and reports would not be sufficient. During the first BRI lawsuit in 1986 involving the Office for Children, its commissioner, Mary Kay Leonard, sought technical assistance from Gary LaVigna and then convened a team of experts to review the variance requests submitted by BRI. To avoid the perception of bias and knowing that BRI had successfully argued that Leonard's handpicked team was biased, Campbell and his team used an open request for proposal (RFP) process to solicit individuals or groups interested in conducting the review as part of the recertification process.[11] But the turnaround time for the RFP was only ten days and there were only two responses. Using an internal review process, DMR hired a nonprofit organization, the Rivendell Team of Minnesota, to conduct a program assessment of BRI. But Rivendell had reservations. In October 1993, Rivendell experts expressed concerns about Israel's "demonstrated propensity for using defamation suits as an intimidation tactic."[12] The Massachusetts attorney general had a policy against indemnification by the commonwealth and advised DMR to either purchase insurance or reimburse the experts for the costs of insurance. The Rivendell Team agreed to this condition and was willing to conduct the program assessment.

BRI took issue with the "propriety of the Department's selection, and the competency of the Rivendell Team to conduct a fair, objective, and unbiased program review."[13] One member of the team, Rick Albin from the University of Oregon, had signed the "Call to Action: Toward the Elimination of Aversives to Control People with Disabilities." In a probate court hearing, on November 1, 1993, BRI stated that it was opposed to the program evaluation and would be seeking appropriate judicial relief in conjunction with the proposed evaluation. It then filed a motion on December 10 seeking a court order "to enjoin Defendant Philip Campbell from requiring, mandating or otherwise directing or causing, BRI, to submit to a program evaluation by Rivendell."[14] The motion filed in court alleged contempt by DMR by ignoring the court order and sought equitable relief.[15]

Meanwhile members of the Rivendell review team responded to BRI's contempt motion and each of its specific allegations. Angela

Amado, a team member, was executive director of the Human Services Research and Development Center of St. Paul, Minnesota, an experienced evaluator and well published in the field of developmental disabilities. She had recently conducted an extensive evaluation of intermediate-care facilities for people with mental retardation for the Minnesota Legislature. In a letter to Tuller, Campbell's special assistant, she responded to the allegation of bias resulting from her membership on the board of directors of the American Association of Mental Deficiency (AAMD), which had a policy statement condemning the use of painful, physically damaging, and dehumanizing procedures:

> It is interesting that virtually every major professional association in the country has made a position statement against the use of painful and degrading aversive methods (Note that most of these statements are not against the use of *all* aversive methods, but rather those which cause pain, physical damage and degradation). Many of BRI's charges against people on the Rivendell team are that they belong to professional associations, which have taken positions against the use of aversive therapies. That gives them a basis for alleging bias against almost any professional in the country.[16]

In fact, the major disability advocacy organizations in the United States did have anti-aversive statements similar to the AAMD's.[17] The Association for Persons with Severe Handicaps (TASH) had a formal resolution calling for an end to all aversive procedures. However, the Association of Applied Behavioral Analysis did not call for the cessation of aversive procedures that caused pain.

In the middle of the Rivendell Team controversy, Campbell was focused on the use of the GED-IV at BRI, the device that delivered a much stronger shock than the original GED. During BRI's license review process, FDA staff conducted a site review of the school the first week of February 1994 and permitted the continued use of the GED and GED-4 devices as long as the devices were not going to be sold.[18] The FDA's involvement prompted MacLeish to once again accuse the state of trying to shut down the school: "They are trying to put us out of business. They are very determined."[19] (See table 2.)

In early February 1994, before the Rivendell evaluation was completed, DMR granted BRI a six-month provisional certification contingent on the organization coming into compliance on a number of regulatory and licensing issues.[20] The violations that DMR cited included "(1) substantiated cases of abuse and neglect; (2) improper use of restraints; (3) failure to advise staff of their obligation to report abuse and neglect to state authorities; (4) using electrical shock devices not approved by the U.S. FDA,[21] and (5) use of the GED to address behaviors that are not extraordinarily difficult or dangerous."[22] The *Boston Globe* reported that allegedly, "a student sat in restraints in a corner during the seven-hour school, was bathed while positioned in a four-point restraint, and was bound at the arms and legs whenever he moved from one location to another."[23] MacLeish responded to the report and provisional certification saying, "We look at this as a positive development, but obviously we want to make sure DMR is acting in good faith and these conditions can be realistically complied with."[24] Robert Sherman, another attorney representing the school, "characterized the report as a 'slipshod and bad-faith investigation' by DMR."[25] BRI had until August 8 to address the compliance issues.

Meanwhile, the review process and Rivendell Team members were reviewed by Judge LaStaiti and mediated by former justice George N. Hurd Jr. as stipulated in the Office for Children settlement agreement that was still in effect. Rivendell president Roger Deneen communicated with Tuller, the commissioner's special assistant, about his frustration in attempting to schedule a conference call with BRI to set up the logistics of the review visit. Deneen was told to contact BRI's attorney, MacLeish, about his request for a conference call. In a letter summarizing the timing and nature of his communications with MacLeish, Deneen reported:

> I explained my request for a conference call. He (MacLeish) replied that a conference call wasn't necessary due to the fact that their [sic] was going to be a hearing next week to discuss the incredibly strong bias of the team members, and it was clear in his mind the hearing would negate the need for Rivendell to even have a conference call to discuss the program review. I stated that all I wanted to do is to discuss the logistics of the program review. He stated that he could tell that I was a nice guy and that he really did not want to waste my time, and a conference call was unnecessary. He then asked for a list of the team members, which I gave him, and he then requested me

to fax him a copy of their CVs. I told him that I would fax him a copy of the CVs I had in my possession.[26]

Eventually BRI and the review team agreed to a confidentiality clause and a condition by Israel that no student would be interviewed unless a staff member was present who was of the same professional level as the interviewer (for example, psychologist to psychologist).[27] The Rivendell Team and DMR viewed these as delaying tactics that indicated a lack of cooperation. On March 22, 1994, during the external review process, BRI reversed its agreement to allow Rivendell to review client records. Murdock wrote to MacLeish: "You and I spent hours yesterday working out an agreed confidentiality agreement to govern Rivendell's need for *copies* of the client records. At no time did you indicate to me that BRI intended to prevent Rivendell from simply *reading* the records."[28] MacLeish responded that BRI was only concerned about the removal of the records, and a new confidentiality agreement was developed.[29] He also expressed concerns that Rivendell did not have the resources to indemnify BRI in the event there was a breach of the confidentiality agreement. Murdock replied that the same was true for DMR and again worked out an agreement for the consultants to see the records.[30] This was all unfolding while Rivendell experts were in Massachusetts attempting to identify and copy records necessary to complete their reports. Murdock was increasingly frustrated: these tactics were slowing the review and hampering the ability of the Rivendell Team to do their work. DMR was constantly reacting and spending valuable resources to move its agenda forward. On March 25, the last day of the review, Murdock, DMR's general counsel, wrote to MacLeish:

> Dear Eric:
> Yesterday, at around 11:00 am, I faxed you a letter proposing a solution to your client's concerns with the photocopying of client records, which is part of the program review. When I spoke to you by telephone at approximately 2:30, you had not yet reviewed my letter. I suggested that we speak in the next five minutes, after you had had time to look at it. Although you stated that you had other matters to attend to immediately, you would call me back that afternoon with your comments. I promised to remain in my office for your call.
> When you had not called by 6:00, I phoned you. Your

recorded message said you were still in your office. I left a message asking you to call me in the morning.

When I did not hear from you the following morning by 11:00, I called your office. I was told that (you) were not there, but that you were expected later in the day. I again left a message asking you to call me.

Rivendell expects to make copies of any records relevant to its review of the BRI program, in order to ensure a more accurate and complete report. It is unacceptable to force the Rivendell consultants to spend an inordinate amount of time in the clerical task of taking notes about records (so they can recall the records' contents), when their time could be much better spent in actually conducting a program review.

I am still hopeful that we can resolve this issue, which is not a complex one at all. The Department seeks resolution, not conflict. When BRI yesterday objected to the photocopying of records, even though they were not being removed from BRI, and even though we had understood your objection to be only record removal at that point in time, we immediately stopped copying any records. The Department also seeks your client's cooperation with this program review, as required by the terms of BRI's certification.[31]

From March 20 through March 25, Roy Froemming, an attorney for the Wisconsin Protection and Advocacy System[32] and a Rivendell team member, visited BRI to review the records and programs of several selected clients. He cited problems getting access to records, some limitations in observations, and problems with the aversive programs being delivered. His summary, clear about the lack of options available to the clients at BRI, captured some of the fundamental issues Massachusetts was facing as it attempted to stop the use of aversives:

> BRI has some important resources for moving toward
> integration and social goals, most notably the location
> of the houses and, energy and commitment of its staff,
> and the abilities of the residents. In closing, my strongest
> recommendation to Massachusetts, is that other resources
> need to be developed to serve people with severely challenging
> behaviors, both to ensure that other alternatives are exhausted
> before people are subject to extraordinary aversives, and to

provide alternatives for people like Mr. M and Ms. S, who seem ready for greater community involvement and could benefit by being closer to family and some community. Mr. M.'s parents are actively seeking alternatives that they can believe in, both residential and vocational. It is not surprising that families and courts have chosen BRI over more positive approaches when no other actual placement or program was available at the time of their admission, and no clear viable alternative picture has been presented to the courts to the treatment program BRI has been prepared to offer.[33]

The Rivendell Team delivered its final report in April. Organized into fourteen program review criteria as required by DMR, the report was overwhelmingly negative. The summary paragraph read:

> The regulations (104 CMR 20:15) are clear that highly intrusive or restrictive behavior modification procedures must meet the heaviest burden of review among all treatments and be subjected to the strictest safeguards and monitoring, however, BRI appears to perceive external review and monitoring functions as bureaucratic "harassment." While seeking "unique" certification from the Commonwealth of Massachusetts to utilize a "unique" and highly intrusive intervention, BRI complains about being singled out for 'unique' treatment by the Commonwealth.
>
> The Rivendell Team is concerned that, despite all the program weaknesses and internal contradictions, BRI interprets its program's ineffectiveness with certain students to mean that the shock must not be powerful enough—thus the quest for certification to create Class IV intervention category.[34]
>
> The staff at BRI appear to be deeply committed to providing services that make a difference. They work hard and obviously invest enormous amounts of energy into their work. An increased emphasis on teaching students new social skills, increasing students' social effectiveness, enhancing student independence, and delivering training in environments of ultimate functioning will further that commitment.[35]

Following the completion of the team report, the Massachusetts Coalition for the Legal Rights of People with Disabilities sent a letter to the state attorney general, Scott Harshbarger, urging the office to vigorously defend the administrative decisions of DMR with respect to the certification and operation of BRI. The coalition feared that BRI's contempt motion and the advocacy by BRI parents would result in little, if any, action:

> The Department is currently facing a contempt motion, essentially for exercising its administrative responsibilities to enforce its regulations and to protect persons with disabilities for whom it is responsible. If DMR decided not to continue BRI's certification, because of the school's unabashed refusal to comply with the agency's certification conditions, further legal action is almost certain. We believe it is essential that the Attorney General's Office vigorously defend the Department. A repetition of the previous legal strategy, which resulted in the 1987 settlement, would be an affront to citizens with disabilities and their families. There is universal opposition within the disability community for an approach which essentially acceded to all of BRI's demands and which sacrificed the rights of persons with disabilities and the prerogatives of the Commonwealth's executive agencies.[36]

Despite the Rivendell's Team's findings and although only four of the twelve conditions cited in the February review had been satisfied, in July 1994 DMR extended BRI's certification to use Level III aversives until December 31. This provided DMR time to find alternative placements for the BRI residents. These unmet conditions related to behavioral intervention planning, medical and psychopharmaceutical assessment, identification of behaviors considered extraordinarily difficult or dangerous, staff training and reporting requirements, communication with agencies and families about the use of mechanical and electrical restraints, research using new devices or interventions, and appointment of two individuals to the human rights committee.

During the period of the Rivendell and licensing reviews, staff members from Massachusetts DMR were interacting with the New York Office of Mental Retardation (OMR). Jean Tuller, special assistant to Campbell, was in regular communication with the New York OMR, assisting it in identifying alternative programs for students from New York who were currently residing at BRI. At the end of February 1994, the New York OMR informed the parents and guardians of sixteen students attending BRI that it wanted to return the students to programs in New York.[37] The loss of these students would clearly be a financial hit to BRI. DMR staff members were coordinating with New York to remove the students from BRI. Tuller said, "I was focused on protecting people. We all wanted to shut BRI down. But Phil [Campbell] was very careful and understood that we had to focus on compliance with the state regulations if we were going to be successful."[38]

EXPERIMENTAL TREATMENT

During this period, DMR engaged in other efforts to examine issues affecting people with disabilities, particularly those in institutional settings. Although not explicitly related to the quality assurance findings, on December 31, 1993, Campbell ordered facilities and programs across the state to search for any records of experiments on people with disabilities.[39] He did not want the concern about experimental treatment to be perceived as specific to BRI. Rather, he was concerned that other facilities in the state might have conducted experiments similar to those at Fernald State School in Waltham, Massachusetts, that exposed teenagers to radioactive milk in the 1940s and 1950s. DMR staff members believed that BRI was experimenting with the GED-IV on students without proper authority or proper scientific and human subject protocols.[40] Highlighting this concern, DMR contacted the U.S. Food and Drug Administration about BRI's development and use of the GED-IV,[41] which was approved for fifty-two of the sixty-six students in the school. The students fitted with a GED-IV wear a battery pack that is attached to electrodes, which are adhered to the person's body parts.[42] An article in *Boston Magazine* in July 2008 described why BRI believed that a stronger shock device was needed:

> The school says that the GED needed more juice. The
> mentally handicapped and behaviorally impaired students
> who attend JRC, who are in fact its lone attendees, weren't
> responding to the machine. So in the early 1990s, a couple of
> years after the GED was first developed, the school made a new
> one—upping the milliamps from 15 to 41 and the voltage to 66,
> and calling it the GED IV. Even at its higher capacity, the GED IV
> still carries less power than a stun gun, a defibrillator, or a cattle
> prod. But the GED IV, as well as the base model, has been found
> in numerous state reports and in the accounts of former JRC

staffers to burn students' skin. Some have been taken off it for a month at a time as a result. And then put back on.[43]

In spring 1994, the anti-aversive advocacy community was working hard to bring the practices of BRI to the forefront. The CBS *Eye to Eye with Connie Chung* that focused on BRI's practices was finally aired on March 3 and created more controversy and attention on BRI.[44] Parents of BRI students issued news and press statements: "CBS News' 'Eye to Eye with Connie Chung' Airs Tabloid Fiction on the Behavior Research Institute" and "Parents of BRI Students Charge CBS Report Abandons Standards in Favor of Ratings and Commercialism."[45] Anne Marie Millard, a former BRI employee, alleged that after she accused the school of abusive tactics, the school investigated her personal life and obtained transcripts of a child custody hearing that involved her daughter.[46] She had accused Dr. Israel of beating a student with a spatula and losing control, which Israel denied. Two other former employees, Gail Lavoie and Collen Seevo, described a student receiving more than 5,000 shocks in one day, another student who received over 350 shocks, the use of liver powder on food to punish misbehavior, burns from the GED unit, and a firsthand description of receiving a shock. Israel responded to these statements by saying that the treatments were necessary to save the life of a teenage student who weighed only 52 pounds, was self-injurious, and habitually vomited.[47]

In March 1994 these former employees, who alleged that BRI was abusing students received draft libel lawsuits in the mail from BRI's attorneys,[48] meant to discourage them from making public statements. An attorney from Michigan critical of BRI also received a letter asking for a retraction of his critical comments.[49] The *Boston Globe* reported on the draft lawsuits:

> Laura Conlon, another former employee said she saw Israel beat a patient so severely with a spatula that the patient needed bed rest for three days. The patient was in four-point restraint at the time-held by wrists and ankles to a board—and Israel was hitting areas that are off limits, including the student's breasts. Israel denied the accusation. He said there was one

occasion when the student was hit, but it was "exactly three applications," and the student was restrained face-down, making it impossible to hit a breast. "The people who made those accusations worked here for a number of years, and were demoted or quit." They vowed revenge. They met as a group to plan revenge against BRI.' He noted that they never made complaints at the time about the alleged abuse as they should have, according to state law. I laughed at the stories.[50]

MacLeish, who sent the draft lawsuits to the four former staff members, commented to the press, "We defend ourselves and we do it vigorously. We can't be trampled over by this. We will not allow people to come in and make irresponsible and outrageous comments . . . We are being hit from every corner and we have to respond. There can be a legitimate debate over aversive therapy, but when people start telling lies, what are we supposed to do? Roll over and say, here are the keys, take it away? We didn't start this battle."[51] MacLeish demanded that the employees recant their accusations or face a lawsuit. State representative David Cohen, the chief sponsor of anti-aversive legislation at the time, responded to the lawsuits, which were sent directly to the individuals and not actually filed in court: "You have to be very brave to speak out against them. It is really an act of courage."[52]

Some parents continued to passionately defend BRI. The compelling stories often spoke to the lack of capacity that states had to serve people with severe behavior disorders. Journalist Tim Greene of the *Middlesex* (Massachusetts) *News* spoke to Duncan McKnight, the father of David, 27 years old and a resident at BRI since 1987. McKnight tried to get his son into more than seventy-two programs. He was accepted by only seven, including BRI. McKnight said, "The other six did nothing but drug him or abuse him. David's self-abuse included digging at his eyes, scratching his ears till they bled and twisting and yanking his own testicles. I hurt, physically hurt, Duncan said, and he would laugh: He never cried; He never cried. Never. I've seen him bleeding and in agony, but he never cried. BRI used its painful therapy on David, and it worked, his father said. He basically has no serious self-abusive behaviors anymore."[53]

Greene also reported that other parents denied that BRI was the only alternative. "Israel preys on the parents' reasonable fears" said Jerry Kelly, the father of a young man in the Delta Project.

"You're so fearful. You know what you have works. What these people need to do is try other alternatives and the end result is their loved ones won't be tortured."[54]

NEW NAME, SAME BATTLES:
THE JUDGE ROTENBERG CENTER

In July, one month before its certification expired in August 1994, BRI announced that it would move its entire operation to Massachusetts. It would also change its name to the Judge Rotenberg Center to honor the late probate court judge who had been responsible for supporting the use of aversive interventions during the certification process and previous lawsuit filed by BRI against Mary Kay Leonard and the Office for Children (Figure 13).[55]

The name change came at a time of difficult negotiations with DMR mediated by Judge George Hurd. After August, the length of the certification for BRI was still not determined, but compliance issues had been addressed with plans for remediation. MacLeish said that BRI would continue to use electric shock with the most difficult students but was in the process of developing new programs that emphasized positive approaches to problem behaviors. The *Boston Globe* reported that MacLeish "insisted that the changes were neither a public relations ploy nor a condition of the state's certification."[56]

BRI was feeling the pressure. Other state agencies in Massachusetts were raising issues. In August 1994, Joseph DeNucci, the Massachusetts state auditor, criticized BRI for refusing to fully cooperate with a review of $1.2 million in legal bills and lobbying expenses. DeNucci said that BRI billed $630,000 in legal expenses as direct care expenses and spent $13,591 to lobby state officials over a three-year period. BRI responded to the audit by claiming that information the auditor sought would violate attorney-client privilege. MacLeish rebutted by saying that BRI would release all of the records as long as DeNucci agreed not to make them public, which the auditor refused to do. MacLeish believed that the records could "reveal legal strategy in ongoing litigation" between BRI and the commonwealth.[57] Lorraine Greiff, deputy director of the Office of Disability,[58] said, "This isn't the first time [BRI] officials have refused to cooperate with an agency. Every time anybody tries to monitor the things that go on there . . . they

Figure 13. Matthew Israel at the Judge Rotenberg Center. Larry Sultan,
Mother Jones *magazine, August 2007. Courtesy of the Estate of Larry Sultan.*

refuse to cooperate. In the meantime, we believe people are being sub-jected to cruel punishment."[59]

With the leadership of Representative David Cohen, members of the legislature once again planned to submit new anti-aversive legis-lation. Aware of the controversy related to the audit, lawmakers sent a letter expressing outrage over the lack of disclosure to other col-leagues in the State House:

> BRI's refusal to provide documentation for an expenditure
> of $1.2 million dollars in state funds, claiming "attorney/client
> privilege" is outrageous. As the appropriating authority, we have
> to take a hard look at the private agency, which obstructs state

agencies in their review of expenditures of state dollars. BRI's response to the Auditor's findings on funds used for lobbying is equally outrageous. When confronted with the Department of Public Safety regulation, BRI did three things: They retroactively changed sworn statements made to the Secretary of State's Office to say that although they had been billed for lobbying they didn't pay for it; They said the lobbying services were part of $51,152 in pro-bono services provided by their law firm, but provided no documentation; They said the lobbying services had been paid for with federal funds, but provided no documentation.[60]

In addition to the controversies surrounding the department's interactions with BRI, Campbell was coming under attack from pro-institution advocates for his actions that were directed at downsizing state institutions. He was committed to deinstitutionalization and the development of a community-based system of services for people with developmental disabilities and mental illness. This was threatening to parents with children and adult sons and daughters living in the state institutional system. Benjamin Ricci, a retired professor in exercise science from the University of Massachusetts–Amherst, had a son in a state institution and was an official in the Advocacy Network, a parent advocacy organization. In a tactic similar to those used by BRI's attorneys, Ricci filed a lawsuit charging the department and Campbell with libel.[61] The lawsuit sought an injunction barring the department from further acts of alleged harassment, defamation, and retaliation. One act of retaliation, according to the lawsuit, was the department's criticism of the Advocacy Network's guardianship of several clients that were served in Massachusetts institutions. The state had sought a contempt order against the Advocacy Network for allegedly failing to supply appropriate annual guardianship accountings. DMR alleged that the group failed to take enough interest in some of the clients and failed to account for the funds of another guardian. The Advocacy Network denied the charges, and the complaint was eventually dismissed.[62] The network urged U.S. District Court Judge Joseph L. Tauro to become reinvolved in the 1972 deinstitutionalization case, from which he had recently stepped down, because he was viewed as supportive of the parents' perspectives. The fact that Campbell was arguing with family organizations that had strong ties to their state legislators created problems for the department and its attempts to create a comprehensive, community-based system that could provide alternatives to institutions and to BRI.

HUMAN RIGHTS

DMR required all provider agencies to have human rights committees, and oversight of BRI's practices was partly the responsibility of its human rights committee. Carol Upshur, an external member of BRI's human rights committee, Harvard educated, and a professor and clinical psychologist at the University of Massachusetts Medical School, was increasingly concerned about BRI's practices and was voting not to approve its treatment plans. In a letter to Rosemary Silva, BRI's human rights officer, Upshur explained reasons for her lack of support for treatment plans: lack of individualization in plans, plans that asked for too broad a range of aversive interventions for too broad a range of behaviors, and some specific interventions that seemed to have a great probability of violating human rights. She wrote:

> My review of the data for one of these clients illustrated that after 18 months of use of the spank, no significant decelerating trend in the behavior was seen. Thus not only is it an unusually degrading procedure, but seemingly ineffective, behaviors are targeted for aversive procedures which are caused by the program environment, some plans do not have appropriate treatment goals, there are not replacement behaviors specifically matched to the behaviors targeted for deceleration, there are no goals set for positive behaviors, and the rewards listed in the contracts are different from the rewards listed as especially meaningful to the client . . . In sum, I have had great difficulty feeling that I would be protecting the human rights of the clients at BRI/JRC if I approved treatment plans that contain so much that I disagree with and that seem to me to violate the behavioral regulations of the DMR.[63]

On January 20, 1995, DMR once again granted only conditional certification of the JRC because it failed to meet DMR's conditions and published rules. DMR found that shock was being used for behaviors such as laughing and staring, which did not meet the criteria for Class III aversives.[64] There were several other findings:

1. JRC failed to implement the behavior modification plans of the six individuals in accordance with applicable requirements of the regulations. DMR found JRC's misuse of aversive techniques on the six individuals to constitute unlawful use of behavior modification interventions. They cited JRC's use of electric shock for such behaviors as refusing to get out of a seat, tearing paper, ripping tags off clothing, and refusing to follow directions.
2. JRC, in violation of 104 CMR 20.15 (4) (b)(3), does not use only those interventions which are, of all available interventions, least restrictive of the individual's freedom of movement and most appropriate given the individuals' needs. DMR cited the fact that in October, 1994, J.F. was squirted in the face with water 2,500 times. J.F. was still being punished with water sprays for inappropriate verbal behaviors even though JRC's data showed that the frequency of those behaviors was lower during the period when the verbal correction procedure "no" was used to address the behaviors.
3. JRC's data collection procedure does not provide for monitoring, evaluating, and documenting the use and effectiveness of each intervention.[65]

Other issues were also cited that related to the technical aspects of how target behaviors were identified; the development of individualized plans; research conducted without permission by DMR; and noncompliance with licensing inspections, including refusing to permit two noted behavioral psychologists, Thomas Linscheid and Brian Iwata, from reviewing the implementation of four behavior plans on December 1 and 2, 1994. Israel wrote to Linscheid and Iwata on November 30 explaining the he viewed their proposed review as a "bad-faith" action by the department and not as an "invited, collegial, constructive visit by two respected behavioral psychologists."[66] This denial of access was curious, since both Linscheid and Iwata were involved with the development and testing of the self-injurious behavior system (SIBIS) and were not opposed to the appropriate clinical application of aversive interventions.

Israel responded harshly to the conditional certification, stating, "DMR could fairly be described as corrupt. This man, DMR commissioner Phillip Campbell is conducting a campaign against us, to decertify us, for over two years now. He has wasted almost $2 million of the taxpayers' money."[67] The conditional certification through May1996 allowed JRC to continue to use Class III aversives on all but six patients who were evaluated by Rivendell. The conditional certification came after a January 3, 1995, investigation report on the death of Linda Cornelison. The report, which took two years to complete, and other DMR findings related to JRC failing to meet state standards led to the conditional recertification. The Massachusetts Disabled Person's Protection Commission and the Department of Mental Retardation released the report,[68] which included interviews of seventy-two witnesses, review of hundreds of documents, and reports by four experts, direct care staff, nursing staff, and administration, as well as several specific staff members. The report concluded that BRI took actions that were "egregious" and "inhumane beyond all reason" and constituted not only violations of legal standards but violations of "universal standards of human decency."[69] "The report stated that Linda arrived at school clutching her stomach. Once there, she lay on a couch, but a nurse thought her illness was an act. After school, Cornelison returned to her BRI-run residence in Attleboro, where staff gave her thirteen spatula spankings, twenty-nine finger pinches, and fourteen muscle squeezes, and they forced her to inhale ammonia five times. She died in the hospital early the next morning from complications related to a gastric perforation. Her mother said Cornelison had never had gastrointestinal problems before, according to a medical report. Though the department's report said the school "violated the most basic codes and standards of decency," it found that neither the dereliction of care nor the administration of aversives had killed her.[70]

MacLeish argued that the report on Linda Cornelison's death was "littered with inaccuracies [and] is designed to do nothing less than implement Phil Campbell's personal agenda to destroy this program. We dispute almost all the allegations . . . Linda's death was tragic but it was not the result of any negligence. We didn't do anything wrong. We loved her . . . No one except DMR has found any fault with what has occurred."[71] It was true that the police and the medical examiner had not found any wrongdoing.

On February 23, 1995, another legislative hearing was scheduled on a bill that would ban aversive therapy. In a press conference the day before, Linda Cornelison's mother, Roberta, said, "I am enraged that no one listened to her cries for help. And I am saddened that she suffered needlessly and that her basic human rights were neglected."[72] Roberta Cornelison later sued JRC and settled out of court for an undisclosed amount.[73]

ANOTHER ATTEMPT TO
LEGISLATE AGAINST AVERSIVES

In February 1995, the Massachusetts legislature held a hearing to once again pass legislation to outlaw Class III aversives, H. 3358, An Act to Protect Disabled Persons. In the hearing room and in front of a large audience of advocates both in support of and against the use of aversives, the vice chair of the Committee on Human Services and Elderly Affairs, State Representative James V. DiPaola, quietly put the shock device on his arm and shocked himself with the GED. He leaped out of his chair yelling and tearing at the device. He described it as torture and as very painful. Testimony opposing the use of aversives was countered by a Harvard professor of government, Paul Peterson, who had administered the powerful shocks to his son, David, 25, to prevent him from shoving his fist down his own throat. Peterson believed the electric shocks had saved his son's life.[74] Despite Peterson's testimony, the legislative committee voted overwhelmingly in support of a ban on aversive therapy on February 28. The committee chairman, Paul Kollios, representative from Millbury, said, "It's against the law to do it to pets. It's child abuse and a crime to do it to children. It's not even allowed on convicted criminals serving time for high crimes."[75] Under questioning at this hearing, "Matthew Israel conceded that one student had received 5,300 shocks from the Graduated Electronic Decelerator (GED) in one day."[76]

The bill went to the House Ways and Means Committee, where a similar bill had been voted down the previous year. The *Boston Herald* reported that Israel had supported the powerful chair of the Ways and Means Committee, Thomas M. Finneran, by contributing to his 1993 reelection campaign. Finneran did not allow any anti-aversive bills out of the Ways and Means Committee to get to the house floor. Israel also contributed to two other members of the committee.[77] The *Providence Journal* responded to the unsuccessful legislative attempt to ban aversives with an article supportive of JRC that accused Massachusetts legislators of "getting caught up in displaying virtue rather than in solving real problems, . . . leaving parents to pick up the pieces."[78]

On March 23, backed by Attorney General Scott Harshbarger and Governor William Weld, Campbell ordered JRC to stop using electric shock as treatment by July 1. DMR issued the ban after JRC refused to comply with a January 20 order to stop using the GED on six clients.[79] That order had come two days after JRC had filed a motion for a preliminary injunction against Campbell that would have prevented DMR from imposing any certification standards on the school. In a letter, Campbell referred to the use of the GED to shock a woman 100 times in one day and to withhold food, which violated several conditions in the recent "conditional certification." MacLeish promised to fight the ban in court as part of an ongoing lawsuit against DMR: "This is the grossest abuse of governmental power by a state agency that I have ever seen. They have wasted millions of dollars in taxpayer funds in this vendetta.[80] We view this as retaliatory. This is an out-of-control agency. It's using hundreds of thousands of dollars to harass this program and more importantly the parents of these kids."[81]

Margaret Chow-Menzer, DMR deputy counsel, said that the school was not acting illegally by simply using electric shock, but shocking for behaviors such as laughing and simply singing was inappropriate. "This is not a witch hunt. We have clinical evidence showing that, in fact, what they are doing is inconsistent with what the regulations require."[82] Susan Phelan, whose son attended the school, countered: "Why don't they leave us alone? We are not bothering anybody. This is what has worked for our children."[83]

The Disabled Persons Protection Commission, an agency that operated independent of DMR, reviewed the various cases in which abuse had been alleged and urged the Massachusetts Supreme Judicial Court to closely monitor the Bristol Probate and Family Court over which Judge LaStaiti presided. The commission argued that the supreme judicial court should intervene "using its power of general superintendent of the courts to review the monitoring system developed by the Bristol Probate and Family Court in order to insure the elimination or reduction of risk to students at BRI from the application of aversive procedures . . . It is our position that, given advances in behavioral sciences and the fact that Massachusetts General Law c. 19c was not and has not been considered by the court in its decisions regarding the use of aversive procedures, the court should not reevaluate the need for using painful aversives which cause serious physical or emotional injury as defined by c. 19C."[84]

On March 24, LaStaiti,[85] Judge Rotenberg's replacement on the Bristol Probate Court, issued a temporary restraining order that stopped the DMR's ban on the use of aversives and Campbell's attempts to decertify the center. Both sides claimed victory. Israel was "delighted, particularly for the parents whose right to choose life-saving treatments had been affirmed by this court."[86] But the order also required that JRC comply with the January 20 directive that granted provisional certification to cease using electric shock on six clients and to stop using food deprivation techniques in treating students, thereby establishing the authority of the state to regulate the center's programs.[87] Gerald Ryan, spokesman for Commissioner Campbell said, "We are very gratified with the decision because it reinforces the state's authority to regulate BRI."[88]

DMR recruited five psychologists to review the treatment plans of these six individuals. All of the psychologists reported that there were no substantial changes in the treatment plans of the six individuals despite recommendations for change. "Essentially all the psychologists found that nothing of substance had been done to improve the plans of the six individuals for whom the Commissioner gave only conditional certification to JRC. Consequently, the plans are still in violation of the behavior modification regulations."[89]

However, LaStaiti ruled that any changes in treatment for students should be approved by the probate court rather than the state administrative agency.[90] Israel said, as he had in 1987 during the battle with the Office for Children, "I'm fighting for my survival . . . The children here are all in good health. They're thriving. The parents are happy. Why am I being subjected to this?"[91]

Several charges of abuse at JRC were being investigated at this time. The state agency charged with oversight of abuse of people with disabilities, the Disabled Persons Protection Commission, released a report on JRC's use of spatulas and pinching as a form of punishment and urged the probate court to "re-examine whether it is necessary to use these procedures."[92] The commission was unable to substantiate three reports involving two students who allegedly received aversive procedures on unapproved parts of the body and one student who was allegedly deprived of food. The fourth allegation involved a student who was ordered "bed rest, but was given a bed in the classroom instead."[93] The commission once again asked the supreme judicial court to review the probate court monitoring of JRC and argued in the report that the treatment protocols used at JRC constituted a form of abuse under state law.

JUDGE ELIZABETH LASTAITI

On April 5, 1995, Judge LaStaiti held a hearing on the global motion filed by DMR: Emergency Motion for Order Directing JRC to Stop Using Certain Class III Interventions on Behalf of 52 Students. Like Rotenberg, she typically dealt with trusts, wills, guardianship, adoption, partition of property, termination of parental rights, and involuntary commitment and had little experience with educational and behavioral interventions and the controversies surrounding them. Subsequent to the hearing, she entered an order that removed DMR's ability to use its certification process to modify the individual behavior plans, essentially nullifying Campbell's January 20 letter. In her order LaStaiti ruled that the 1987 Mary Kay Leonard OFC settlement agreement superseded the authority of DMR:

> All treatment decisions or changes in treatment plans must be addressed in the substituted judgment proceedings in the individual guardianship cases after due notice and an opportunity to be heard. Said proceedings are not governed by the January 20, 1995, letter from DMR to BRI re: certification. The Department of Mental Retardation's contention that their letter of January 20, 1995, supersedes this Court's order of January 7, 1987, is at odds with the plain language of the settlement agreement filed with this Court on December 12, 1986. The Department of Mental Retardation cannot by implementation of its certification process subvert the provisions of said settlement agreement and also the jurisdiction of this Court to render substituted judgment determinations on a case-by-case basis.[94]

Essentially, LaStaiti ruled that DMR could not use its regulations or its quality assurance and certification processes to modify the treatment plans of the students at BRI. Following the precedent set by

Rotenberg, she held that the court could modify treatment plans only through substituted judgment proceedings. This was a major blow to Campbell and DMR.

BACK TO COURT

In late spring 1995, Campbell and his senior team members were being deposed in preparation for the trial on the contempt charges filed by JRC in 1993 for alleged violation of the OFC settlement agreement when DMR refused to certify Class III aversives. The contempt allegations would be heard in a bench trial beginning in June 1995 in front of Judge LaStaiti. Mary Cerreto, assistant commissioner for the office of quality enhancement at DMR, was deposed by JRC's attorney, Robert Sherman, on April 21, 1995. This occurred out of court, under oath, and was recorded by an authorized officer to be used later in the trial. Sherman, who worked with MacLeish, pursued a line of questioning that targeted several issues: DMR's bias against the use of aversives, a targeted attempt by DMR to shut down JRC, and dishonesty about the purpose and intentions of the Tuesday Morning Group. Attorney Holmes represented Cerreto. The following exchanges between Cerreto and the skillful Sherman capture the issues of morality and advocacy versus objective science that permeated the cross-examination:

> Sherman: In terms of the moral issues involved with the employment of aversives, do you have a position on that?
> Cerreto: I'm trying to figure out whether my moral position can be separated from my position. I don't think it can. I think when I make my statement about my position it includes having thought about the morals, the ethics and the professional need.
> Mr. Holmes: Objection.
> Sherman: Okay.
> Cerreto: Okay?
> Sherman: Would you characterize yourself as philosophically and morally opposed to the implementation of aversives?
> Mr. Holmes: Objection.
> Cerreto: My concern about responding to that with a no, which would be my first response, is that there are then a whole host of qualifiers. So I am not morally or philosophically or professionally opposed to the use of aversives under specific conditions.

Sherman: Do you believe that there is another way, quote, unquote, another way to treat individuals with severe behavior problems other than the use of aversives?

Cerreto: Yes.

Sherman: Do you believe that that applied to all individuals with severe behavior problems?

Mr. Holmes: Objection.

Cerreto: I don't believe anything applies to all individuals with severe behavior problems.

Sherman: Then in terms of your belief, when I asked you the question before, do you believe there is another way, you said yes. What do you mean by that?

Cerreto: That with appropriate assessment of an individual with severe behavior problems, there is a wide range of techniques. For some, medication is indeed appropriate. For some change in environment. For some, an aversive. Extremely restricted or extremely dependent on the particular individual whom you are trying to decrease and eliminate this type of behavior on.

Sherman: Do you recall writing a memo in October of 1992, to Commissioner Campbell, regarding Class III approval for an individual that resided at the Templeton program?

Cerreto: No

Sherman: Let me show you this document. Why don't we have this marked? If I could ask you to take a minute and just refresh your recollection about the memorandum that you wrote?

Cerreto: Yes.

[There are several questions clarifying Cerreto's role and responsibilities for quality assurance at DMR.]

Sherman: Now, directing your attention to Paragraph 1 of Exhibit 1, you start with the phrase: "It is with a great deal of regret, given the philosophical and moral issues involved, that I recommend approval of the attached request for Templeton for the implementation of Class III program for—and then it's the individual whose name is blacked out, correct?"

Cerreto: Yes

Sherman: Why did you have a great deal of regret?

Cerreto: The issue here for me became one of approving a highly restrictive program when he probably should not have been there at all, at Templeton at all.

[...]

Sherman: Now at some point, did you become part of a group that became known as the ad hoc committee on BRI?

Cerreto: I never heard it referred to as the ad hoc committee on BRI, but there was a group of us who met around BRI.

Sherman: Just to use a phrase—what was the group referred to as?

Cerreto: The Tuesday morning meeting. I don't think the group was referred to by anything.

Sherman: Did you ever hear people refer to it as a task force on BRI?

Cerreto: No.

Sherman: No?

Cerreto: No.

Sherman: Other than your group, to your knowledge, was there ever another group that constituted a task force on BRI?

Cerreto: Not that I know of.

Sherman: Was the Tuesday Morning Group aware of a report in which it was concluded that the GED 4 and the specialized food program were being carried out within the mandates of the regulations of the Department of Mental Retardation?

Mr. Holmes: Objection.

Cerreto: I don't know if the group was aware.

Sherman: You were not aware, correct?

Cerreto: I was not aware.

Sherman: And you were also not aware, were you, of the ultimate recommendation in the report that says the team recommends that the Behavior Research Institute be certified to employ Class III interventions in behavior modification programs with the following provisions and a list of the two provisions which are contained on page 11. You weren't aware of that either, were you?

Cerreto: I think that I was aware that the team had no opposition to certifying BRI.

Sherman: You at least had been aware that there had been a team that had no opposition to certifying BRI? Is that your language?

Cerreto: Yes.

Sherman: Did you know they affirmatively recommended certification of BRI?

Cerreto: I don't recall.
Sherman: Did you know who the members of the team were?
Cerreto: I know three of the members of the team.
Sherman: Did you ever contact them?
Cerreto: No.[95]

Sherman was elucidating the fact that a certification team had previously approved of BRI's food program and Class III aversives in 1993 and had reported, "There is no indication that BRI was failing to adhere to the regulations of the Department of Mental Retardation in implementing these interventions." Sherman was pointing out the inconsistency in certification decisions, which would be highlighted in the upcoming court proceedings. After JRC applied for recertification in 1991, DMR assigned a team to make a site visit that included George Casey, a DMR attorney, and Kevin Reilly, the chief psychologist at Wrentham State School. After visiting, they recommended recertification subject to five minor conditions and complimented the center. There was no action on the Casey report. In May 1993, another team, which included a nutritionist and physician, was sent to review the specialized food and GED programs. The team determined that JRC had complied with all five conditions cited in the Casey report, concluded that the specialized food and GED program were being carried out within the mandate of DMR, and recommended that JRC be certified to use Class III interventions with two minor provisions. Apparently there was no follow-up to the report, even after it was submitted to the DMR attorney, Murdoch. This became a major issue during testimony, and Judge LaStaiti later cited it in her findings.[96]

There were several depositions during this time and more media attention. Brian Jenkins from CNN reported on JRC in a segment entitled: "Treatment or Torture, Aversive Therapy in Use." Carlo Casoria, Susan Phelan, Phyllis Shields, and Duncan McKnight, parents of students at JRC and outspoken pro-aversive advocates, once again testified to the program's effectiveness and their inability to find suitable alternatives. Lorraine Greiff, executive director of the Massachusetts Office for Disability, was also interviewed and argued that "it can never be justified to abuse another person like this, no matter what the situation is."[97]

10 : CONTEMPT

In May 1995, in what DMR leadership perceived as a defiant and distracting move, Israel announced that he was going to move the entire Judge Rotenberg Center operation from Providence, Rhode Island, to Massachusetts for its permanent home. The group homes were already located in the state, but JRC had been officially a program of Rhode Island. Now it would be wholly the responsibility of the commonwealth. Massachusetts legislators David Cohen and James Di-Paola were upset and began an unsuccessful campaign to prevent the move. "I am hopeful people in this state will become more aware of the abuse and that it will energize people to end this barbaric program,"[1] Cohen said. This was happening as DMR was about to face contempt charges brought by JRC.

The depositions had been taken and the line of questioning posed by JRC and the parents' attorneys was focused on proving that DMR intentionally undermined the Office of Families and Children Settlement decree, which basically ruled that treatment decisions were to be made by the probate court, not by the DMR, which normally was responsible for overseeing treatment and quality assurance. The JRC attorneys argued that DMR's Tuesday Morning Group was scheming and laying plans for JRC's demise. The two-week trial before Judge Elizabeth LaStaiti extended from June 26 to July 14, 1995, on a contempt action against the DMR filed by JRC and its students' parents.[2] On June 26, nine attorneys appeared. Judith Yogman for the attorney general's office represented DMR and commissioner Campbell, along with Margaret Chow-Menzer and Lucy Wall. Seven attorneys—Eric MacLeish, Michael Flammia, Bettina Briggs, Eugene Curry, Paul Cataldo, C. Michele Dorsey, and Christopher Fiset—represented JRC and the class of parents/students. Briggs was the guardian appointed by the court to act in the best interests of JRC students.[3] The state was clearly outnumbered, and its attorneys had neither MacLeish's courtroom skills nor LaStaiti's sympathies. Anti-aversive advocates saw this case as an opportunity to restrict the use of aversives and to alter the

234

use of substituted judgment, which took control from the state department and gave it to the courts to approve and disapprove treatment plans. The court made clear that the trial was not about these two issues. Rather, it was a contempt complaint against Phillip Campbell, in his capacity as DMR commissioner, for violation of the 1987 Settlement Agreement with Mary Kay Leonard as director of the Office for Children.[4]

In his opening remarks, MacLeish emphasized the provisions of the 1987 Office of Families and Children Settlement Agreement that required mediation of disputes between DMR and JRC and the fact that two DMR certification reviews stated that there were no violations of DMR regulations, a fact that he claimed Campbell and his team ignored. Furthermore, JRC argued that the Tuesday Morning Group, which they referred to as the "Tuesday Morning Club," was actively trying to shut down BRI:

> MacLeish: Now your Honor, at the same time that this was all happening, a team was assembled from the Department of Mental Retardation. It's called the Tuesday morning club and it would meet at 8 o'clock in the mornings on Tuesday. There was a small group and then there was a large group. The small group was comprised of the commissioner of the department of Mental Retardation, Dr. Maury Sorettson, special assistants, Jean Tuller, Richard Cohen, and I believe Kim Murdock.
>
> Now, it's curious that Richard Cohen was involved in these meetings at all, your Honor. He's the director of investigation for DMR and these documents, which were just produced to us last Friday demonstrate that the director of investigation was involved in what was called policy development. And there is notes from those meetings and there is agendas from those meetings; and what they show, your Honor, is a full battle plan for how we sink and destroy this program.
>
> The commissioner will testify as he testified at his deposition that these meetings were only about certification. Well, now we have the records, your Honor. We know what they were about. They were about going to placement agencies, the out of the state placement agencies, and getting clients out of those programs.
>
> They were about going to the Food and Drug Administration

to try to persuade the Food and Drug Administration to take action against BRI. They were about getting as much dirt on BRI as possibly could be imagined. They were about a misuse of the investigation process. For example, investigations of the guardian ad litem. One of the agenda items, it stated, "Is Bettina Briggs related to the medical examiner who did the autopsy on Linda Cornelison?" who was a student who died at BRI.

A report was filed with the Court but the Department felt the need to take this up several years later, and that was a directive of the investigation to investigate if Bettina Briggs was related to the medical examiner?

Now I should mention, your Honor, that all throughout this process, attacks were being made on anyone who was deemed to be sympathetic with the position of JRC, whether it was the guardian ad litem Bettina Briggs. And that memorandum—that agenda will be in front of us.

There was a very interesting meeting which took place on Tuesday morning club on October 19, 1993, Your Honor. And again, this was at the time, your Honor, that the Rivendell program was going to be coming to BRI in the fall and evaluating supposedly to do an independent program review. And we'll have evidence, your Honor, about how independent that program was and in fact we provided the information to the Department of Mental Retardation showing that the members of the Rivendell program are all—had agendas that made their involvement with doing an independent review withdraws them, but that was October 19, 1993.

But they were coming. And the Commissioner in his pleading to your Honor says I just want to make a fair decision on certification. Well this is what happened on October 19. This is a note that someone attended the meeting. We don't know who it is. We just got the notes. I asked this gentleman if he can tell me. At the bottom of the page, your Honor, December 15, that would be December 15, 1993 "BRI" "D" day. D day is, as I'm sure the Commissioner will remember, was the largest invasion of a country ever undertaken in the history of the world.

And then on the next line, your Honor, the following very significant statement appears, "What would BRI have to do to not be certified? Top two areas are capacity to obey laws and efficacy of treatment." What would BRI have to do not to be certified? These are discussions with the Commissioner of Mental Retardation who has testified under oath in his deposition that these meetings were being undertaken as part of a very neutral certification process.[5]

. . . DMR has spent unlimited amounts of funds in an effort to violate the settlement agreement and to destroy this program and to eliminate the very fabric of that settlement agreement and the process by which these very, very difficult decisions involving some very difficult clients are made. They have gone to every agency, most of them unsuccessfully, like the FDA. They urged that the FDA take some regulatory action against BRI to stop the use of the GED which the FDA declined to do. They approved the GED procedures for pre-market notification at a time when BRI just having to deal with this regulatory assault was occurring [incurring] legal fees. We request reimbursement. They go to the rate setting agencies and they say well these legal fees aren't reimbursable because they involve litigation against the Commonwealth.

The Commissioner sent his Deputy Commissioner down to do that. They go to the Department of Labor to argue that clients who work in the workshop program violate the fair standards act. They have utilized every tool available to them including the funds that belong to the taxpayers of the Commonwealth. They have utilized every bit of regulatory authority that they have and a lot of regulatory authority that they don't have.

They have utilized thousands, tens of thousands of man hours of their own employees, the evidence will be that for the past 15 months according to DMR's own documents they have had two to three full-time investigators assigned at BRI doing investigations, trying to dig up dirt. This process is about fundamentally a violation of specific provisions of the Settlement Agreement but more importantly it is about a gross abuse of governmental powers by individuals who pre-determined what they were going to do and then did not stop at anything to do it, including the law, including the court process, including the settlement agreement . . . The sanctions that will be requested will be significant sanctions. The damage which has been done to the program, to these students is significant, is substantial. The violations of the law are clear. They range from misrepresentations to this court, to bad faith, and a variety of other actions and I have not described everything, Your Honor, in my opening statements, and I apologize for going on.[6]

Assistant Attorney General Yogman followed MacLeish and the other attorneys who were representing the families and students at JRC.[7] In her opening remarks, she appeared to irritate Judge LaStaiti from the very beginning. She immediately moved to dismiss the case arguing that DMR's certification process should not be the subject of the contempt complaint. She asserted that Campbell had been properly exercising his regulatory authority, and the focus of the trial should be whether Campbell violated any clear and unequivocal order of the court. Her opening strategy was not successful:

> Yogman: Your Honor, in response to that opening statement, I would like to renew the point of my motion to dismiss that even if all the statements made are absolutely true, that those . . .
> LaStaiti: Attorney Yogman, I indicated at our last conference that we would try the case. So would you please make your opening statements.
> Yogman: Yes, Your Honor, but for the record though I am moving to . . .
> LaStaiti: Attorney Yogman, the record is made. Please make your opening statements.
> Yogman: Yes, Your Honor. With the Court's permission I need to make . . .
> LaStaiti: Attorney Yogman, make your opening statements, please.
> Yogman: Your Honor, as the Court pointed out, this is a contempt action. This is a contempt action brought by the Judge Rotenberg Educational Center against Philip Campbell, the Commissioner of the Department of Mental Retardation. This is not an action for judicial review of the Commissioner's certification decisions or of the procedures that the Commissioner has used in conducting that certification process, that after relief was available to the JRC and they declined to pursue.
>
> This is not an action for declarative or injunctive relief with a Court who would have an opportunity to construe ambiguous provisions and provide relief for clarification to the parties.

This is an action for contempt. As such, as the Court has already pointed out the issue is this: Whether Commissioner Campbell directly, not indirectly, directly and undoubtedly violated any clear and unequivocal order of this Court. More specifically whether Commissioner Campbell clearly and unequivocally directly violated any provision of the Settlement Agreement, any clear and unequivocal provision of the settlement agreement in this case. When the parties entered into the settlement agreement in this case, the agreement was intended to end the underlying litigation.

All that remains is for this Court to enforce any clear and unequivocal litigation practice of the settlement agreement by contempt sanctions. The evidence will show that far from violating any provision of the settlement agreement, Commissioner Campbell has been carefully and prudently exercising his regulatory authority. The Department's regulations at 104 CMR section 20:15 expressly authorized and mandate that even if a program is already certified, this type of structure that was undertaken in this case is required. The regulation says it is the Department's policy that such procedures are to be used only in programs which are especially qualified and certified to use such procedures with appropriate care.

It is further that the policy of the Department that the application of a procedure comply even after it has been approved must be strictly monitored by the program as well as the Department itself. In summary, it's the purpose of these regulations to insure that the behavior modification procedures are used to enhance the dignity, health and safety of the clients and that extraordinary procedures which cause a risk to such health and dignity should be used as a last resort by certified programs subject to the strictest safety guards and monitoring. And it is that regulatory authority that the Commissioner is exercising and has been exercising over the JRC. Not without substantial resistance from BRI . . .[8]

At every turn BRI resists the Department's regulatory authority, claiming at every turn that it's a violation of the settlement agreement, bad faith, anything else. There is no other provider in the Commonwealth of Massachusetts that provides so much resistance to being regulated by the Department of Mental Retardation and this provider is the only provider in the Commonwealth of Massachusetts that used aversive procedures to the extent used by BRI and so is [in] need of more scrutiny that other providers.

On the other hand, the evidence will show that JRC has consistently and repeatedly violated its many specific obligations under the settlement agreement and that is the subject of our counter claims that we filed as part of our answer in this case.[9]

After hearing opening arguments, LaStaiti urged the attorneys to meet with Judge George Hurd and attempt to mediate the dispute rather than pursue the litigation. Hurd was appointed as the mediator for the settlement decree after Dr. Daignault requested that he be replaced as the mediator. Daignault felt that he was a distraction because DMR was arguing that he could no longer serve as an unbiased arbiter because of his financial relationship with MacLeish's office, where he was working on a case focused on clergy sex abuse. LaStaiti urged the parties to get together:

I also note for the record that there is a great deal of resource that is involved in this particular contempt action. A tremendous collection of legal talent and an enormous financial commitment is represented by all of you here. As I indicated earlier, the issues before the court presently are contempt issues. They do not directly affect students. The students are affected by the treatment plans and the individual guardianships. It is my considered opinion that the resources, the expertise, the financing and backing of this litigation would be better directed in litigating the treatment issues in the individual guardianship proceedings. I am going to give you one last chance to meet with Judge Hurd to see if there is any resolution that might be made of any or all of these issues."[10]

The attorneys did not appear before Judge Hurd. They were tired of compromise and wanted a resolution. During the thirteen-day trial, JRC's attorneys focused on several key issues: the purpose of the Tuesday Morning Group, the fact that a DMR certification team recommended that JRC be certified,[11] and alleged violations and disregard for the settlement agreement. When the Tuesday Morning Group began meeting, DMR's attorney incorrectly advised the members that they could take notes and would be protected by client/attorney privilege. Instead, notes from the group were obtained through the legal discovery process and were used throughout the trial. Four hundred and eight exhibits were produced, and fourteen witnesses testified. The following exchange between MacLeish and Campbell highlighted the issue of the intent of the Tuesday Morning Group, which Campbell had described as focused only on JRC's certification application.[12]

MacLeish: You never did anything in anticipation of the Connie Chung show about BRI?

Campbell: No, I was not motivated by that.

MacLeish: But you never did anything in connection with that program, correct, concerning BRI, concerning the regulation of BRI? Correct?

Campbell: That's correct.

[Campbell was then presented with notes from the Tuesday Morning Group dated October 18, 1993.]

MacLeish: Could you turn to Page 3? You see the item there that says "Respond to parents as follow-up to parents meetings," then underneath that, "repeat major themes in the letter, send prior to Connie Chung show as well as commitment to ongoing communication." Then it says, "Second letter after the Chung show."

Campbell: Yes.

MacLeish: This didn't relate to BRI's application for certification; did it?

Campbell: It related to parents having information of what the department was doing.

MacLeish: It didn't relate to the application; did it?

Campbell: No.

Campbell: Didn't you testify earlier today that you never did anything at these meetings because of what the Connie Chung show was or wasn't going to do? Wasn't that your testimony here earlier today?

Campbell: Yes.

MacLeish: Would you like to correct that testimony now, Commissioner?

Campbell: No.

Similar exchanges between JRC attorneys and Mary Cerreto, assistant commissioner for the Office of Quality Enhancement, and Richard Cohen, director of investigations, also took place. Three months later, in October, LaStaiti issued a scathing 126-page decision blasting DMR and ordering the state to pay JRC $1.1 million. She wrote: "Based upon the Finding of Fact and Conclusion of Law entered in this matter, it is ordered and adjudged that the Defendant, Philip Campbell, in his capacity as Commissioner of the Department of Mental Retardation ('DMR'), has acted in contempt of this Court's Order dated January 7, 1987 which incorporates the Settlement Agreement dated December 12, 1986."[13] Furthermore, "high-ranking government officials have been deliberately untruthful on the witness stand, have expended public funds in order to pursue baseless allegations, and launched investigations on court personnel."[14] She accused both Cerreto and Campbell of lying to the court with specific mention of their involvement with the *Eye to Eye with Connie Chung* show and concealing two favorable reports on the school conducted by the DMR certification team. LaStaiti wrote:

> The Court concludes that a plan was developed at the September 7, 1993, meeting . . . to disrupt the operation of JRC by every conceivable means — to allege that clients were being abused; to interfere with financial operations, to disrupt JRC's relationships with funding agencies, as well as parents; and other activities which have absolutely no bearing on the legitimate exercise of regulatory authority.
>
> This Court found most of DMR's witnesses not to be credible, and the Court felt the need on numerous occasions, after repeated instances of contradictory sworn testimony, to remind witnesses that they were under oath and had to tell the truth. The testimony of Commissioner Campbell and Assistant Commissioner Cerreto was deliberately false on matters material to the issues in question in this case. The Court finds that the materially false statements under oath of Commissioner Campbell and Assistant Commissioner Cerreto would support a prosecution for perjury under G.L.C. 268, § 1.

The Court is referring this matter to the District Attorney of Bristol County for a determination as to whether a prosecution for perjury and/or criminal contempt should be initiated against these two government officials. . . . The extraordinary remedies including the appointment of a Receiver are justified and necessitated by the extraordinary history of bad faith conduct by DMR in its dealing with JRC which spans a ten year period. This conduct is continuing during the very course of this trial and infects the entire Administrative Agency.[15]

LaStaiti denied DMR's counterclaim alleging that JRC had violated the OFC settlement agreement.[16] The basis of the denial was that she believed the 1987 agreement was clear that all conflicts between parties were subject to the dispute resolution process set forth in the agreement before they would be adjudicated in the court. She held that DMR presented no evidence to show that any of the alleged violations of the settlement agreement were subject to any mediation or arbitration. DMR never requested that JRC mediate any matters alleged in its counterclaim. Therefore, LaStaiti stated, the counterclaim was improper since DMR failed to follow the dispute resolution process. She went further with the dismissal and wrote that even if the mediation or arbitration processes had been followed, she would have dismissed the counterclaims. Throughout, she found DMR's witnesses—Carol Upshur, Michael Dorsey, and attorney Richard Cohen—not credible; declared the Rivendell Team biased; and reiterated that DMR had acted in bad faith. She ordered DMR to pay JRC, counsel for the parents, and counsel for the class of students their legal fees and expenses totaling $1,098,087.50. "The Court finds that the enormous expenditure of legal resources by DMR in its contemptuous attack on JRC more than justifies the legal commitment JRC was obliged to make to repel those efforts. The Commissioner himself, testified that he authorized an inordinate and unusual amount of legal resources to be devoted to the pursuit of JRC. The Affidavits filed by Assistant Attorney General Yogman, Assistant Attorney General Wall and Deputy General Chow-Menzer understate the expenditure of legal and financial resources."[17]

In the final paragraph of her ruling, LaStaiti noted, "Despite the herculean effort of my predecessor, Judge Ernest I. Rotenberg, the Settlement Agreement of 1986 did not put an end to the war upon JRC begun by DMR's predecessor in interest, OFC. It merely effected a temporary cease fire. The deep-seated passions with DMR against JRC, with blind disregard to the best interests of the students, grew stronger and resurfaced with greater force in 1993. It is a sad chapter in the history of the Commonwealth."[18]

Clearly pleased with the ruling, Israel said, "We knew the trial went well. We didn't know how courageous this judge would be."[19] Campbell was "so caught up in his own personal philosophical position that he's unable to administer his agency in an equitable way."[20] MacLeish added, "This is more of a case of government misconduct. This guy lied and engaged in a campaign of dirty tricks to destroy this program." JRC considered filing civil rights claims against the state officials.[21] DMR responded to the decision in a brief statement: "We believe that the court's decision attempts to usurp the executive branch's authority to regulate and monitor services."[22] Governor Weld's office issued a statements: "We have confidence in Commissioner Campbell and both the attorney general's office and the DMR feel strongly the agency was operating consistent with the settlement agreement. Weld said his staff would look into the judge's allegations, but indicated he didn't believe Campbell perjured himself.[23] Representative Cohen commented, "I believe that the court decision was a travesty of justice and that the losers are the patients." MacLeish immediately responded: "Cohen should keep his mouth shut and that the self-appointed zealots don't know any of these children."[24] Groups such as the Massachusetts Disability Law Center believed that the decision would have a chilling effect on the rights of people with disabilities because it stripped the state of its ability to oversee and regulate the use of aversive interventions.[25] "The Eckert Seamans lawyers and the center have been successful at deflecting the public's attention from the dangers of aversive therapy to the 'big bad state using its authority in order to harass people who don't agree with their point of view,' said Robert Agoglia of the Center for Public Representation."[26]

DEPARTMENT OF MENTAL RETARDATION IN RECEIVERSHIP

LaStaiti appointed a retired justice of the superior court, James J. Nixon, as receiver on October 6, 1995, to stand in place of Campbell in his interactions and relations with JRC.[27] Nixon in turn appointed Peter M. Gately, a family law attorney in Franklin, Massachusetts, as the investigator of the complaints the DMR had received for abuse and neglect. These two appointments removed Campbell's and DMR's ability to regulate JRC's practices. On February 12, 1996, Nixon granted JRC interim certification to conduct Class III interventions and rescinded Campbell's letters decertifying the use of Class III aversives.[28] The state was no longer in the driver's seat. Nixon had a great deal of authority to make decisions.

INCONSISTENCIES IN TESTIMONY: FEEDING THE JUDGE?

After LaStaiti's decision, Governor Weld referred to Campbell as a man of integrity and continued to show his support. Yogman, the assistant attorney general, criticized by LaStaiti for not correcting Campbell's false testimony, expressed her concern that LaStaiti had adopted the same language used by lawyers representing JRC and had mischaracterized statements that Yogman had made during the trial. Yogman denied any unethical conduct.[29] Attorney General Scott Harshbarger, who had a strong record as a civil rights attorney, appealed LaStaiti's decision.[30]

After the conclusion of a hearing, attorneys on each side submit findings of fact for the judge to review. MacLeish was trying to persuade LaStaiti that there was a basis for a perjury claim against Campbell and Cerreto, thereby compelling DMR and its attorneys to ensure that the court record and finding of facts were accurate. In October 1995, DMR attorneys Margaret Chow-Menzer and Jackie Berman analyzed JRC's addendum to its proposed findings of fact and conclusions of law in which there were fifty-seven allegations of contradictions and inconsistencies in Campbell's testimony.[31] A similar addendum was directed at Cerreto. Berman pointed out that JRC's attorneys had introduced evidence into the record after the trial that was not allowed; had mischaracterized testimony; had used testimony out of context that was misleadingly ascribed to Campbell's inconsistency when he testified to being unsure or not remembering; and had alleged that statements had been made or conclusions drawn that were not supported by record. An example where DMR counsel claimed that JRC's counsel included inaccurate information in their addendum focused on an allegation[32] regarding Campbell's knowledge of Gunnar Dybwad's objection to the use of aversives:

STATEMENT. At his deposition, Commissioner Campbell stated that he was aware that Dr. Dybwad did not support the use of any aversives. (Tr. June 28, p. 131. 1.5-1.5-14)

INCONSISTENCY. At the trial, however, the Commissioner denied that he was aware of this. (Tr. June 2, p. 131, 1.4)

DMR Response to Allegation #20. The trial transcript reveals consistency in Campbell's statements that he was aware that Professor Dybwad did not support the use of *some* aversives procedures and not that he was aware, that Professor Dybwad did not support the use of any aversives.

This allegation is a pure misstatement of Commissioner Campbell's testimony with respect to Professor Dybwad. JRC attempt(s) to put words into Commissioner Campbell's mouth in an effort to show that he was aware, when appointing Professor Dybwad to the JRC HRC (Human Rights Committee) that Dybwad was opposed to all aversives.

JRC framed Campbell's testimony in the following way:

> At his deposition, Commissioner Campbell stated that he was aware that Dr. Dybwad did not support the use of any aversives. At the trial, however, the Commissioner denied that he was aware of this." (from JRC's addendum to Proposed Findings of Fact).

This is the actual testimony:

> MacLeish: You were aware, were you not, commissioner, that Mr. Dybwad did not support the use of aversive procedures?
> Campbell: Yes.
> MacLeish: In fact, you were aware, were you not, that Mr. Dybwad did not support the use of any aversive procedures; is that correct?
> Campbell: No.
> MacLeish: But you knew when you appointed Mr. Dybwad that he opposed all such procedures; did you not?
> Campbell: No.
> MacLeish: Are you aware of some aversive procedures that Mr. Dybwad did support?
> Campbell: I'm not aware that he's against all of them.

Campbell and Cerreto were represented by Bruce Singal, an attorney who specialized in white-collar crimes and complaints against professionals, to represent them in the event of perjury charges. On December 1, 1995, Singal traveled to the Bristol County Court to review the binder that MacLeish's office had assembled to make the perjury claims. In a memo to Cerreto,[33] Singal described his conversation with Gilbert "Gil" Nadeau, Bristol assistant attorney general, which focused on the neutrality of the court, its commitment to follow through with Rotenberg's decision in the OFC case, and MacLeish and JRC's intimidating practices:

> [Nadeau] then asked how I was enjoying working on this case, and I told him that frankly I had not felt the need to work much on it at this time because I hoped and expected they would reach the conclusion I thought they would, namely that there was not any need to investigate further or any basis to prosecute (for perjury). He then said that the people in the Probate Court felt quite strongly about it, and then mentioned Judge Hurd (Superior Court), who apparently had had some prior involvement with the case, had communicated (either with Nadeau or someone else in the office) that based on Hurd's involvement in the case, he believed Judge LaStaiti had the "right take" on the case. Nadeau said that he knew LaStaiti from before she had become a judge, and described her as "the last person to go out on a limb." Nadeau indicated that there seemed to be an effort by the Court to align with the late Judge Rotenberg and to ensure that his efforts in the BRI proceedings were continued. I responded that I was concerned about any pressure being brought to bear on his office, first just by virtue of a judge making findings of perjury (which I explained to him came largely by her adopting the findings submitted by MacLeish), and secondly by others in the court system chiming in, as Judge Hurd apparently had done. I then questioned why it was that so much work was being put into the "perjury" end of this case, starting with the extensive Proposed Findings submitted to the Court by MacLeish on perjury (which had nothing to do with the outcome of the case), and the extensive work put into this binder submitted to their office. I suggested that, although I was not there to make any presentation at this

point, it appeared to me this was part of a continuing effort by BRI/JRC to intimidate regulators so as to avert regulation altogether. By pursuing criminal perjury allegations in an aggressive fashion, I indicated that JRC hoped to "stamp out" regulators and frighten them from pursuing future regulatory actions.

Nadeau then asked me if it was MacLeish who was putting these perjury allegations together, and I responded that it was him (along with people from his office). He indicated that he had gotten to know MacLeish from the Father Porter case,[34] in which MacLeish had represented the victims of alleged sexual abuse, and he noted that MacLeish liked to latch onto these kinds of "victim" cases. He also said MacLeish was "not shy about pushing his agenda." I then noted that this was his latest and perhaps most aggressive agenda.[35]

MORE TROUBLE FOR COMMISSIONER CAMPBELL

Soon after LaStaiti's ruling that Commissioner Campbell acted in contempt of the OFC settlement agreement and ordering the state to pay JRC $1.1 million, he was accused of not including all of his earnings in his financial report to the state Ethics Commission. These records were obtained as part of the lawsuit and leaked to the *Boston Globe*.[36] Campbell had been consulting with the state of Texas, which paid him $25,376 in 1992 (a third of the payment was travel costs). Although Campbell used vacation time to consult, the lack of financial disclosure fueled critics who called for his resignation.[37] Campbell had also received twenty-four calls from Texas state officials between 1992 and 1995. During this time, Texas hired him to review plans to shut down two state institutions and review community-based programs. The lawyer who represented the families in the Texas case was David Ferleger, whom Campbell had retained as a legal consultant to assist with the monitoring and regulation of BRI.[38]

Governor Weld had stood by Campbell throughout the JRC ordeal, but now he was asking his legal counsel to review Campbell's consulting work. The *Globe* revealed soon after that several other DMR senior officials had not reported outside earnings to the Ethics Commission.[39] Gerald Whitburn, the health and human services secretary who oversaw DMR, said, "The sloppiness around ethics filings is not

PAIN AND SHOCK IN AMERICA

good. I am very concerned by several ethics filings omissions in the DMR front office. This shouldn't happen."[40] After the ethics investigation, Witburn said, "He didn't know the rules, and some mistakes were made. I am confident these mistakes will not be repeated. Phil is doing a tough job well. He has my confidence and the governor's confidence."[41] The *Globe* also showed some level of support for Campbell in an editorial that addressed concerns about several cases of alleged abuse in the community care system.[42] The editorial acknowledged that despite claims by Campbell's critics, he had expanded employment and training for Massachusetts residents with disabilities who received services funded through the DMR, increased Medicaid coverage for thousands of people, and made efforts to ensure that people with disabilities living at home received services. In January, Campbell agreed to pay $1,500 to the state for violating state ethics guidelines.[43]

The commissioner filed multiple injunctive and receivership orders during the last months of 1995. All of them were denied. On February 1, 1996, the state appealed LaStaiti's decision, arguing in a 190-page brief that she had copied extensively from the briefs submitted by JRC and had made several legal errors in her analyses and findings. Lawyers for DMR argued that the judge relied so heavily on JRC's briefs that she included mistakes related to dates and mischaracterizations in her ruling. Attorney General Harshbarger argued, "This court should scrutinize the findings particularly close, because they are adopted nearly verbatim from the proposed findings submitted" by JRC. MacLeish responded that this was another form of harassment that would squander state funds to persecute a small treatment program and its clients.[44]

Pro-institution groups were using this time as an opportunity to air their concerns about Campbell. The *Globe* reported on pro-institution advocacy groups that were requesting that he resign because of poor leadership. Campbell, who, with Weld's support, was developing community-based services for people with intellectual disabilities was accused of compromising their safety as he shifted them from large institutions to community residences.[45] It was argued that Campbell showed "poor leadership, people skills, and judgment."[46] People with children in institutional settings strongly opposed Campbell and his team. The Advocacy Network, a group of families of children residing in state institutions, did not like Campbell's and his Mary Cerreto's efforts to offer people with disabilities more community inclusion and valued social roles. DMR was promoting the use of a training method, social role valorization, developed by Wolf Wolfensberger at Syracuse University. This training, based on the belief that people with disabilities should live in and be valued members of their communities, ran counter to the beliefs of some people who believed that institutional placements were necessary. In the Advocacy Network's March 1996 newsletter, William Knauss, the group's vice president, wrote, "Members of the elite sect of the Social Role Valorization movement parade about with V.I.P. on their shirts. These are the 'Wolfies,' a term that describes members of the Wolfensberger cult. Philip Campbell continues to shove this Wolfie ideology down our throats. Throughout the country, Wolfies or their close ideological allies, have repeatedly made aggressive attacks against parent groups and advocacy organizations for the mentally retarded. Using lawyers to take action against parent groups, anti-congregate facility zealots seek to shut down institutions for the mentally retarded."[47]

Anti-aversive advocates, in particular members of TASH–New England, were closely monitoring the actions of the court-appointed receiver, James J. Nixon. They reported in April that Nixon had sent a letter to DMR listing a set of requirements for it. The first that Nixon listed was that DMR was required by the court to move twenty-five students within the next sixty days to JRC. LaStaiti stated that DMR was responsible for JRC's loss of over twenty-five placements, and this was a way for the facility to recoup financial losses. Nixon was responding to her directive and was requiring that an equal number of students lost now be sent to JRC. In a stern letter to the DMR deputy commissioner, Gerald Morrissey, Nixon wrote:

> I reviewed some of the records from 1994 and 1995, and it appears that twenty-five persons were removed from JRC. Three of the persons so removed were mentioned by you at our meeting on March 20, 1996 and were the only three that were funded by DMR. JRC, however, suggests the remaining persons were removed as a result of the adverse influence by Commissioner Campbell. As an example, [a resident] was returned to New Mexico by DMR officials. Obviously, that type of conduct tends to substantiate JRC's view point. I do not need to argue whether the view is correct or not, since Justice LaStaiti

has already made that determination. My position as Receiver is remedial. I am to remedy the wrongs committed in the past.

To the extent that these twenty-five persons were removed as a result of DMR's wrong-doing, then it is my position to make certain that these placements are restored, either with the same persons who were removed, or with other persons . . . The reconstitution of the JRC population must be accomplished swiftly if it is to be remedial. We do not have the time, nor the staff resources, to review all of the RFPs and Sole Source Contracts that have been awarded. I must rely on you to accomplish this. I do not wish to micromanage the operation.

I have the authority to order DMR to do this, and I have the directive from Justice LaStaiti's Findings and Order. If my directions are not complied with, I also have the power to seek individual contempts against the persons ordered to reconstitute the population, and who fail to do so . . . My preference is to handle this in a manner in which everyone is working together to accomplish the same goal. The Supreme Judicial Court refused to issue a Stay of Justice LaStaiti's Judgment and Order, including her appointment of me as Receiver so I suspect that we will be involved with each other for the foreseeable future.

It is in our mutual interests to reconstitute JRC's population, and to have DMR eliminate any remaining anti-JRC bias, and replace it with a positive attitude towards JRC. Once this occurs, and JRC is playing on a level playing field, this would enhance a DMR petition to either eliminate or modify the controls that exist over DMR. The failure to foster this attitude, and reconstitute JRC's population will only result in further contempt findings and the potential penalties escalating.[48]

Nixon also issued the following additional requirements:

2) No sole source contracts were to be awarded to any other vendors where JRC could perform such services;

3) No Consumer-Driven RFPs were to be awarded until the receiver allowed it;

4) The Receiver wanted a list of all Individual Service Plans coming up for review by DMR with a list of all vendors;

5) The Receiver specifically wanted to know how many contracts were awarded to the May Institute and Amego [programs that serve individuals with behavioral disabilities] between 1993 and 1996;

6) The Receiver let it be known that he would choose who will go to JRC and that the consumers or their parents/guardians will not have the right of refusal. Anyone turning 22 years old, for example, could be sent to BRI/JRC upon the receiver's order and no one according to him, could appeal the decision.[49]

Margaret Chow-Menzer from DMR pushed back, arguing that it would not be feasible or consistent with DMR regulations to send twenty-five people to BRI. She argued that this would violate individual service plan regulations, a transfer statute, and procurement regulations. The principle of providing services that are individually designed and tailored to each person's needs and desires is generally fundamental to the beliefs and values of people who work in disability service systems. The idea of assigning twenty-five people to JRC to correct a financial situation, or returning people who had transitioned from JRC to another setting, was antithetical to the department's commitment to flexible, responsive person-centered service delivery. Furthermore, Chow-Menzer argued, "The Department would have to find $4,000,000 to comply with your directive. Since the state finance law prohibits state officials from incurring obligations in excess of appropriations and as noted above this year's appropriation is obligated, you are in essence requiring the Department to deny or withdraw services and supports from DMR clients in order to fund the JRC placements."[50]

In April 1996, JRC received permission from the town of Canton, Massachusetts, to relocate its day educational program there. But the legal battles were not over. JRC was taking aim and confidently filing class action suits against DMR officials, targeting specific individuals. On August 15, 1996, MacLeish, representing JRC and Israel, and Eugene Curry, the attorney for JRC parents, filed a class action suit against Campbell and Kim Murdock, DMR counsel, in a civil action in superior court in Bristol.[51] The introduction to the complaint read, "This is an action for damages arising out of a violation of civil rights and other tortuous conduct by the Commissioner of the Department [of] Mental Retardation and his general counsel who, individually and acting under cover of state law, grossly abused governmental power and exploited state resources in order to further their corrupt and perverse campaign to close a private treatment program for severely handicapped students." JRC's and the parents' attorneys cited eight violations: three involved the Massachusetts Civil Rights Act, one cited the Federal Civil Rights Act of 1983, and the remainder involved intentional interference with advantageous business relations, defamation, and intentional infliction of emotional distress.

THE COMMISSIONER RESIGNS

On March 13, 1997, eighteen months after LaStaiti's decision charging DMR with public corruption, the supreme judicial court remanded to the probate court and rejected the appeal by Attorney General Harshbarger on behalf of DMR and Campbell.[52] It also affirmed LaStaiti's finding of contempt and the court's appointment of Nixon as receiver. However, the court ruled that "in the absence of express statutory authority, we are unable to affirm the award of attorney's fees against the Commonwealth."[53] Justice Neil Lynch, a member of the supreme judicial court, wrote, "We recognize that direct judicial intervention into the operation of a state agency is not to be undertaken lightly, but in this case, it was necessary because there was no reasonable alternative. The JRC devoted an enormous amount of time, effort, and money to fight off the department's indirect attacks on aversive therapies through needless and excessive regulatory demands."[54] MacLeish immediately asserted that this was grounds to fire Campbell. He said, "They had their staff working full time to put the Judge Rotenberg Center out of business. They've now lost and lost in a very damning way. They've told untruths continually, for 25 years. The real judges are the parents who are deeply involved in their children's care. The parents approve the treatment. We want the governor to appoint someone with mainstream treatment philosophies and someone who will make peace with the parents and the patients at the Rotenberg Center. This is a great day for the mentally retarded, but now we have to make sure there is a major house-cleaning in this agency."[55]

The parent group at JRC, under the leadership of Marie Washington, praised the decision. "These are not kids who sit in a corner rocking back and forth," she said. "They're different. They are self-abusive and no other place can maintain them without medication. This is a drug-free place."[56] She said her son, Jack, was obese and on psychotropic medications before he entered JRC. She described him as "happy" and said that now she could "go on with her life."[57]

Governor Weld's support for Campbell began to waver under increasing pressure from JRC and other groups concerned about Campbell's desire to close institutions, as well as several reported instances of abuse in the community service system. Weld asked for Campbell's resignation after reading only one-third of the Supreme Judicial Court's decision. The governor's office was quoted in the *Globe*: "Both he [the governor] and Campbell thought given the Supreme Court's opinion, it was going to be tough for him to advance our agenda into the immediate future at the Department of Mental Retardation. So, we thought the better course was for him to retire from the field and let someone else carry the ball. The Governor stated, 'I made it plain to the department years ago that I am not personally opposed to aversive therapy. In fact, I am somewhat of a believer.'"[58]

The day after the ruling, Campbell resigned as DMR commissioner. He was never prosecuted for perjury. Some groups were happy with his departure, and others saw his departure as a loss for safe and humane community-based services.[59] Many credited him with increasing community placements and Medicaid payments for community-based services and family supports. His attempts to focus on community-based placements were not unusual in the region. New Hampshire, Vermont, and Maine closed their public residential institutions for people with intellectual disabilities in the 1990s. However, for some time, Massachusetts remained resistant to closing institutions and moving away from approving aversive procedures.[60] On April 15, 1997, Secretary of Health and Human Services Joseph Gallant appointed Gerald J. Morrissey, the DMR deputy commissioner, as DMR commissioner.[61]

In December 1997, the *Globe* reported that Massachusetts had quietly paid $1.5 million to settle a civil rights lawsuit filed against Phillip Campbell and Kim Murdock, DMR counsel, for grossly abusing regulatory power in an attempt to close JRC. Payment of the settlement was split among JRC ($950,000), Matthew Israel ($175,000), and the parent association ($375,000). In addition, Massachusetts was made to pay for the costs of having a receiver. Morrissey, who was involved in the development of the settlement, publicly said, "We've turned a page with the settlement and look forward to working with the Judge Rotenberg Center in the future."[62]

It was a loss for anti-aversive advocates. Many believed Campbell and his team tried, using the quality assurance process and DMR's authority as a state agency, to do its job without malice and with the best of intentions. DMR was responsible for protecting the health and welfare of the residents of JRC. It had to follow existing laws and regulations. JRC argued that this oversight and restrictions were a violation of the OFC settlement agreement. The use of extreme aversives was not endorsed by the major national disability organization, and the use of alternative strategies and placements was prevalent. Yet JRC succeeded in convincing LaStaiti that Campbell and his team were dishonest and intent on closing down the center. DMR was in a difficult position. If it claimed it was opposed to the use of aversives, it was seen as biased. If it claimed that it supported the use of aversives, it was dishonest. Judge Rotenberg, who was highly regarded by the community and probate court system, had created a settlement agreement that positioned the state as the oppressor and JRC as the victim. Campbell was unable to overcome the language of the agreement, the capability of JRC's attorneys, the strength of parental testimony in favor of aversives, professional disagreements over the use of aversives, and a society ambivalent and possibly ignorant about alternative interventions such as positive behavioral supports and the rights of people with disabilities.

Six months later, on May 5, 1998, a 16-year-old JRC student, Silverio Gonzalez, was critically injured in a bus accident. Gonzalez, diagnosed with paranoid schizophrenia, had been at JRC just shy of one year. He was on a school bus being transported from the JRC center to the JRC residence in Rehoboth. At some point, he bolted down the bus aisle, opened the rear emergency exit door, and either fell or jumped onto Interstate 95 in Attleboro.[63] He suffered traumatic head injuries and was transferred to Massachusetts General hospital in Boston. Gonzalez, a student from New York, died the next day. Sergeant Larry Gillis of the state police reported that a female staff member had attempted to restrain Gonzales, who was six feet tall and weighed 200 pounds, but he overpowered her and ran toward the back of the bus.[64] JRC's attorney said that Gonzalez, "without warning, broke loose from the three counselors and leaped out. This happened in a matter of seconds. It is a very tragic and unfortunate situation."[65] Gonzalez's mother brought a lawsuit against the JRC attending psychiatrist, Dr. David Kass, who had weaned Sylverio from his antipsychotic medications in favor of electric shock. The Bristol Probate Court accepted Kass's motion to dismiss the case. Anti-aversive advocates claimed they knew why Silverio was trying to escape.

11 : MORE LEGAL ISSUES, AND ADVOCATES TAKE ACTION

Nancy R. Weiss and Jan Nisbet

When Cheryl McCollins visited the Judge Rotenberg Center in the fall of 2000, she was impressed by its beauty and pleased that the facility did not feel like an institution. Her son, Andre, had a history of behavioral incidents that included breaking things, kicking or hitting, and running away.[1] Doctors diagnosed him as having a pervasive developmental disorder, attention-deficit/hyperactivity disorder, impulse-control disorder, and conduct disorder. When Andre was 10 years old, Cheryl made the tough decision to send him to a residential school to get help with his learning and behavioral issues. He was moved to a second residential program by age 12. Although the new facility was in Pennsylvania, Cheryl made the trip from her home in Brooklyn, New York, to visit her son almost every week. After three years at that facility, Cheryl learned that Andre had been sexually abused by another resident.[2] She needed to find another program for him. The school system in her home district recommended the Judge Rotenberg Center in Massachusetts. During her first visit there, she was reassured by all the video cameras that recorded activities in every room in the main building and in the group homes where residents lived. She felt that this level of surveillance would ensure that Andre would be safe from abuse at JRC. McCollins could not have known that those cameras would eventually record the first video documentation to be made public of the electric shock delivered by the GED or that this footage would be instrumental in advancing the efforts of professionals and self-advocates to achieve an FDA ban on electric shock devices used for behavior modification.

When Andre entered JRC in February 2001 at age 16, the psychologist at the facility described him as a "well-groomed young man with a pleasant disposition."[3] In his initial interview, Andre, an African American teenager, spoke of wanting to get his driver's license, become a police officer, and have a girlfriend. The psychologist's report also noted that Andre "expressed a fear of strangers and of being hurt by others."[4] As is done with almost all residents upon admission to JRC, Andre was taken off his psychotropic medicines. He had been taking Risperal, an antipsychotic drug used to treat schizophrenia, bipolar disorder, and symptoms of irritability in autistic children.[5] Matthew Israel was an outspoken critic of the use of psychotropic medications, even when there was a diagnosis of schizophrenia, major depression, anxiety, or bipolar disorder.[6] He believed that behavioral interventions were more effective.

Nine months after Andre's admission, the center sought and received permission from both his mother and the probate court to begin using the GED device on him.[7] When Cheryl McCollins first heard about the shock device during an early visit to JRC, she was excited by its potential and thought it might offer her son the opportunity to stop aggressive behaviors that seemed uncontrollable. She asked JRC officials if the GED offered a cure for behaviors like fighting and breaking furniture and was told, "Yes, this device does it."[8] Andre's treatment plan "eventually listed 29 behaviors for which he would receive a shock. These included aggressive acts (like kicking or biting), nonviolent acts (screaming, any attempt to remove his electrodes), and also 'health-dangerous behaviors' (including tensing up his entire body)."[9]

Over the next six months, Andre received one or two shocks during a typical week. During many weeks, he received none at all. On one occasion, he received a shock in error: he had done nothing wrong.[10] These are known as "misapplications."[11] Sometimes staff would shock the wrong person, and sometimes the devices "misfired."[12] Reports of the devices shocking people in error were not unusual. One former resident recalled getting out of the shower when the device malfunctioned, which resulted in her being shocked ten times.[13]

When Andre went home to Brooklyn for a visit in mid-October 2002, his mother reported that he was talking to himself and behaving erratically.[14] When she brought him back to JRC earlier than planned, she urged the staff to reconsider using medication. She felt that Andre's behavior was changing; he was showing the psychiatric symptoms he had exhibited in the past, and she felt that medication was needed.[15] Within days of Andre's return from his home visit, on October 25, 2002, Andre McCollins was shocked using the GED-4, the strongest shock device used at JRC, for failing to take off his jacket when he entered the classroom that morning. He did not verbally refuse or make defiant gestures; he simply did not take off his jacket when instructed to do so by a staff member. That day McCollins was shocked thirty-one times over seven hours. The first shock was for failing to follow the instruction to take off his jacket and the other thirty were either for screaming while being shocked or tensing his muscles in anticipation of the next shock.[16] Over the seven hours during which he was shocked, he was tied to a board face-down in a spread-eagle position.

Andre's mother brought a medical malpractice civil suit against the facility. The lawsuit went to trial in 2012, almost ten years after the incident. At the trial, Cheryl McCollins testified, "I never signed up for him to be tortured, terrorized and abused. I had no idea—no idea—that they tortured the children in the school."[17] Marc Whaley, a psychiatrist, served as an expert witness on behalf of Andre and his family. During the trial, he stated that there was "ample evidence to show that the treatment was harming the individual at this time and certainly not helping him."[18] Whaley characterized the shock as it was used on McCollins that day as a "gross deviation from accepted standards."[19] He said, "He's crying out, pleading really not to be shocked and those pleadings are ignored."[20] Whaley testified that Andre "had become so psychotic it was impossible for him to control his behavior" and that "there is no reputable, qualified, psychiatrist or psychologist that would ever recommend aversive therapy as a treatment for acute psychotic symptoms. That was done in the 1800s."[21] Whaley also testified that McCollins never recovered from what happened that day: "Now we have an individual who is heavily medicated, state institutionalized, with no immediate prospect of any kind of independent functioning and all of that turned on October 25, 2002, when his psychotic disorder was traumatized by the 31 or so shocks he got on that day."[22]

Mike Beaudet, a reporter for Boston's Fox 25 television news, covered the trial, and television reports were aired nightly over the six-day trial. The videotape of Andre being shocked was shown in the courtroom. Attorneys for JRC attempted to keep the video from being made public, but Judge Barbara Dortch-Okara permitted Fox 25 to make a recording of the video with their courtroom cameras. Benjamin Novotny, the attorney who represented Andre and his family, was able to convince the judge to release the footage to the public. The footage of Andre being shocked was shown multiple times on Boston's Fox TV news and eventually was made widely available on YouTube. Shain Neumeier, an attorney and disability advocate who attended the trial, reported with daily blog postings: "In what was perhaps a surprising turn of events given the JRC's reputation for being highly successful in litigation and the fact that video footage of the incident was suppressed by court order 8 years before, Judge Dortch-Okara allowed the tapes not only to come into evidence, but to be recorded by news cameras to be shown on television to the public. This was made over objections by counsel for JRC and the other defendants, who insisted that viewers would not be able to judge the appropriateness of the shocks and restraints without having more context by which to understand their use."[23]

In his closing argument, Novotny said, "You can tell a lot about a society by how it treats its most vulnerable people."[24] He asked the jury to send a message to the world, and specifically to the defendants, about how Andre was treated at JRC. After the trial but before the jury reached a verdict, Cheryl McCollins settled her civil suit against the JRC for an undisclosed sum.[25] Novotny's website described the impact of the McCollins trial: "This was the first time in JRC's 41-year history that such a videotape had been released. The story quickly spread across the United States and internationally. Before the end of the trial, hundreds of thousands of people signed petitions to end the use of electro-shock therapy. Since then, Andre's case has been publicized on news networks and in magazines such as *New York Magazine*, BBC and CNN."[26]

For years, JRC had described the shock as a hard pinch or similar to a beesting.[27] People assumed that it was a mildly uncomfortable reminder to interrupt unwanted or dangerous behavior. Access to the footage of Andre being shocked changed the public's understanding of the intensity and pain of the shock delivered by the GED-4. The video showed Andre falling on the floor in response to the first shock, screaming out in pain and crying and pleading for them to stop shocking him over the seven hours during which he was restrained and shocked.[28] The video also raised questions about the kinds of behaviors for which shocks were being administered. JRC argued that a brief electric shock was preferable to allowing people to bang their head or gouge their skin or eyes. But in this instance, the shock was given for nondangerous behaviors. Anti-aversive advocates who reviewed years of behavioral programs from the facility pointed out that people were

PAIN AND SHOCK IN AMERICA

being shocked for behaviors as innocuous as nagging, swearing, refusing to follow staff directions, failure to maintain a neat appearance, stopping work for more than ten seconds, getting out of seat, interrupting others, whispering, slouching, swearing, talking loudly, clicking their teeth, shaking their head, blinking their eyes rapidly, holding their head to their shoulder, shaking their leg, or not answering a question within five seconds.[29]

The video of McCollins's experience that day in October 2002 altered anti-aversive advocates' strategies. Now, people who for years had been advocating against the use of electric shock and other painful procedures used to modify behavior could show policymakers and others the impact of the painful shocks. In 2016, four years after the McCollins trial, the FDA proposed a ban against the electric shock device used at JRC. In the view of advocates who had fought for this ban over the years, the ability to show the intensity and impact of the shock delivered by these devices was instrumental to the success of the effort.

The McCollins lawsuit was not the first civil suit brought against JRC. Mary Ann Milletich filed one in 1986. In 2006, attorney Ken Mollins represented 17-year-old Antwone Nicholson, his mother, Evelyn Nicholson, and his family of Freeport, New York. Nicholson had been at JRC for approximately four years and had received shock interventions. The suit claimed that "education officials were negligent by failing to ensure that her son was not mistreated at JRC."[30] The family received $65,000 to settle the lawsuit, which asserted that the use of electric shock was inhumane and violated the student's civil rights.[31] In that lawsuit, JRC's attorney, Kevin Ryan, claimed that Evelyn Nicholson, Antwone's mother, had "been made fully aware of the shock treatment when she signed an individualized education plan for her son."[32] But Mollins asserted that Antwone's mother "believed that the therapy would only be used to prevent Antwone from hurting himself or others, but that was not the case."[33] "There was a whole list of criteria by which he would be shocked. If he just said no to a directive, they would shock him. If he failed to pay attention to a directive, they would shock him,"[34] said Mollins. At the conclusion of the case, JRC issued a statement calling the settlement "minimal."[35]

Since 1995, Nancy Weiss had been the executive director of TASH, a progressive international disability advocacy association whose mission was to "support the inclusion and full participation of children and adults with disabilities in all aspects of their communities as determined by personalized visions of quality of life." In 2001, with the organization's Positive Behavioral Supports Committee, she spearheaded the passage of a new TASH resolution to codify the organization's opposition to the use of aversive and restrictive procedures. This resolution stated:

> Although it has been believed that aversive and restrictive procedures are necessary to control dangerous or disruptive behaviors, it has now been irrefutably proven that a wide range of methods are available which are not only more effective in managing dangerous or disruptive behaviors, but which do not inflict pain on, humiliate, dehumanize or overly control or manipulate individuals with disabilities. Alternative approaches that are proven to be effective attempt to identify the individual's purposes in behaving as he or she does and offer support and education to replace dangerous or disruptive behaviors with alternative behaviors that are positive and will achieve the individual's needs . . . TASH is unequivocally opposed to the inappropriate use of restraint and to the use of overly restrictive and aversive procedures under any circumstance and calls for the cessation of the use of all such procedures.[36]

The TASH board of directors established a goal of recruiting a wide range of disability organizations to work together with it to focus on reducing and eliminating the use of aversive procedures, seclusion, and restraint as methods of behavior control. In 2004, a steering committee was convened to consider the establishment of an interorganizational group that would work to end the use of restrictive procedures.[37] This group, originally called the State and National Alliance to Prevent Aversives, Restraint and Seclusion, sent a letter to other organizations inviting their participation. The letter said in part, "We are asking you to support a powerful new initiative aimed at one of the most fundamental and dangerous problems facing our nationwide disabilities community: the use of aversive procedures, seclusion, and restraints in the name of 'treatment.' While our organizations have made great strides in advancing the human rights and civil rights of the people for whom we advocate, over the years this problem has remained stubbornly entrenched, slowing our progress and harming countless lives."[38] Eventually the group changed its name to the Alliance to Prevent Restraint, Aversive Interventions and Seclusion (APRAIS). The group continues to operate, add organizational members, and advocate for humane behavioral approaches.[39]

A FORMER EMPLOYEE SPEAKS OUT

As part of APRAIS's efforts, Nancy Weiss contacted former JRC employees. While many residents, by virtue of the significance of their disabilities, were unable to tell their stories in a way they could be heard and understood, it was felt that staff accounts might add information about JRC practices that would strengthen advocacy efforts. One former employee, Greg Miller, became an important voice.

Miller was certified as a teacher in Massachusetts and worked at JRC as a teacher's aide from January 2003 until he resigned in March 2006.[40] He understood that people often questioned how parents could allow their sons and daughters to be treated in the manner that they were at JRC. In most cases, parents had signed treatment plans allowing for the electric shock to be administered, but Miller felt that parents didn't fully understand what was being done to their sons and daughters or that they thought they had no choice but to agree to the center's recommendations. A month after Miller resigned from JRC, he wrote an article, "I Wonder If Parents Really Know What Happens to Their Children at the Judge Rotenberg Center." In that article he asks whether parents, judges, and state authorities know that:

· A non-verbal student with autism gets shocked for closing his eyes for more than five seconds while sitting at his desk;
· Some students get shocked for standing up from their seat, raising their hand, and politely asking, "I would like to go to the bathroom, please";
· Some students get shocked for going to the bathroom in their pants—even if they have been asking for the bathroom for nearly two hours;

- Some students get shocked for yelling when they think they are about to get an electrical shock;
- Some students get shocked for instinctively trying to remove the electrode while the electrode is shocking and burning through their skin for two seconds.[41]

Miller also made public an affidavit that spoke about the responses of students when they thought a shock was for them when it was not. Miller wrote,

> They scream or stand up out of their seat or attempt to remove their electrodes off their arms and legs because they think they are about to get shocked . . . All of these behaviors had to be consequated with a GED electric shock, and if staff did not shock the students, staff would get evaluated and suspended, and might even lose their jobs . . . Staff were absolutely required to follow student programs and shock any student for screaming or for "out of seat without permission," or any other behavior, even though they were reacting out of fear and panic.[42]

He concluded, "I resigned from Judge Rotenberg Center when my doctor pointed out physical signs that my stress levels were too high. If my feelings were affecting my health, I have no doubt that students' health is also affected at JRC."[43] Israel countered that Miller had not raised any safety concerns while employed, was reprimanded for insubordination, and resigned.[44] Miller continued to advocate on behalf of the people at JRC for many years after he left the facility's employment.

AN INVESTIGATION INTO
PROFESSIONAL LICENSING AT JRC

The same month that Miller made public his article describing his experiences at JRC, the Massachusetts Division of Professional Licensure reviewed the names and credentials of staff members who were listed on JRC's website as psychologists.[45] This investigation was sparked by Ken Mollins, the New York state attorney who first became aware of the facility when representing former resident Antwone Nicholson.[46] The Massachusetts Department of Professional Licensure cited JRC after discovering that fourteen of the seventeen individuals listed as psychologists on the facility's website were not in fact psychologists.

JRC agreed to pay $43,000 in fines for identifying staff as psychologists when they were not licensed as such.[47] Five of the fourteen unlicensed staff members admitted that they had represented themselves as psychologists in Massachusetts probate court when seeking approval of treatment plans.[48] JRC's attorney, Michael Flammia, defended JRC's actions, asserting that since four of the people employed at JRC were in fact licensed psychologists, it wasn't necessary for all of their psychologists to be licensed. He added, "We have acknowledged we were giving the incorrect title."[49] Israel argued that psychologists are not required to have a license to work at the center[50] and stated, "I believe that we and our professional staff were singled out because of a bias against aversive therapy, and not because of our mistake."[51] In a statement, Israel said that JRC had always employed clinical staff with training and graduate degrees in psychology and that "these professionals provide diagnostic evaluations and develop treatment plans. JRC assigned the job title 'psychologist' to these persons though not all of them had chosen to become licensed psychologists."[52]

The commonwealth of Massachusetts viewed the misrepresentation of the licensure status of JRC staff as more serious than a mere oversight. On March 1, 2007, Marianne Meacham, general counsel for the DMR, wrote in a letter to Gregory Sullivan, inspector general,

> My inquiry stemmed from an investigation by the Division of Professional Licensure (the Division) that concluded that unlicensed clinicians had been referring to themselves as psychologists. This violates state law . . . I strongly recommend that the Department review the potential for recovery.[53]

Meacham noted that the rates that Massachusetts paid for services at JRC were "among the highest for human service providers with state contracts and that "if the services provided at JRC didn't meet contractual and/or regulatory requirements, there may have been an overcharge by JRC of almost $400,000 on all state contracts since 2002 or approximately $13,000 per enrolled student."[54] The state Department of Developmental Disabilities pursued the claim in conjunction with other Massachusetts agencies that had been financially affected by the overcharges and recovered $213,548 from JRC in addition to the $43,000 in fines that it had paid.[55]

In February 2007 the Massachusetts Department of Education published a sixty-nine-page report of its private special education school program review of JRC.[56] According to the report, a four-member team from the department visited the center during the week of January 23, 2006, and made additional visits in April and May. They interviewed forty-one staff members and one parent of a JRC resident from Massachusetts. The Department of Education reviewed the school on several hundred criteria, finding no deficiencies in areas such as behavior management and restraint training, nutritional requirements, toileting programs, parent and student involvement, health and medical services, or transportation safety. Only one standard, related to serving students who have limited English proficiency, was determined to have not been implemented, and a written response to this issue was requested, to be provided within a year. A similarly positive review was conducted in 2012.[57] After both reports were made public, advocates questioned how a facility with as many documented concerns and potential human rights issues could be assessed so positively.[58]

Like Massachusetts, New York State had to provide oversight of students from the state who were in out-of-state facilities. The majority of residents at JRC came from New York.[59] In 2006, about 255 people were served at JRC, and well more than half were sent from and paid for by school districts across New York State.[60] Over the years, the New York State Education Department (NYSED) and the New York Office of Mental Retardation had conducted a number of site reviews of the JRC facility and its programs. The NYSED reviews of JRC in 1978 and 1979 documented a number of serious concerns, but little had changed in response to these reports. In spring 2006, the New York State Education Department conducted visits and a review of JRC's programs.[61] The 2006 assessment was conducted by four NYSED staff members[62] and by three consultants hired by the department: Caroline Magyar, Daniel Crimmins, and David Roll, all highly regarded in the field of behavioral psychology.[63] The April 25–26 site review was an announced visit, while the May 16–18 review was unannounced. Unlike the Massachusetts Department of Education review, the twenty-six-page report contained numerous findings reflecting serious concerns:

1. The integrity of the behavioral programming was not sufficiently monitored by appropriate professionals and in

many cases the background and preparation of staff was not sufficient to oversee treatment of children with challenging emotional and behavioral problems;

2. Level III aversive behavioral interventions were applied to students with a broad range of disabilities, many without a clear history of self-injurious behaviors; JRC employs a general use of Level III aversive behavioral interventions to students for behaviors that are not aggressive, health dangerous or destructive, such as nagging, swearing and failing to maintain a neat appearance;[64]

3. The use of the electric skin shock conditioning devices as used at JRC raises health and safety concerns;

4. The Contingent Food Program and Specialized Food Program may impose unnecessary risks affecting the normal growth and development and overall nutritional/health status of students subjected to this aversive behavior intervention;

5. The education program is organized around the elimination of problem behaviors largely through punishment, including the use of delayed punishment practices.

6. Behavioral Intervention Plans are developed to support the use of aversive behavioral interventions with limited evidence of students "being faded" from the electric skin shock conditioning devices or other aversive interventions;

7. Students are provided insufficient academic and special education instruction, including limited provision of related services;

8. JRC often does not support the continuation of related services that have been previously recommended on students' IEPs and/or promote the transition of students to less restrictive environments;

9. The privacy and dignity of students is compromised in the course of JRC's program implementation; and,

10. The collateral effects (e.g., increased fear, anxiety or aggression) on students resulting from JRC's punishment model are not adequately assessed, monitored or addressed.[65]

Advocates believed that the 2006 New York State Education Department report would have significant impact, but there were no discernable changes following its release. Israel believed that the review was inaccurate[66] and that "it was prepared as part of a campaign to deny New York students the possibility of aversive therapy — a campaign . . . challenged in federal court by 50 JRC parents from New York State."[67]

By 2006, the population served at JRC began shifting away from people with autism and intellectual/developmental disabilities toward young people who were predominantly from the New York City boroughs and had psychological or behavioral issues or involvement with the criminal justice system. In response to the criticism of JRC's behavioral approaches and because positive behavioral approaches were increasingly favored, many states stopped sending children and adults with autism and other developmental disabilities to JRC. The facility shifted its focus to recruiting young people with psychiatric conditions including behavioral issues resulting from past abuse, post traumatic stress disorder, and conditions as mild as learning disabilities and attention deficit disorder.[68] Weiss described this shift in 2010:

> Everything JRC puts forth in defense of its unorthodox behavioral techniques hinges on the argument that these are children who have severe developmental disabilities and life-threatening behaviors who (in their view) without electric shock, would be eye gouging, mutilating themselves and banging their heads. JRC's census has fallen dramatically in recent years. When states stopped being willing to send kids with significant cognitive disabilities or autism to JRC (or when some states stopped sending kids at all) JRC shifted its focus. Many of the people there now and for the past number of years, are not kids with severe autism or other developmental disabilities but represent another group that can push the limits of families, professionals and systems — tough, oppositional kids from urban areas who had gotten in trouble multiple times and who schools were anxious to see go elsewhere. If an argument could be made that "surely aversive procedures are better than letting a child gouge his eyes out or bang his head against the wall" — it just doesn't hold water when you're working with kids whose biggest issue may be that they come from families that didn't have the resources, skills or support to help their kids

268   PAIN AND SHOCK IN AMERICA

grow up with controls. Because as a society we (like every other industrialized nation in the world) are clear that we would not allow painful electric shock to be used even against hardened criminals or political prisoners, JRC would have a much harder time defending the use of these practices against kids who are simply troubled.[69]

A New York State Department of Education psychologist who visited JRC in 2006 said, "When I visited the place, I was expecting much more difficult, non-communicative behavior in these children. It was a total surprise to me to find out that half to two thirds of the kids from NY had learning disabilities or emotional problems—street kids, kids of color—carrying these shock backpacks. It is prison-like and they are prisoners of the apparatus."[70] A report by Disability Right International notes,

> In the early days of the facility, most students were diagnosed with autism or mental retardation and accompanying self-injurious behaviors. As of 2006, however, according to a New York State Department of Education (NYSED) report, most students from New York State—have the disability classification 'emotional disturbance' with IQ scores that fall in the low average to average range of intelligence. A number of students have a history of abuse and abandonment. More recently, some adolescents have also been coming to JRC through the juvenile justice system and transfers from Rikers Island prison in New York.[71]

In 2011, a New York City News Service investigation documented that JRC advertised for New York students on the FM station Hot 97, one of the city's most popular hip-hop stations. JRC's radio commercial asked, "Is your child autistic or emotionally disturbed? Unmanageable, failing in school, refusing to attend or stuck in a psychiatric or correctional setting?" At the conclusion of the ad, JRC provided a phone number to call for "free consultation and placement assistance."[72] The National Center for Education Statistics provided data on the JRC educational program for the 2017–18 school year. In that year the center served 121 school-aged residents. Of these, 100 (83 percent) were students of color: African American (64 students), Hispanic (33 students) or Asian (3 students).[73]

On August 8, 2007, an event occurred that would change the course of history for the Judge Rotenberg Center. The changes in its population played an important role in this event. Staff members working the overnight shift at a JRC group home received a phone call that they believed to be from one of its quality control monitors, who view multiple on-site live camera feeds throughout the day. In the middle of the night, a former resident who had run away from JRC phoned the group home posing as a JRC monitor. He instructed the staff members to awaken two residents and administer shocks for behaviors that they had allegedly exhibited earlier in the day but for which they had not been punished.[74] The caller assured the staff on duty that he was following the orders of the residents' clinicians and told them that if they did not follow his instructions they would lose their jobs.[75] When the staff woke up the two residents, ages 16 and 18, both denied having done anything wrong. Nevertheless, as instructed, staff administered seventy-seven shocks to one of the young men and twenty-nine shocks to the other. The program of only one of the two residents allowed for "movement limitation," but both were strapped to four-point restraint boards for the administration of the shocks. It was eventually discovered that the call had been a hoax.

An investigative report from the Massachusetts Department of Early Education and Care found sufficient evidence to determine that staff were physically abusive and neglectful in their care of the residents.[76] However, the report also stated that staff had not been in agreement with the instructions to awaken and shock the two young men, but believed that they would be negatively evaluated if they did not comply.[77] Although one of the residents complained afterward of pain in his leg and asked that a nurse be called and the other resident told staff that he was sweaty, his mouth was dry, his blood pressure was racing, and he felt as though he was about to have a stroke, nursing staff were not notified.[78] An Associated Press report about the incident, which became known as "the prank," noted,

> Seven people have been fired over electrical shocks given to two emotionally disturbed teenagers at the direction of what turned out to be a prank caller, the operator of the group home where the incident occurred said Thursday. At the time of the

call, five of the six staffers had worked double or triple shifts, and most had been on the job less than three months. The staffers were described as concerned and reluctant about the orders, but they failed to verify them with the central office or check treatment plans to make sure the teens could receive that level of shock therapy, the report said. Staffers also did not know who the shift supervisor was that night. Staff members realized their mistake after someone finally called the central office. One reason staffers might not have been suspicious of the phone call is that the Rotenberg Center uses surveillance cameras in its group homes to monitor residents and staff, and a central office employee is allowed to initiate discipline by phone. As a result of the investigation, the center has expanded staff training, implemented new telephone verification procedures, added oversight at group homes and eliminated delayed punishment.[79]

During the course of the investigation of staff actions, it was discovered that the events of the evening had been video-recorded. Within days, Israel ordered the recording equipment and the recording of that night's events to be removed from the group home and brought to JRC's main building. There, investigators from the Massachusetts Department of Social Services, the Disabled Persons Protection Committee, and the Early Education and Care Division reviewed the video, and investigators ordered JRC to save the recording. It was later determined that Israel acted in defiance of this directive, instead instructing a JRC employee to destroy the recording, telling the employee that it was no longer needed because the investigation had been concluded.[80] Eventually Israel's actions led to an indictment on charges of accessory after the fact and misleading an investigator or a witness and forced his resignation.[81]

The change in the type of residents at JRC contributed to the prank on the night of August 8, 2007. Previously, most of JRC's residents had had significant developmental disabilities, making it less likely that they would be able to carry out a prank of this kind. The change in the type of person housed at JRC had even more far-reaching implications as residents who were more capable left the facility and were able to tell their stories. The advocacy of former residents, or JRC survivors as they sometimes refer to themselves, became an important force for change.

In August 2007, *Mother Jones* magazine published an in-depth article on the history of the JRC titled, "School of Shock."[82] The article reported that eight states were sending people to JRC at that time and
that, "of the 234 current residents, about half are wired to receive
shocks, including some as young as 9 or 10."[83] Journalist Jennifer Gonnerman reported,

> The Rotenberg Center is the only facility in the country that
> disciplines students by shocking them, a form of punishment
> not inflicted on serial killers or child molesters or any of the 2.2
> million inmates now incarcerated in U.S. jails and prisons. Over
> its 36-year history, six children have died in its care, prompting
> numerous lawsuits and government investigations. Last year,
> New York state investigators filed a blistering report that made
> the place sound like a high school version of Abu Ghraib. Yet
> the program continues to thrive—in large part because no one
> except desperate parents, and a few state legislators, seems
> to care about what happens to the hundreds of kids who pass
> through its gates.[84]

Gonnerman's article gained national attention and generated a
considerable number of responses on the *Mother Jones* website. Israel wrote a response to the *Mother Jones* article in which he noted that
many surgical, dental, or medical treatments involve discomfort and
have risks, but these need to be weighed against the potential benefits.
He expressed concern that the article was one-sided, failing to let readers know "that JRC is the only program in the country that is able to
offer effective, lifesaving treatment to students with severe self-abuse
and aggression or that other programs that try to serve such students,
but which are unable to serve them successfully, often expel those students and refer them to JRC for successful treatment."[85] He concluded
his response to the article by saying that Gonnerman

> fails to put the risks/intrusiveness of aversive therapy with
> skin-shock into proper perspective. Behavioral treatment
> with skin shock at JRC involves a brief, two-second period of
> discomfort that has no significant side effects. It is a procedure
> which, when combined with a program that is overwhelmingly
> based on rewards and educational procedures, enables JRC

to take students off of all psychotropic medication, give them an education for the first time in their lives, and give them and their parents hope and optimism for their future where none had previously existed. Without aversive therapy, the alternatives, for many of the students who are referred to JRC, are being heavily drugged with life-shortening and medically dangerous psychotropic medications, being warehoused in institutions or jails without receiving any treatment at all, being confined and/or frequently restrained in padded isolation rooms, bouncing in and out of psychiatric hospitals with no improvement, killing or maiming themselves or others with their own self-abusive behaviors or aggressive behaviors, or simply ending up homeless on the streets.[86]

ADVOCACY ON A VARIETY OF FRONTS

Anti-aversive advocates continued to urge federal agencies to regulate against the use of electric shock at JRC and to press national organizations to take a position in opposition to the use of shock as punishment. By 2007, almost every mainstream disability organization had a resolution clarifying their position against the use of pain for behavior modification. The American Psychological Association (APA) was one of the only major national organizations that did not have a statement addressing this issue. In October 2007, Nancy Weiss and Derrick Jeffries, the latter a parent of a child with a disability and a person who had Asperger syndrome himself, wrote a letter to the APA that 154 disability professionals and organizations eventually signed. The letter called on the APA and professionals who adhere to its code of ethics to act in a manner that is ethical and consistent with that code of ethics and asked the association "to declare your position regarding the use of skin-shock 'treatments,' food deprivation, and any other aversives that inflict pain or deprive basic human rights at JRC or elsewhere."[87] The letter referenced two recent APA documents: the 2006 "Resolution against Torture and Other Cruel, Inhuman, and Degrading Treatment or Punishment" and the 2007 "Reaffirmation of the American Psychological Association Position against Torture and Other Cruel, Inhuman, or Degrading Treatment or Punishment and Its Application to Individuals Defined in the United States Code as 'Enemy Combatants.'" The APA has never taken a position against aversives.[88]

People with disabilities and their supporters were organizing against the use of electric shock. The Autistic Self Advocacy Network (ASAN) and other organizations, such as ADAPT, Occupy JRC, and Brandeis Students United against the Judge Rotenberg Center, assumed important roles in the anti-aversive advocacy efforts. ASAN was founded in 2006 and is "run by and for autistic people."[89] Its work focuses on advancing civil rights, supporting self-advocacy, improving public perceptions of autism, empowering autistic people to take control of their own lives, and seeking to organize the autistic community to ensure their voices are heard in the national conversation.[90] Lydia X. Z. Brown and Shain Neumeier, both affiliated with ASAN, have published op-eds, letters to the editor, articles, and blog postings describing their outrage at the way in which people at JRC were treated.[91] In 2011 Brown began creating an archive that remains current and documents the history of JRC-related advocacy, events, and issues. Brown calls it a "Living Archive and Repository on the Judge Rotenberg Center's Abuses."[92]

In this thorough compendium, Brown captures links to news articles, videos, state and federal agency actions, court cases, independent and nonprofit organization reports and letters, advocate/activist testimony, op-eds, editorials and letters to the editor, blog posts, and scholarly articles. In August 2014, ASAN published a detailed article about JRC, "Prisoners of the Apparatus," written by member Quentin Davies.[93] Another advocacy group, Occupy JRC, was established in 2012.[94] It developed a website and organized a number of well-attended demonstrations at the JRC and at the Massachusetts State House.

Ari Ne'eman,[95] a disability rights activist, was ASAN's founder and first president. Speaking about ASAN's advocacy against the use of electric shock and other aversive interventions, Ne'eman said, "This issue is deeply personal—this could be happening to us."[96] He and others from ASAN contacted Weiss in 2006 to ask for her help in developing effective advocacy strategies against the use of aversive procedures at JRC. ASAN advocates wanted help crafting a letter to Amnesty International. Weiss was pessimistic because she had tried to engage Amnesty International in 1993 and many times over the ensuing years without success. However, these discussions were taking place during the time when Americans were hearing about abuses at the U.S. military prison at Guantanamo Bay in Cuba and the Abu Ghraib prison in Iraq.[97] They agreed that the climate was possibly right to raise the issue with Amnesty International again.

A four-page letter and ten-page addendum, documenting practices and abuses at JRC and calling for the elimination of the use of aversive and other inhumane practices, was developed and signed by thirty-one national disability organizations.[98] Although the letter was first intended for Amnesty International specifically, it was sent to seven federal agencies and three human rights organizations on September 30, 2009: Amnesty International U.S., Human Rights Watch, and Physicians for Human Rights.[99] The letter called on these groups and federal agencies to take action against the continued abuse of people with disabilities through painful methods of behavior control.[100]

Despite numerous attempts to follow up, there was little response. None of the human rights organizations showed interest in this issue. On January 26, 2010, Weiss and the ASAN advocates received a response to the September 2009 letter from Arne Duncan, the U.S. secretary of education. He wrote that he too was concerned about ensuring that schools are safe and that the use of seclusion and restraint is "very limited."[101] Although the use of seclusion and restraint was also of concern to advocates, the letter had focused on the use of electric shock and other aversive procedures and hadn't addressed these issues. Duncan described policies that the U.S. Department of Education was putting into place to limit seclusion and restraint procedures and said that the decision to use any restrictive procedures with children in schools is a decision left to each state.[102]

In January, the Disability Rights Section of the Civil Rights Division of the U.S. Department of Justice (DOJ) sent an email to Weiss asking to be updated on whether any other office within the federal government had addressed the issue of the use of aversive procedures at the JRC. The letter said that the DOJ "may determine that their office should investigate" or they "may determine that they have overlapping jurisdiction with other agencies that are better suited to investigate."[103]

On February 18, 2010, Renee Wohlenhaus, deputy chief of the Disability Rights Section of the Civil Rights Division of the DOJ, sent a letter to Weiss: "The Department of Justice has received your complaint alleging that the Judge Rotenberg Center has violated title III of the Americans with Disabilities Act of 1990 (ADA), 42 U.S.C. §§ 12181–

12189. This office has opened a routine investigation of the complaint. Please note that our decision to investigate does not reflect any determination as to the merits of the complaint. Our goal is to investigate this matter in a fair and impartial manner and to work with all parties to reach a productive and amicable resolution . . . We look forward to working with you to bring this matter to a prompt resolution." Two years later, there was still no conclusion or report. In 2012 Jonathan Young, chairman of the National Council on Disability, wrote to the DOJ urging it to expedite its investigation and quickly move forward with its findings.[104] The DOJ did carry out the investigation, but ten years after the announcement of their intent to investigate and their statement that they hoped to bring the matter to a prompt resolution, no results or report were ever released. As recently as fall 2019, a Freedom of Information request was made to access the findings of the DOJ investigation of the Judge Rotenberg Center. At that time, over eight and a half years after the investigation was announced, the requesting party was told that no findings could be provided because the investigation remained ongoing.[105]

MATTHEW ISRAEL FORCED TO RESIGN

On May 20, 2011, more than three and a half years after the August 2007 incident in which JRC residents were woken up in the middle of the night and shocked in error at the instruction of a prank caller, Attorney General Martha Coakley brought criminal charges against Matthew Israel. A Norfolk County grand jury returned indictments against Israel on charges of accessory after the fact and misleading an investigator or a witness.[106] At his arraignment, Israel entered into a sentencing agreement for pretrial probation. Under the terms of his probation, he was required to resign from his position as executive director of the JRC within the month and was prohibited from working for it or serving as a member of its board of directors. Coakley said, "Today's action removed Dr. Israel from the school and should ensure better protection for students in the future . . . We believe that Dr. Israel created a system and environment at the JRC that failed to prevent a lapse of this magnitude."[107] While Israel dismissed the severity of the indictment, saying in his resignation letter, "I am now almost 78 years old, and it is time for me to move over and let others take the reins,"[108] this legal action was clearly significant: it ended a forty-year career devoted to gaining support for JRC's controversial behavioral approaches.[109]

In addition to the requirement that Israel discontinue his relationship with JRC, the court required that an independent monitor be appointed to ensure that an incident similar to the response to the prank call would not happen again.[110] Attorney General Coakley and the JRC's board of directors entered into a deferred prosecution agreement "whereby an Independent Monitor would be appointed to review and assess safety at JRC."[111] On May 25, 2011, Judge Isaac Borenstein was retained as the independent monitor. He and his team reviewed dozens of documents, including many internal to JRC operations,[112] as well as reports and assessments of the facility by other agencies. They also reviewed state regulations and interviewed forty-five people, including staff, board members, parents, guardians, and two students who were receiving GED intervention.[113]

On February 22, 2013, Borenstein submitted a 128-page report to the Massachusetts Attorney General's Office and the JRC board of directors. The report indicated that at the time of the review, 39 percent of JRC's clients had the GED as part of their program. At that time, there were 236 residents at JRC, 35 percent of whom Borenstein described as "emotionally disturbed, behaviorally disordered adolescents," and 65 percent were described as "autistic, developmentally delayed children and adults." Of those approved for use of electric shock, 99.9% were autistic and developmentally delayed. The facility acknowledged that a significant portion of their residents were adults at the time of the review.[114]

The report expressed concern about staff retention, noting that many prospective staff members did not graduate from basic training, and in the one-year period preceding the report, 44.25 percent of staff members had resigned within six months of being hired.[115] In the three-month period prior to Borenstein's investigation, forty-eight staff members had resigned. Of these, thirty-five had been at JRC less than a year. Borenstein's report noted that JRC policy "did not encourage staff questioning orders or actions of other staff members, took decision-making away from direct care staff . . . and staff were unfamiliar with the administration of GEDs but did not ask questions."[116] This was of particular concern the night of the prank call incident in which shocks were given in error, because staff understood what they were told to do was not ordinary procedure but they feared questioning the directive.[117]

The report also warned of the risks of JRC policies that specified that staff cannot engage in social or informal conversation with residents. It noted that resident-raised human rights issues investigated by a staff person were frequently dismissed[118] and that although JRC residents were informed of their right to bring concerns to the Human Rights Committee, no resident-raised concerns were ever reviewed by that committee.[119] The report recommended that JRC improve quality control and monitoring, staff hiring, training and retention, staff independent judgment, staff supervision and safety, use of the GED and restraints, response to emergencies, student health, and human rights.[120] Under the prosecution agreement, JRC had one month to vote on whether to adopt the recommendations in the monitor's report.[121] JRC did agree to adopt the recommendations.[122]

DISABILITY RIGHTS INTERNATIONAL
AND THE UNITED NATIONS GET INVOLVED

In April 2010, Mental Disability Rights International (now Disability Rights International), an organization founded in 1993 by attorney Eric Rosenthal and "dedicated to promoting human rights and the full participation in society of children and adults with disabilities worldwide,"[123] published a fifty-four-page report on its investigation into "the human rights abuses of children and young adults with mental disabilities residing at the Judge Rotenberg Center."[124] The report was titled, "Torture Not Treatment: Electric Shock and Long-Term Restraint in the United States on Children and Adults with Disabilities at the Judge Rotenberg Center, an Urgent Appeal to the United Nations Special Rapporteur on Torture."[125]

The report was effective in getting the attention of the United Nations Special Rapporteur on Torture, Manfred Nowak, an Austrian human rights lawyer and a professor of constitutional and international law and human rights at Vienna University. Nowak called on the U.S. federal government to investigate this potential human rights abuse.[126] In a follow-up interview with *ABC News*, Nowak confirmed that the use of electric shock at JRC amounted to torture: "I have no doubts about it. It is inflicted in a situation where a victim is powerless. And, I mean, a child being subjected to electric shocks, how much more powerless can you be?"[127] Nowak also said that the same practices employed at the JRC would not be legal if they were used on a convicted terrorist.[128] Three years later, in March 2013, Juan Méndez, Nowak's successor, issued an international report on torture and other cruel, inhuman, or degrading forms of treatment of punishment. The report condemned the use of electric shock and physical restraint used at the JRC and noted that the U.S. government acknowledged that "the use of aversive therapy by JRC has been challenged through a variety of state and federal legislative and judicial actions, including the Department of Justice's investigation into possible violations of civil rights laws, which remains open and ongoing."[129]

MASSACHUSETTS DEPARTMENT OF DEVELOPMENTAL SERVICES REGULATES

There was increasing pressure on the Massachusetts Department of Developmental Services (DDS), previously named the Department of Mental Retardation, to pass regulations eliminating or restricting the use of electric shock. In October 2011, DDS passed regulations that prohibited the use of electric shock on any resident of JRC unless a previous court-approved plan allowing for the use of the GED was in place at that time. DDS sought and received public testimony and written comments. In a twenty-one-page review of the procedures that the department undertook to propose the regulation and receive testimony and written comments, DDS said, "After careful deliberation, the department finds that the current standard of care for individuals with intellectual disability with the most severe behavioral challenges is positive behavior intervention and does not include aversive interventions or punishment. The department concludes that there has been an evolution in the treatment of severe behavioral disturbances in persons with intellectual disability over the past 30 years, and particularly in the last two decades, which has moved towards forms of treatment that are non-aversive and involve positive behavioral supports."[130]

The October 2011 amended behavior modification regulations for Massachusetts stated that "no program which is operated, funded or licensed by DDS shall employ the use of Level III Aversive Interventions."[131] However, the amended regulations provided an exception on an individual basis for people "who as of September 1, 2011, have an existing court-approved treatment plan which includes the use of Level III Aversive Interventions." The amended regulations also required that such exceptions needed to be reapproved by the courts

Figure 14. JRC student with GED holsters and backpack.
© *2020 Rick Friedman Photography.*

each year thereafter. This meant that anyone who was a JRC resident in August 2011 and had a court-approved plan that included electric shock could continue to receive that intervention with regular reapprovals from the courts. However, no one who was admitted after that date or who did not already have court approval for use of the GED as of August 2011 could receive Level III aversives; essentially, people who currently had the GED as part of their behavioral plan were grandfathered in (Figure 14).

NEW YORK AGAIN

After a series of site reviews that revealed continued concerns and during the time when the commonwealth of Massachusetts passed regulations to limit the use of electric shock, the New York State Education Department (NYSED) notified JRC on March 23, 2009, that the center continued to have policies and procedures inconsistent with New York State regulations and noted that it had been working with

JRC since June 2007 to address these matters.[132] An issue of particular concern was the use of aversive procedures for behaviors that were not self-injurious, aggressive, or otherwise threatened the well-being of the student or others.[133] The NYSED issued a compliance assurance plan to JRC on May 23, 2011, that required the facility to take corrective actions in order to comply with New York State regulations. Soon after, in July 2011, the NYSED conducted an unannounced visit to JRC. The New York team randomly selected a sample of 10 students from a list of 126 New York students who were at JRC at that time. A report of their findings, sent to JRC on February 15, 2012, described that while JRC had completed some student-specific corrective actions, "significant and serious noncompliance" issues continued to be found relative to the use of aversive procedures and emergency interventions.[134] Specific findings included that JRC continued to use aversive interventions with students whose Individual Education Plans (IEPs) did not include them and overused mechanical restraints such as the five-point restraint chair "not as protective equipment due to documented medical necessity but as a planned response to modify students' behavior."[135]

Despite persistent concerns about the use and misuse of aversive procedures, New York continued to send students to JRC. A New York City News Service investigation in 2011 found that JRC spent hundreds of thousands of dollars annually to press New York State to continue to fund students to be sent to their facility. According to the investigation, JRC's "efforts have ensured that New York state spends millions of dollars every year to send more than 100 students to the school, and to keep more coming."[136] The report noted the success of JRC's efforts to continue a steady stream of New York State–funded residents: "At a time when New York state education officials are slashing programs because of budget shortfalls, New York City alone paid more than $30 million last year to the private Boston school. That covers about two-thirds of the facility's annual operating budget, according to its most recent publicly available financial statements."[137] In spring 2010, there were 144 school-aged children at JRC, of these, 118 were from New York City, funded with New York tax dollars. New York City comptroller records showed that the city "paid nearly $32.5 million to the Rotenberg Center during fiscal year 2011."[138] Of this amount, $16.8 million came from the city's Department of Education and the remainder from the New York City Administration for Children Services.[139]

The investigation also revealed that between 2005 and 2011, JRC spent over $1.2 million to lobby against legislation that would limit their use of aversive procedures.[140] Federal records documented that in 2011, JRC spent over $116,000 to lobby against such legislation: "The bulk of that went to Bracewell and Giuliani, the firm of former New York City mayor Rudolf Giuliani."[141] JRC also contracted with Steven Sanders, a lobbyist and former New York State assemblyman who served on the state's education committee.[142] Even as recently as 2014, nearly 90 percent (121 of the 137 people at JRC) were from New York City, including 29 who had been sent there between 2013 and 2014.[143]

In an effort to recruit students, JRC ran radio ads in the New York City area[144] and contracted with marketing representatives who provided information to families and made presentations to staff at some New York State psychiatric facilities.[145] "JRC's marketing representatives visit the homes and provide the family with information and gifts for both the family and student, e.g., a gift bag for the family, basketball for the student."[146] Marketing strategies also include exhibiting at conferences such as the American Probation and Parole Association, the Virginia Juvenile Justice Association, the National Council of Juvenile and Family Court Judges, the New York City Young Child Expo and Conference, and the conference of the National Association of School Psychologists.[147] This marketing strategy helped to yield a steady supply of clients and ensure payment for services, usually through New York school systems. By 2014, when the annual cost of sending a student to JRC was $248,000, New York City taxpayers paid JRC $30 million.[148]

The New York State Education Department's comment to the FDA in 2014 described the shock as used at JRC as "demeaning, demoralizing, and dehumanizing" and said that its use poses "health and safety risks to the individuals receiving the shocks and to those who observe it."[149] They said that it "has no place in the treatment of children and individuals with disabilities."[150] Their 2006 site visit report had noted that the "use of electric skin shock conditioning devices as used at JRC raises health and safety concerns," that "students are provided insufficient academic and special education instruction," and that "the integrity of the behavioral programming at JRC is not sufficiently monitored by appropriate professionals."[151] The same department wrote to JRC in 2009 making it clear that the use of aversive procedures is prohibited in New York State.[152] In another state site visit report, the team described their review of JRC as "the singularly most depressing experience that team members have had in numerous visits to human service programs,"[153] yet as of the date of this writing, the JRC continues to be included on the New York State list of approved out-of-state schools serving students with disabilities. It is approved as a placement for children ages 5 to 21 who have labels of autism, emotional disturbance, multiple disabilities, and intellectual disabilities.[154]

MORE INCIDENTS REPORTED:
FIGHTS AND BRAWLS

Records obtained by the New England Center for Investigative Reporting confirmed that JRC was cited frequently for violations related to abuse and neglect.[155] Only one other center had a higher number of violations of state regulations between 2011 and 2016, according to the reports of the Massachusetts Department of Early Education and Care, the state agency that licenses Massachusetts residential facilities that serve students under the age of 22.[156] During the same five-year period, JRC was cited for abuse of adult residents more than any other Massachusetts facility by the state Disabled Persons Protection Commission.[157] In 2016 the school was cited twenty-seven times, mostly for abuse and neglect, by the two state agencies that monitor care at special education schools.[158] In one incident in December 2016, two former employees of JRC were charged with beating a resident multiple times over the course of months. The police reported that video surveillance in one resident's room showed that staff had whipped, spat on, and beaten the resident with a belt and punched and shoved him several times throughout October and the start of November that year.[159] The Massachusetts Disabled Persons Protection Commission investigated the incident and other substantiated claims of abuse and found that the two former employees had been abusing this resident "from time to time for nearly a year," noting that the amount of time that this abuse continued without detection was of particular concern.[160] They recommended "that the Judge Rotenberg Educational Center take a hard look at its policies after two now-former employees were charged with assaulting a patient."[161] In its report, the commission wrote, "That [the two employees] acted with so little regard to [the victim's] dignity and his behavioral program for such a period of time suggests that staff is either insufficiently trained or supported to carry out complex treatment programs for individuals with disabilities."[162] At the trial related to this incident, prosecutors said that the staff member used the buckle end of his belt to whip the resident. The accused staff member testified, "That client is very aggressive. You have to match aggression with aggression. I'm not going to get broken bones for minimum wage."[163]

In another 2016 incident, a former staff member pleaded guilty and served ninety days in jail for three incidents with three residents, one of whom was kicked, one thrown against a wall, and a third punched.[164] In December 2017, police responded to an incident at a JRC group home and arrested a staff person for assaulting an 18-year old resident while helping to restrain him. The staff member pleaded guilty to assault and battery and was given two years of probation and ordered to obtain anger management counseling.[165] Many similar incidents were reported over the years by the New England Center on Investigative Reporting.[166]

Glenda Crookes, JRC's executive director who replaced Matthew Israel, said that the facility "does everything it can do to protect its residents"[167] and that caring for residents who are between the ages of 10 and 59 can be challenging. Crookes had been Israel's second in command (Figure 15). She confirmed that the facility's 1,000 staff members receive ongoing training, but that this doesn't always stop abuses from happening. She added, "Sometimes people don't react the way they should. We self-report everything."[168] Critics asserted that mistreatment at JRC was a "natural extension of a culture that espouses the use of painful stimuli as a way to control students."[169] Shain Neumeier, a disability rights attorney representing a California family who claimed their 17-year-old daughter was assaulted at the center in February 2018, expressed concern about the culture of the facility: "People focus on the shock aspect of it. But well before, they were doing other things that are abusive. It's a culture of institutional abuse."[170]

THE GRADUATED ELECTRONIC DECELERATOR AND THE FDA

Over the years, advocates tried to convince the Food and Drug Administration (FDA) to take action to ban the use of the graduated electronic decelerator.[171] In March 2010 Nancy Weiss sent a letter to Jeffrey Shuren, director of the Center for Devices and Radiological Health of

Figure 15. Glenda Crookes, JRC executive director.
© *2020 Rick Friedman Photography*

the FDA, requesting that the agency take action to outlaw the GED. The letter raised concerns about JRC's claims on its website that the electric shock device was approved by the FDA, although this was not the case. In this letter to the FDA, Weiss suggested that the JRC's assertion that the shock devices are FDA approved "implies a certain level of trust or safety, which in this case appears unfounded."[172] The letter reminded the FDA that the June 2006 New York State Education Department JRC program visitation report noted that "the GED is manufactured by the JRC. While JRC has information posted on their website and in written articles which represents the GED device as 'approved,' it has not been approved by the Food and Drug Administration (FDA),"[173] yet the FDA had taken no action to correct this inaccuracy.

Weiss's letter also contained a review of an article published on the JRC website but had not been peer reviewed: "A Remote-Controlled Electric Shock Device for Behavior Modification."[174] The review of the article was written by James Angelo Ruggieri, an electrical engineer and board-certified forensic engineer. The article first described an electronic shock device that had been used previously, the self-injurious behavior inhibiting system (SIBIS). The article noted that the GED was modeled on this device, but that JRC felt that the SIBIS device "may not be strong enough to decelerate the target behavior."[175] Matthew Israel and the other JRC-affiliated authors wrote that even if the electric shock delivered by the SIBIS " does have a mildly decelerative effect, numerous applications may be required to accomplish any significant deceleration, and this frequent use increases the likelihood of adaptation . . . Research with both animals and humans suggests that for maximal effectiveness, an electrical stimulus should be as intense as possible, consistent with safety."[176] The SIBIS device had been FDA approved in 1986.[177] Ruggieri did not have a GED to test, but after reviewing the article, he concluded: "Their numbers regarding current and their use of electrical units are problematic. For instance, the article says, '[The] SIBIS device produced a 0.2 second shock to the surface of the skin that had an average intensity of 2.02 mA (root mean squared). It's either rms or peak — and when I see terms like 'average' and how such terms have been misused in the past, it sends a red flag. Another problem is that [it] reads 'Peak 90 mA rms.' Again, it's either peak or rms — not both. If the FDA registered this device, I'm sure it was based on the numbers and claims the center furnished — and I am certain the FDA did not instrument and test the device."[178]

The FDA did not reply to the letter from Weiss, but fourteen months later, in May 2011, the FDA sent a letter to JRC explaining that the FDA had made an error. The letter clarified that while the FDA cleared a premarket notification of the GED on December 5, 1994 (that is, it determined that the GED was not subject to premarket approval because it was as safe and effective as a substantially equivalent, legally marketed device)[179] and while the FDA told JRC in a February 2000 letter[180] that the GED devices were exempt from the 510(k) requirement [a premarket submission made to the FDA to demonstrate that the device is as safe and effective as a legally marketed device],[181] the decision that the FDA had conveyed—that premarket approval was not needed for the GED—was not correct."[182]

On June 29, 2012, the FDA sent another letter to JRC stating it had reviewed eleven responses from JRC to its May 2011 letter, but the responses were inadequate. In the FDA's view, JRC had not provided "sufficient evidence to support the safety and effectiveness of these devices . . . or any information regarding the physical and/or psychological consequences of a student being placed in a pseudo restraint via the holster."[183] The holster is a device with two deep pockets that is attached to a chair or a belt around a person's waist. The person must keep his or her hands inside the pockets of the holster; removing the hands from the holster triggers an automatic shock when activated.[184]

In December 2012 the FDA sent JRC a third letter, this time a warning letter.[185] The letter noted that an investigator from the FDA had inspected JRC and that the GED-3A and GED-4 devices (the two stronger versions of the shock device) violated the federal Food, Drug, and Cosmetic Act because JRC had failed to obtain FDA clearance or approval for these devices. The letter stated, "Your facility should take prompt action to correct the violations addressed in this letter. Failure to promptly correct these violations may result in regulatory action being initiated by the FDA without further notice."[186] The letter also scheduled a meeting with JRC for January 9, 2013, to discuss the center's plan for corrective action.

JRC responded to the FDA's warning letter on December 21, 2012, expressing that it took the issues raised in the warning letter seriously, that it was continuing to make significant progress on its corrective action plan, and that it was prepared to discuss an appropriate transition of the GED versions 3A and 4:

> JRC also intends to discuss the physical and emotional harm that would be caused by any further FDA action that would require the removal, or transition from treatment, of the GED to other therapies which have previously been determined to be not effective for these clients . . . any action by the agency that would remove or require the removal of the GED from the clients who currently rely on this therapy would have dire consequences from a client safety and health perspective.[187]

Advocacy encouraging the FDA to take action against the shock devices used at JRC continued on many fronts. On January 8, 2013,

Massachusetts State senator Brian Joyce sent a letter to the FDA. Joyce had supported unsuccessful efforts to pass legislation in Massachusetts that would eliminate the use of electric shock. He wrote that he believed that "government must stop the use of this device on innocent, disabled children and adults, which is contrary to the public good and human decency . . . As a society, we can be judged by how we treat our most vulnerable members, and these children, strapped to painful shock devices 24-hours a day, are certainly among that group. I implore you to ensure that these devices are not FDA approved, and be removed from JRC as soon as practicable."[188]

A month later, the Boston Center for Independent Living also sent a letter to the FDA to urge it "to move swiftly to prohibit, and if necessary seize these unsafe and ineffective devices which are neither cleared nor approved by the FDA."[189] On March 29, Weiss sent a letter on behalf of fifteen national organizations requesting a meeting with the FDA.[190] The FDA granted this request, and advocates met with FDA representatives on April 16, 2013. In advance of that meeting, the advocates sent the FDA information indicating that the GED should not be approved on the basis of its being "substantially equivalent" to the previously approved SIBIS device because the stronger GED that was being used at JRC had been modified from the original FDA-cleared device and because electric shock was being used at JRC for behaviors beyond those for which the SIBIS device had originally been approved.

At the April 2013 meeting with the FDA, advocates presented information confirming that the use of aversive procedures was prohibited in most states, that there were case reports of psychological trauma and posttraumatic stress disorder symptoms in response to having been subjected to electric shock at JRC, and that "alternative treatments such as positive environmental and reinforcement strategies had been developed and are currently effective for severe and refractory self-injury."[191] The Massachusetts Disability Law Center sent a follow-up letter to the FDA on April 22, providing thirty-six pages of information in support of the FDA taking action to prevent the use of electric shock for the purpose of behavior modification. The letter included an analysis by the Occupational Safety and Health Administration on the effects of electric shock on the human body,[192] which identified voltages comparable to those delivered by the GED-3A and GED-4 as unsafe.[193] Over the next several years, Julia Bascom, Ari Ne'eman's successor as executive director of the Autistic Self Advocacy

Figure 16. Jennifer Msumba. Courtesy of Brittany Simcic.

Network, organized a series of meetings during which advocates met with FDA and Department of Health and Human Services officials in an effort to urge the FDA to ban the electric shock devices.

A FORMER JRC RESIDENT

MAKES A DIFFERENCE

While national experts and advocacy groups were writing to and meeting with the FDA to urge it to regulate against the use of electric shock for behavior control, possibly the most influential voice came from Jennifer Msumba, a former JRC resident who was then living in Florida (Figure 16). Msumba's self-advocacy and heart-felt story of her experience receiving electric shocks at JRC inspired action.

Jennifer is a highly intelligent young woman.[194] Many residents at JRC had been unable to find a way for their story to be heard because the severity of their disability made it nearly impossible for them to articulate what happened to them. Msumba had been shocked at JRC for seven years. Her ability to tell her story to the FDA with astonishing recall for detail appeared to motivate the FDA to take action. In

January 2013, Msumba sent the letter opening this book to Weiss, who was now the director of the National Leadership Consortium on Developmental Disabilities at the University of Delaware. The letter would have far-reaching consequences. Msumba told Weiss that she wanted her letter to be made public, that she wanted to tell her story to the FDA, and that she wanted Weiss to help ensure that her voice would be heard.[195]

Msumba became a folk hero of the anti-aversive community. She let the world know that she saw aversive procedures as ineffective and inhumane. She was by this time in a setting that provided her options and caring and responsive support. Reflecting on her time at JRC, she wrote, "I was so low in society, it was okay for me to be tortured without appeal. I felt I was no longer American. The country I was raised to believe in, denounced torture of a citizen. I mattered so little that this didn't even apply to me."[196]

In the same way that the release of the video evidence of Andre McCollins being shocked opened the eyes of many to the real-life impact of experiencing the GED, Msumba's self-testament changed the course and impact of advocacy efforts. At her request, a copy of her letter was sent to the U.S. Department of Justice and to the FDA requesting action and a ban of the electric shock devices. Both agencies requested phone interviews with Msumba, presumably in an effort to establish whether she was authentic. Hearing firsthand from a person who experienced the shock at JRC proved to be influential. Jennifer also shared her experiences being shocked with the restraint board, elevating the agencies' concerns:

> The most sickening, horrifying experience of my life was being shocked on the restraint board. What is the board? It is a large, door sized contraption made out of hard plastic, with locking restraint cuffs on each corner where your wrists and ankles get locked in. Your body becomes stretched spread eagle style, pinned tight, rendering you completely helpless, combined with an overwhelming feeling of vulnerability. It is a torture that you would expect to see in a horror movie. The kind that makes you cringe and scream while you watch. The kind you can't get out of your head even after it's over. Only this was happening for real, to me. They added the restraint board, which for me was 5 shocks over 10 minutes to my program

after a few months, which means getting shocked 5 different times, over a period of 10 minutes for having just one single behavior. If you have just one of those behaviors on your sheet, which can be getting out of your seat without permission (even without doing anything violent), tensing your body, anything they decide to put in your program. A behavior is anything you do that JRC considers a problem. Anything from hitting your head, to talking to yourself, saying a swear word, rocking, even screaming from fear and pain of the shocks, is a "behavior." The staff grab you, put you in restraints, walk or drag you to where the board is kept (usually right in the middle of the classroom with all the other students watching and stepping around you), and then restrain you to the board. Arms and legs locked in. Then the terror starts. You have to wait for it. You never know when it's coming. The staff shocking you usually hides behind a door or desk so you cannot see them.[197]

MEDICAID FUNDING PROHIBITED

On December 14, 2012, the Centers for Medicare and Medicaid Services (CMS) sent a letter to the Massachusetts Executive Office of Health and Human Services stating that while CMS acknowledged that the use of aversive interventions and food deprivation is regulated by the states, "reasonable people will agree that electric shock and withholding of meals have no place in their homes or communities." This letter requested immediate assurance that Level III aversive interventions are eliminated for anyone receiving home- and community-based services (HCBS) Medicaid waiver funds and that any settings in which waiver participants are served must not allow the use of such aversive procedures.[198]

All services at JRC are publicly funded. The admissions page of its website says, "Students are funded by public school districts and various state agencies."[199] The vast majority of adults with developmental disabilities in the United States (people over the age of 22) who receive services are served using HCBS Medicaid waiver funds, which allows states to share the cost of services using a combination of state and federal funds.[200] CMS's decision to disallow waiver funds for services at JRC (regardless of whether the person being supported there has electric shock in their plan or not) was a financial blow to states that were supporting adults at JRC. Now those services, which cost states upward of $278,000 per resident per year, now needed to be funded entirely with state dollars.

At least one state balked at this. Two young men from Delaware were at JRC, and the electric shock device was part of both men's programs. After CMS ruled that Medicaid funds could not be used to support people there, the Delaware Department of Health and Social Services (DHSS) terminated JRC as a qualified provider and sought to return the men to Delaware and provide appropriate support services there. JRC and both sets of the young men's parents took legal action in an effort to reverse the Delaware Department of Health and Social Services' decision to bring the two men back to Delaware. The parents appealed the state's decision to discontinue funding to JRC on the basis that the GED was "medically necessary and that by removing GED services, DHSS has threatened the recipients' ability to remain in a community-based setting."[201] Delaware paid the cost of the two men to stay at JRC while the state planned for their transition to a qualified Delaware service agency, but Delaware stopped making payments to JRC in 2014 after Delaware's contract with JRC expired. Later, the state agreed to pay JRC retroactively for the care of the two men once their transition back to Delaware was complete.[202]

At a hearing held in April 2016, the hearing officer's decision upheld the right of the state to require JRC to stop using the GED on the two Delaware residents. The officer ruled that the use of this procedure was disallowed by both state policy and Medicaid regulations."[203] The case was appealed to the Delaware Supreme Court,[204] which also ruled that the state of Delaware was within its rights to cease payments to JRC and to return the two men to the state.[205] Staff of the Delaware DHSS spent months planning the transition to bring the men back. They sought and identified an appropriate in-state agency to serve them and worked with the agency to plan for a successful transition. In fall 2020, the two men returned to Delaware. The agency that provides services to them in Delaware uses no aversive behavioral procedures. The two men are currently being served in a shared apartment. Although JRC warned of serious behavioral crises should the state of Delaware remove these two Delaware residents from the JRC program, there have been no significant behavioral incidents.[206] The transition has been judged by the state as well as by the parents of the two men to have been enormously successful.

In February 2013, Massachusetts Attorney General Martha Coakley filed a motion to vacate the 1987 Office for Children consent decree that had taken the power to regulate the treatment plans at the Judge Rotenberg Center away from the state.[207] The attorney general's office argued that the consent decree was over 25 years old at that point, and knowledge about best practices to serve people with challenging behaviors had changed significantly. But in June 2013, Bristol County Probate Court judge Katherine Field ruled in the center's favor, with the effect that the consent decree would remain in place and could be used to overrule the Massachusetts Department of Developmental Services' regulations that were intended to prohibit the use of the GED for anyone who had not already had electric shock as part of an approved behavior plan as of August 2011.

Unsatisfied with Judge Field's decision, in February 2016, the commonwealth again tried to have the 1987 consent decree vacated. The trial did not conclude until October 2016 after forty-four days of evidentiary hearings and six hundred exhibits. In her closing argument, the assistant attorney general, Frances Cohen, said, "We're here because under the consent decree, Judge Rotenberg Center has a permanent guarantee to use a brutal painful treatment that is not used anywhere else in the world for this purpose."[208] Attorneys for JRC argued that the state was "bending to the will of public opinion and media coverage, wanting to end a controversial practice despite its benefits."[209] On June 20, 2018, almost five and a half years after the motion to vacate the consent decree was first filed, the petition to eliminate the consent decree was again denied. Judge Field ruled in the center's favor, writing that the commonwealth "failed to demonstrate that there is now a professional consensus that the Level III aversive treatment used at JRC does not conform to the accepted standard of care for treating individuals with intellectual and developmental disabilities."[210] The state secretary of health and human services, Marylou Sudders, discussing whether to appeal the decision of the county probate and family court, said, "Obviously it's controversial, but there is a use of aversives in the Commonwealth under probate court and I obviously need to review all the findings and determine whether we accept the judgment or, in fact, whether we appeal . . . I think the use of aversives in very controlled environments for individuals who are at extraordinarily high risk of harm to themselves or others—in a very controlled environment, there is evidence that it can interrupt the negative behavior in order for you to introduce positives."[211] The following month, Mary Lou Sudders announced that she had asked Attorney General Maura Healey to appeal the probate court decision that continued the consent decree.[212] As of the date of this writing, over two years after the intent to appeal was announced, an appeal has not been filed.

12 : THE FDA BANS THE ELECTRIC SHOCK DEVICE

A FINAL RULING?

Nancy R. Weiss and Jan Nisbet

On March 21, 2014, the FDA announced that an open meeting of the Neurological Devices Panel of the Medical Devices Advisory Committee would be held on April 24, 2014. The purpose of the hearing was to "provide advice and recommendations to the agency" as the Medical Devices Advisory Committee considered "the current knowledge about safety and effectiveness of aversive conditioning devices that are intended to deliver a noxious electrical stimulus to a patient to modify undesirable behavioral characteristics"[1] and "considered a ban on electrical stimulation devices (ESDs)."[2] The announcement noted that the "FDA was convening the committee to seek clinical and scientific expert opinion on the risks and benefits of certain aversive conditioning devices and invited people to submit data, information, or views, orally or in writing."[3]

The FDA noted that while holding a panel meeting before banning a device is not required, it "decided to do so in the interest of gathering as much data and information as possible, from experts in relevant medical fields as well as all interested stakeholders, and in the interest of obtaining independent expert advice on the scientific and clinical matters at issue."[4] In considering whether to ban electric shock devices, the FDA wrote that it also conducted an extensive, systematic literature review to assess the benefits and risks associated with electrical stimulation devices, as well as alternative treatments for people exhibiting self-injurious and aggressive behaviors.[5] The announcement clarified that in order to ban a device, the "FDA must make a finding that a device 'presents substantial deception or an unreasonable and substantial risk of illness or injury' based on all available data and information."[6] The nineteen members of the advisory panel were considered experts in program evaluation, nursing, neurosurgery, psy-

295

chiatry, statistical science, public policy and behavioral psychology, as well as a patient representative, a consumer representative, and an industry representative.[7]

As far as was known, the Judge Rotenberg Center was the only facility in the world that used electric shock in an effort to modify behavior.[8] Although JRC was not specifically mentioned in the March 2014 FDA announcement, a ban would directly affect the practices used there. Advocates immediately organized on both sides of the issue: those supporting the continued use of electric shock devices and those who supported a ban. Anti-aversive advocates worked hard to ensure that comments were submitted to the FDA in advance of the open meeting and that experts, people who had been JRC residents, and people who had worked at JRC would testify. Jennifer Msumba, the former JRC resident who had written the letter that gained Department of Justice and FDA attention, was not able to travel to the Washington, DC, to testify, but she recorded a twenty-minute video hoping it would be shown at the public meeting.

The FDA accepted public comment for a month prior to and a month following the April 24 meeting.[9] During the original comment period, it received 297 comments. In total, including those received during extended comment periods, the FDA received over fifteen hundred comments regarding the proposal to ban devices that deliver a noxious electrical stimulus.[10] The FDA described these comments as coming from several types of stakeholders, including hundreds from parents of children and adults with intellectual and developmental disabilities. They also received comments from several people who had themselves manifested self-injurious or aggressive behavior in their lifetimes.[11] Dozens of state agencies, other public agencies, and private organizations sent comments. "State and federal legislators also expressed interest, as did state and national advocacy groups."[12] The New York State Education Department sent a letter urging the FDA to ban the use of electric shock for the purposes of behavior modification, arguing that noxious electrical stimuli "provide an unreasonable and substantial risk of illness or injury to the individuals subject to their use."[13]

JRC also sent comments, which the FDA described as "the affected manufacturer and residential facility," some of its employees, and parents of individual residents.[14] The FDA noted that "the overwhelming majority of comments supported this ban. The comments in opposition to this ban were primarily from the JRC and people affiliated with it.[15]

The JRC submitted a sixty-nine-page comment that included the following comments:

> FDA's proposed ban is not supported by any evidence demonstrating that ESD (electrical stimulation device) therapy presents "substantial deception" or an unreasonable and substantial risk of illness or injury. To the contrary, FDA has largely disregarded, dismissed or distorted evidence contrary to its position, over-weighted evidence it deems supportive, engaged in speculation, cited unreliable and even anecdotal information, and mischaracterized the data. Although one would never know it from reading FDA's proposal, many prominent and national experts in the field of behavioral therapy, including members of FDA's own Neurological Devices Advisory Panel (the "Advisory Panel"), support the safety and efficacy of ESDs (electrical stimulation devices) for treatment of refractory patients with self-injurious or aggressive behavior. In fact, the balance of data and professional opinions does not remotely support a ban and leads to the undeniable conclusion that the proposed ban will lead to real and substantial harm to the very patients FDA purports to be protecting.[16]

JRC asserted further that any decision "that would precipitously remove or require the eventual removal of the GED from the patients who currently rely on this court-ordered therapy would have dire consequences from a patient safety and health perspective" and that the GED "is the only treatment available to these patients; all others were tried and failed."[17] As an example of what could result from a mandated, sudden removal of the GED, JRC described one person whose GED was removed against the medical advice of JRC health professionals. The individual soon resumed self-injurious scratching and picking behaviors that led to serious blood and bone infections, paralysis of his legs, and eventual death three years after leaving JRC.[18]

Because the FDA considered the JRC to be the only "affected firm" at the April 24 open meeting of the Neurological Devices Panel, four people spoke on behalf of the facility.[19] Seventeen people testified on behalf of professional societies or organizations, all but one of those in support of the ban.[20] And finally, sixteen people spoke during the public hearing's general session, eight in favor of banning the device and eight opposed.[21] The people who spoke during the general session included five former JRC residents (two who supported the ban and three who opposed it), five family members of JRC residents (one who supported the ban and four who opposed it), one former employee who supported the ban, and five concerned citizens (four who supported the ban and one who opposed it).[22]

The FDA would not agree to show Jennifer Msumba's entire video. She was required to edit it down to three minutes to comply with the rules that applied to other speakers, and it was shown in lieu of her speaking in person.[23] Ari Ne'eman, an autistic advocate and founder of the Autistic Self Advocacy Network, said in his testimony,

> Had my life been different, I could have ended up at the Judge Rotenberg Center. I have the same diagnosis, Asperger syndrome, as a number of those who ended up there, subject to the devices now under review. As a child and into young adulthood, I self-injured, I was aggressive. I was removed from my neighborhood school because of behavioral problems and elopement (running away). If I had been born in a different place or to a different family, the years I spent graduating high school and college and building and running an organization could have been spent subject to a treatment that the United Nations has rightly deemed torture. If I had been slightly less lucky, instead of serving as a presidential appointee and working on public policy, I could be living a life in which not a single moment would be free from the threat of pain. Luck and circumstance, not biology, make the difference. Not every person in the Judge Rotenberg Center is like me, but every person there has someone who is like them in the broader community being successfully supported without aversives. You don't have to be able to go to college or work or even be able to talk right or type in order to live and succeed without aversives. People with severe cognitive, behavioral, and communication-related challenges are served throughout the country through positive means of support, including many with self-injurious and aggressive behaviors.[24]

Other former residents, as well as parents of residents of the JRC, offered emotional testimonies, some speaking against continued use of the devices and some calling the device a "godsend" and a last re-sort for people who hadn't responded to other types of interventions.[25] It was reported that "nearly 20 disability advocacy and patient repre-sentative groups testified that the products were 'unsafe,' 'inhumane', and a form of torture, calling for their outright ban from the market."[26] Jennifer Bellamy, legislative counsel for the American Civil Liberties Union, testified, "The use of noxious electrical stimulants is inhu-mane. The fact that we consider using it on people with disabilities, and only people with disabilities, is evidence of significant bias and discrimination. We urge you to ban the use of these devices."[27]

Rick Glassman, director of advocacy at the Disability Law Center in Boston, the state protection and advocacy agency,[28] testified that the Disability Law Center had retained James Eason, a biomedical engi-neer who specialized in the physical effects of electric shock on the human body, to provide an affidavit.[29] In a previous *New York Times* ar-ticle, Eason had been quoted as saying, "Technically, the lowest shock given by Rotenberg is roughly twice what pain researchers have said is tolerable for most humans."[30] In his affidavit, he described the po-tential hazards posed by three electrical stimulation devices: the SIBIS (which had been cleared by the FDA in 1986), the original GED device and GED-1 (cleared by the FDA in 1994), and the GED-4 (neither FDA cleared nor approved).[31] "Dr. Easton compared the SIBIS (4.1 mA), GED-1 (30 mA), and GED-4 (90 mA), with an electrical fence (4 mA), a dog training collar (2-4 mA), and a cattle prod (10 mA), respectively."[32] He concluded that "the SIBIS shock falls below the range usually con-sidered painful; the GED-1 shock falls within the range of pain thresh-olds, meaning some would find it painful and some may not" and that "the GED-4 shock would be painful or extremely painful to anyone" and "presents a risk of heart palpitations, long-term psychological dis-orders, and neurological effects."[33]

At the conclusion of the open meeting, the advisory panel mem-bers were asked six questions to determine their opinions relevant to the reasonableness of the risk of illness or injury posed by electri-cal stimulation devices; whether other treatments would be adequate to address self-injurious and aggressive behavior; whether available evidence presented at the panel meeting showed a benefit to using electrical stimulation devices, and if so, for what subpopulation; and whether the devices present a substantial and unreasonable risk of ill-ness or injury. The members were also asked to identify potential risk mitigations and discuss how they would address identified risks, the risks and benefits of applying the ban to devices currently in use, any recommendations regarding how people who currently had electric shock as part of their program should be transitioned to alternative treatments, and what concerns panelists had about conducting a clinical study with these devices involving either children or adults.[34]

Members of the panel were not asked to vote on a decision regarding banning the electrical stimulation devices; rather, each panelist's responses to the questions posed at the end of the meeting were recorded. A large majority of panelists expressed that the devices *did* pose an unreasonable and substantial risk of illness or injury, noting as well that any further clinical study of the devices, using either children or adults as subjects, would be unethical.[35] The panel was more evenly split regarding the benefit to people who have electrical stimulation devices as part of their current treatment program, with some panel members strongly expressing that the devices did not provide benefit while others indicated that they believed that there were benefits when electric shock was used as a last resort in certain instances.[36]

Steven Miles, a professor of medicine and bioethics at the University of Minnesota Medical School, commented on the fact that there was very little recent research on the use of electric shock for punishment: "The data is more than 50 to 55 years old. I can't think of any other comparable risk therapy that is allowed to persist on such old data. The plural of anecdotes is not data, especially when it comes from a single treatment center with a conflict of interest . . . There are no subpopulations within the treatment facility for which selective efficacy exists."[37] As the April 24 hearing ended, the FDA was clear that it had not yet made any decision regarding whether the devices would be banned and stated that their primary concern in making a determination regarding the continued use of the devices was for the safety and well-being of people who were receiving shock as part of their treatment protocol.[38]

Anti-aversive advocates understood that it might take some time for the FDA to issue a decision. They knew that the agency needed to consider fully the input received through comments and documents that had been submitted, the testimony of over thirty speakers, and the discussion in response to the questions that were posed to the advisory panel members at the meeting. Still, a year later, there was mounting frustration about the FDA's lack of a decision regarding a ban. On

June 4, 2015, forty-one national and twenty-nine state and local disability rights advocacy organizations sent a letter to the FDA urging them to act on the recommendations of the agency's advisory panel to ban the devices.[39] The letter concluded, "We call for the FDA to issue a total ban on any aversive conditioning devices used for contingent electric shock in order to protect the public's right to safe, evidence-based treatment and the inherent human rights and dignity of people with disabilities."[40]

Five months later, on September 11, 2015, a follow-up letter was sent to FDA commissioner Ostroff from the Autistic Self Advocacy Network; the Disability Law Center of Massachusetts; Disability Rights, New York; and the National Leadership Consortium on Developmental Disabilities at the University of Delaware,[41] expressing support for the advisory panel's finding that the risks and dangers associated with contingent electric shock meet the regulatory standard for banning a medical device: "As representatives of national and state-based organizations with years of experience working with people with disabilities, we know from research and practice that aversive interventions have little efficacy and many potential risks. Our organizations advocate for access to evidence-based interventions and supportive services that respect human dignity and maximize autonomy in place of outdated and harmful interventions like aversives."[42]

After advocating for FDA action for so many years, anti-aversive advocates were delighted when, on April 22, 2016, the FDA published a 124-page document proposing a ban of electrical stimulation devices used to treat aggressive or self-injurious behavior.[43] The FDA's press release stated that it was proposing to ban electrical stimulation devices (ESDs) used for self-injurious or aggressive behavior because they present an unreasonable and substantial risk to public health that cannot be corrected or eliminated through changes to the labeling:[44]

> The FDA takes the act of banning a device only on rare
> occasions when it is necessary to protect public health. . . .
> Evidence indicates a number of significant psychological and
> physical risks are associated with the use of these devices,
> including depression, anxiety, worsening of self-injury
> behaviors and symptoms of post-traumatic stress disorder,
> pain, burns, tissue damage and errant shocks from a device
> malfunction. In addition, many people who are exposed to

these devices have intellectual or developmental disabilities that make it difficult to communicate their pain or consent. As these risks cannot be eliminated through new or updated labeling, banning the product is necessary to protect public health.[45]

In this announcement, William Maisel, acting director of the Office of Device Evaluation in the FDA's Center for Devices and Radiological Health, noted, "Our primary concern is the safety and well-being of the individuals who are exposed to these devices. These devices are dangerous and a risk to public health—and we believe they should not be used."[46] The FDA further stated that it "has information that indicates only one facility is using these devices in the United States, the Judge Rotenberg Educational Center (JRC) in Canton, Massachusetts, and estimates between 45 and 50 individuals are currently being exposed to the device. The FDA believes that state-of-the-art behavioral treatments, such as positive behavioral support, and medications can enable health care providers to find alternative approaches for curbing self-injurious or aggressive behaviors in their patients."[47]

With the publication of the proposed ban of the devices, the FDA announced a thirty-day public comment period set to conclude on May 26, 2016. However, a few days before the comment period was to close, the FDA announced a sixty-day extension of it. Anti-aversive advocates were frustrated by this decision. On June 1, a letter signed by 194 disability organizations was sent expressing concern about the extension of the comment period.[48] Advocates wrote, "The FDA took a full two years before announcing on April 22, 2016, that it had determined that these devices present an unreasonable and substantial risk of illness or injury that cannot be corrected or eliminated by labeling. We were pleased that the FDA finally recognized what the United Nations, disability advocates, researchers, psychiatrists and psychologists, families and people with disabilities have long claimed—these are devices of torture and abuse—and that their use would finally be ended. But FDA's delay in finalizing these rules, by providing an additional two months of public comment raises concerns about whether these rules will be finalized during this Administration."[49]

On June 3, Tom Kraus, chief of staff for the FDA, sent a letter to Hogan Lovells, a Washington, DC, law firm retained by the JRC. Hogan Lovells describes itself as a firm designed to help "clients navigate an increasingly complex legal and regulatory landscape" with "more than a century of experience representing clients before the federal courts, executive branch departments and agencies, and the U.S. Congress."[50] The firm had requested, on behalf of JRC, that the FDA provide an opportunity for an informal regulatory hearing. The reply from the FDA indicated that while the "FDA may, as a matter of discretion, offer an opportunity for a regulatory hearing on a regulatory action in order to obtain additional information before making a decision or taking action," that it had "decided not to offer your client an opportunity for a hearing on the above referenced ban."[51] The letter from the FDA indicated that it had already provided JRC an opportunity for a hearing and an opportunity to present information. They added, however, "In response to your request we extended the comment period on the proposed rule from 30 to 90 days to provide JRC and other interested parties additional time to submit information and other comments."[52]

Over one thousand additional comments were collected during the extended period, with 1,532 comments submitted in total. The Civil Rights Division of the U.S. Department of Justice submitted a five-page comment, with ninety-nine pages of exhibits, supporting the ban. Their comment stated in part, "Through its work enforcing laws that protect the civil rights of people with disabilities, including people with behavioral health needs, the Department has gained extensive experience in assessing whether treatment practices are harmful or fail to meet generally accepted standards of care."[53] The Department of Justice said that the devices "not only fail to meet the Food and Drug Administration's minimum standards for the protection of the public . . . but they have also been rejected by the Department as physically and psychologically harmful."[54] The American Academy of Pediatrics also submitted comments in support of the ban.[55] JRC submitted a sixty-nine-page comment with an additional twenty-one attachments. Comments were also submitted by the JRC Parents and Friends Association.[56]

Disability advocates met with leaders from the Department of Health and Human Services, including representatives from the secretary's office, the Office of Civil Rights, and the Administration on Community Living on July 14, 2016.[57] The goal of the meeting was to establish that finalizing the ban of the electric shock devices was still a priority for the Obama administration. At that meeting, advocates were assured that finalizing the rules remained a priority, and it was the Department of Health and Human Services' goal to finalize the proposed ban before the end of the Obama administration. This failed to occur.

In September 2016, Senators Tammy Baldwin, Richard Blumenthal, Cory Booker, Robert Casey, Al Franken, and Christopher Murphy sent a letter to the FDA urging passage of the proposed rule to ban electrical stimulation devices.[58] They wrote, "The use of these shock devices as aversive therapy for individuals with developmental disabilities is inhumane, especially since many of these individuals have difficulty communicating and alternative effective treatment options are available. Put simply, it is outrageous that this practice is allowed in the United States for this vulnerable population and it should be stopped immediately . . . The harmful, antiquated, and inhumane use of ESDs as part of aversive conditioning has no place in the 21st Century."[59] The same month, twelve members of the U.S House of Representatives also sent a letter to the FDA expressing their strong support for the ban to be finalized expeditiously.[60]

Advocates were increasingly concerned that the FDA would not take action before the end of the Obama administration, which was fast approaching. They knew that delays could be anticipated regardless of the result of the upcoming presidential election and that staff changes would occur if there was a new administration. On October 12, advocates again wrote to the FDA urging it to finalize the rule banning electrical stimulation devices.[61] Disability advocates were even more concerned after the results of the election were in, fearing that under a new administration, the ban would be in jeopardy. Anticipating a potential shift in priorities, on December 21, 2016, another letter signed by over eighty disability organizations was sent to the FDA.[62]

In November 2016 the *Washington Post Magazine* published an in-depth story on JRC based on some of the testimony presented at the FDA open meeting. It described the use of electric shock at JRC as "aversive therapy of the most extreme kind" but explained that for many parents whose sons and daughters were at JRC, "the GED has been life-changing."[63] The article noted that "parents who have turned to the graduated electronic decelerator (GED), usually after exhausting other options, say a ban would force caregivers to rely more on restraints and drugs."[64] The article described that "opponents of the center argue that even if the electric shocks stop bad behavior, the behavior resumes as soon as the devices are removed. They also instill fear in students, who watch their classmates get shocked. Some have reported symptoms of posttraumatic stress disorder."[65] Susan Mizner, disability counsel with the American Civil Liberties Union, was quoted in the article: "Using electric shocks is incredibly barbaric treatment that exemplifies how much we treat people with disabilities differently. There are few loving families who would consider this if they weren't desperate. What we as a society have to figure out is why they haven't been given other options."[66]

The *Washington Post Magazine* article also quoted Brian Iwata, one of the experts on the FDA's advisory panel at the April 2014 hearing. Iwata, who helped develop the self-injurious behavior inhibiting system (SIBIS), said, "It's time to phase it out. The SIBIS is no longer manufactured. We found other ways to deal with the problem."[67] Iwata said that he had treated hundreds of people who exhibited self-injurious behavior at the Kennedy Krieger Institute at Johns Hopkins Children's Center and the University of Florida where he is a professor of psychology and psychiatry and the director of the Florida Center on Self-Injury. He described the people he had treated as including "the most difficult cases there were to see" and said that he had had success with milder forms of punishment, from time-outs to restraints, as well as rewards. "It might take longer," he told the *Washington Post*. "If we shocked everyone who came in the door, we could probably do things quickly, but most professionals in the field do not regard shock as an acceptable form of treatment for problem behavior."[68]

In March 2018, ADAPT held a multiday protest in front of the home of the FDA commissioner, Scott Gottlieb, and at the White House, "demanding that Gottlieb release the regulations that would immediately end the use of an electric shock device to control disabled children and adults at the Judge Rotenberg Center."[69] ADAPT describes itself as "a national grassroots community that organizes disability rights activists to engage in nonviolent direct action, including civil disobedience, to assure the civil and human rights of people with disabilities to live in freedom."[70] Two years earlier, in October 2016, ADAPT, skilled at national protests across the United States, organized an action that attracted over one hundred activists at the Judge Rotenberg Center and in front of the Massachusetts State House.[71]

ADAPT protesters camped out in front of Gottlieb's house for ten days (Figure 17). In explaining their purpose for the action, ADAPT said that the regulations that they were asking the FDA to release had

Figure 17. An ADAPT protest. AP Photo/Tetona Dunlap.

been finished for two years.[72] It added, "Two administrations have sat on them while disabled children and adults are being tortured at the JRC."[73] Cal Montgomery of ADAPT said, "The FDA's job is to protect Americans from harmful practices in the name of medicine, and if torture doesn't count, I don't know what does. We will not stop fighting the JRC until the barbaric practices of this institution are ended once and for all."[74]

On April 7, 2017, well after the close of the extended FDA comment period, JRC's attorney, Michael Flammia from Eckert Seamans, submitted an additional ninety-page comment on behalf of the JRC to the FDA. The accompanying letter noted that this "supplemental comment" was "submitted in response to the numerous factually false comments that the United States Food and Drug Administration received from the public concerning its Proposal to Ban Electrical Stimulation Devices Used to Treat Self-Injurious or Aggressive Behavior." On behalf of JRC, Flammia asked for the document to be made part of the administrative record.[75]

Once again, on April 23, 2018, a letter signed by 217 disability organizations and advocates was sent to the Department of Health and Human Services, the FDA, and the Office of Management and Budget, urging these federal agencies and the White House "to prioritize and take all actions necessary to ensure this critical rule is immediately finalized and implemented."[76] On June 4, more than four years after the 2014 FDA hearing on the ban, disability advocates[77] again met with the FDA.[78] The advocates presented the FDA representatives with printed copies of a petition signed by over 290,000 people calling for the ban to be finalized.[79] Ten cartons containing the signed petitions were rolled in on carts (Figure 18).

The advocates urged the FDA to finalize the ban on the devices and then followed up with a detailed letter addressing questions that had been raised during the meeting, providing related case law and emphasizing the FDA's authority to finalize the ban.[80]

While the FDA process marched on, an important development occurred. On December 18, 2018, the Inter-American Commission on Human Rights (IACHR) issued a "rare formal notice"[81] calling on the United States to "adopt the necessary measures to protect the rights to life and personal integrity of all the persons with disabilities who reside at the Judge Rotenberg Educational Center"[82] and ensure that JRC immediately cease the use of all aversive procedures, including the

Figure 18. Nancy Weiss and colleagues deliver petitions to FDA.
Private photo.

use of electric shock. The IACHR describes itself as "a principal and autonomous organ of the Organization of American States whose mission is to promote and protect human rights in the American hemisphere."[83] The request for the precautionary measures was filed by Disability Rights International, TASH, Mental Health Legal Advisors Committee, and the Massachusetts Disability Law Center.[84] In their seven-page resolution,[85] the Inter-American Commission said that the practice of using electric shock for behavior control poses a "serious impact on the rights" of the vulnerable children at the facility, "particularly on their right to personal integrity which may be subjected to a form of torture."[86] In the resolution, the IACHR gave the Trump administration fifteen days to impose a ban on the practice. An article in the *Guardian* noted that while an IACHR call for a prohibition was nonbinding, "for a member state of the OAS (Organization of American States) to willfully ignore the call of its human rights arm would open the United States to international condemnation."[87] The commission cited the work of the 2013 United Nations Special Rapporteur on Torture, Juan Méndez, who found JRC's use of electric shock to be a potential violation of the convention against torture and other international laws.[88]

MASSACHUSETTS MAKES ANOTHER ATTEMPT TO CHANGE BEHAVIOR MODIFICATION REGULATIONS

Over the years, there were numerous failed attempts to pass legislation in Massachusetts restricting the use of aversive procedures. Massachusetts state senator Brian Joyce, who represented the district in which JRC is located, introduced several bills attempting to get electric shock outlawed. In 2010 his bill passed the state senate but failed to pass in the house. In 2012 he filed two additional bills, one that would strengthen developmental disability service regulations and another that would have required a complete ban on the use of aversives. Neither bill passed, and in 2016, following an unrelated ethics investigation related to campaign spending, Joyce announced that he would not seek reelection.[89]

In March 2019, the Massachusetts Department of Developmental Services announced public hearings and the opportunity for public comment pertaining to proposed amendments that would modify state regulations relating to behavior modification. The department proposed replacing current regulations with regulations that promoted a system of positive behavior supports. They described the proposed regulations as "a widely accepted and utilized framework for both systems change and individual treatment which supports individuals to grow and reach their maximum potential,"[90] and they characterized the new regulations as "an attempt to update a rulebook that has not been touched since 1986."[91] State officials described the goal of the proposed amendments as being to promote dignity.[92]

Chris Klaskin, the legislative liaison for the Department of Developmental Services (DDS), said, "There is a plethora of research supporting Positive Behavior Supports. It is the purpose of DDS to assure the dignity, health, and safety of its clients. The amendment supports this goal."[93] The proposed changes eliminated the use of mechanical restraint (those using straps, boards, and other devices to restrict movement) and limited the use of physical (or hands-on) restraint to certain, well-defined emergency situations. An article in the *MetroWest Daily News*, a Framingham, Massachusetts, newspaper, noted that the proposed amendment "would directly affect the controversial use of a shock device to modify behavior at the Judge Rotenberg Educational Center in Canton."[94] Klaskin said the proposed amendments would not eliminate the use of the shock device altogether but would change the process for approval. "The amendments create a system of peer review when providers seek to use graduated electronic decelerators," he said. "Providers would be required to conduct an internal review and consult with clinical staff. This step would occur prior to petitioning the courts and submitting a request to DDS Human Rights, which is the current process."[95]

The amendments to the DDS regulations, promulgated on February 21, 2020, provide guidance related to restraint (to be used only in cases of emergency; therefore, not as punishment) and require the use of positive behavior support approaches. The new regulations provide additional protections related to the use of aversive procedures but do not exclude their use under specified circumstances and with significant controls.[96] Because the consent decree is still in place, the degree to which JRC is required to comply with the regulations is not certain.

MATTHEW ISRAEL, AGAIN

When Matthew Israel, JRC's founder, was indicted by a grand jury in Massachusetts in May 2011 on charges of being an accessory after the fact and misleading an investigator, he resigned, saying publicly that since he was almost 78 years old, it was time for him to step down and let a successor take over the operation of the facility.[97] Advocates thought that they had seen the last of his involvement in the treatment of people with disabilities, but in 2015, it was revealed that Israel was working as a consultant in California at special education schools run by his wife, Judy Weber-Israel. Controversy over the discovery of Israel's involvement in the California schools may have fueled their closure in late 2019.

After Israel was indicted in Massachusetts in 2011, he moved to California, where his wife was operating three private special education schools, Tobinworld I, II, and III. Israel and Weber, a widow, had married in 2006. She continued to operate special education schools in California while Israel continued operation of the JRC in Massachusetts.[98] The Tobinworld schools had long asserted that they had no relationship with JRC or with Matthew Israel, and, over the years, they had tried to distance themselves from the controversies that surrounded JRC.[99]

Weber-Israel's third school opened in April 2014 with a ribbon-cutting event that Matthew Israel attended. In September , the mother of a student at one of Weber's other schools claimed that staff members had twice pinned her 7-year-old son to the ground, leaving him with a bloody nose and bruises.[100] A state probe into this and other complaints alleged that the Tobinworld schools promoted a culture of abuse.[101] In addition, the investigation revealed that the facility's administrators had not been forthcoming with California education monitors, had incomplete background checks, and allowed Israel to work at the facility without appropriate credentials.[102] It was determined that Israel had been employed at Tobinworld II since September 2013, "providing administrative and behavioral implementation design and planning" services, although he was not licensed and not qualified to do so.[103] His psychology license had expired in 1987.[104] The state suspended the certification of Tobinworld II and III in August 2015. The two schools were allowed to continue to operate under this suspension, but they could not accept new students. In January 2016, a video was circulated on the Internet showing a teacher's aide at Tobinworld II hitting a 9-year-old boy.[105] The incident prompted another investigation by the California Department of Education that found that the facility had taken appropriate corrective action.

In July 2016, Judy Weber-Israel announced that two of the Tobinworld schools would be closing. Her letter to families of students said that the loss of funding had made it impossible to continue to operate.[106] The letter referred to "an unfortunate series of events, sparked originally by a set of false and misleading media attacks against Tobinworld II" led to the closure.[107] In November 2019 Weber-Israel announced that the third and final Tobinworld school was closing, saying that the school had experienced "severe financial difficulties" and that their "financial difficulties were further worsened" by a severe drop in both referrals and enrollment over the past year.[108] Tobinworld's website now advertises that it offers community mental health services, including assessment, evaluation, therapy, rehabilitation, crisis intervention, and therapeutic behavioral services.[109]

FDA ACTION AT LAST

In December 2019, five and a half years after the FDA's Medical Devices Advisory Committee's Neurological Devices Panel met and recommended that the electric shock devices be banned, and three and a half years after the FDA announced that it was proposing a ban, advocates[110] once again met with a representative of the Department of Health and Human Services to urge that agency to encourage the FDA to finalize the ban. In July 2016, three and a half years prior, disability advocates had met with the Department of Health and Human Services and others, expressing concern that the ban would not be finalized before the end of the Obama administration.[111] Now advocates saw the end of Trump's first term looming and anticipated additional potential delays if the ban was postponed further.

A few months later, in February 2020, Senator Patty Murray, ranking member of the U.S. Senate Health, Education, Labor, and Pensions (HELP) Committee, and Senator Christopher Murphy, along with six other senators, wrote a letter to the FDA commissioner calling for an immediate ban on the use of electrical stimulation devices.[112] The senators noted that the FDA had issued a proposed ban nearly four years prior and had announced their intent to finalize the rule in 2019, but that the FDA had "missed its deadline, allowing the continued use of electric shock on people with disabilities including children."[113] The senators signing the letter described this use of electric shock as unacceptable and went further, saying, "The proposed rule would end a barbaric—and disproven practice."[114] Murray added, "It is unconscionable that in 2020, it is still legal to shock children and adults with disabilities as a method to control behavior. We have an obligation to protect children and adults with disabilities from archaic and inhumane forms of punishment—no more excuses, the FDA needs to finalize this rule immediately."[115]

On March 4, 2020, ten years almost to the day after Nancy Weiss first wrote to the FDA urging it to take action to make the electric shock device used by JRC unlawful, the FDA published a final rule to ban electrical stimulation devices used for self-injurious or aggressive behavior."[116] The FDA's ban provided an extended period of time to transition people who had the GED in their plan off the device: "In light of concerns about thorough assessments of the behaviors' functions and corresponding development of appropriate treatment plans, FDA recognizes that affected parties may need some period of time to establish or adjust treatment plans." With regard to effective dates, the FDA wrote, "For devices in use on specific individuals as of the date of publication and subject to a physician-directed transition plan, compliance is required 180 days after the date of publication of this rule. For all other devices, compliance is required 30 days after publication in the Federal Register."[117] Essentially, the FDA was providing a six-month period during which people subjected to the device at the time of the ruling could be transitioned to other behavioral programs. The FDA clarified the specific effective dates as follows: "This rule is effective April 6, 2020. However, compliance for devices currently in use and subject to a physician-directed transition plan is required on September 2, 2020. Compliance for all other devices is required on April 6, 2020."[118]

RESPONSE OF THE DISABILITY COMMUNITIES

While disability advocates celebrated the FDA's decision to ban the device, many felt it had been too long coming. Ari Ne'eman, the founder of the Autistic Self Advocacy Network and one of President Obama's appointees to the National Council on Disability, said, "It is simply not the case the Judge Rotenberg Center is serving the most severely disabled people in the country. For every person in the Judge Rotenberg Center who is subject to this device, there are people outside the center receiving community-based services without the use of aversives that are just as severely disabled." Many advocates believed the ban was not sufficient. "A ban will do nothing to undo the decades of torture that people confined to JRC have had to suffer through until now," said Lydia X. Z. Brown, a disability rights activist, attorney, associate for disability rights at Georgetown Law's Institute for Tech Law and Policy, and an adjunct lecturer in disability studies at Georgetown University. Brown pointed to the multiple opportunities Massachusetts had to stop the use of electric shock for behavior modification, saying, "Massachusetts has a responsibility to make reparations to the survivors." Brown raised concerns about how long it took for this decision to be enacted. "It's been condemned twice by the United Nations, the Department of Justice opened a civil rights investigation," Brown said. "And yet (alluding to the extended transition period), it's still legal. Technically, it is still legal for 30 days in general. And up to six months for some other people."[119]

In the FDA's publication of the final rule, William Maisel, director of the Office of Product Evaluation and Quality in the FDA's Center for Devices and Radiological Health said, "Since Electrical Shock Devices (ESDs) were first marketed more than 20 years ago, we have gained a better understanding of the danger these devices present to public health. Through advancements in medical science, there are now more treatment options available to reduce or stop self-injurious or aggressive behavior, thus avoiding the substantial risk ESDs present."[120] The FDA made clear in the publication of the final rule that it believed that state-of-the-art behavioral treatments, such as positive behavioral support and medications, can enable health care providers to find alternative approaches for curbing self-injurious or aggressive behaviors.[121] The FDA noted that it had banned only two other medical devices since gaining the authority to do so.[122] In the FDA's press release regarding the final rule, it said,

> Evidence indicates a number of significant psychological and physical risks are associated with the use of these devices, including worsening of underlying symptoms, depression, anxiety, post-traumatic stress disorder, pain, burns and tissue damage. In addition, many people who are exposed to these devices have intellectual or developmental disabilities that make it difficult to communicate their pain. Evidence of the device's effectiveness is weak and evidence supporting the benefit-risk profiles of alternatives is strong. As the risks presented by ESDs meet the agency's definition of unreasonable and substantial and cannot be corrected or eliminated through new or updated labeling, banning the product is necessary to protect public health. The act of banning a device is rare and the circumstances under which the agency can take this action is stringent, but the FDA has the authority to take this action when necessary to protect the health of the public.[123]

Michael Flammia, JRC's attorney who had represented the center for over twenty-eight years, immediately announced that they planned to appeal the ban: "The FDA isn't entitled under the law to abandon the science and abandon the scientists and to do something that is politically expedient to them."[124] In response to the publication of the ban, Glenda Crookes, JRC's executive director, defended the use of electric shock for behavior modification. Clarifying that out of JRC's 282 clients at that time, only 55 had the electric shock device as part of their plan,[125] Crookes said, "The treatment is safe and effective and has been in use for almost 30 years with minimal side effects. The GED treatment is only used when court approved and after all other treatment options have failed."[126] The Judge Rotenberg Educational Center Parents Association also defended the use of the GED: "The FDA's actions can only be interpreted one way: The FDA is saying our children's lives do not matter. A government agency offering no effective alternative treatments for our loved ones is moving to take away the only treatment that has successfully allowed them to stop maiming themselves, spend time with their family and to learn and engage in the community instead of being in a locked room while physically, mechanically or chemically restrained by drugs. It is a matter of life and death."[127]

A statement issued by JRC said in part, "The Judge Rotenberg Educational Center will continue to advocate for and will litigate to preserve this court-approved, life-saving treatment. FDA made a decision based on politics, not facts, to deny this life-saving, court approved treatment."[128] The parents' group added, "Let us be clear: we will fight any attempt to remove this treatment from their available care and treatment plan."[129]

On March 27, 2020, the JRC filed a motion for an administrative stay with the U.S. Court of Appeals.[130] A motion to stay suspends all proceedings in the action to which it applies.[131] Prepared by the law firm Eckert Seamans Cherin & Mellott, the petition was 182 pages in addition to hundreds of pages of exhibits. The petition requested that the FDA delay the effective dates for banning electrical stimulation devices[132] and requested that any action to ban the devices be delayed "until the latest of the following . . . (1) the full and final adjudication of resolution of all legal challenges to the Ban, including the appeal of the Ban filed, or to be filed with the D.C. Circuit . . . or (2) until such time as the Commissioner rules on JRC's instant Petition and, in the event the Petition is denied, such time as is necessary for JRC to seek and obtain a stay from the D.C. Circuit in connection with the appeal."[133] Through this action, JRC sought to allow the continued use of the devices not only when a JRC resident already had electric shock applied as part of his or her program, but also to allow use of the GED on people who were not currently using the device but who may "need such treatment because they have not meaningfully improved with other forms of treatment."[134] The petition said that if a stay was not granted, "JRC and its patients would suffer irreparable injury" and that granting the stay would "be in the public interest and in the interest of justice."[135] JRC additionally requested that the FDA grant the stay "in light of the recent presidential declaration of a national emergency concerning the novel coronavirus disease (COVID-19)."[136] The petition sought to make the case that "harm will occur if FDA fails to promptly act to ensure that the life-saving aversive treatment with GED for each patient can continue without interruption, including any attempt to transition the patients."[137] The petition concluded that if the FDA reversed its decision and allowed use of the electric shock device, it would "avoid irreparable injuries to JRC and its patients" and that such a decision would be "in the public interest and the interest of justice."[138] A response was requested within seven days.

The FDA provided a response to JRC on the same day that JRC submitted the petition for a stay.[139] The FDA agreed to a limited stay. They explained that their decision to grant the stay was made in light of the COVID-19 pandemic, in consideration of the fact that people were advised to limit contact with health care providers, acknowledging that the creation or implementation of a physician-directed transition plan had the potential to increase the risk of transmission or exposure to the virus, and acknowledging that health care resources may be diverted elsewhere during the pandemic. The FDA's letter to JRC said that it "finds that it is in the public interest and interest of justice"[140] to grant a limited stay "intended to remain in effect for the duration of the public health emergency related to COVID-19 declared by HHS."[141] Once the public health emergency ended and while JRC's legal challenge to the ban was pending, the stay would remain in effect until the FDA substantively responded to JRC's petition. If the FDA did not grant the petition, JRC would be assured adequate time and reasonable opportunity to obtain a ruling from the D.C. Circuit Court. The

FDA clarified that this partial stay affected only the effective date for those devices currently in use on specific individuals. However, the effective date for all other devices that JRC might recommend for a person who did not already have electric shock in their plan would remain at April 6, 2020, thirty days after the rule was published.[142]

Antiaversive advocates anticipated many additional months of strategizing to effectively end the use of electric shock for behavior management, once and for all. *Mother Jones* reported that since 2010, JRC had spent more than $431,000 on lobbying in an effort to sway the FDA's rule-making on the shock devices and prevent legislation aimed at prohibiting the kind of aversive interventions practiced at JRC.[143] As expected, JRC filed a Petition for Review of a Final Rule of the FDA on November 16, 2020. The sixty-three-page brief challenged both the FDA's decision to ban the devices and their right to make a decision of this nature. The U.S. Department of Justice filed a brief on behalf of the FDA (that is, in support of the decision to ban the devices) on January 15, 2021, and a number of disability groups filed a brief on January 22 urging that the ban of these devices go into effect. Shock devices can continue to be used at JRC until the pandemic is no longer a national emergency *and* all legal challenges to the FDA's ban are resolved.

On July 6, 2021, the U.S. Court of Appeals, DC Circuit, in a two to one decision overturned the FDA's ban on the use of electrical stimulation devices to reduce or stop self-injurious or aggressive behavior. The court said that Congress has explicitly prohibited the FDA from regulating the practice of medicine, leaving that to the states. Judge David Sentelle wrote that a "use-specific ban interferes with a practitioner's authority by restricting the available range of devices through regulatory action." Mike Flammia, JRC's attorney, stated he was glad the decision is being left up to the doctors not the FDA. Frustrated antiaversive advocates knew that they had more work to do and continued to be up against a formidable adversary.

EPILOGUE

I never intended for this book to take more than twenty years to write. I began collecting information on the Judge Rotenberg Center in 1998, after Herb Lovett's death, and continue to do as I write this epilogue. There have been some recent changes. There are fewer people with autism at JRC and many more who have been involved in the criminal justice system. The FDA has issued a ban of electrical stimulation devices, with a temporary stay until the end of the COVID-19 pandemic and until JRC has a chance to challenge the ban in court. The National Institutes of Health issued a disclaimer to the consensus statement on the Treatment of Destructive Behaviors in Persons with Developmental Disabilities: "This statement is more than five years old and is provided solely for historical purposes. Due to the cumulative nature of medical research, new knowledge has inevitably accumulated in this subject area in the time since the statement was initially prepared. Thus, some of the material is likely to be out of date, and at worst simply wrong."[1] I hope this is a recognition of the evolution of positive behavioral supports.

But some things have not changed. Massachusetts continues as the only state in the country that allows this type of painful intervention. I hope that this book explains why that is the case. It would be easy to argue that very good lawyers from a top-notch law firms skilled at deploying families and the media to support the use of aversives and sympathetic probate judges paved the way. But that is too simplistic. In our country, there can be a general distrust of government. Thus, it can be difficult for legislatures or state agencies to intervene in decisions supported by families who fiercely defended aversive interventions. The story of the Judge Rotenberg Center also resides in our history of stigmatizing, institutionalizing, and underestimating children and adults with disabilities, insisting that they are out of control and thereby deserving or needing punishment.

It is impossible not to be moved by the stories of families with children with severe behavior disorders who interacted with hundreds of human service professionals, residential settings, and physicians whose first instinct was to prescribe medications rather than positive behavioral supports that do not "stigmatize, humiliate, or inflict pain."[2] The families were and are indeed desperate for something to work, to fix, to change, or to modify their loved one's difficult and sometimes dangerous behaviors. Despite progress in developing individualized and self-directed community-based services, many families were and still are poorly served. There was a time, thirty years ago, in which people with autism, for example, were routinely institutionalized, and their behaviors were often dramatic, or destructive, or both. They were removed from society and given few, if any, strategies for expression other than their behavior. If behavior is viewed as communication rather than something manifest in the disability itself, the intervention will be different. Robert Cutler, son of Massachusetts advocate Barbara Cutler, who was a central figure in the early organizing against aversives, described what it is like to have a poorly understood disability: "I am autistic. My life has been hell because nobody truly understands autism. I want to tell you, behaviorism almost destroyed my mind and soul. I was asked to act like a seal. Being fed food to do nonsense jobs because I was different. I live a life hunting to survive. I enjoy the opportunity to choose who helps me. This was not always the case. My acting out was the cry for freedom." The self-advocacy movement has empowered people with disabilities to represent themselves, to speak up and out against injustice, and to inform the world about their experiences and needed changes. It was Jennifer Msumba's powerful testimony about receiving the GED shocks that helped advance the FDA ban on electrical stimulation devices. Without the self-advocacy and disability rights movements, the arguments would remain disagreements among lawyers, parents, and professionals. To date, I have not read or heard one self-advocate argue in favor of the use of electric shock or other painful or demeaning procedures.

Today, with early identification and intervention, children and adults with autism and other related disabilities are no longer relegated to institutions. They live at home, have access to early intervention services, go to school in the neighborhood, and live and work in the community. In many states, their families are afforded family support services. They have relationships and although some may have challenging behaviors, there are well-documented strategies used to help people and their families manage them. That is progress. That is in part the reason that JRC is now serving a different population: many from Black and Latinx communities who are more likely to encounter law enforcement officials.[3] Judges and lawyers argue that nothing else has worked. What does that mean? The absence of expertise in local communities, and in facilities in some cases, is not an adequate justification for using aversive electric shock on people who have disabilities or who have had repeated engagement with the criminal justice system. The minute that one accepts the premise that nothing else has or can work, the argument is over. The lack of expertise and knowledge about "what works" should not be an excuse for using aversives. As I researched and wrote this book, I repeatedly reflected on the work of three scholars: Herb Lovett, Murray Sidman, and John O'Brien. Each contemplated the use of punishment from three different perspectives: learning to listen, behavioral analysis and the negative effects of punishment, and professional ethics and community building.

Herb Lovett helped me reframe my relationships with people with disabilities. He explained this new lens:

> People who used to be difficult to serve have been my collaborators in trying to put together services that make sense for them. I have found more and more that there are not so many people who are behaviorally disordered as there are people who have been systematically excluded and inaccurately served. I have stopped thinking about people as clients who need some extra measure of therapy so much as they are freedom fighters who have insisted, often at great personal cost, that what we have done is not what they need. Rather than struggle with people, I have learned it is far more sensible to work with them, to speculate, to guess; to ask the "what ifs . . . we all need to ask as we work out lives to shape ourselves.[4]

This expression of learning to listen and understand is a significant departure from that of coercion and control. Ideally, schools and communities would have the resources necessary to engage and support people over the long haul and not be forced to send children and adults with challenging behaviors away to separate facilities. That is not to say that there are not very good professionals and programs capable of positively supporting people with very difficult behaviors. There are. But there are still not enough of them, which leaves room for those who advocate for the use of punishment.

The professional disagreements presented throughout the book still exist. I suspect they always will. There is probably no study that will convince those with strongly held views that positive behavioral supports are the most effective and morally sound. For example, in 2005, Richard Foxx, who argued for the use of aversives in the Office for Children trial, wrote a chapter entitled, "Severe Aggressive and Self-Destructive Behavior: The Myth of Nonaversive Treatment of Severe Behavior."[5] Similarly, the same year James A. Mulick and Eric M. Butter wrote in a chapter entitled, "Positive Behavior Support: A Paternalistic Utopian Delusion" that said, "whatever else it may be, Positive Behavior Supports is not science, but rather a form of illusion that leads to dangerously biased decision-making."[6] Some are persuaded by their characterizations and arguments but not Murray Sidman.

Murray Sidman, author of *Coercion and Its Fallout*, an important text in the field of behavior analysis, argues that we are a country of punishment.[7] For example, children are told if you don't do this, you won't get that or, worse, you will be physically punished. Unlike Europe, corporal punishment is still permitted in the United States in family homes and even in public schools in some states. I was required to read several of Dr. Sidman's articles as a Ph.D. student in behavioral disabilities at the University of Wisconsin. At that time, I was not fully cognizant of his concerns about punishment and coercion. In his 1989 book, he explains: "I wrote this book to say some things I have long thought need saying not just to professional colleagues but to all the thoughtful people who are concerned about where we are going as a species."

More than once, as I wrote and referenced chapter after chapter, I too wondered how we got here and where are we going. Sidman argues that rigorous laboratory research "supports the contention that coercion is both undesirable and unnecessary" and that punishment stops behavior, but it does not teach new skills, and while it might accomplish something in the moment, its side effects are self-defeating.[8] Furthermore, the argument that nothing else works is unlikely if people are highly skilled in behavioral analysis or functional behavioral assessment and positive behavioral supports. Interviews conducted with four mothers with children who were placed at JRC and later left that setting revealed that none of the mothers had heard of the terms *behavioral analysis* or *functional behavioral assessment* prior to their children being placed at JRC, and they were not involved in planning interventions for their children.[9]

"Knee jerk-coercion is not behavior analysis," writes Sidman.[10] Punishment leads to avoidance and a need to escape. When the 16-year-old JRC student Silverio Gonzales jumped out of the bus onto Interstate 95, one can posit that he was trying to avoid punishment and escape:

> People are always escaping from schools for [people with disabilities]; we react with pity, attributing such seemingly nonadaptive actions to the escapee's lack of intelligence. In many such "schools," however, the residents learn only to adapt to avoidance contingencies that the keepers set up for their own convenience. Escape from the environment does not always indicate low intelligence; it is just as likely to represent a perfectly rational adjustment to coercive control. We should regard escapes by [people with disabilities] as cries not for pity but for help.[11]

I take seriously Sidman's recommendation to ignore those advocating for punishment and electric shock because to not do so, we might be reinforcing the practices with attention. Our attention should be focused on positive behavioral interventions and supports and creating positive and constructive learning communities. However, I also embrace Boston-based philosopher George Santayana, who said, "Those who cannot remember the past are condemned to repeat it." So my hope is that this book does not reinforce those advocating the use of aversive interventions; rather, I hope it educates students, policymakers, lawyers, judges, families, and people with disabilities about what was and still is possible in the United States in such a way that we will no longer permit the use of painful electric shock and other painful and overly restrictive procedures on anyone.

Like John O'Brien, I oppose "the professional use of pain as a tool because it undermines each of the conditions for creating the community which decreases the occurrence of pain and sustains us to live together in our times of joy and our times of suffering." I was an assistant professor at Syracuse University in the 1980s when John O'Brien was working with its Center on Human Policy. That shared opposition to pain as a tool guided me as I wrote this book. It is likely obvious to most readers. In my opposition, I also have empathy for all the families who have been convinced and coerced by professionals to use pain along the way and for the people with disabilities and families that systems of services have failed. My heart still breaks for all the people with disabilities who have endured the extreme forms of punishment described throughout the book. And I am filled with hope by the organization and expression of self-advocates who have given voice to the pain and torment.

Jennifer Msumba introduced the book with her powerful letter to the FDA. It is appropriate that she help to close it. Her experience being shocked at JRC and her testimony helped to achieve a ban on electrical stimulation devices designed to punish. Today, she lives in Florida, makes documentary films, blogs, manages the Rebranding Autism YouTube Channel, plays piano, goes fishing, writes songs and performs, and advocates for people with autism. Last year she won best film prize for her *The Fish Don't Care When It Rains*, her story of survival and growth.[12] Jennifer writes, "My confidence is so much better now. I'm more sure of myself. I'll take more chances, I used to feel anxiety before an experience. I still get anxiety, but now I also feel excitement. I like to do a new thing and then be honest about how I'm feeling doing it—before and after. I like to record my feelings, so people can say, 'Oh, she was nervous and anxious about it—and it's okay to feel that way.' I have been through it—state hospitals, residential schools, horrible treatments for behavior, strong medications. So, I felt like I could help people because I really understand all the parts of it, now that I'm on the other side."

CHRONOLOGY

1971—Matthew Israel founded the Behavior Research Institute in Providence, Rhode Island, with two students.

1972—The Behavior Research Institute's first residential program was started within a private home in Rhode Island.

1973—Judge Ernest Rotenberg appointed to the Probate and Family Court of Bristol County.

April 1976—Matthew Israel and Judy Weber opened a related program in Van Nuys, California; later called Tobinworld. Israel and Weber later opened two other programs in Antioch, California. They married in 2006.

1976—Rhode Island removed all students from BRI.

1978—The New York Education Department inspected BRI in Rhode Island and found it to be out of compliance with regulations. New York made efforts to remove their fifteen students. The state was sued by a group of parents whose children were at BRI. New York lost the case in federal court.

February 15, 1979—U.S. District Court of New York temporarily restrained the state Education Department from withdrawing funding for the New Yorkers at BRI.

January 1979—A team from the New York Department on Developmental Disabilities made a three-day unannounced visit to BRI. The state restricted BRI's use of physical punishment on students from New York, allowing the use only when a child was likely to cause "serious physical danger" to self or others.

January 1979—The board of directors of the North Los Angeles County Regional Center voted to halt funding to the California BRI. Parents went to court to block the move and prevailed.

October 30, 1980—Robert Cooper, a 25-year-old student at BRI in Massachusetts, died of a bowel obstruction. BRI was exonerated but criticized for transporting him to the hospital by private vehicle rather than calling an ambulance.

July 17, 1981—Danny Aswad was found dead in his bed in the

Northridge group home run by California BRI. He was found face down; his legs and left arm were strapped to the bed with plastic cuffs, and his right hand was covered with a sock and tied to the bedpost with a belt-like strap. The staff reported that the straps were used to prevent him from injuring himself, including gouging his eyes.

July 24, 1985 — Vincent Milletich died while being punished for "making inappropriate sounds" while at his group home in Seekonk, Massachusetts. His death occurred while being shackled, with a helmet emitting white noise, his head forced down between the knees of a staff member.

July 1985 — The self-injurious behavior system (SIBIS) device was submitted to the FDA for premarket notification.

October 1, 1985 — Mary Kay Leonard, director of the Massachusetts Office for Children, announced an emergency order to close the seven group homes in Massachusetts, but in response to protest, a Massachusetts administrative law judge ruled that BRI could stay open pending further hearings.

October 9, 1985 — U.S. District Court Judge Joseph L. Tauro upheld the Office for Children's decision to close the group homes as long as other administrative procedures were available to parents protesting the suspension of BRI's license.

October 23, 1985 — Magistrate Joan Fink of the Division of Administrative Law Appeals issued a nonbinding order that the BRI homes remain open temporarily.

November 26, 1985 — The *Boston Phoenix* published "Doctor Hurt: The Aversive Therapist and His Painful Record," by Ric Kahn.

February 1986 — Oxford Medilog was notified by the FDA that SIBIS was deemed "substantially equivalent" to the Whistle Stop Device and thus approved for marketing, with the caveat that Oxford Medilog could not represent the device or its labeling as being approved by the FDA.

February 1986 — BRI filed a class action suit in Judge Rotenberg's Bristol Probate Court against Mary Kay Leonard on behalf of sixty-two students who resided in group homes in Massachusetts. The suit sought a temporary restraining order and preliminary injunction that would allow the use of aversive therapy.

June 13, 1986 — The Bristol County Probate Court ruled that residents of BRI may receive physical punishment. The ruling by Judge Ernest Rotenberg overruled actions taken by the Massachusetts Office for Children.

July 22, 1986—A hearing was held in the Massachusetts legislature on Senator Jack Backman's anti-aversive bill in the Massachusetts legislature. The bill did not pass.

July 30, 1986—The Massachusetts appellate court upheld Rotenberg's ruling that dismissed OFC's ban on the use of aversives at BRI. Chief Justice John Greany denied OFC's appeal and upheld the decision that Mary Kay Leonard was acting in bad faith. She was enjoined from doing anything that would affect or impede BRI's operations without probate court approval.

August 7, 1986—BRI and parents of students residing at BRI filed a $15.4 million civil suit in superior court in Attleboro against the Massachusetts Office for Children.

November 6, 1986—Judge Rotenberg ordered the state to pay $580,605 in legal fees to the eleven plaintiff attorneys involved in the lawsuit against the Office for Children.

December 9, 1986—District Court Judge Paul E. Ryan said in a report that Israel was negligent in the July 1985 death of Vincent Milletich but that no charges were brought because there was no evidence the treatment caused the death.

December 13, 1986—In a fourteen-page settlement agreement, Massachusetts agreed to allow BRI to use spankings, pinches, vapor sprays, and other disciplinary techniques subject to review by the Department of Mental Health and approval by Judge Rotenberg.

January 7, 1987—The settlement agreement, executed in 1976, became a consent decree after it was incorporated as an order by the Bristol County Probate and Family Court.

February 19, 1987—A bill was filed by the Massachusetts Developmental Disabilities Law Center attempting to outlaw aversive therapy. It did not pass.

June 22, 1987—Rotenberg ruled that he would indefinitely oversee the settlement agreement. This permanently (or until it was overturned) took away the power from the state of Massachusetts to regulate treatment plans at BRI.

June 25, 1987—Abigail Gibson, a student at BRI, suffered a heart attack and died. The plan for her treatment of spanking, pinching, and cold water showers had been approved only three days prior to her death.

July 2, 1987—New behavior regulations were promulgated by the Massachusetts Department of Mental Health. They classified interventions as restrictive, such as use of restraint and physical punishment, or nonrestrictive, which did not involve physical contact.

1989—California requested that BRI's license be revoked, leading to a four-month administrative hearing.

September 12, 1989—National Institutes of Health Consensus Conference on the Control of Destructive Behaviors by Developmentally Disabled Individuals. One of the conclusions of the conference appeared to support the use of aversive procedures under some circumstances.

December 1990–August 1992—BRI manufactured seventy-one graduated electronic decelerators and used them on fifty-two students.

December 12, 1990—Nineteen-year-old Linda Cornelison died. The previous day, she was reported to be pale and disoriented, and she kept attempting unsuccessfully to vomit. Because staff mistook her attempts to communicate for target behaviors, she was punished, repeatedly receiving sixty-one aversives on the day she died. Her mother filed suit against BRI and its director, which was settled out of court.

March 26, 1992—The Massachusetts legislature's Human Services Committee held a hearing to pass legislation outlawing aversives. It was unsuccessful

July 7, 1992—Judge Ernest Rotenberg died at the age of 67.

November 1992—Nancy Weiss visited BRI and in early 1993 published "Eliminating the Use of Aversive Procedures to Control Individuals with Disabilities: A Call to Action to Amnesty International." In the ensuing months, she shared the "Call to Action with Human Rights Watch and Physicians for Human Rights."

May 1993—The Hughes bill outlawing the use of aversive procedures and unnecessary restraint was passed in California.

August 6, 1993—Massachusetts Department of Mental Retardation granted BRI interim certification with several conditions.

September 2, 1993—BRI's attorney, Eric MacLeish, filed a motion declaring that the Department of Mental Retardation was violating the Office for Children settlement decree.

October 7, 1993—Three former BRI employees charged that the

center routinely subjected residents to electric shocks and other punishments for behavior as innocuous as mumbling. One stated, "I have seen clients shocked, pinched, spanked . . . for not raising their hand before speaking."

December 1993—Oprah Winfrey aired a show on the use of electric shock.

March 1994—Massachusetts Department of Mental Retardation hires the Rivendell review team to complete an evaluation of BRI. They delivered their final report in April 1994.

March 3, 1994—*Eye to Eye with Connie Chung* TV show about the Behavior Research Institute aired.

July 1, 1994—The Behavior Research Institute announced plans to move its headquarters and school/day center to Canton, Massachusetts, from Providence, Rhode Island, and to change its name to the Judge Rotenberg Center (JRC).

December 5, 1994—The Food and Drug Administration cleared a premarket notification of the graduated electronic decelerator noting that it was substantially equivalent to the self-injurious behavior system device.

February 23, 1995—In Massachusetts, a hearing was held to attempt to pass legislation to outlaw Class III aversives: H. 3358, An Act to Protect Disabled Persons. Lawmakers heard testimony for and against BRI's continued use of electric shock and other aversive procedures. Israel conceded that one student had received 5,300 shocks in one day, stating that over a 24-hour period, a teenager who weighed only 52 pounds was subjected to an average of one shock every 16 seconds, and during some periods, he was shocked every second if he lifted his hand off a paddle. The legislation did not pass.

March 23, 1995—DMR's commissioner, Philip Campbell, ordered the JRC to stop using electric shock as treatment by July 1.

March 24, 1995—Judge Elizabeth LaStaiti issued a temporary restraining order that stopped the DMR's ban on the use of aversives and Campbell's attempts to decertify the center.

April 5, 1995—Judge LaStaiti held a hearing on DMR's emergency motion to stop JRC from using certain Class III interventions. She ruled that DMR could not use its regulations or its quality assurance and certification processes to modify the treatment plans of the BRI students.

June 26, 1995–July 14, 1995 — A trial was held before Judge LaStaiti on a contempt action against the Department of Mental Retardation filed by JRC and its students' parents.

October 6, 1995 — LaStaiti appointed a retired Justice of the superior court, James J. Nixon, as receiver for the Department of Mental Retardation.

October 10, 1995 — Judge LaStaiti concluded in a 126-page ruling that the Massachusetts Department of Mental Retardation had abused governmental power and that the DMR commissioner tried to shut down JRC illegally. The state was ordered to pay the Judge Rotenberg Center $1.1 million for legal fees.

February 1, 1996 — The commonwealth of Massachusetts appealed LaStaiti's decision, arguing that the judge had copied extensively from the briefs submitted by JRC's attorney and had made several legal errors in her analyses and findings.

March 13, 1997 — The Massachusetts Supreme Judicial Court of rejected the appeal on behalf of DMR and Campbell. LaStaiti's finding of contempt and the court's appointment of Nixon as receiver were affirmed, but the award of attorney's fees against the commonwealth was denied.

March 14, 1997 — Embattled state DMR commissioner Philip Campbell and deputy commissioner Mary Cerreto resigned after the state's highest court concluded that department officials tried to force JRC to close.

May 5, 1998 — Silverio Gonzalez, a 16-year-old JRC student, died. He had been at JRC just shy of one year, was diagnosed with paranoid schizophrenia, and had been taken off his psychotropic medication. He was on a school bus being transported from the JRC center to a JRC-run group home when he bolted down the bus aisle, opened the rear emergency exit door, and either fell or jumped onto Interstate 95 in Attleboro, Massachusetts.

February 2000 — The FDA sent a letter to JRC saying that the GED devices were exempt from the 510(k) requirement, a premarket submission made to the FDA to demonstrate that the device is as safe and effective as (i.e., substantially equivalent to) a legally marketed device

October 25, 2002 — Andre McCollins, a JRC student, was shocked using the GED-4 for failing to take off his jacket when he entered the classroom. He was shocked thirty-one times over seven hours

—the first shock for failing to follow the instruction to take off his jacket and the additional thirty shocks either for screaming while being shocked or tensing his muscles in anticipation of the next shock. The incident was videotaped and the footage eventually made public.

2006—Attorney Ken Mollins represented 17-year-old Antwone Nicholson and his family of Freeport, New York. Nicholson had been at JRC for approximately four years and had received shock interventions. The suit claimed that "education officials were negligent by failing to ensure that [Antwone] was not mistreated at JRC."

January, April, and May 2006—The Massachusetts Department of Education conducted a program review of JRC; it noted no deficiencies were found in areas such as behavior management and restraint training, nutritional requirements, toileting programs, parent and student involvement, health and medical services, or transportation safety.

April 2006—The Massachusetts Division of Professional Licensure reviewed the names of seventeen workers listed on JRC's site as psychologists and found that fourteen were not licensed or appropriately trained.

April 17, 2006—Greg Miller, a former JRC employee, circulated an article titled, "I Wonder if Parents Really Know What Happens to Their Children at the Judge Rotenberg Center."

April 25–26 and May 16–18, 2006—The New York State Education Department conducted a visit and review of JRC's program and published a scathing twenty-six-page report, including that electric shock was used for behaviors that are not aggressive, dangerous to health, or destructive, such as nagging, swearing, and failing to maintain a neat appearance. They stated that the use of the electric skin shock as used at JRC raises health and safety concerns.

October 2006—The Massachusetts Department of Professional Licensure cited JRC after discovering that fourteen of the seventeen individuals listed as psychologists on the JRC website were not in fact psychologists. JRC was required to pay $43,000 in fines and later an additional $213,548 to the state for overcharges related to the misrepresentation of psychologists.

August 8, 2007—A former resident, who had run away from JRC, phoned group home staff, posing as one of JRC's quality control monitors, and gave instructions to awaken two residents and administer shocks for behaviors allegedly exhibited earlier in the day. Two students were awoken and strapped to boards. Seventy-seven shocks were administered to one student and twenty-nine to the other.

August 20, 2007—Jennifer Gonnerman's "School of Shock" article was published in *Mother Jones* magazine.

October 2007—Nancy Weiss and Derrick Jeffries sent a letter to the American Psychological Association calling on it to take action against JRC and a position against the use of aversive procedures in a manner that is consistent with its code of ethics.

December 25, 2007—A *New York Times* article noted, "A former teacher from the school . . . said he had seen children scream and writhe on the floor from the shock." The article quoted James Eason, a professor of biomedical engineering at Washington and Lee University: "Technically, the lowest shock given by Rotenberg is roughly twice what pain researchers have said is tolerable for most humans."

March 23, 2009—The New York State Education Department notified JRC that it continued to have policies and procedures inconsistent with New York State regulations and noted that it had been working with JRC since June 2007 to address these matters.

September 2009—Nancy Weiss wrote a letter documenting abuses at JRC and calling for the elimination of the use of aversive and other inhumane practices. The letter was signed by thirty-one national disability organizations and sent to the Office on Disability, U.S. Department of Health and Human Services; the secretary of the U.S. Department of Health and Human Services; the secretary of the U.S. Department of Education; the attorney general of the United States; the U.S. Department of Justice; the House Committee on Education and Labor; the Senate Committee on Health, Education, Labor, and Pensions; Amnesty International; Human Rights Watch; and Physicians for Human Rights.

February 18, 2010—In response to the September 2009 letter, the Disability Rights Section of the Civil Rights Division of the U.S. Department of Justice announced an investigation of the JRC. No report was ever made public.

March 26, 2010—Nancy Weiss sent a letter to Jeffrey Shuren, M.D., the director of the Center for Devices and Radiological Health of the FDA, requesting that the agency take action to outlaw the GED.

April 2010—Disability Rights International published, "Torture Not Treatment: Electric Shock and Long-Term Restraint in the United States on Children and Adults with Disabilities at the Judge Rotenberg Center, an Urgent Appeal to the United Nations Special Rapporteur on Torture." Manfred Nowak, U.N. Special Rapporteur on Torture, when asked if the JRC's use of electric shock for punishment constituted torture, said, "Yes, I have no doubts about it."

September 15, 2010—The lawsuit on behalf of Antwone Nicholson settled for $65,000.

2011—Lydia Brown begins documenting and creating an archive about the Judge Rotenberg Center issue on the blog Autistic Hoya --https://autistichoya.net/judge-rotenberg-center/.

May 20, 2011—Matthew Israel was indicted on charges of destroying evidence and misleading a witness in connection with a series of events at JRC's Stoughton facility where two students were injured as a result of improperly administered contingent electric shock (see the August 2007 description of event) and resigns.

May 23, 2011—The New York State Education Department issued a compliance assurance plan to JRC that required the facility to take corrective actions in order to comply with New York State regulations.

May 23, 2011—The FDA sent a letter to JRC explaining that it had made an error. When it had cleared a premarket notification of the GED on December 5, 1994, and told JRC in a February 2000 letter that the GED devices were exempt from the 510(k) requirement (a premarket submission made to the FDA to demonstrate that the device is as safe and effective as a legally marketed device), it had incorrectly conveyed that premarket approval was not needed for the GED.

May 25, 2011—Judge Isaac Borenstein was retained as an independent monitor to review and assess safety at JRC. His 128-page report was submitted on February 22, 2013, to the Massachusetts Attorney General's Office and the JRC board of directors. The report called for improvements in the areas of quality control and monitoring; staff hiring, training, and retention; staff independent judgment; staff supervision and safety; use of the GED and restraints; response to emergencies; and student health and human rights.

September 1, 2011—The Massachusetts Department of Developmental Services banned the use of painful aversive interventions on any resident of JRC unless a court-approved plan was in place by this date.

April 2012—A medical malpractice lawsuit brought by the family of Andre McCollins went to trial, and video footage of the shocks was made public for the first. In 2002, McCollins, an African American autistic teenager, had been shocked thirty-one times in seven hours while restrained face-down in four-point restraints.

June 29, 2012—FDA sent JRC a warning letter that JRC had failed to obtain FDA clearance or approval for the GED-3A and GED-4 devices and stating that failure to promptly correct violations might result in regulatory action being initiated by the FDA without further notice.

December 14, 2012—The Centers for Medicare and Medicaid Services (CMS) sent a letter to the Massachusetts Executive Office of Health and Human Services prohibiting any federal Medicaid money used for any person who lives at any facility that uses electric shock interventions, even if the person in question isn't being shocked.

December 21, 2012—JRC responded to the FDA's warning letter expressing that it took the issues raised in the letter seriously. It said it was continuing to make significant progress on its corrective action plan and was prepared to discuss an appropriate transition of the GED versions 3A and 4.

January 11, 2013—Jennifer Msumba, a former JRC resident who had received electric shock, sent a letter describing her seven years at JRC to Nancy Weiss asking for help to get word out about her experiences there. At first, Jennifer wanted to remain anonymous but later changed her mind and became an important and outspoken advocate. Her letter was shared with the Department of Justice and the Food and Drug Administration and was instrumental in the FDA's initiation of action toward a ban of electric shock devices.

February 2013—The Massachusetts attorney general filed a motion to vacate the settlement agreement. The Attorney General's Office argued that the settlement agreement was over twenty-five years old, and both circumstances and knowledge about best practice in serving people with challenging behaviors had changed significantly. Probate judge Katherine Fields ruled in favor of JRC.

March 4, 2013—Juan Méndez, the UN's Special Rapporteur on Torture, issued an international report on torture and other cruel, inhuman, or degrading forms of treatment of punishment. The report condemned the use of electric shock and physical restraint used at the JRC and noted that the U.S. Department of Justice's investigation into possible violations of civil rights laws remained ongoing.

April 2013—The New York State Department of Education announced that it was requiring that JRC stop using the electric shock on any New York State student within thirty days.

April 16, 2013—In response to a letter on behalf of fifteen national organizations, advocates met with FDA representatives. In advance, the advocates had sent the FDA information indicating that the stronger GED that was being used at JRC had been modified from the original FDA-cleared device and that shock was being used for behaviors beyond those for which the SIBIS device had been approved.

March 21, 2014—FDA announced that an open meeting of the Neurological Devices Panel of the Medical Devices Advisory Committee would be held on April 24, 2014.

April 24, 2014—FDA's Neurological Devices Advisory Panel convened a committee of experts to seek clinical and scientific opinion on whether to ban aversive conditioning devices that are intended to administer a noxious electrical stimulus to modify undesirable behavior. The committee advised eliminating the use of such devices.

August 2015—California suspended the certification of Tobinworld II and III.

April 22, 2016—The FDA announced that it had determined that the electrical stimulation devices should be banned, including a ban of those used to treat aggressive or self-injurious behavior, as they presented an unreasonable and substantial risk of illness or injury.

July 2016—Judy Weber-Israel announced that two of the Tobinworld schools in California were closing.

December 13, 2016—Two former JRC employees were charged with beating a resident multiple times over the course of months. The police reported that staff had whipped, spat on, and beaten the resident with a belt, punched him, and shoved him several times throughout October and the start of November that year.

March 2018—ADAPT held a multiday protest in front of the home of FDA commissioner Scott Gottlieb and at the White House demanding an end to the use of the electric shock device at the JRC.

June 20, 2018—Bristol County Probate and Family Court judge Katherine Fields denied the motion to vacate the consent decree ruling in favor of JRC.

July 24, 2018—The Massachusetts Office of Health and Human Services announced its decision to appeal the probate court decision that continued the consent decree. No appeal has yet been filed.

October 17, 2018—The FDA announced that it would ban electric shock devices before the end of 2019.

December 18, 2018—The Inter-American Commission on Human Rights called on the United States to "adopt the necessary measures to protect the rights to life and personal integrity of all the persons with disabilities who reside at the Judge Rotenberg Educational Center."

May 2019—The Massachusetts Department of Developmental Services proposed amendments to regulations concerning behavior modification practices that could have an impact on the use of shock at JRC. State officials described the amendments as "standards to promote dignity" and would replace current standards with positive behavior supports.

May 22, 2019—The FDA's Spring 2019 Unified Agenda announced that the ban on electric shock devices was in the final rule stage.

November 2019—Judy Weber-Israel announced that the third and final Tobinworld school was closing in California.

February 21, 2020—The Massachusetts Department of Developmental Services promulgated regulations providing that restraint can be used only in cases of emergency (therefore, not as punishment) and requiring the use of positive behavior support approaches. The regulations provide additional protections related to the use of aversive procedures but do not exclude their use under specified circumstances and with significant controls.

March 4, 2020 — The FDA published a final rule to ban electrical stimulation devices used for self-injurious or aggressive behavior. The ban provided an extended period of time to transition people who had the GED in their plan off the device. The ban was to be effective April 6, 2020. However, compliance for devices currently in use and subject to a physician-directed transition plan would not be required until September 2, 2020.

March 27, 2020 — JRC filed a motion for an administrative stay on the ban with the U.S. Court of Appeals.

March 27, 2020 — The FDA agreed to a limited stay. The decision to grant it was made in light of the COVID-19 pandemic, acknowledging that the creation or implementation of a physician-directed transition plan had the potential to increase the risk of exposure to the virus and acknowledging that health care resources might be diverted elsewhere during the pandemic. The FDA's letter to JRC said that it "finds that it is in the public interest and interest of justice" to grant a limited stay "intended to remain in effect for the duration of the public health emergency related to COVID-19 declared by HHS.

November 16, 2020 — JRC filed a Petition for Review of a Final Rule of the FDA, and a separate lawsuit was filed on behalf of families with children or family members at JRC. The petitions have been combined.

November 24, 2020 — The New Civil Liberties Alliance filed an amicus brief in the U.S. Court of Appeals for the District of Columbia Circuit Court supporting JRC's challenge to the final rule issued by the FDA. The alliance argued that the statute on which FDA relies does not provide FDA the rulemaking authority it seeks to exercise. Congress adopted the statute to permit FDA to move swiftly to prevent manufacturers from continuing to distribute fraudulent or hazardous medical devices commercially during the time it would take for FDA to prevail in a court proceeding. The NCLA brief says that this rationale is inapplicable because no manufacturer is seeking to distribute the devices commercially.

January 15, 2021 — The Department of Justice filed a brief on behalf of the FDA that was followed by another brief supporting the FDA decision signed by the American Academy of Pediatrics, the American Association on Intellectual and Developmental

Disabilities, the American Academy of Developmental Medicine and Dentistry, the International Association for the Scientific Study of Intellectual and Developmental Disabilities, the National Association of State Directors of Developmental Disabilities Services, the National Association of State Directors of Special Education, and the National Association of the Dually Diagnosed.

July 6, 2021 — The U.S. Court of Appeals, DC Circuit, in a two to one decision overturned the FDA's ban on the use of electrical stimulation devices to reduce or stop self-injurious or aggressive behavior.

NOTES

1. A LONG STORY

1. J. Gonnerman discussed the mistaken use of shock in a *Mother Jones* article: "School of shock." *Mother Jones*, 20 August 2007: "Jamie Z. was getting his battery changed; Louie G. received a shock. A former student reports being shocked in error dozens of times, sometimes when the shock was meant for another student or when the device malfunctioned and began to give shock after shock after shock, until staff could get to her backpack and disconnect the wires."

2. Jennifer Msumba to Nancy Weiss. Correspondence, December 2012.

3. Nussi and DeMarco worked at BRI.

4. Walker, Jackie, and Ricci, John. "Report to Captain, Juvenile Division, Providence, RI, Police Department," 19 October 1976.

5. The Behavior Research Institute was renamed the Judge Rotenberg Center in 1994.

6. Comerford, Richard H., and Conn, Joseph R. "Report to Captain, Juvenile Bureau, Providence Police Department," 20 October 1976.

7. Sargent, Richard H. Comerford, Juvenile Bureau and Conn, Joseph R. Detective Juvenile Bureau. "Report to Captain, Juvenile Bureau, Providence Police Department," 20 October 1976.

8. Handwritten draft letter to Dr. Israel. 29 April 1978.

9. Crookes, Glenda. Testimony and PowerPoint presentation on behalf of the Judge Rotenberg Center entitled, "Aversive Conditioning Devices," 5, FDA Neurological Devices Panel Meeting. 24 April 2014.

10. Gonnerman, J. "School of shock." *Mother Jones*, 20 August 2007.

11. Special education pricing details. https://www.mass.gov/service-details/special-education-tuition-pricing-details.

12. Allen, Scott. "N.Y. report denounces shock use at school: Says students are living in fear." *Boston Globe*, 15 June 2006.

13. TASH, an international association located in Washington, DC, remains an ardent opponent of all aversives and promotes positive behavioral interventions and supports.

14. Lovett preferred to use the word *reputations* rather than *disabilities* to make the point that over time, the reputation of an individual was a bigger barrier than the disability itself.

15. Lovett, Herbert, untitled speech. Dallas, May 1996.

16. At that time, her name was Anne Walsh. She later moved to the University

of Wisconsin, where she was a professor specializing in autism spectrum disorders. I was a student at the University of Wisconsin-Madison when she was there.

17. More than thirty years later, in July 2006, she married Matthew Israel in a ceremony in Los Angeles.

18. BRI in California was closed in the late 1980s after reports of abuse, the death of a resident, and numerous regulatory and licensing violations. California, unlike the commonwealth of Massachusetts, succeeded in using its state regulatory authority to close the facility. Danny Aswad's death, staffing issues, injuries, and the lack of licensed psychologists overseeing the program in California justified the state's decision not to recertify the program.

19. "Operant Conditioning," *Merriam Webster Dictionary*, entry 1941.

20. Israel, M., application for certification, Massachusetts Board of Certification in Psychology, 11 January 1972.

21. The Association for Retarded Citizens changed its name to ARC in 1992.

22. Mesa, Ricardo. "A parent's view of treatment." *Boston Globe*, 29 May 2006, A10.

23. "Report of the National Institutes of Health Consensus Conference on the Treatment of Destructive Behaviors in Persons with Disabilities 1989," 11–13 September 1989 , 108–109.

24. After doing something wrong or unacceptable, an individual must repeatedly practice the correct behavior for that situation. For example, someone who stuffs food into his or her mouth has to repeatedly practice eating small bites slowly.

25. Extinction reduces behavior by withdrawing or terminating the positive reinforcer that maintains an inappropriate target behavior. For example, a child may whine at the table and his mother will ignore him until he asks politely.

26. There is also a GED-4, which delivers a stronger shock for a longer duration.

27. Bristol Probate and Family Court, Commonwealth of Massachusetts, Motion to Amend Treatment Plan. Docket No: 86P1168, Order No: 86-P1168-GI, 9 February 1989;

28. A magistrate mandated cessation of the procedures for thirty days.

29. Armstrong, David. "BRI defends 5000-shock therapy." *Boston Globe*, 28 April 1994, 29.

30. Ibid.

31. LaStaiti, Judge Elizabeth O'Neill. Judgment and Order. Behavior Research Institute, Inc. also called Judge Rotenberg Center, Inc. v. Philip Campbell, in His Capacity as Commissioner of the Department of Mental Retardation. Superior Court Department of the Trial Court, and the Probate and Family Court Dept. of the Trial Court. Docket no 86E0018-G1, 6 October 1995.

32. Murphy, Jarrett. "School of shock." *Village Voice*, 3 October 2006.

33. Gonnerman, J. "School of shock." *Mother Jones*, 20 August 2007, 40.

34. There have not been any approved clinical trials that document the effectiveness of or the problems associated with the device.

NOTES (CHAPTER 1)

35. Wen, Patricia. "Showdown over shock therapy testimony moves some critics; new bill would limit, not ban, treatment." *Boston Globe*, 17 January 2008, http://www.boston.com/news/local/articles/2008/01/17/showdown_over_shock_therapy/.

36. Wen, Patricia. "Prank led school to treat two with shock: Special education center duped, report says." *Boston Globe*, 18 December 2007, B1.

37. Goss, Angela. *Investigation Report*. Taunton, MA: Department of Early Education and Care, 1 November 2007, 2.

38. Wen, Patricia. "A parent describes toll taken by shocks: Victim's father blames poor weekend staffing." *Boston Globe*, 19 January 2008, B4:1.

39. Wen, Patricia. "Report says shock tapes destroyed against order." *Boston Globe*, 18 January 2008, A1–A12.

40. Wen, Patricia, and McGrory, Brian. "Rotenberg founder set to face charges." Boston.com. 25 May 2011, http://archive.boston.com/news/local/massachusetts/articles/2011/05/25/rotenberg_founder_set_to_face_charges/.

41. Ahern, Laurie, and Rosenthal, Eric. "Torture not treatment: Electric shock and long-term restraint in the United States on children and adults with disabilities at the Judge Rotenberg Center. Urgent appeal to the United Nations Special Rapporteur on Torture." Washington, DC: Mental Disability Right International, 2010.

42. Hinman, Katie, and Brown, Kimberly. "UN calls shock treatment at Mass School torture." *ABC News*, 30 June 2010.

2. HOW WE GOT TO THIS PLACE

1. Laties, Victor G. "Society for the Experimental Analysis of Behavior: The first thirty years (1958–1987)." *Journal of the Experimental Analysis of Behavior* 48 (1987): 495–512.

2. Lovaas, I. O., and Simmons, J. Q. "Manipulation of self-destruction in three retarded children." *Journal of Applied Behavior Analysis* 2:3 (1969): 143–157; Foxx, R. M., and Azrin, N. H. "The elimination of autistic self-stimulatory behavior by overcorrection." *Journal of Applied Behavior Analysis* 6:1 (1973): 1–14; Risley, T. R. "The effects and side effects of punishing the autistic behaviors of a deviant child." *Journal of Applied Behavior Analysis* 1:1 (1968): 21–34; Azrin, N. H., and Fox R. M. "A rapid method of toilet training the institutionalized retarded." *Journal of Applied Behavior Analysis* 4:2 (1971): 89–99.

3. Brown, Lou. "Who are they and what do they want? An essay on TASH. University of Wisconsin-Madison, September 1990, 1.

4. Opton, Edward M. "Institutional behavior modification as a fraud and sham." *Arizona Law Review* 17:1 (1975): 20–28.

5. Foxx, Richard. "Severe Aggressive and Self-Destructive Behavior: The Myth of Nonaversive Treatment of Severe Behavior." In J. W. Jacobsen, R. M. Foxx, and J. A. Muick (Eds.), *Controversial therapies for developmental disabilities: Fad, fashion, and science in professional practice* (p. 296). Mahwah, NJ: Erlbaum.

6. Kuhlmann, Hike. *Living "Walden Two": B. F. Skinner's Behaviorist Utopia and Experimental Communities.* Champaign: University of Illinois Press, 2005.

7. Kixe, Paul. "The shocking truth." Boston.com, 17 June 2008.

8. DaSilva, Bruce. BRI was David's last resort. *Providence Journal*, 3 March 1974, A12.

9. "History of JRC." Retrieved 20 April 2008 from www.Judgerc.org.

10. Wade, Bert. "Behavior modification has a new home." *Providence Journal*, July 1974.

11. Matthew Rossi to Dr. Harvey Lapin. 29 September 1976.

12. Dr. Israel was fired because of his "radical behaviorist" approach. *Providence Journal*, 5 April 1981. BRI was incorporated in Massachusetts on March 3, 1971, as a nonprofit corporation, and was registered to do business in Rhode Island on July 10, 1972.

13. The 1971 date must be a mistake.

14. This letter reflects Dr. Rossi's perception of what transpired. The facts have not been independently corroborated. Israel may have disputed the events.

15. The committee was established in response to the 1970 Developmental Disabilities Services and Facilities Construction Act of 1970 (P.L. 91-517) - (Amended Mental Retardation Facilities and Community Health Facilities Construction Act of 1963)

16. Rhode Island Planning and Advisory Council on Developmental Disabilities Human Rights Committee: *A Report on the Behavior Research Institute.* February 1973, Unpublished manuscript.

17. "Court orders state to pay for disturbed boy's learning." *Pawtucket Times*, 27 August 1974.

18. Stuart, Richard B. Letter to Ms. Sandra Poirier summarizing BRI review findings, 15 May 1975.

19. Ibid..

20. Ibid.

21. The numbers range from eleven to twenty in various records and correspondence.

22. Later called the June Groden Center after its founder.

23. Baxter, Alice M. Letter to Dr. Harvey Lapin, 12 October 1976.

24. In another letter to Edward Rivo, associate professor of psychiatry, University of California, Los Angeles, August 25,1978, Mrs. Ciric elaborates by saying that the police handcuffs were used to keep him chained to bed all day and to his bed at night—even to a fire escape—hands behind his back on a stool with water squirts in the face.

25. The commercial principle that the buyer is responsible for making sure that goods bought are of a reasonable quality, unless the seller is offering a guarantee of their quality (Encarta Online World English Dictionary. 2011. Microsoft Corporation. 8 August 2011 http://encarta.msn.com/encnet/features/dictionary/dictionaryhome.aspx.

26. Mehegan, David. "Putting Skinner's behaviorism to work." *Boston Globe*, 12 July 1981.

27. Nazareth had chaired the Human Rights Committee Report on BRI in 1973.

28. Nazareth, G. Letter to Governor Edward DiPrete, 26 June 1986.

29. Dennehy, P. Letter to George Nazareth, 24 July 1986.

30. Joseph Temble, then president of the RI Society for Autistic Children, a state chapter, admonished the national organization in a letter dated October 31, 1975, for unilaterally advising member organizations and executives of the national office not to make referrals or have dealings with Matthew Israel. The Rhode Island chapter had only nine members at the time, and two were involved with BRI.

3. ENCOURAGED TO EXPAND TO CALIFORNIA

1. At the time, her name was Anne D. Walsh.

2. Walsh, Anne, D. Letter to Matthew Israel, 16 August 1974.

3. When Anne Walsh divorced, she used her original name: Anne Donnellan. She received her Ph.D. from University of Santa Barbara in 1980, was a professor at the University of Wisconsin–Madison, and is on faculty at the University of San Diego. She is recognized internationally for her work on autism.

4. Assembly Bill No. 2586. Hughes. Chapter 959: An Act to Add Chapter 5.5 (commencing with Section 56520) to Part 30 of the Education Code, relating to Education. Approved by Governor September 17, 1990. Filed with Secretary of State September 18, 1990. The bill provided parameters for the use of behavioral interventions with individuals with exceptional needs receiving special education and related services.

5. On April 30, 1976, the California Community for Autistic Persons endorsed and sponsored a branch of BRI, the same year that Rhode Island transferred all of its students out of the Providence-based program.

6. Weber, Jordan, Secretary Pro Tem. Minutes of Los Angeles NSAC Pacific Center Special Fund Committee, 17 June 1975.

7. Los Angeles County Chapter of the California Society for Autistic Children and the National Society for Autistic Children. Resolution #1/10-28-75. Attested by Connie Bowles, Recording Secretary and Robert Fredricks, President. Northridge, CA, 28 October 1975.

8. Fredricks, Robert W. Letter to Mr. Dennis Amundson, director, North Los Angeles County Regional Center, 6 November 1975.

9. Fredericks, Robert. Letter to Hon. Evelle J. Younger, Attorney General, State of California, 17 June 1976.

10. Gonnerman, Jennifer. "Matthew Israel interviewed by Jennifer Gonnerman: From sugar-coated lollipops to electric shocks, the road to discipline. Jennifer Gonnerman talks with the Rotenberg Center's founder Matthew Israel." *Mother Jones*, 20 August 2007.

11. Dr. Rossi's letter appears in chapter 2.

12. Unsigned letter to Dr. Harvey Lapin, July 21, 1976.

13. Barrera, Edward. "Profile: Radical, Physician, William Bronston on single payer and how med school lacks soul." Retrieved 8 October 2020 from https://medium.com/@edwardbarrera/radical-physician-william-bronston-on-single-payer-and-how med-school-lacks-soul-5b3a00e79bca.

14. See Rothman, D. J., and Rothman, S. M. *The Willowbrook Wars*. Hawthorne, NY: De Gruyter, 1984.

15. Israel, Matthew. Letter to William Bronston, 7 December1976.

16. The letter was copied to Hon. Arlen Gregorio, Hon. Gary Hart, Hon. Howard Berman, Hon. James Mills, Hon. Frank Lanterman, Hon. Leona Egeland, Hon. Albert Rodda, Jerome Lackner, M.D., and Dorothy Miller.

17. Lapin, Harvey. Letter to Katherine Lester, Department of Health, Los Angeles, CA,13 January 1977.

18. Letter from Helen Gray, consumer service representative, California Board of Medical Quality Assurance, Sacramento, CA 95825. Letter to Harvey Lapin, 20 May 1977.

19. Harrington, Charlene, deputy director for Licensing and Certification Division. Letter to Matthew Israel, 17 January 1977.

20. Brock, Stephen E. "Functional assessment of behavior, EDS 240: Philosophical, legal and ethical issues." Presentation at California State University, Sacramento, n.d.

21. Lester, Katherine. Memo to Mari Goldman, chief, Community Care Licensing Branch, Department of Social Services, 14 July 1978.

22. Joseph Bevilacqua has over twenty-five years of experience. He served as state commissioner of mental health services in Rhode Island, Virginia, and South Carolina and as assistant commissioner for community services for four years in Virginia.

23. Joseph J. Bevilacqua, director, Department of Mental Health, Retardation and Hospitals, Office of the Director, Cranston, RI. Letter to Jordan Weber, attorney at law, Panorama City, CA, 25 August 1976.

24. Founded in 1975 by the Autism Society of California, Jay Nolan Community Services was named after the son of film actor Lloyd Nolan, in honor of the elder Nolan's financial contribution to the Autism Society.

25. Gary LaVigna, executive director of the Jay Nolan Center, would emerge as a critic of BRI.

26. This letter is written by an attorney, a parent of a child who has autism. At the time, he was not a member of the board of directors.

27. Lemon Boyd to Godfrey Isaac, Esq. (cc Harvey Lapin, DDS), 5 March 1980.

28. Rafael, Robert A., and Fairbanks, Ronald. Letter to Matthew Buttigileri, president, board of trustees, North Los Angeles County Regional Center, 12 December 1978.

29. Horowitz, Joy. "Controversy on therapy for autism. Part IV." *Los Angeles Times*, 29 June 1979.

30. Horowitz, Joy. "Autistic children: Treatment or abuse? Hearing to determine future of valley school." *Lost Angeles Times*, 14 March 1979. Retrieved 20 December 2012 from ProQuest Historical Newspapers L.A. Times (1881–1987).

31. Horowitz, Joy. "Controversy on therapy for autism." Part IV. *Los Angeles Times*, 29 June 1979.

32. Uttley, Lois. "State probes school for autistic." *Knickerbocker News*, 19 December 1978.

33. Loberg, David E., Department of Developmental Services, California. Director's Decision in the Fair Hearing of Mr. and Mrs. Jack Krieger, Mr. and Mrs. Gerard McCallum, Mr. and Mrs. Sheldon Rosenbloom, Mr. and Mrs. Jordan Weber, and North Los Angeles County Regional Center, 6 June 1980.

34. Bersinger, Anne, deputy director, Community Care Licensing Division, California Department of Social Services. In the Matter of the Accusation against Behavior Research Institute of California. No. L230-1278. First amended accusation/statement of issues, 29 January 1982.

35. Horowitz, Joy. "Controversy on therapy for autism." Part IV. *Los Angeles Times*, 29 June 1979, 8–13.

36. Bronston, William, medical director. Memorandum to Department of Developmental Services to David Loberg, director, Department of Developmental Services, State of California, 29 April 1979.

37. Loberg, David, E., Department of Developmental Services, California. Director's Decision in the Fair Hearing of Mr. and Mrs. Jack Krieger, Mr. and Mrs. Gerard McCallum, Mr. and Mrs. Sheldon Rosenbloom, Mr. and Mrs. Jordan Weber, and North Los Angeles County Regional Center. 6 June 1980.

38. Loberg, D. E., director, Department of Developmental Services, California. Memorandum to Marion Woods, director, Department of Social Services, State of California, 3 May 1979.

39. Woods, Marion J., director, Department of Social Services, State of California–Health and Welfare Agency. Letter to Mrs. Judith Weber, President, Behavior Research Institute, Northridge, CA, 24 May 1979.

40. Pseudonyms are used.

41. Carr, Andrew, personal affidavit to Sylvester Bell, Department of Social Services, Client Protection Services Bureau, 31 May 1979.

42. The former governor of California, Edmund G. "Pat" Brown. His son, Edmund G. Brown Jr., was the governor of California.

43. H. Albert, attorney at law, Law Offices of Ball, Hunt, Hart, Brown and Baerwitz, Beverly Hills, CA. Letter to Marion J. Woods, Director, Department of Social Services, Sacramento, CA, 31 May 1979.

44. Brown, Edmund G., Law Offices of Ball, Hunt, Hart, Brown and Baerwitz, Beverly Hills, CA. Letter to Gray Davis, executive assistant, Governor's Office, State Capitol, Sacramento, CA, 5 June 1979.

45. Isaac, Godfre, and Marks, Rosalind, attorneys for the North Los Angeles Regional Center, Memorandum of Points and Authority, 7 August 1980, 1.

46. Calderon, Benjamin N. State of California, Department of Social Services,

Client Protection Services Branch, Department of Social Services, Community Care Licensing Division, Los Angeles, CA. Personal affidavit, 9 August 1979.

47. Woods, Marion J., director, Department of Social Services, Sacramento, CA. Letter to Mrs. Judith Weber, president, Behavior Research Institute, Northridge, CA, 9 August 1979.

48. *Kate School v. Department of Health*, 156 Cal. Rptr. 529. 5th Dist., June 28, 1979.

49. Ebright, Albert, B. Ball, Hunt, Hart, Brown, & Baerwitz. Letter to Marion J. Woods, director, Department of Social Services, Sacramento, CA, 14 August 1979.

50. Title 22, California Administrative Code, Sections 80341(a) (3) and 81207 (a) (10) 9G).

51. Woods, Marion J. Woods, director, Department of Social Services. Letter to Albert H. Ebright, Law Offices of Ball, Hunt, Hart, Brown and Baerwitz, 15 October 1979.

52. Torres, Art, chairman, Committee on Health, Assembly California Legislature, to Marion J. Woods, director, Department of Social Services, Sacramento, CA, 3 December 1979.

53. The state's attention to the use of aversives was intensified when the state closed the Kate School for Children in October after a forty-seven-month legal battle. The program for children with autism located in Fresno used slapping, pulling children's hair, pinching of ears, spanking and electrical shocks via cattle prod.

54. Horowitz, Joy. "Controversy on therapy for autism." *Los Angeles Times*, 29 June 1979, 1, 8, 9, 12.

55. Ibid., 8.

56. Ibid., 9.

57. Consultant report in author's possession cited in State of California Assembly Health Committee Transcript of Interim Hearing on Aversive Behavior Interventions. No. 781, 1–2, Los Angeles, 17 December 1979.

58. State of California Assembly Health Committee Transcript of Interim Hearing on Aversive Behavior Interventions. No. 781, 1-2, Los Angeles, 17 December 1979.

59. Moser, D. "Screams, slaps and love: A surprising, shocking treatment helps far-gone mental cripples." *Life Magazine*, 7 May 1965, 90–102.

60. Josh Greenfield wrote several books about his experiences raising Noah (*A Place for Noah*; *A Child Called Noah*).

61. Officer Jordan, 273rd PC, Los Angeles Police Department, Investigating Officer, Report of Physical Abuse, 1 May 1980.

62. Although both sets of parents (Rosses and Greenfelds) gave written permission to BRI, which allowed their sons to be spanked, it was only on the buttocks.

63. Director's Decision in the Fair Hearing of: Mr. and Mrs. Jack Krieger, Mr. and Mrs. Gerard McCallum, Mr. and Mrs. Sheldon Rosenbloom and Mr. and Mrs. Jordan Weber, and North Los Angeles County Regional Center, 11 June 1980.

64. Smith, Janice, and Wolberd, Patrick, Licensing Report, Department of Social Services, Community Care Licensing Branch, Los Angeles District Office, 3 March 1981.

65. Smith, Janice, Licensing Report, Department of Social Services, Community Care Licensing Branch, Lost Angeles District Office, 13 April 1981.

66. Notice of Payment. Penalty Assessment #101024. State Department of Social Services, Community Care Licensing Division, Los Angeles District Office, 3 April 1981.

67. Smith, Janice, Licensing Report, State Department of Social Services, Community Care Licensing Division, Los Angeles District Office, 5 June 1981.

68. Wharton, David. "After a troubled past, autistic home reopens. *Los Angeles Times*, 14 August 1986. V-C 30, 32–33,

69. Case staffing report, Confidential Client Information, North Los Angeles Country Regional Center, 29 November 1979.

70. Ibid.

71. Soble, Ronald L. "Controversy over institute is rekindled." *Los Angeles Times*, 18 November 1981, D1.

72. Soble, Ronald L. "Institute broke law, coroner's jury told: Investigator says restraints used on boy who died were illegal," *Los Angeles Times*, 19 November 1981. E7.

73. Soble, Ronald L., "Autistic child's death laid to natural causes," *Los Angeles Times*, 20 November 1981, E1, E3

74. Ibid.

75. Bersinger, Anne, deputy director, Community Licensing Division, California Department of Social Services. In the Matter of the Accusation Against: Behavior Research Institute of California, 9342 Zelzah Avenue, Northridge, California, no. L230-1278 First Amended Accusation/Statement of Issues, 29 January 1992.

76. DSS continued to have concerns and imposed two threshold restrictions: no aversive could be used on any resident for more than six months and use of an aversive was limited to reduction or extinction of "resident behaviors that threat or cause: (1) physical harm to the residents or others; (2) severe property damage; or (3) other serious disruption in the program of the resident or in the program at the facility in general."

77. Marsha Jacobson, staff attorney, California Department of Social Services, to Kim Murdock, Attorney General's Office, Boston, MA, 14 July 1986.

78. Tom Morioka, area director, Regional Center of the East Bay, letter to the Office of Human Rights, Department of Developmental Services, 8 July 1987.

79. Candy J. Cooper, "Homes for autistic accused of abuse: State says staff of 2 East Bay facilities have physically mistreated residents." *San Francisco Examiner*, 28 March 1988, 1.

80. Paul Smith memorandum to Paul Ginsberg, Attorney DSS/CCL, 13 September 1989.

81. Kahn, Ric. "Doctor Hurt: The aversive therapist and his painful record," *Boston Phoenix*, 26 November 1985, 21.

82. Gonnerman, Jennifer. "Interview with Matthew Israel." *Mother Jones Daily*, 20 August 2007. https://www.motherjones.com/politics/2007/08/matthew-israel-interviewed-jennifer-gonnerman/. Retrieved 9 October 2020.

83. Beaudet, Mike. "Graphic video of teen being restrained, shocked played in court." FOX 25 TV/MyFoxBoston.com, 11 April 2012.

84. California Assembly Bill 2586.

85. Brock, S. E. "Functional assessment of behavior." Presentation at California State University, Sacramento, n.d.

86. A functional behavior analysis is a comprehensive and individualized strategy to identify the purpose or function of a student's problem behavior(s), develop and implement a plan to modify variables that maintain the problem behavior, and teach appropriate replacement behaviors using positive interventions. http://www.ideapartnership.org/documents/ASD-Collection/asd-dg_Brief_FBA.pdf. Retrieved 9 October 2020.

87. Hughes Bill. Adapted from SERR Manual, as Revised Feb. 1997. Chapter 8, Discipline of Students with Disabilities.

88. 5 Cal. Code Regs. Sec. 3001 (d), 3052 (a) (5).

89. 5 Cal. Code Regs. Sec. 3052 (i), (l).

90. Tobinworld was named after Judy Weber's son. The name change did not wipe out BRI's history in California; it did, however, provide an opportunity to operate a program without BRI's name and without aversive interventions.

91. "Matthew Israel interviewed by Jennifer Gonnerman: From sugar-coated lollipops to electric shocks, the road to discipline. Jennifer Gonnerman talk with the Rotenberg Center's founder Matthew Israel." *Mother Jones*, 20 August 2007. http://www.motherjones.com/politics/2007/08/matthew-israel-interviewed-jennifer-gonnerman. Retrieved 4 April 2020.

4. PUSHING BACK

1. Rimland, B. "Risks and benefits in the treatment of autistic children: A risk/benefit perspective on the use of aversives." *Journal of Autism and Childhood Schizophrenia* 8:1 (1978), 100.

2. Ibid.

3. Ibid., 100–104.

4. Israel, Matthew L,. director, Behavior Research Institute. Letter to Susan Leary, Massachusetts Department of Education, Division of Special Education, Boston, MA, 3 January 1977.

5. Lester, Katherine S., district administrator, Licensing and Certification Division, Department of Health, Los Angeles, CA, to Jessica Weld, Division of Special Education, Commonwealth of Massachusetts, Boston, MA, 20 January 1977.

6. Leary, Susan, chairperson, Massachusetts State Review Board, Commonwealth of Massachusetts, Department of Education, Boston, MA. Letter to Matthew Israel, director, Behavior Research Institute, 21 June 1977.

7. Leary, Susan, chairperson, State Review Board, Division of Special Educa-

tion, Massachusetts Department of Education, to Matthew Israel, director, Behavior Research Institute, 24 March 1978.

8. The Office for Children (OFC) is a branch of the Massachusetts Executive Office of Health and Human Services (EOHHS). It was established by state legislation in 1972 and is responsible for maintaining the quality of child care services available to children in the commonwealth. The OFC is responsible for establishing licensing regulations for child care operations, issuing licenses, monitoring compliance with licensing regulations, license renewal, and granting provisional licenses and approvals.

9. Judy Weber replaced Israel as the director of BRI-California.

10. Leary, Susan. Letter to Dr. Matthew Israel, director, Behavior Research Institute, 24 March 1978.

11. Slattery, Shirley, and Cull, Mary. Letter to Susan Leary, Department of Education, Boston, MA, 11 April 1978.

12. Israel, Matthew L., Ph.D. Letter to Susan Leary, Massachusetts Department of Education, 17 April 1978.

13. Murphy, Paul J., director Group Care and Placement, Licensing and Consultation Unit, Office for Children, Commonwealth of Massachusetts. Letter to Matthew Israel, 5 July 1978.

14. Cohen, Muriel, and Kenney, Michael. "Providence and Framingham centers: Two schools for troubled earn scrutiny." *Boston Globe*, 21 December 1978, 18.

15. Position paper by Matthew King, assistant director, Bureau of Program Audit and Assistance with the assistance of Mr. Lewis P. Williams, director, Office of Child Placement and Registry, Bureau of Program Audit and Assistance, Division of Special Education, Commonwealth of Massachusetts, Department of Education, 23 March 1979.

16. Ibid., 13.

17. Dr. Matthew King, assistant director, Bureau of Program Audit and Assistance with the assistance of Mr. Lewis P. Williams, director, Office of Child Placement and Registry, Bureau of Program Audit and Assistance, Division of Special Education Commonwealth of Massachusetts, Department of Education, 23 March 1979.

18. Kenney, Michael, "Program for the autistic gets go-ahead in Mass." *Boston Globe*, 27 March 1979.

19. Jack Backman served in the Massachusetts Senate from 1971 to 1987 and was actively involved in BRI litigation and legislation for many years.

20. Loth, Renee. "Jack H. Backman." *Boston Globe*, 23 July 2002.

21. Loth, R. "Obituary of Jack H. Backman." *Boston Globe*, 23 July 2002.

22. Shepard-Kegel, James. Letter to Senator Jack Backman, 2 December 1980.

23. Order Establishing the Special Committee to Investigate Seclusion, Restraint, and Deaths in State Supported Facilities. Commonwealth of Massachusetts Senate-No. 2033, 2 October 1979.

24. Black, Chris. "Parents fight state over R.I. autism center." *Boston Globe*, 4 December 1980, 21.

25. Perl, Peter. "Bay Stater to probe death of Mass. man at Providence Center." *Providence Journal-Bulletin*, 22 November 1980, A10.

26. Perl, Peter. "A life of pain ends for a son who wouldn't be just a zero." *Providence Journal-Bulletin*, 5 April 1981.

27. Black, Chris. "Parents fight state over R.I. autism center." *Boston Globe*, 4 December 1980, 21.

28. Perl, Peter. "Bay Stater to probe death of Mass. man at Providence Center." *Providence Journal-Bulletin*, 22 November 1980, A-10.

29. Ibid.

30. Winship, Thomas. "Eleven troubling children." *Boston Globe*, 23 December 1980.

31. Gerald Koocher was a psychology professor at Simmons College. He is dean emeritus of the School of Allied Health Sciences at Simmons University. He later served as an expert witness in a case that was settled out of court brought by the parents of Linda Cornelison who died while a student at BRI.

32. Senator Jack Backman to Dr. Gerald Koocher, 10 December 1980.

33. Under the federal Developmental Disabilities Assistance and Bill of Rights Act of 1975 (Public Law 94-103), each state was required to have a statewide protection and advocacy system in place by October 1, 1977. Its purpose was to safeguard the rights of people with developmental disabilities. It had to be independent of any state agency that provided residential or other services to people with developmental disabilities. Retrieved 15 January 2020 from https://www.pandasc.org/about/history/.

34. Ted Kurl memo to Dr. R. Guarino, University of the State of New York, State Education Department, "Site visit to Behavior Research Institute," 16 December 1977.

35. Uttley, Lois. "R.I. school for autistic abused students, state says." *Knickerbocker News*, 20 December 1978, 3B.

36. Hermon, Frank. Office for the Education of Children with Handicapping Condition, New York State Education Department, Albany NY. *Review of Educational and Residential Program at Behavior Research Institute*, 28–30 November 1978; Guarino, Robert, director, Division of Supervision, Office for Education of Children with Handicapping Conditions, NY State Education Department. "Site visit report. Behavior Research Institute, Providence, Rhode Island," 13–14 February 1979.

37. Doctor, Norman, S.E.D. regional associate, NY State Education Department, BRI site visit report conducted, 20 March 1978.

38. Uttley, Lois. "State probes school for autistic." *Knickerbocker News*, 19 December 1978.

39. Ibid.

40. Ibid.

41. Meislin, Richard. L. "Doctor insists on punishment of retarded children." *New York Times*, 21 December 1978, B12.

42. Ibid.

43. Meislin, Richard. "Disturbed state children are spanked at institute." *New York Times*, 19 December 1978, B-3.

44. Ibid.

45. "Place is found for 14 retardates in treatment dispute." *New York Times*, 10 January 1979, B4. ProQuest Historical Newspapers.

46. Hawes, Barbara, director of program services. Memorandum and NY Team Program Review Report addressed to Fred F. Finn, Deputy Commissioner for Program Operations, n.d. [1971], 25–26. The following observations were also included in the report: "If——makes noises, she may receive a muscle squeeze to the shoulder. If she makes mouth movements, she may be spanked on the buttocks. If——drools, or brings his hands to his head or refuses to comply, he may be squirted in the face. If——looks away, makes noises, or engages in hand play, he may receive a rolling pinch to his buttocks" (2).

47. Kahn, Ric. "Doctor Hurt: The aversive therapist and his painful record." *Boston Phoenix*, 26 November 1985.

48. Grumet later served as the executive director of the New York State School Boards Association. He closed seventy-five private publicly funded facilities for students with disabilities that didn't meet state standards and moved five thousand students into less restrictive educational environments.

49. Uttley, Louis. "R.I. school for autistic abused students, state says." *Knickerbocker News*, 20 December 1978, 3B.

50. Stanger v. Ambach, 501 F. Supp. 1237 (1980). U.S. District Court, S.D. New York. 2 December 1980, https://advance-lexis-com.unh.idm.oclc.org/api/document?collection=cases&id=urn:contentItem:3S4N-VXP0-0039-S3H8-00000-00&context=1516831; Meislin, Richard J. "New York is blocked in move of 12 disturbed children." *New York Times*, 16 February 1979, B14.

51. Herman, Frank G., State Education Department, Albany, New York. Letter to Dr. Matthew Israel, 7 March 1979, 27.

52. Ibid., 29.

53. Doctor, Norman, *BRI Site Visit Report*, 6 April 1979.

54. Ibid., 4.

55. Ibid., 8.

56. Meislin, Richard. "Disturbed state children are spanked at Institute." *New York Times*, 19 December 1978, B-3.

57. Stanger v. Ambach.

58. Mrs. J. M. Coon, Esq., State Education Department, Albany, NY. Letter to Peter L. Danzinger, Esq., O'Connell and Aronowitz, P.C., Albany, NY, 2 June 1980.

59. Grumet, Louis, Office of the Commissioner for Education of Children with Handicapping Conditions, NY State Education Department, Albany, NY. Letter to Matthew Israel, 4 June 1981.

5. THE DEATH OF VINCENT

1. Harris, Sandra L., and Handleman, J. S. (Eds.). *Aversive and nonaversive interventions: Controlling life-threatening behavior by the developmentally disabled.*

New York: Springer, 1990. There is a clarification that "the aversive procedures were not found to have caused Mr. Milletich's death." Stanley Herr's chapter was contested by BRI as inaccurate because it inferred that the aversive procedures were related to Vincent's death.

2. Only a few years later, screening newborns for PKU lead to preventive treatment of this genetic disorder.

3. Inquest in the matter of Vincent Milletich, Commonwealth of Massachusetts, District Court Department, Taunton Division, 4 December 1986.

4. Impemba, John, and Carrol, Matt. "'Disturbed' teen died during mind-bend therapy." *Boston Herald*, 26 July 1985.

5. Associated Press. "Family doesn't blame death on autism center." *Boston Globe*, 27 July 1985, 15; Zuckoff, M., "Autistic man dies after 'white noise' therapy. A.P. 26 July 1985.

6. Dietz, Jean. "Two parents want Mass. patients out of controversial autism home." *Boston Globe*, 21 August 1985.

7. Ibid., 19.

8. Martha Ziegler, a civil and educational rights pioneer, died September 13, 2016.

9. Senator Jack Backman sponsored legislation that led to its formation in 1982.

10. Dietz, Jean. "Two parents want Mass. patients out of controversial autism home." *Boston Globe*," 21 August 1985.

11. Ibid., 22.

12. Ibid.

13. Ibid., 19.

14. "Section 13. Subject to the requirements of Chapter 30A of the General Laws, the office (OFC) may suspend, revoke, make probationary, refuse to issue or renew the license of any person, assess a civil fine within the limits prescribed by section ten of this chapter, or impose any other sanctions it deems appropriate, in accordance with rules and regulations promulgated by the office. Such action may be taken if such person (1) fails to comply with applicable rules and regulations; (2) furnishes or makes any misleading or false statement or report required under such rules and regulations; (3) refuses to submit any reports or make available any records required by such rules and regulations; or (4) refuses to admit representatives of the office at any reasonable time for purposes of investigation or inspection. The office may temporarily suspend a license in an emergency situation without a prior hearing; provided, however, that upon request of an aggrieved party, a hearing shall be held as soon after the license is suspended as is reasonably possible. Any party aggrieved by a final decision of the office in any adjudicatory proceeding under this section may petition for judicial review in accordance with the provisions of section fourteen of chapter thirty A."

15. Commonwealth of Massachusetts, Executive Office of Human Services, Office for Children. "OFC issues emergency suspension of BRI's license to operate." Press release, 26 September 1985.

16. Ibid., 3.

17. Cooper, Kenneth. "State suspended licenses of program for autistic." *Boston Globe*, 27 September 1985, 21.

18. Dietz, Jean. "Magistrate told of autism center's treatments." *Boston Globe*, 9 October 1985, 30.

19. Office for Children, Commonwealth of Massachusetts. "Order to Show Cause Why Group Care Facility License Nos. 319-P, 394, 396, 397 398, and 399 of Behavior Research Institute, Inc., Should Not Be Suspended, Revoked and Not Renewed and why Group Care Facility License No. 364-P Should Not Be Suspended." Division of Administrative Appeals, OFC No. 1.54. 26 September 1985, 16–17.

20. McClure, Bette, Director Substitute Care, "Office for Children's Decision on the Behavior Research Institute's Request for the General 50 Individual Variance Requests. General variance: Contingent food, file 303," 24 April 1986.

21. Impemba, John, and Carrol, Matt. "'Disturbed' teen died during mind-bend therapy." *Boston Herald*, 26 July 1985.

22. Office for Children (Group Care Facilities License Nos. 319-P, 394, 396, 397, 398, 399, 364-P), Petitioner v. Behavior Research Institute, Respondent, 23 October 1985.

23. Fink, Joan Freiman, administrative magistrate. Recommended Decision. Office for Children Petitioner v. Behavior Research Institute, Respondent, Division of Administrative Law Appeals, Commonwealth of Massachusetts, 23 October 1985.

24. MacLeish, Roderick, Jr., and Roitman, Michael B., Fine & Ambrogne. Post-trial Brief of Respondent Behavior Research Institute, 21 October 1985.

25. Robert Sherman, the attorney for the families, received the Association for Behavior Analysis Humanitarian Award in 1987. He was an effective litigator and includes in the biography of his law firm, Greenberg Traurig, LLP, the fact that he "represented educational center in landmark case resulting in Massachusetts state agency being ordered into receivership." He also published at least two articles related to aversives, fundamental rights, and the courts: "Applying the Least Restrictive Alternative Principle to Treatment Decisions: A Legal and Behavioral Analysis," *Behavior Analyst* 16:1 (1993), and "Aversives, Fundamental Rights and the Courts," *Behavior Analyst* 14:2 (1991).

26. Dietz, Jean. "Parents protest decision to halt controversial program for autistic youth." *Boston Globe*, 1 October 1985, 26.

27. Ibid.

28. Ibid.

29. Cooper, Kenneth. "State suspends licenses of program for autistic." *Boston Globe*, 27 September 1985.

30. Dietz, Joan. "Autism treatment institute appeals suspension." *Boston Globe*, 3 October 1985, p. 36.

31. Spataro, Michael J. "This is where they start to live." *Regional News, UPI*. 6 October 1985.

32. Dietz, Joan. "Parents in confrontation over plans to shut autism center's group homes." *Boston Globe*, 23 October 1985, 21.

33. "Top ten winning trial lawyers, 2003." *National Law Journal*, retrieved 18 April 2021 from https://www.chelaw.com/the-sexual-abuse-survivors-law-group .html.

34. Matchan, Linda. "For accusers' attorney, case's high profile is a plus." *Boston Globe*, 24 September 1992, 59.

35. Wallace, Christina. "Eric MacLeish: JRC's right hand man." *Neponset Valley Daily News*, 20 January 2000.

36. Dockser, Amy. "Making the wheels squeak." *American Lawyer* (May 1988): 112.

37. Ibid., 111.

38. Ibid., 112.

39. English, Bella. "Hole in the heart of a star." *Boston Globe*, 18 April 2010, A1, A18.

40. MacLeish, who represented BRI, had clerked for Judge Tauro in 1978 and 1979.

41. Deitz, Jean. "Judge backs plan to close school for autistic." *Boston Globe*, 10 October 1985, 35.

42. Ibid.

43. Associated Press. "Gain for parents in autism dispute." *New York Times*, 13 October 1985, 68.

44. Reflecting on the development of behaviorism associated with Skinner, the National Institute on Mental Health (NIMH) published in *Behavior Modification: Perspective on a Current Issue* in 1976. The report stated: "Aversive procedures can be and have been seriously misused so that they become a means by which a person in power can exercise control or retribution over those in his charge. The abusive treatment may be justified by calling it therapeutic and labeling it behavior modification. While many behavior modification techniques, such as shock and time-out are effective, it is unfortunately true that they are also cheap and easy to apply, requiring little if any specialized knowledge on the part of the person using—or misusing them."

45. Dietz, Joan. "Psychologist B. F. Skinner come to defense of autistic center leader." *Boston Globe*, 17 October 1985, 33.

46. Ibid.

47. Kahn, R. "Doctor Hurt." *Boston Phoenix*, 26 November 1985, 3.

48. Dietz, Joan. "Autism school gets a go-ahead for now." *Boston Globe*, 24 October 1985, 25.

49. Rattray, Jim. *Regional News*. UPI. 23 October 1985.

50. Dietz, Jean. "Mass. to pull clients from autism school." *Boston Globe*, 25 October 1985, 28.

51. Callahan, Christopher. "Prosecutor begins probe in death of autistic man." *Boston Globe*, 26 October 1985, 23.

52. Dietz, Joan. "Mass. to pull clients from autism school." *Boston Globe*, 25 October 1985, 28.

53. "Autistic children's needs." *Boston Globe*, 25 October 1985, 22.

54. Kahn, R. "Doctor Hurt." *Boston Phoenix*, 26 November 1985.

55. Moser, Don, and Grant, Allan. "Screams, slaps and love." *Life Magazine*, 7 May 1965, 90, 93.

56. Among the many researchers conducting work in the area of positive approaches were Doug Guess, Glen Dunlap, Robert Horner, Ted Carr, and Ian Evans.

57. LaVigna, G. W., and Donnellan, A. M. *Alternatives to punishment: Solving behavior problems with non-aversive strategies*. New York: Irvington, 1986.

58. I was a graduate student at the University of Wisconsin-Madison at the time and knew Dr. Donnellan and her graduate students.

59. Donnellan, A., ed. *Classic readings in autism*. New York: Teachers College Press, 1985.

60. Dietz, Joan. "Head of autism center seeks recommendations: Asks specialist for alternatives to some treatments." *Boston Globe*, 19 November 1985, 23.

61. Rattray, Jim. *Regional News, UPI*. 21 November 1985.

62. In 2000 Richard J. Landau was an attorney in Ann Arbor, Michigan, and is recognized in the area of disability rights and special education.

63. Donnellan, Anne, M. Letter to Board of Bar Overseers, Boston, MA, 11 November 1985.

64. Attorney Sherman served in the attorney general's office during the lawsuit that followed the one against OFC and later became a partner at Greenberg Traurig with BRI's attorney, Eric MacLeish.

65. Sherman, Robert. Letter to Dermot Meagher, First Assistant Bar Counsel, Board of Overseers, Boston, MA, 20 December 1985.

66. Donnellan, Anne M. Letter to Dermot Meagher, First Assistant Bar Counsel, Office of the Bar Counsel, Boston, MA, 3 February 1986.

67. Plummer, W. "Some call it torture, but a New England school says that its therapy is taming autistic students." *People Magazine Weekly*, 14 April 1986, 63–69.

68. Dietz, Jean. "Head of autism center seeks recommendations." *Boston Globe*, 19 November 1985.

69. Deitz, Jean. "Psychologist to offer other ways to deal with center's autistic clients." *Boston Globe*, 8 December 1985, 49; Donnellan, Anne. Letter to Dr. Matthew Israel, director, Behavior Research Institute, Providence, RI, 25 November 1985.

70. I contacted Ric Kahn later when he was a reporter for the *Boston Globe*. He was reluctant to speak to me because he had been legally challenged by BRI for lack of accuracy in his reporting. According to Kahn, it was related to specific dates and time lines rather than the content of the story itself.

71. New York was threatening to withdraw students at the same time the OFC case was developing and being heard.

72. Kahn, Ric. Letter to Dr. Anne M. Donnellan, University of Wisconsin–Madison, 26 November 1985.

73. Kahn, Ric. "Doctor Hurt: The aversive therapist and his painful record." *Boston Phoenix*, 26 November 1985, 29.

74. Ibid., 28.

75. Dietz, Joan. "Judge rules center can resume punishment therapy for 5 despite ban." *Boston Globe*, 4 February 1985, 65.

76. Rattray, Jim. No title. UPI, *Regional News*. 5 December 1985.

77. Wicker, L. Letter to William Bradford Reynolds, U.S. Department of Justice, 23 January 1986.

78. Gould, Lark Ellen. *Regional News*. UPI. 26 December 1985. Retrieved February 15, 2000.

79. Professionals opposed to the use of aversives sometimes were considered biased, and therefore their expertise was questioned. Twenty years later, Judge Elizabeth LaStaiti, Rotenberg's successor, dismissed the expert testimony of professionals who argued that aversives were not necessary.

80. Gould, Lark Ellen. UPI, *Regional News*, 26 December 1985.

81. Dietz, Jean. "Autism center will appeal ruling to allow examination." *Boston Globe*, 27 December 1985, 30.

82. Ibid.

83. Leonard v. BRI. Commonwealth of Massachusetts, Appeals Court. MK [Mary Kay Leonard]. 28 January 1986.

84. Dietz, Joan. "Task force appointed on treatment for autistic." *Boston Globe*, 27 November 1985, 50.

85. Israel, Matthew. Letter to Mr. James Gleich, Director, Office of Handicapped Affairs, 10 January 1986, 7.

86. Superintendent of Belchertown State School v. Saikewicz, 373 Mass. 728 (1977).

87. Rattray, Jim. UPI, *Regional News*, 3 December 1985.

88. He was considered a child advocate and in 1988 received the annual American Bar Association's prestigious Franklin N. Flaschner Award recognizing him as one of the nation's outstanding trial court judges. He was the first judge from Massachusetts to ever receive the award. Richard Brink, who worked at BRI, nominated Rotenberg for the award, saying he demonstrated "integrity, intellectual courage, impartiality, [and] diligence in judicial duties," as well as sound judgment in deciding cases. In several news articles, he described the impact of visiting BRI and seeing Janine regress after having the electric shock terminated.

89. Butterfield, Fox. "Discipline ruling at autism facility." *New York Times*, 31 December 1985, 5 B.

90. Shapiro, Joe. *No pity: People with disabilities forging a new civil rights movement*. New York: Random House, 1993.

91. Janine had been at the Judge Rotenberg Center since at least 1981 when she was 11 years old. Jennifer Gonnerman met her when she wrote "School of

Shock" for *Mother Jones*, 20 August 2007): "Nearly half her life — Janine has been hooked up to Israel's shock device. A couple years ago, when the shocks began to lose their effect, the staff switched the devices inside her backpack to the much more painful ged-4." In October 2020 the center posted on its social media that Janine, who was still at the facility, had celebrated her fiftieth birthday.

92. Linscheid, Thomas R., and Reichenbach, Heidi. "Multiple factors in the long-term effectiveness of contingent electric shock treatment for self-injurious behavior: A case example." *Research in Developmental Disabilities* 23:2 (2002): 161–177.

93. UPI, *Regional News*, 18 December 1985.

94. Butterfield, Fox. "Discipline ruling at autism facility." *New York Times*, 31 December 1985, 5.

95. Associated Press. "Aversive therapy is working." *Boston Globe*, 10 January 1986, 26.

96. Fink, Joan Freiman, administrative magistrate, Division of Administrative Law Appeals, Commonwealth of Massachusetts. Interim Order. Office for Children, Petitioner, v. Behavior Research Institute, Inc., Respondent. 30 December 1985.

97. Ibid.

98. Dietz, Jean. "Autism center's therapy ban modified." *Boston Globe*, 31 December 1985, 13; Dietz, Jean. "Parents of autistic students appeal to judge." *Boston Globe*, 1 February 1986, 23.

99. Beaton, B., Office for Children. Letter to Eric MacLeish, 24 January 1986.

100. Ibid.

101. McLeish, E. Letter to Brenda Beaton, Esq., Office for Children, Boston, MA, 29 January 1986.

102. Findings in Support of Preliminary Injunctive Relief, Procedural History Behavior Research Institute, Inc. and Leo Soucy, Individually and as Parent and Next Friend of Brendon Soucy: Peter Biscardi, Individually and as Parent and Next Friend of P. J. Biscardi; on Behalf of the Class of All Students at the Behavior Research Institute, Inc., Their Parents and Guardians v. Mary Kay Leonard, in Her Capacity as Director of the Massachusetts Office for Children, 4 June 1986, 3.

103. Ibid., 4.

104. Ibid.

105. Ibid., 5.

106. Castellucci, John. "Mass DA asks inquest in death of BRI patient who was undergoing aversive therapy for autism." *Providence Journal*, 15 February 1986. http://archives.Projo.com.

107. Pina in an informal meeting told Barbara Cutler with the Autism Services Association and Bill Crane, executive director of the Developmental Disabilities Law Center, both ardent opponents of BRI, that Vincent's hip had been broken.

108. Deitz, Joan. "Questions remain on aversive therapy for the autistic." *Boston Globe*, 16 February 1986, 46.

109. Castellucci, John. "Judge orders OFC chief to explain therapy ban." *Providence Journal*, 25 February 1986, A3.

110. Commonwealth of Massachusetts, Trial Court, Probate and Family Court Department. Docket 86E0018-G1; cross reference 85P 2137, 86P 0192-G1, 86P 0193-G1, 86P 0194-G1, 86P 0195-G1, 86P 0211-G1.

111. LaPlante, Joseph, R. "BRI, parents ask court to appoint 'neutral party' to oversee institute. Mass. Department director is defendant." *Providence Journal*, 2 March 1986, C2.

112. Ibid.

113. Ibid.

114. UPI, *Regional News*, 28 February 1986.

115. LaPlante, Joseph R. "BRI parents ask court to appoint 'neutral party' to oversee institute, Mass. Department director is defendant." *Providence Journal*, 2 March 1986, C2.

116. Findings in Support of Preliminary Injunctive Relief. Procedural History Behavior Research Institute, Inc. and Leo Soucy, Individually and as Parent and Next Friend of Brendon Soucy: Peter Biscardi, Individually and as Parent and Next Friend of P. J. Biscardi; on Behalf of the Class of All Students at the Behavior Research Institute, Inc., Their Parents and Guardians v. Mary Kay Leonard, in Her Capacity as Director of the Massachusetts Office for Children, 4 June 1986. Probate and Family Court Department No. 0018-G1.

117. LaPlante, Joseph, P. "Panel set to consider physical punishment at BRI." *Providence Journal*, 8 March 1986, A5.

118. Findings in Support of Preliminary Injunctive Relief. Procedural History Behavior Research Institute, Inc. and Leo Soucy, Individually and as Parent and Next Friend of Brendon Soucy: Peter Biscardi, Individually and as Parent and Next Friend of P. J. Biscardi; on Behalf of the Class of All Students at the Behavior Research Institute, Inc., Their Parents and Guardians v. Mary Kay Leonard, in her capacity as Director of the Massachusetts Office for Children, 4 June 1986. Probate and Family Court Department No. 0018-G1, 6.

119. Dietz, Jean. "Parents of autistic students appeal to judge." *Boston Globe*, 1 February 1986, 23.

120. LaPlante, J. "State administrator defends decision to ban punishment of autistic by BRI." *Providence Journal*, 22 May 1986, A10. Third Amended Complaint. Behavior Research Institute, Inc. Dr. Matthew Israel: Leo Soucy, Individually and as Parent and Next Friend of Brendon Soucy: Peter Biscardi, Individually and as Parent and Next Friend of P. J. Biscardi; on Behalf of the Class of All Students at the Behavior Research Institute, Inc., Their Parents and Guardians v. Mary Kay Leonard, in Her Capacity as Director of the Massachusetts Office for Children, 4 June 1986, 20.

121. Commonwealth of Massachusetts, Office of Handicapped Affairs, Board of Education meeting minutes, 25 March 1986.

122. MacLeish, Eric. Letter to Kenneth Schwatz, Executive Office of Human

Services re: Behavior Research Institute, State Office of Handicapped Affairs, 27 March 1986.

123. Ibid., 2.

124. Beaton, Brenda. Office for Children. Letter to Roderick MacLeish, Fine and Ambrogne, 28 March 1986.

125. "Mass. judge restores punishment of autistics." *Providence Journal*, 3 February 1986, C4.

126. Favel, J., Laski, F., Lovaas, I., Meyer, L., & Ratey, J. "Report of the panel appointed by the Commonwealth of Massachusetts, Office for Children to review variance requests submitted by Behavior Research Institute," 28 March 1986, 15.

127. Ibid., 18.

128. DMH was funding many BRI students. OFC had the regulatory authority for licensing of group homes but was not the funding agent.

129. LaPlante, Joseph R. "Thirty autistic pupils, 2.6 million in fees to be pulled from BRI by Mass., N.Y." *Providence Journal Bulletin*, 29 May 1986, A3.

130. Ibid.

131. Ibid.

132. Massachusetts Developmental Disabilities Council, "A Chronology of Recent Development Involving the Office for Children and BRI," 13 June 1986.

133. Barnes, Martie. "Massachusetts orders aversive therapy ban at RI behavioral center for autism." *Boston Globe*, 26 April 1986, 14.

134. Matson later formed the Committee for the Right to Treatment. Its expressed purpose was "to develop a membership advocacy organization composed of persons willing to write letters and provide other appropriate assistance to oppose anti-behavioral bills," to be available for commenting on proposed guidelines to regulate behavioral interventions, as well as to serve as a resource to speak out for effective behavioral interventions. He urged interested members to oppose proposed legislation to regulate aversives in California and Massachusetts.

135. LaPlante, Joseph, R. "Psychologist rips ban on BRI punishments. Says state order threatens treatment of autistic patients." *Providence Journal*, 13 May 1986, A3.

136. LaPlante, Joseph R. "Proposals on BRI due in court Tuesday. Judge wants school, state to submit final positions on ban for aversive therapy." *Providence Journal*, 23 May 1986, A14.

137. Paul Dever School was the state institution in Taunton. In the 1973 case of Massachusetts Association for Retarded Citizens v. Dukakis, the Massachusetts ARC along with local ARC parent groups from the Wrentham and Paul A. Dever State Schools, filed this case in federal court, challenging that the constitutional rights of residents in these facilities had been violated. In 1975, a consent decree was signed by Governor Michael Dukakis agreeing to bring these five facilities—Belchertown, Dever, Fernald, Monson, and Wrentham—up to

Federal Title 19 Medicaid status. Retrieved 16 January 2011, from http://www.arcmass.org/ArcMassHome/WhoWeAre/lawsuits/tabid/615/Default.aspx.

138. LaPlante, Joseph. "Massachusetts Travis accuses state of harassing BRI: Legislator contends autistic children are being left in limbo." *Providence Journal*, 15 May 1986, A10.

139. Ibid.

140. Ibid.

141. "The purpose of a temporary injunction is to maintain the status quo and prevent irreparable damage or change before the legal questions are determined. After the trial, the court may issue a 'permanent injunction' (making the temporary injunction a lasting rule) or 'dissolve' (cancel) the temporary injunction." Retrieved 29 July 2008, from http://dictionary.law.com.

142. LaPlante, Joseph R. "State administrator defends decision to ban punishment of autistic by BRI." *Providence Journal*, 22 May 1986, A10.

143. Ibid.

144. LaPlante, Joseph, R. "State administrator defends decision to ban punishment of autistic by BRI." *Providence Journal*, 22 May 1986, A-10.

145. A preliminary injunction is a court order made in the early stages of a lawsuit or petition that prohibits the parties from doing an act that is in dispute, thereby maintaining the status quo until there is a final judgment after trial.

146. Associated Press. "Dukakis, groups reaffirm opposition to BRI aversives." *Providence Journal*, 6 June 1986, A2.

147. LaPlante, Joseph R. "Court bans state from closing homes for the autistic: Ruling leaves open possibility of restoring aversives." *Providence Journal*, 5 June 1986, A3.

148. Butterfield, Fox. "Judge backs discipline at institute for autistic." *New York Times*, 5 June 1986, A16.

149. LaPlante, J. R. "Court bans state from closing homes for the autistic: Ruling leaves open possibility of restoring aversives." *Providence Journal*, 5 June 1986, A3.

150. Dietz, Jean. "Judge reinstates punishment therapy." *Boston Globe*, 5 June 1986, 29.

151. Ibid.

152. Associated Press. "Dukakis, groups reaffirm opposition to BRI aversives." *Providence Journal*, 6 June 1986, A2.

153. Developmental Disabilities Law Center. "Parents and advocates criticize probate court order on use of aversive therapy." Press release, 5 June 1986.

154. Roberts, John, Kramer, Eileen, Larking, Thomas, and Crane, William. "Aversive treatment violates standards of care." *Boston Globe*, 20 June 1986, 10.

155. States and territories are funded by the U.S. Department of Health and Human Services to have a protection and advocacy center to protect the legal rights of citizens with developmental disabilities.

156. Crane, William, executive director, Developmental Disabilities Law Center. Memo re: Recent developments. 6 June 1986.

157. Shaw, J., and Larkin, T., MA Developmental Disabilities Council. Letter to Justices Mason, Podolski, and Morse, 11 June 1986.

158. Williams, J. Memo to Lorraine Grieff. "Correspondence involving Council's request to administrative justices requesting they assign a judge not involved in the BRI cases to the superior court review; and follow-up criticizing me." Massachusetts Developmental Disabilities Council." 21 April 1992.

159. "Severely afflicted children's care." *Boston Globe*, 13 June 1986, 10.

160. UPI. "Judge upholds ruling for BRI." *Regional News*, 30 July1986.

161. Associated Press. "Appeal court rules Mass. can't prohibit BRI treatment." *Providence Journal*, 31 July 1986, A3.

162. Ibid.

163. Ribadeneira, Diego. "Justice upholds punishment therapy ruling." *Boston Globe*, 31 July 1986, 28.

164. Ferleger, David. "Preliminary comments on investigatory and legal options with regard to Behavior Research Institute, Inc.," 21 July 1986.

165. Hoey, John. "Inquest set for September in death of autistic student." *Taunton Daily Gazette*, 23 July 1986, 7.

166. Associated Press. "Use of physical punishments in treating disabled is debated." *Providence Journal*, 23 July 1986, A3.

167. Fuller, Brian. "Parents sue agency head for $15 million." UPI, Regional News, 7 August 1986.

168. Fuller, Brian. "Autism center regrouping amid court battle." UPI, Regional News, 8 August 1986.

169. Mintz, Jim. Letter to Roone Arledge, 7 August 1986.

170. Hoey, John. "Inquest set for September in death of autistic student." *Taunton Daily Gazette*, 23 July 1986, 7.

171. LaPlante, Joseph. R. "Inquest to be held in death of autistic man who received aversive therapy at BRI." *Providence Journal-Bulletin*, 23 July 1986, A3.

172. Harris, Allyson. "Vigil to mark anniversary of BRI death. Parents, advocates march in Taunton." *Sun Chronicle*, 22 July 1986, 3.

173. Milletich, Mary Ann. Letter to Mrs. Lorraine Greiff and Family, 17 October 1986.

174. "BRI director disputes account of treatment." *Providence Journal*, 10 September 1986, A14. Boundy, Marcia. "Court inquest into death of BRI student is completed; ruling awaited." *Providence Journal*, 17 October 1986, A3.

175. Kennedy, John H. "Judge awards fees in autism therapy case." *Boston Globe*, 7 November 1986, 23.

176. LaPlante, Joseph R. "Judge orders state to pay legal fees of BRI, parents. Founder expresses mixed emotions about the decision." *Providence Journal*, 7 November 1986, A3.

177. Ibid.

178. Ibid.

179. Ibid.

180. Ibid.

181. Associated Press. "State to appeal award of lawyers' fees to Providence-based school for autistics." *Providence Journal*, 8 November 1986, A5.

182. LaPlante, Joseph, R. "Judge pushes for settlement in school suit. R.I. school charges Mass. agency trying to force it to close." *Providence Journal*, 2 December 1986, C7.

183. Crane, William, Schwartz, Stephen, & Weber, R. H. An Appeal from a Preliminary Injunction Issued by the Probate and Family Court of Bristol County. Brief for the MA Chapter of the National Society for Adults and Children with Autism, the New England Chapter for The Association for Persons with Severe Handicaps, the Association for Retarded Citizens/Massachusetts, Inc., the Coalition for the Legal Rights of the Disabled, and the Civil Liberties Union of Massachusetts, 1986.

184. Fuller, Brian. "Settlement reached in autism therapy battle." Regional News, 12 December 1986.

185. LaPlante, Joseph R. "BRI, Children's Office works out deal on therapy." *Providence Journal*, 13 December 1986, A1.

186. "Autistic children's needs." *Boston Globe*, 16 December 1986, 14.

187. "A fresh start in dealing with autistic behavior." *Providence Journal*, 17 December 1986, A2.

188. Inquest in the Matter of Vincent Milletich, District Court Department, Taunton Division, Bristol, SS, 4 December 1986.

189. Commonwealth v. Vanderpool, 367 Mass 743 (1975): "Wanton and reckless conduct is intentional conduct, involving either the commission of an act or an omission of one where there is a duty to act. This intentional conduct involves a high degree of likelihood that substantial harm or injury will occur to another person." Commonwealth v. Welansky, 316 Mass. 383, 399 (1944): "Wanton and reckless conduct amounts to what has been variously described as indifference to or disregard of probable consequences to that other . . . or rights of that other."

190. "If the grave danger was in fact realized by the defendant, his subsequent voluntary act or omission which caused the harm amounts to wanton or reckless conduct, no matter whether the ordinary man would have realized the gravity of the danger or not." Commonwealth v. Welansky, 316 Mass. 383, 398 (1944).

191. Inquest in the Matter of Vincent Milletich, District Court Department. Taunton Division, Bristol, SS, 4 December 1986.

192. LaPlante, Joseph, R. "Mother seeks no retribution against BRI in son's death." *Providence Journal*, 10 December 1986, A3.

193. Ibid.

194. Witcher, Gregory. "Judge says he'll keep overseeing BRI case: Treatment of autism at heart of dispute." *Boston Globe*, 23 June 1987, 17.

195. "Judge allows BRI therapy to continue six months." *Providence Journal*, 24 June 1987, A24.

6. THE FDA PERMITS THE USE OF ELECTRIC SHOCK ON PEOPLE WITH DISABILITIES

1. Salsberg, Bob. "Feds probe Mass. special needs school." *Washington Post*, 25 February 2010.

2. FDA. "FDA takes rare step to ban electrical stimulation devices for self-injurious or aggressive behavior: Devices found to present unreasonable and substantial risk of illness or injury." News release, 4 March 2020.

3. Lovaas, O. I., Schaeffer, B., and Simmons, J. Q. "Building social behavior in autistic children by use of electric shock." *Journal of Experimental Research in Personality* 1 (1965): 99–109.

4. The twins lived in a residential setting.

5. Gonnerman, J. "School of shock." *Mother Jones*, 20 August 2007.

6. Lichstein, K. L., and Schreibman, L. "Employing electric shock with autistic children: A review of side effects." *Journal of Autism and Childhood Schizophrenia* (June 1976): 170.

7. Ibid., 171.

8. Personal communication with Brian Miller, 2008.

9. Cutler, Barbara Coyne. *You, your child, and "special" education: A guide to making the system work*. Baltimore: Paul H. Brookes, 1993.

10. Pennhurst State School and Hospital v. Halderman, 465 U.S. 89 (1984).

11. Brian Iwata is a highly regarded researcher and teacher at Florida State University. He was a professor of pediatrics at John Hopkins University between 1978 and 1986. Prior to that, he was an assistant professor at Western Michigan University, 1974–1978. He is active in the field of applied behavioral analysis and served as editor of *Journal of Applied Behavior Analysis*.

12. The company developing the device, Human Technologies, had close associations with the Applied Physics Laboratory and the Kennedy Institute at John Hopkins University.

13. Cutler, Barbara, Autism Services Association. Letter to Gunnar Dybwad, professor emeritus, Brandeis University, 16 May 1987.

14. The use of aversive stimulation to prevent certain types of behavior is known in the art. U.S. Patent No. 3,998,209, issued to Gilbert Macvaugh on December 21, 1976, teaches the application of electric shock pulses for conditioning snoring. U.S. Patent No. 3,885,576, issued to Elliott Symmes on May 26, 1975, teaches the use of electric shock as a means to deter smoking. In that patent, a mercury switch is mounted on a wristband so that when the user moves his arm (for example, to place a cigarette in his lips), the mercury switch closes and allows an electric current to flow to electrodes on the user's wristband. Retrieved August 19, 2010, from http://www.freepatentsonline.com/4524773.html. The use of aversive stimulation to inhibit self-injurious behavior was first described by Mooza Grant in U.S. Patent No. 3,834,379, issued September 10, 1974. Mooza Grant describes an apparatus that conditions self-destructive patients against self-injurious blows to the head. The apparatus contains a helmet mounted on the patient's head to absorb self-injurious blows. The helmet contains a metallic

cylinder and a movable pin disposed centrally therein. When a patient strikes the helmet, the pin contacts with the cylinder and establishes an electrical contact that activates an electronic package (described as being disposed within a jacket in patients' clothing). An electric pulse generated in the electronic package is sent to the electrodes contained in an armband and provides an aversive electric shock to the patient's arm. The helmet, electronic package, and stimulation electrodes are all connected by electrical wires. The use of a wireless communication link between a sensor module and a stimulus module was first described by R. E. Fischell et al. in U.S. Patent No. 4,440,160, issued April 3, 1984. The Fischell et al. apparatus includes a means for setting an acceleration threshold so that an aversive blow to the head can be distinguished from acceleration due to the patient's regular activities. The device teaches the use of an event counter located in both the sensor and stimulus modules to record the occurrence of both a self-injurious blow and the application of aversive stimulation.

15. Johns Hopkins University, Applied Physics Laboratory. "SIBIS gives hope to the self-injurious." Press release, 8 September 1987.

16. Grant, Mooza V.P. *SIBIS . . . the result of a mother's plight*. St. Petersburg, FL: Human Technologies.

17. Johns Hopkins University, Applied Physics Laboratory. Media release, 8 September 1987.

18. Ibid.

19. NASA. Life and Microgravity Sciences and Applications. Life Sciences, n.d.

20. 510 clearances. Retrieved 17 January 2011 from http://www.fda.gov /MedicalDevices/ProductsandMedicalProcedures/DeviceApprovalsand Clearances/510kClearances/default.htm.

21. Carr, E. G., and Lovaas, O. I. "Contingent electric shock as a treatment for severe behavior problems." In S. Axelrod and T. Apsche (Eds.), *The effects of punishment on human behavior* (221–245). New York: Academic Press, 1983.

22. Chissler, Robert II. Premarket notification coordinator, Office of Device Evaluation, Center for Devices and Radiological Health, FDA. Letter to Oxford Medilog. Attn: John K. Laurie, Clearwater, FL, 15 October 1985.

23. Mohan, K., Office of Device Evaluation, FDA. Letter to Mr. Smith, Oxford Medilog, 7 January 1986.

24. There is a distinct difference between voluntary use of aversive stimulation to deter smoking, and the use of pain to reduce behaviors of people who had little, if any, voice about their treatment. People with disabilities, particularly children, have little ability to refuse shock. People who are trying to stop smoking can terminate the shock at any time.

25. Mohan, K., Office of Device Evaluation, FDA. Letter to Mr. Smith, Oxford Medilog, 7 January 1986.

26. The use of aversive stimulation to prevent certain types of behavior is known in the art. U.S. Patent No. 3,998,209, issued to Gilbert Macvaugh on December 21, 1976, teaches the application of electric shock pulses for condi-

tioning snoring. U.S. Patent No. 3,885,576, issued to Elliott Symmes, on May 26, 1975, teaches the use of electric shock as a means to deter smoking. In that patent, a mercury switch is mounted on a wristband so that when the user moves his arm (e.g., to place a cigarette in his lips), the mercury switch closes and allows an electric current to flow to electrodes on the user's wristband.

27. Meier, Barry. "Medical device approval process is called flawed." *New York Times*, 30 July 2011, B1, B6.

28. Murray, G. C., director, Division of Anesthesiology, Neurology, and Radiology Devices, Office of Device Evaluation, Center for Devices and Radiological Health. FDA, U.S. Department of Health and Human Services. Letter to James N. Deering, Human Technologies, 29 May 1987.

29. Linscheid, T. R., Iwata, B. A., Ricketts, R. W., Williams, D. E., and Griffin, J. C. "Clinical evaluation of the self-injurious behavior inhibiting system (SIBIS)." *Journal of Applied Behavioral Analysis* 23 (1990): 53–78.

30. Israel, M. L., von Heyn, R. E., Connolly, D. A., and Marsh, D. "A remote-controlled electric shock device for behavior modification." JRC pub. 92-3, n.d.

31. CDRH Consumer Information. "Learn if a medical device has been cleared by FDA for marketing." U.S. Food and Drug Administration, Center for Devices and Radiological Health, 2004. http://www.fda.gov/cdrh/consumer/geninfo.html.

32. McWhorter, Celane. TASH Western Union mailgram message, 8 April 1988.

33. This argument regarding protection versus the right to treatment would become the foundation for future legal arguments that ensued in the numerous legal cases in Massachusetts.

34. Skinner believed that punishment could be effective, but over time, he raised caution about its use and misuse.

35. Will, M., and Reynolds, W. B. "Concerns about electroshock therapy." *Washington Post*, 29 September 1987, A18.

36. Food, Drug and Cosmetics Act. P.L. 94-295. 90 Stat. 593. 1976.

37. The graduated electrical decelerator was later developed by Matthew Israel at BRI to deliver a stronger electric shock.

38. Israel, M. L., von Heyn, R. E., Connolly, D. A. and Marsh, D. "A remote-controlled electric shock device for behavior modification." JRC pub. 92-3, n.d. http://www.effectivetreatment.org/remote.html

7. HERE COMES THE NATIONAL INSTITUTES OF HEALTH

1. Israel, Matthew. Letter to Dr. Rosemary Dybwad, Nathan and Toby Starr, Center on Mental Retardation, Brandeis University, 23 January 1987.

2. Rud Turnbull specialized in disability law and policy. He had a son with Down syndrome, was president of the American Association on Mental Deficiency from 1985 to 1986, and was a professor at the University of Kansas. Madeline Will also had a son with Down syndrome and was an opponent of aversive interventions.

3. Turnbull, Rutherford. "An analysis of the court settlement in the BRI case." *TASH Newsletter* 13:4 (1997).

4. Turnbull, R. Memorandum to Assistant Secretary Madeleine Will, 13 January 1987.Turnbull, R. "An analysis of the court settlement in the BRI case." *TASH Newsletter* 13:4 (1997).

5. Community Services for Autistic Citizens' executive director, Pat Juhrs, would later vigorously object to the outcome of an NIH consensus conference on the use of punishment.

6. This act authorized the attorney general to conduct investigations and litigation relating to conditions of confinement in state institutions. CRIPA, 42 U.S.C. sec. 1997a et seq.

7. Reynolds, William Bradford. Address at the Community Services for Autistic Adults and Children's Annual Symposium for the Advancement of Non-Aversive Behavioral Technology, Rockville, MD, 22 September 1987.

8. Morris, Edward. Memo to ABA/SABA Council Board Members, 18 November 1986.

9. Warren, Frank. "ABA award sparks wide controversy." *Community News: Newsletter of Community Services for Autistic Adults and Children* [Rockville, MD] 3:2 (Summer 1987).

10. Meyer, Luanna, Division of Special Education and Rehabilitation, Syracuse University. Memo to ABA Council Members re: Planned awards to an attorney and family on the "right to most effective treatment" at the 1987 ABA conference, 22 November 1986.

11. Du Verglas, Gabrielle, executive director, Autism Training Center, Marshall University, Huntington, WV. Memo to ABA Council re: ABA right to effective treatment award, 4 May 1987, 1.

12. Tom Nerney began editing and publishing the *Wallenberg Papers*, a newsletter that highlighted SIBIS and what he described as torture of people with disabilities as well as other issues related to disability and ethics. He also held positions as executive director of the CT ARC, Autism Society director, program director for the National Legal Services initiatives on medical discrimination, and codirector of the Robert Wood Johnson National Program Office on Self-Determination.

13. OHA had the responsibility for overseeing the equal rights of persons with disabilities in Massachusetts. The Office of Handicapped Affairs had the responsibility, pursuant to M.G.L. c.6 s.187 and 188, for promoting the advancement of the legal rights of handicapped individuals, as well as for promoting and securing the maximum possible opportunities, supportive services, accommodations, and accessibility toward the end of full and equal participation of the commonwealth's handicapped citizenry in all aspects of life within the commonwealth.

14. MacLeish, Roderick. Letter to James Gleich, director, Office of Handicapped Affairs, 15 December 1987.

15. Israel, Matthew. *History of JRC*. Retrieved 14 August 2011 from http://www .judgerc.org/history.html.

16. Ibid.

17. "Legislating Therapy." *Boston Globe*, 21 April 1987, 18.

18. Retrieved 16 September 2008 from http://www.judgerc.org/history.html.

19. 104 CMR 20.15 Behavior Management and Behavior Modification.

20. Crane, William. "DMR promulgates aversive regulations." Unpublished memorandum, July 1987.

21. Ibid.

22. MacLeish, Roderick. Letter to James Gleich, director, Office of Handicapped Affairs, 15 December 1987.

23. "Another student dies at school for the autistic." *New York Times*, 26 June 1987, B4.

24. Laplante, Joseph R. "BRI resident dies 2 days after coronary arrest." *Providence Journal*, 26 June 1987, C-7.

25. Cobb, Polyxane S. *A short history of aversives in Massachusetts*, n.d. Retrieved 7 October 2007, https://autistichoya.files.wordpress.com/2016/04/jrc -history-2005-polyxane-cobb.pdf.

26. King, John. "Student at controversial school for autistic dies after heart attack." *Providence Journal*, 24 June 1987.

27. To my knowledge, there was not a coroner's inquest.

28. Sullivan, Louis W., secretary, Department of Health and Human Services. Letter to Barbara Sackett, president, Association for Retarded Citizens of the United States, Arlington, TX, 20 July 1990.

29. "Review of NIH Consensus Conference," unpublished document, 3 May 2000.

30. Coulter, David L. Letter to Itzhak Jacoby, Office of Medical Applications of Research, National Institutes of Health, Bethesda, MD, 11 December 1986.

31. Cerreto, in her role as director of quality assurance for Massachusetts, was later fired along with six other colleagues, including the director of the Department of Mental Retardation, Philip Campbell, after BRI sued the commonwealth using similar arguments and actions that were used against Mary Kay Leonard.

32. Cerreto, Mary. Letter to Itzhak Jacoby, Office of Medical Applications of Research, National Institutes of Health, Bethesda, MD, 17 December 1986.

33. Jacoby, Itzhak, acting director, Office of Medical Application of Research, NIH, Bethesda, MD. Letters to David Coulter and Mary C. Cerreto, 16 January 1987.

34. Cerreto, Mary. Letter to Itzhak Jacoby, Office of Medical Applications of Research, National Institutes of Health. Bethesda, MD, 6 March 1987.

35. Ibid.

36. Lovett, H. *Learning to listen*. Baltimore: Paul H. Brookes, 1996, 75.

37. John Matson provided testimony that supported BRI in the OFC lawsuit involving Mary Kay Leonard.

38. Robb, W. S. Letter to M.A.R.C Board member, International Association for the Right to Effective Treatment, November 1989.

39. The SIBIS was introduced to the field in 1987.

40. Sherman, R. "Aversives, fundamental rights and the courts." *Behavior Analyst* 14 (1991): 204.

41. Stobbe, M. "Otisville girl gets shock therapy: First in state to wear the device." *Flint Journal*, 21 July 1989, A11.

42. Linscheid, T. R. "SIBIS article facts disputed." *AAMR News and Notes* 2:2 (1989): 6.

43. Foxx, Richard M. "The National Institutes of Health Consensus Development Conference: A study in professional politics." In John W. Jacobson, Richard M. Foxx, and James A. Mulick (Eds.), *Controversial therapies for developmental disabilities: Fad, fashion, and science professional practice* (461–476). Hillsdale, NJ: Erlbaum, 1989.

44. Robert Cooke, Jo Ann Simons Derr, Leonard Krasner, Marty Krauss, Gene Sackett, Thomas Bellamy, Murray Sidman, Gary LaVigna, Sharon Landesman, Sara Sparrow, David Braddock, Naomi Zigmond, Joseph Noshpitz, Gerald Nord and several more.

45. Foxx, Richard M. "The National Institutes of Health Consensus Development Conference: A study in professional politics." In John W. Jacobson, Richard M. Foxx, and James A. Mulick (Eds.), *Controversial therapies for developmental disabilities: Fad, fashion, and science professional practice* (pp. 461–476). Hillsdale, NJ: Erlbaum, 1989.

46. Cataldo presented a paper entitled, "The effects of punishment and other behavior reducing procedures of the destructive behaviors of persons with developmental disabilities."

47. Smith, Marcia Datlow, Community Services for Autistic Adults and Children, Rockville, MD. Letter to Dwayne Alexander, national director of the Institute of Child Health, Bethesda, MD, 31 August 1989.

48. National Institutes of Health. *Participant's guide to consensus development conferences*. Bethesda, MD: National Institutes of Health, 1989.

49. Foxx, Richard M. "The National Institutes of Health Consensus Development Conference: A study in professional politics." In John W. Jacobson, Richard M. Foxx, NS James A. Mulick (Eds.), *Controversial therapies for developmental disabilities: Fad, fashion, and science professional practice* (pp. 461–476). Hillsdale, NJ: Erlbaum, 1989.

50. National Institutes of Health. *Treatment of destructive behaviors in persons with developmental disabilities*. NIH Publication No. 91-2410. Washington, DC: U.S. Department of Health and Human Services, Public Health Service, July 1991.

51. Foxx, Richard. M. "The National Institutes of Health Consensus Development Conference: A study in professional politics." In John W. Jacobson, Richard M. Foxx , and James A. Mulick (Eds.), *Controversial therapies for developmental disabilities: Fad, fashion, and science professional practice*. Hillsdale, NJ: Erlbaum, 1989, 465.

52. Among the opponents of aversives, the Center for Human Policy at Syra-

cuse University and its faculty, including Douglas Biklen, Stephen Taylor, and Luanna Meyer and associates, were the most vocal. The center had made strong policy statements against institutionalization and segregation of people with disabilities, arguing for the least restrictive environment and humane supports.

53. "To stop a child from acting in a particular way, you may allow him to continue (or insist that he continue) performing the undesired act until he tires of it." Huitt, W. "Principles for using behavior modification." In *Educational psychology interactive*. Valdosta, GA: Valdosta State University, 1994.

54. Time-out from reinforcement ("time-out") is a procedure in which a child is placed in a different, less-rewarding situation or setting whenever he or she engages in undesirable or inappropriate behaviors. Retrieved 20 July 2009 from http://www.interventioncentral.org/htmdocs/interventions/behavior/timeout.php

55. O'Brien, John. *Against pain as a tool in professional work on people with severe disabilities*. Syracuse, NY: Center on Human Policy, Syracuse University, 1988, later published in *Disability, Handicap and Society* 6:2 (1991): 81–90.

56. Smith, Marsha Datlow. Letter to Duane Alexander, National Director of Institute of Child Health, Bethesda, MD, 31 August 1989.

57. Ibid.

58. Bernard Rimland, founder of the Autism Society of America and supporter of the use of aversives, referred to Datlow as "an anti-aversive ideologue" despite the fact that she provided evidence for the utility of nonaversive approaches.

59. Wortman, P. M., Vinokar, A., and Sechrest, L. "Do consensus conferences work? A process evaluation of the NIH Consensus Development Program." *Journal of Health Politics, Policy and Law* 13:3 (1988): 469–498.

60. Public Citizen Litigation Group, founded in 1972, is a public interest law firm that litigates cases at all levels of the federal and state judiciaries. It has a substantial practice before federal regulatory agencies and specializes in health and safety regulation, consumer rights, including class actions and access to the courts, open government, and the First Amendment, including Internet free speech.

61. Meyer, Katherine A., and Morrison, Alan B. Letter to William Raub, acting director, NIH, and Duane Alexander, director, Bethesda, MD, 8 September 1989.

62. Raub, William F. Letter to Katherine A. Meyer, Esquire, and Alan B. Morrison, Esquire, Public Citizen Litigation Group, Washington, DC, 11 September, 1989.

63. National Institutes of Health. *Treatment of destructive behaviors in persons with developmental disabilities*. NIH pub. 91-2410., Bethesda, MD: U.S. Department of Health and Human Services, July 1991, 513.

64. Ibid., 124.

65. Ibid.

66. Sackett, Barbara. Letter to Louis W. Sullivan, secretary of health and human services, Washington, DC, 30 October 1989.

67. Ibid.

68. Duane Alexander was the director of the National Institute of Child Health and Development.

69. Sackett, Barbara. Letter to Louis W. Sullivan, secretary of health and human services, Washington, DC, 23 January 1990.

70. Sullivan, Louis W., secretary of health and human services. Letter to Barbara Sackett, president, Association for Retarded Citizens, Arlington, TX, 20 July 1990.

71. Mikulski, Barbara, A. Letter to Office of Government Relations, National Institutes of Health, Bethesda, MD, 24 October 1989.

72. Holden, C. "What's holding up 'aversives' report?" *Science* 249:4972 (1990): 980–981.

73. Rimland, Bernard. Letter to Louis W. Sullivan, secretary of health and human services, Washington, DC, 20 November 1990.

74. Foxx, Richard. M. "The National Institutes of Health Consensus Development Conference: A study in professional politics." In John W. Jacobson, Richard M. Foxx, and James A. Mulick (Eds.), *Controversial therapies for developmental disabilities: Fad, fashion, and science professional practice* (p. 473). Hillsdale, NJ: Erlbaum, 1989.

8. STAGING THE NEXT BATTLEGROUND

1. Behavior Research Institute; Dr. Matthew L. Israel: Leo Soucy, Individually and as Parent and Next Friend of Brendon Soucy; Peter Biscardi, Individually and as Parent and Next Friend of P.J. Biscardi; and All Parents and Guardians of Students at the Behavior Institute; on Behalf of Themselves, Their Children and Ward, Plaintiffs v. Mary Kay Leonard, Individually and in Her Capacity as the Director of the Massachusetts Office for Children, Defendant. Settlement Agreement, Superior Court Department of the Trial Court, and the Probate Court Department of the Trial Court, Docket No. 86E—0018-GI. Filed 12 December 1986.

2. Behavior Research Institute, Inc., et al. v. Mary Kay Leonard, Findings of Fact and Conclusion of Law in Support of Approval of Settlement Agreement Pursuant to Mass. R. Civ. P.23 (c) Probate and Family Court Department, Superior Court Department, No. 86E-0018-GI, 3, 7 January 1987.

3. "Aversive therapy protested at hearing on DMH rules." *Providence Journal*, 13 June 1987, A1.

4. Ibid.

5. "House votes to eliminate 'aversive therapy," *Boston Globe*, 15 June 1988, 64.

6. Caprioglio, Carolyn. "Health bills with local ties signed into law. Measure bans electric shock use." *Middletown Press*, 29 June 1993, 11.

7. Hanafin, Teresa M. "Weld names new head of retardation department." *Boston Globe*, 18 July 1991, 25.

8. Cafarell, Ken. "Order requiring availability of aversive therapy is overturned." UPI, 6 March 1990. In the Matter of Christopher David McKnight, Supreme Judicial Court of Massachusetts, 406 Mass. 787 550 N.E.2d 856, 6 March 1990.

9. Retrieved 5 February 2020 from https://www.law.cornell.edu/wex/preliminary_injunction.

10. Cafarell, Ken. "Order requiring availability of aversive therapy is overturned." UPI, 6 March 1990.

11. In the matter of Christopher David McKnight. 406 Mass. 787. 4 October–6 March 1989. Retrieved 16 August 2011 from http://masscases.com/cases/sjc/406/406mass787.html.

12. Warren, Catherine. "School officials ignore recommendations that autistic boy be removed from facility." *Star-Tribune*, 3 November 1985, A3.

13. Nelson, Eric. "Torture comes cheaper in state." *Tribune Star Letters*, 17 December 1985.

14. In the Matter of Christopher David McKnight. 406 Mass. 787. October 4–March 6, 1989. Retrieved 16 August 2011 from http://masscases.com/cases/sjc/406/406mass787.html.

15. Ibid., 799.

16. Cafarell, Ken. "Order requiring availability of aversive therapy is overturned." UPI, 6 March 1990.

17. Behavior Research Institute, Inc., & Joseph A. Ferrara, by His Parent and Guardian, Nancy B. Ferrara; and Timothy E. Green, by His Parents and Co-Guardians, Robert E. and Elena J. Green v. Secretary of Administration & the Rate Setting Commission; the Department of Mental Retardation; the Department of Education, the Division of Purchased Services; and the Commonwealth. 411 Mass. 73; 577 N.E.2d 297; 1991 Mass., 4 September 1991.

18. In the Matter of Marc Sturtz, Supreme Judicial Court of Massachusetts, Bristol, 410 Mass. 58; 570 N.E.2d 1024; 1991 Mass. Lexis 213, 6, 8 March 1991.

19. Marc Sturtz appeals from a judgment appointing his parents as his permanent guardians and authorizing a behavior modification treatment plan at the JRC. The SJC does not answer the legal questions raised, finding that the case is moot because the guardianship was discharged before the decision. Sturtz had argued that the judges' substituted judgment standard was incorrect. Matter of Sturtz, 570 N.E.2d 1024 (Mass., 1991).

20. Thurmond, R., and Reilly, H. "Judge Rotenberg dies at 67." *Sun Chronicle*, 8 July 1992.

21. "Ernest Rotenberg, first justice of Bristol Probate Court; at 67." *Boston Globe*, 9 July 1982, 43.

22. Armstrong, David. "BRI at a critical juncture." *Boston Herald*, 10 August 1992, 6.

23. Ibid., 5.

24. Lindsley studied under B. F. Skinner and was well known for precision teaching. He coined the term *behavior therapy* and started the Behavior Research Laboratory at Harvard Medical School in 1953. In 1965, he moved into the area of special education teacher training at the University of Kansas.

25. Armstrong, David. "BRI at a critical juncture." *Boston Herald*, 10 August 1992, 5.

26. Working group members included Ogden Lindsley (SIBIS collaborator), Bea Barrett, Joe Morrow, Pancho Barrerra of the Southwestern Regional Center of Ontario, and Don Williams of Richmond State School in Texas. Also in attendance were staff members; BRI counsel, Eric MacLeish; the court monitor, John Daignault; and court-appointed attorneys Ellen Nelson and Elizabeth Balashak.

27. Israel, M. L., von Heyn, R., Connolly, D., and Marsh, D. (1993). "A remote-controlled electric shock device for behavior modification," JRC pub. no. 92-3, n.d., http://www.effectivetreatment.org/remote.html.

28. Horner, R. H., Dunla, G., Koegel, R. L., Carr, E. G., Sailor, W., Anderson, J., Albin, R. W., and O'Neill, R. E. "Toward a technology of 'nonaversive' behavior support." *Journal of The Association for Persons with Severe Handicaps* 15:3 (1990): 125–132.

29. Israel, von Heyn, Connolly, and Marsh. "A remote-controlled electric shock device for behavior modification." JRC pub. no. 92-3. Unpublished manuscript. http://www.effectivetreatment.org/remote.html.

30. Ibid., 11. The draft manuscript was later published as part of a BRI series (BRI pub. 92-3). No data on the effectiveness of the GED appeared in the report.

31. Latin for "that you have the body." In the United States, federal courts can use a writ of habeas corpus to determine if a state's detention of a prisoner is valid. The writ is used to bring a prisoner or other detainee (e.g., an institutionalized mental patient) before the court to determine if the person's imprisonment or detention is lawful. A habeas petition proceeds as a civil action against the state agent (usually a warden) who holds the defendant in custody. Retrieved 30 March 2021 from https://www.law.cornell.edu/wex/habeas_corpus.

32. John Kauffman, petitioner (and a consolidated case), Supreme Judicial Court of Massachusetts, 413 Mass. 101; 604 N.E.2d 1285; 15 December 1992.

33. Ibid.

34. Ibid.

35. Hanafin, Theresa. "Aversive therapy is hearing topic." *Boston Globe*, 27 March 1992, 19.

36. Ibid.

37. "Short circuits." *Boston Globe*, May 6, 1992.

38. Cutler, Barbara D. Letter to Philip Campbell, commissioner, Department of Mental Retardation, Boston, MA, 29 July 1992.

39. Weiss, Nancy. Letter to the Oprah Winfrey Show, 11 August 1992.

40. Winfrey, Oprah. "Electric shock therapy for children with disabilities." 13 December 1993. https://mn.gov/mnddc/parallels2/one/video/OprahElectroshockTherapy.html.

41. Chalmers, Amanda, J. Letter to Matthew Israel, director, Behavior Research Institute, 10 June 1992.

42. Israel, Matthew, Letter to Amanda J. Chalmers, Massachusetts Department of Mental Retardation, 16 July 1992.

43. Israel, Matthew. Letter to Commissioner Philip Campbell, Massachusetts

Department of Mental Retardation. Re: Response to DMR certification, 28 August 1993, 3.

44. Jansen, a clinical psychologist, opposed BRI's methods. See the probate court order of 12 March 1992, paragraphs 20–22.

45. Ibid., 6.

46. Campbell, P. Letter to Matthew Israel, 31 August 1993, 2.

47. Ibid., 6.

48. Behavior Research Institute Parents and Friends Association, Inc. Co-Chairs, Marie Washington and Paul E. Peterson. "Parents of BRI students to hold press conference to refute so-called CBS report," 7 March 1994.

49. Behavior Research Institute, Inc. Dr. Matthew Israel; Leo Soucy, Individually and as Parent and Next Friend of Brendon Soucy; Peter Biscardi, Individually and as Parent and Next Friend of P. J. Biscardi; and All Parents and Guardians of Students at the Behavior Research Institute, Inc., on Behalf of Themselves; Their Children and Wards, Plaintiffs v. Philip Campbell, in his capacity as Commissioner of the Department of Mental Retardation. Amend the Complaint, for Preliminary Injunctive Relief and for Periodic Review; a Verified Amended Complaint; and a Complaint for Contempt Pursuant to Rule 65.3 of the Massachusetts Rules of Civil Procedures. Superior Court Department of the Trial Court, and the Probate and Family Court Department of the Trial Court Docket No. 86E-0018-GI, 3 September 1993.

50. Daignault was a psychiatrist associated with McLean Hospital and Harvard Medical School. He later worked with MacLeish on the Catholic Church child abuse case.

51. Motion of BRI, Inc. to Amend the Complaint. For preliminary Injunctive Relief and for Periodic Review. Immediate Hearing Requested. BRI, Inc., Dr. Matthew Israel; Leo Soucy, Individually and as Parent and Next Friend of Brendon Soucy; Peter Biscardi, Individually and as Parent and Next Friend of P. J. Biscardi; and All Parents and Guardians of Students at the Behavior Research Institute, Inc., on Behalf of Themselves, Their Children and Wards, Plaintiffs, v. Philip Campbell, in his capacity as Commissioner of the Department of Mental Retardation, 2 September 1993.

52. Behavior Research Institute; Dr. Matthew L. Israel: Leo Soucy, Individually and as Parent and Next Friend of Brendon Soucy; Peter Biscardi, Individually and as Parent and Next Friend of P. J. Biscardi; and All Parents and Guardians of students at the Behavior Institute; on Behalf of Themselves, Their Children and Ward, Plaintiffs v. Mary Kay Leonard, Individually and In Her Capacity as the Director of the Massachusetts Office for Children, Defendant. Settlement Agreement, Superior Court Department of the Trial Court, and the Probate Court Department of the Trial Court, Docket No. 86E—0018-GI. Filed 12 December 1986.

53. Motion of BRI, Inc. to Amend the Complaint. For Preliminary Injunctive Relief and for Periodic Review. Immediate Hearing Requested. BRI, Inc., Dr. Matthew Israel; Leo Soucy, Individually and as Parent and Next Friend of Brendon Souncy; Peter Biscardi, Individually and as Parent and Next Friend of P. J.

Biscardi; and All Parents and Guardians of Students at the Behavior Research Institute, Inc., on Behalf of Themselves, Their Children and Wards, Plaintiffs, v. Philip Campbell, in his capacity as Commissioner of the Department of Mental Retardation. 2 September 1993, 6.

54. Ibid., 7–8.

55. Ibid., 5.

56. Ibid., 24.

57. Pennhurst State School v. Halderman, 465 U.S. 89 (1984).

58. Laski, Frank. Personal communication with the author, November 2007.

59. Armstrong, David. "Mental retardation lawyer's pay cut after complaints." *Boston Globe*, 21 May 1994, 27.

60. MA Department of Mental Retardation's Report to the Court: Status of Behavior Research Institute, Inc. Re: BRI Inc. v. Mary Kay Leonard, Defendant. Bristol Superior Court Department of the Trial Court, and the Probate and Family Court Department of the Trial Court, Docket no. 86E-0018-GI, 22 September 1993.

61. MA Department of Mental Retardation's Report to the Court: Status of Behavior Research Institute, Inc. re: BRI Inc. v. Mary Kay Leonard, Defendant. Bristol Superior Court Department of the Trial Court, and the Probate and Family Court Department of the Trial Court, Docket no. 86E-0018-GI, 22 September 1993, 1–3.

62. Weiss, Nancy. "Toward the elimination of the use of aversive procedures to control individuals with disabilities." TASH, 3, 1993.

63. Previously titled in 1993: "The Application of Aversive Procedures to Individuals with Developmental Disabilities: A Call to Action."

64. Several people who signed the document would be involved in an evaluation of BRI a few years later. Their signatures on "Call to Action" supported BRI's contention that they were biased against the center and part of a deliberate strategy by DMR to close BRI. In the next round of litigation, the document, signed by hundreds of professionals and family members across the country, ended up being used as a tool to eliminate individuals as experts and consultants as biased and therefore not objective.

65. Gwin, Lucy. Letter to Nancy Weiss. Re: Renewing the effort to put an end to aversives, 21 January 1993.

66. Judy Rybak has produced, written and directed for several national news magazine shows, including ABC's *Primetime Live*, *Eye to Eye with Connie Chung*, as well as *Extra!* and *Entertainment Tonight*.

67. Weiss, Nancy. Personal communication with the author, February 2006.

68. Israel, Matthew. Letter to Campbell, P.

69. Campbell, P. Letter to Matthew Israel, 31 August 1993, 2.

70. Shapiro, Joseph. *No pity: People with disabilities forging a new civil rights movement*. New York: Random House, 1993, 154.

71. Biddle, F. M. "Behavior Institute slams 'Eye to Eye.'" *Boston Globe*, 1 March 1994, 58.

72. Martin, J. "Connie Chung vs. BRI parents." *Providence Journal*, 3 March 1994, F7.

73. Biddle, Frederic M. "Behavior Institute slams 'Eye to Eye.'" *Boston Globe*, 1 March 1994, 58.

74. Armstrong, D. "School says CBS altered sound in report on its shock therapy." *Boston Globe*, 9 March 1994, 22.

75. Armstrong, D. "School aims at therapy critics; ex-workers at BRI got lawsuit drafts," *Boston Globe*, 23 March 1994, 17.

76. Ibid.

77. Heyward, A. "Eye to Eye; of autism and critics." *New York Times*, 10 April 1994, 2:9.

78. Aucoin, D. "Former institute workers charge clients are often beaten, shocked." *Boston Globe*, 8 October 1993, 34.

79. Milliard, Anne Marie. Testimony at Massachusetts State House news conference, 8 October 1993.

80. Aucoin, D. "Former institute workers charge clients are often beaten, shocked." *Boston Globe*, 8 October 1993, 34.

81. CPR is dedicated to enforcing and expanding the rights of people with disabilities and others who are in segregated settings. CPR uses legal strategies, advocacy, and policy to design and implement systemic reform initiatives to promote their integration and full community participation. Working on state, national, and international levels, CPR is committed to equality, diversity, and social justice in all its activities." Retrieved 16 October 2020 from https://www .centerforpublicre.org.

82. Aucoin, D. "Former institute workers charge clients are often beaten, shocked." *Boston Globe*, 8 October 1993, 34.

83. Greene, T. "Gain worth the pain? Autistic institute's methods come under attack." *Middlesex News*, 8 March 1994.

84. Fehrnstrom, E. "Unreported death renews R.I. mental institute flap," *Boston Herald*, 9 February 1994, 012.

9. BAD FAITH OR RESPONSIBLE GOVERNMENT?

1. The Deposition of Mary Cerreto, a Witness Called by the Plaintiffs, taken Pursuant to the Applicable Provisions of the Massachusetts Rules of Civil Procedure, before Kathleen L. Good, Registered Professional Reporter and Notary Public, 21 April 1995.

2. Cerreto, M. *Review of psychiatric evaluations, BRI*. Boston: Department of Mental Retardation, Executive Office of Health and Human Services, Commonwealth of Massachusetts, 5 December 1993.

3. Jansen, Paul, Family Psychological Associates, Norwood, MA. Letter to Attorney John Coyne, Barros and Coyne, P.C., New Bedford, MA, 1 August 1993. Campbell, Philip, Commissioner, Department of Mental Retardation to Matthew Israel, executive director, Behavior Research Institute, 31 August 1993, 7.

4. I tried several times to meet with Mary Cerreto, but she was reluctant given the gag order that Judge LaStaiti had imposed on her.

5. Governor's Commission on Mental Retardation. "Trends in Community Based Day Services." January 1997.

6. The term *mental retardation* is no longer used. *Intellectual disability* is the preferred terminology.

7. Bradley, V. J., Jaskulski, T., Feinstein, C., Brown, L., Silver, J., and Rabb, B. "Intermediate care facilities for persons with mental retardation. Compendium of state quality assurance systems." Cambridge, MA: Human Services Research Institute, 31 October 1996.

8. Cerreto, M. *Review of psychiatric evaluations, BRI.* Boston: Department of Mental Retardation, Executive Office of Health and Human Services, Commonwealth of Massachusetts, 5 December 1993.

9. Ibid., 3–4.

10. Behavior Research Institute, Dr. Matthew Israel; Leo Soucy, Individually and as Parent and Next Friend of Brendon Soucy; Peter Biscardi, Individually and as Parent and Next Friend of P. J. Biscardi; and All Parents and Guardians of Students at the Behavior Research Institute, Inc., on behalf of Themselves; Their Children and Wards, Plaintiffs v. Philip Campbell, in his capacity as Commissioner of the Department of Mental Retardation. Amend the Complaint, for Preliminary Injunctive Relief and for Periodic Review; a Verified Amended Complaint; and a Complaint for Contempt Pursuant to Rule 65.3 of the Massachusetts Rules of Civil Procedures. Superior Court Department of the Trial Court, and the Probate and Family Court Department of the Trial Court Docket No. 86E-0018-GI, 2 September 1993.

11. Cerreto, Mary C., assistant commissioner, Office for Quality Enhancement. Memo to Colleagues in the Field of Psychology and Development Disabilities Re: Request for Proposals, 30 August 1993.

12. Murdock, K. Memo to Philip Campbell, Fred Misilo, Jean Tuller, Mary Cerreto, and Dick Cohen, Indemnification of experts, 14 October 1993.

13. Members of the team were Angela Amado, Ph.D.; Richard Amado, Ph.D.; Roger Deneen; Michael Tessneer; Betty Ferris; Roy Froemming, J.D.; and Kathryn Kirigin-Ram, Ph.D. Flammia, M. Letter to Kim E. Murdock, general counsel, MA DMR, 7 March 1994.

14. Ferris, B. *Program evaluation report of BRI to Executive Office of Health and Human Services.* Boston: DMR, Commonwealth of Massachusetts, April 1994, 5.

15. Equitable relief involves court-ordered remedies that require certain acts or contracts. Retrieved 27 July 2009 from http://www.answers.com/topic/equity.

16. Amado, A. executive director, Human Services Research & Development Center, St. Paul, MN. Letter to Jean Tuller, general counsel, DMR, Boston, MA, 6 January 1993, 4.

17. AAMD was later renamed the American Association on Mental Retardation (AAMR), then later, the American Association on Intellectual and Developmental Disabilities (AAIDD).

18. On December 20, 1994, DMR received written confirmation from the FDA that the GED had been cleared for marketing on December 5, 1994. Yet there was no approval for the GED-4. DMR officials had complained to the FDA about their approval process, arguing that this was a dangerous device and not "substantially equivalent" to previously approved medical devices.

19. Armstrong, D. "DMR probes school's use of shock treatments." *Boston Globe*, 9 February 1994, 20.

20. The Department of Mental Retardation Report on Compliance by the Judge Rotenberg Center, Inc. with the Requirements of the Behavior Modification Regulations and the Terms of Certification to Use Level III Interventions, January 1995.

21. Fernstrom, E. "Institute gets 6-month OK on disputed therapy." *Boston Herald*, 10 February 1994, 12.

22. Campbell, P. commissioner, DMR. Letter to Matthew Israel, 9 February 1994.

23. Armstrong, David. "State says school's use of restraints violated youth's human rights." *Boston Globe*, 10 February 1994, 34.

24. Fehrnstrom, Eric. "Institute gets 6-month OK on disputed therapy." *Boston Herald*, 10 February 1994, 12.

25. Armstrong, David. "State says school's use of restraints violated youth's human rights." *Boston Globe*, 10 February 1994, 34.

26. Deneen. R. A., president, Rivendell, Cambridge, MN. Letter to Jean Tuller, Executive Offices, DMR, 16 March 1994.

27. Murdock, Kim, general counsel, DMR. Letter to Eric MacLeish Jr. Esq. Re: Confidentiality agreement, 21 March 1994.

28. Murdock, Kim E., general counsel, DMR. Letter to Eric MacLeish Jr. Esq. Re: Program review, 22 March 1994.

29. Murdock, Kim E., general counsel, DMR. Letter to Eric MacLeish Jr. Esq. Re: Rivendell, 23 March 1994.

30. Murdock, Kim E., general counsel, DMR. Letter to Eric MacLeish Jr. Esq. Re: Confidentiality agreement, 24 March 1994.

31. Murdock, Kim. E., general counsel, DMR. Letter to Eric MacLeish Jr. Esq. Re: Program review, 25 March 1994.

32. All states and territories have a protection and advocacy program funded by the U.S. Department of Health and Human Services to protect the rights of children and adults with disabilities.

33. Froemming, R. "Behavioral Research Institute Program review. Dates reviewed: March 20–25, 1994," 23 April 1994.

34. The state of Massachusetts had only a Class III category for aversives. A Class IV category was proposed but never adopted. Ferris, B. "Program Evaluation Report of BRI to Executive Office of Health and Human Services, DMR, Commonwealth of Massachusetts," April 1994, 43.

35. Amado, Richard S., Rivendell reviewer. Behavioral Research Institute Program Review, Individual Report, 28 April 1994.

36. Connelly, M. et al. Coalition for the Legal Rights of the Disabled. Letter to L. Scott Harshberger, attorney general, 27 April 1994.

37. Armstrong, David. "N.Y. seeks to remove 16 pupils from BRI." *Boston Globe*, 24 March 1994, 38.

38. Tuller, Jean. Personal communication to the author. April 2004.

39. Armstrong, David. "Experiment records search ordered at state facilities." *Boston Globe*, 31 December 1993, 12.

40. Ibid.

41. Israel, M. L., von Heyn, R. E., Connolly, D. A., and Marsh, D. "A remote-controlled electric shock device for behavior modification." 1992.

42. "Each GED system was comprised of a remote control transmitter, a shock generator (the GED device itself), a battery and an electrode. The transmitter, a SECO-LARM (model SK-919TD2A) two channel RF transmitter, operated at 315 MHz and transmitted a uniquely coded signal to the receiver worn by the participant. The transmitter was housed in a lexan box (104 mm × 76 mm × 38 mm) with the participant's name and photo on the outside. The shock generator consisted of a receiver (SECO-LARM model SK-910) set to the same code as the transmitter, a shock controller circuit board that created the shock stimulus, and a stimulation indication beeper (Mallory piezoelectric ceramic buzzer model PLD-27A 35W). The shock generator was housed in a lexan box (140 mm × 89 mm × 38 mm) and the unit weighed 269 g. A 12 V rechargeable nickel metal hydride battery pack (Panasonic P/N HHR-AAB 2000 mAh) provided power to the shock generator and was housed in a lexan box with the same dimensions as those of the shock generator. The battery unit weighed 397 g. The battery was attached by Velcro to the shock generator and connected to it electrically by a short cable (Hirose Electric Co., Ltd., Part # H0063-ND). The battery and shock generator were both carried in a back pack or fanny pack worn by the participant. A cable (Hirose Electric Co., Ltd., Part # H0063-ND) connected the shock generator to the electrode. Each electrode was attached to one of several preapproved locations, typically the arms, legs, or torso. The electrode and connecting cable were hidden by the participant's clothing. The electrodes employed during the 3-year period were of two types: (1) a "concentric" electrode which consisted of a stainless steel button (diameter 9.5 mm, thickness 3.25 mm) surrounded by a stainless steel ring (outer diameter 21.5 mm, inner diameter 16.5 mm, thickness 3.25 mm) with 2.35 mm between the outer edge of the button and the inner edge of the ring; or (2) a "distanced" electrode consisted of two stainless steel buttons (diameter 9.5 mm, thickness 3.25 mm) mounted up to 15.24 cm apart on flexible nonconductive material. During the 3-year period covered in this report, the vast majority of the participants wore distanced electrodes. Each participant wore from one to five GED sets (each consisting of battery, shock generator, and associated electrode), depending on the decision of the participant's clinician. Each remote control unit sent a signal to only one particular GED shock generator and that shock generator was connected to one electrode on the participant's body. When a participant wore more than one GED set, the therapist possessed

a separate remote control for each set. In these cases, on any given application the participant did not know which electrode would deliver the skin-shock (i.e., which remote control device the staff member would employ)." Excerpt from Israel, M., Blenkush, N. A., von Heyn, R. E., and Rivera, P. M. "Treatment of aggression with behavioral programming that includes supplementary skin-shock." Unpublished manuscript. Judge Rotenberg Center, 2007. Retrieved 24 July 2009 from http://www.judgerc.org/.

43. Kix, P. "The shocking truth." *Boston Magazine*, 1 July 2008.

44. Goodman, Walter. "A few scary pictures can go a long way." *New York Times*, 20 March 1994, 28.

45. Behavior Research Institute Parents and Friends Association. News and press statement, 8 March 1994.

46. Armstrong, David. "School aims at therapy critics; ex-workers at BRI got lawsuit drafts." *Boston Globe*, 23 March 1994, 17.

47. Armstrong, David. "BRI defends 5,000-shock therapy; president says student given them in one day to save his life." *Boston Globe*, 28 April 1994, 29.

48. Armstrong, David. "School aims at therapy critics; ex-workers at BRI got lawsuit drafts." *Boston Globe*, 23 March 1994, 17.

49. Ibid

50. Greene, Tim. "BRI founder, under fire, defends record." *Middlesex News*, 8 March 1994.

51. Armstrong, David. "School aims at therapy critics; ex-workers at BRI got lawsuit drafts." *Boston Globe*, 23 March 1994, 17.

52. Armstrong, David. "School aims at therapy critics; ex-workers at BRI got lawsuit drafts." *Boston Globe*, 23 March 1994, 17.

53. Greene, Tim. "BRI parents: Strong praise, strong disdain." *Middlesex News*, 9 March 1994.

54. Greene, Tim. "BRI Parents: Strong praise, strong disdain." *Middlesex News*, 9 March 1994.

55. Armstrong, David. "School that uses shock therapy plans new programs, name change." *Boston Globe*, 1 July 1994, 21.

56. Ibid.

57. Aucoin, Don. "State auditor wants facility for disabled to open books." *Boston Globe*, 31 August 1994, 25.

58. The Massachusetts Office on Disability (originally named the Office of Handicapped Affairs) was established by statute as an independent agency. Independence allowed it to monitor the provision of state services for people with disabilities without interference. The director of the office reported directly to the governor. http://www.mass.gov/mod/Director.html.

59. Meyer, J. "Auditor blasts firm treating mentally ill." *Boston Herald*, 31 August 1994, 25.

60. Cohen, D. B., et al. Commonwealth of Massachusetts, General Court, State House, Boston. Letter to Colleague, 4 October 1994.

61. Advocacy Network, Benjamin Ricci and Jonathan Hallett, Plaintiffs v. The

Massachusetts Department of Mental Retardation, Region I, Philip Campbell, Steven F. Bradley, Catherine Rossi and Laurie Robert, Defendants. Summary Judgment. Massachusetts Superior Court, Civil Action No. 94-295, 20 October 1995.

62. Armstrong, David. "Advocacy group sues state; alleges effort to discredit by agency for retarded." *Boston Globe*, 12 September 1994.

63. Upshur, Carol. Letter to Ms. Rosemary Silva, human rights officer, BRI/JRC, 31 October 1994.

64. Paige, Connie. "State pulls plug on group home; autism center ordered to stop shock treatments." *Boston Herald*, 24 March 1995, 1.

65. Campbell, Philip, commissioner, DMR. Letter to Matthew Israel. Re: January 20, 1995, Decision on Certification to Use Level III Interventions, 20 January 1995.

66. Ibid., 7.

67. McLaughlin, Stephanie. "Embattled BRI receives only conditional certification." *Boston Globe*, 21 January 1995, 30.

68. Cabral, Donna. "Investigation report." DMR Agency Case 2540-94-076, DPPC Case 12440, 3 January 1995.

69. LaSalandra, Michael. "Group home OK'd despite death: Retarded resident died after 'inhuman' treatment." *Boston Herald*, 16 February 1995, 1, 26.

70. Kixe, Paul. "The shocking truth." Boston.com, 17 June 2008. https://www.bostonmagazine.com/2008/06/17/the-shocking-truth/.

71. Ibid., 26.

72. LaSalandra, Michael. "Mom to lawmakers: End aversive therapy." *Boston Herald*, 23 February 1995, 16.

73. Gerry Koocher, a well-known psychologist and author, president of the American Psychological Association in 2006, and dean of the School of Health Studies at Simmons College, served as an expert witness on behalf of Linda's mother.

74. Paige, Connie. "BRI shock treatment probed by lawmakers." *Boston Herald*, 24 February 1995.

75. Paige, Connie. "Panel votes to ban aversive therapy." *Boston Herald*, 1 March 1995.

76. Paige, Connie. "BRI shock treatment probed by lawmakers." *Boston Herald*, 24 February 1995.

77. Paige, Connie. "BRI boss contributed $$ to key House pol." *Boston Herald*, 27 March 1995, 6.

78. Patinkin, M. "Aversive therapy is shocking but necessary." *Providence Journal*, 2 March 1995, E2.

79. Paige, Connie. "Ban on aversive therapy clocked; group home calls judge's temporary order a victory." *Boston Herald*, 25 March 1995, 7

80. Armstrong, David. "State orders school to end shock punishment for autistic students." *Boston Globe*, 24 March 1995, 37.

81. Paige, Connie. "State pulls plug on group home; autism center ordered to stop shock treatments." *Boston Herald*, 24 March 1995, 1.

82. Armstrong, David. "State orders school to end shock punishment for autistic students." *Boston Globe*, 24 March 1995, 37.

83. Ibid.

84. Vesey, K. M., D'Arcangelo, A., and Cavallo, M. Statement of the Disabled Persons Protection Commissioners Regarding Commissioners' Investigation at BRI, 14 March 1995.

85. Prior to her appointment as Bristol probate judge, LaStaiti served as the assistant town counsel, Dartmouth, MA, 1979–1988; legal assistant district attorney, Southern District, 1978–1979; and was in private practice in New Bedford, 1970–1988.

86. Paige, Connie. "Ban on aversive therapy clocked; group home calls judge's temporary order a victory." *Boston Herald*, 25 March 1995, 7.

87. Ibid.

88. Ibid.

89. Berman, J. Memorandum to Margaret Chow-Menzer. JRC's revised plans of J.C., P.M., B.S., M.S., J.F., D.P., *Analysis of Psychologists' Reviews*, 15 September 1995.

90. Paige, Connie. "Inside an aversion therapy facility." *Boston Herald*, 29 March 1995, 1.

91. Ibid.

92. "Probe funds BRI therapy abusive." *Boston Herald*, 30 March 1995, 18.

93. Ferdinand, Pamela. "SJC called to review handling of BRI case." *Boston Globe*, 30 March 1995, 23.

94. LaStaiti, Elizabeth, judge of probate and family court. Bristol, SS. Heard April 5, 1995. Re: JRC vs. Philip Campbell, Commissioner of the Department of Mental Retardation. Entered 14 April 1995.

95. Deposition of Mary C. Cerreto, a Witness Called by the Plaintiffs, in JRC et al. v. Philip Campbell, Superior Court Civil Action No. 86E-0018-GI, 21 April 1995, at Eckert, Seamans, Cherin & Mellot, 37–41.

96. LaStaiti, Judge Elizabeth O'Neil. Findings of Fact, 6 October 1995. Retrieved 15 November 2020 from https://www.clearinghouse.net/chDocs/public/ID-MA-0002-0002.pdf.

97. Jenkins, Brian. "Treatment or torture, aversive therapy in use." CNN transcript 21, 8 July 1996.

10. CONTEMPT

1. Paige, Connie. "Lawmakers push for ban of BRI aversive therapy." *Boston Herald*, 4 May 1995, 18.

2. Judge Rotenberg Educational Center, Inc. v. Commissioner of the Department of Mental Retardation, JRC, 424 Mass. 432, 434.

3. Goudreau & Goudreau Reporting Service. Court transcript. Behavior Re-

search Institute, Inc., et al. v. Philip Campbell, in His Capacity as Commissioner of the Department of Mental Retardation, 26 June 1995.

4. The parties executed the settlement agreement in 1986, and it was adopted as an order of the court on January 7, 1987 (docket 86E0018-G1).

5. Roderick MacLeish, Attorney. BRI, Inc. et al., v. Philip Campbell, 26 June 1995, New Bedford Probate Court, Judge LaStaiti, 34–36.

6. Ibid., 45–47.

7. Kim Murdock, DMR's attorney who also represented OFC, was present in court but did not address the court or examine any witnesses or experts.

8. Judith Yogman, Assistant Attorney General. BRI, Inc. et al v. Philip Campbell, New Bedford Probate Court. Judge LaStaiti, 26 June 1995. 48–52.

9. Ibid., 48–52.

10. LaStaiti, E. Judge, Judith Yogman, Assistant Attorney General. BRI, Inc. et al. v. Philip Campbell, 26 June 1995, New Bedford Probate Court. Judge LaStaiti, 90.

11. Certification and licensing are different. A state has the authority to determine who or what receives a license according to its rules and regulations. Certification is often granted by a nongovernmental agency as an endorsement after completing certain professional requirements. A certification maybe required to obtain a license.

12. Commissioner Campbell's Trial Testimony, June 28, 1995. Bristol Probate Court.

13. BRI et al. v. Mary Kay Leonard, Settlement Agreement, Superior Court Department of the Trial Court, and the Probate and Family Court, Department of the Trial Court, Civil Action No. 86E-0018-G1.

14. Hon. Elizabeth O'Neill LaStaiti. Judgment and Order. Behavior Research Institute, Inc. also called Judge Rotenberg Educational Center, Inc. v. Philip Campbell, in His Capacity as Commissioner of the Department of Mental Retardation. Conclusions of Law, 6 October 1995, 1, 17–18, 48, 86, para. 22 (Corollary Findings: Improper Conduct by DMR and Its Attorneys).

15. Ibid., 27.

16. BRI et al. v. Mary Kay Leonard, Settlement Agreement, Superior Court Department of the Trial Court, and the Probate and Family Court, Department of the Trial Court, Civil Action No. 86E-0018-G1, 12 December 1985.

17. Judge Rotenberg Educational Center, also known as Behavior Research Institute, Inc., v. Philip Campbell, in His Capacity as Commissioner of the Department of Mental Retardation, Conclusion of Law, 6 October 1995, 22.

18. Ibid., 27.

19. Jenkins, Brian. "Behavioral treatment under fire: Parents of autistic, retarded support controversial approach." CNN, 13 November 1995.

20. Paige, Connie. "Judge blasts DMR in $1.1 M ruling." *Boston Herald*, 11 October 1995, 1.

21. Daly, Christopher B. "School for autistic wins 'war' with Massachusetts:

Judge suggests officials lied in opposing therapy." *Washington Post*, 10 October 1995.

22. Ibid.

23. Armstrong, David. "Judge raps state agency in treatment center case." *Boston Globe*, 11 October 1995, 1.

24. Paige, Connie. "AG appeals fine and loss of state control over BRI." *Boston Herald*, 13 October 1995, 25.

25. Armstrong, David. "Ruling on aversive therapy center attacked as a miscarriage of justice." *Boston Globe*, 13 October 1995, 33.

26. "Judge: Agency's lawyers schemed to shut clinic." *National Law Journal*, 13 November 1995.

27. Nixon, James J., receiver. Letter to Commissioner, DMR, 17 November 1995.

28. Nixon, J. J., receiver, Letter to Matthew Israel, 12 February 1996.

29. Armstrong, D. "Judge raps state agency in treatment center case." *Boston Globe*, 11 October 1995, 1.

30. Paige, Connie. "AG appeals fine and loss of state control over BRI." *Boston Globe*, 13 October 1995, 25.

31. Berman, J. Memo to Margaret Chow-Menzer. Re: JRC's addendum to its proposed findings of fact and conclusions of law. Massachusetts Department of Mental Retardation, October 1995.

32. Ibid., JRC Allegation 20, p. 37.

33. Singal, B. Memorandum to Campbell File. Privileged and Confidential Subject to Attorney-Client Privilege, Attorney Work Product. Re: Meeting with Gil Nadeau (the First Assistant District Attorney for Bristol County), 1 December 1995.

34. Eric MacLeish represented sixty-eight accusers of Father Porter, a Massachusetts Catholic priest accused of sexual abuse. The case revealed that the Roman Catholic Church had extensive files on abusers. Daignault, who was the court monitor, was the psychologist who tested each of the victims. The suit resulted in a settlement that involved a large sum of money being paid to the accusers. Daignault's involvement in the case was a concern to the Massachusetts DMR, which felt that his alliance with MacLeish made him biased.

35. Singal, B. Memorandum to Campbell File, 1 December 1995.

36. Armstrong, David. "Call log rebuts DMR chief: Shows Texas work on Bay State Time." *Boston Globe*, 26 October 1995, 29.

37. Armstrong, David. "Agency chief free-lancing in question: Campbell's financial report didn't include all his earnings." *Boston Globe*, 25 October 1995, 21.

38. Armstrong, David. "Call log rebuts DMR chief: Shows Texas work on Bay State Time." *Boston Globe*, 26 October 1995, 29.

39. Armstrong, David. "Top DMR aides did outside work; Some failed to report income, records say." *Boston Globe*, 16 November 1995, 29.

40. Ibid.

41. Armstrong, David. "Official is fined, to stay at DMR." *Boston Globe*, 6 January 1996, 13.

42. "Meeting the needs of the retarded." *Boston Globe*, 31 October 1995.

43. Armstrong, David. "Official is fined, to stay at DMR." *Boston Globe*, 6 January 1996, 13.

44. Armstrong, David. "Ruling backing shock-care school is appealed." *Boston Globe*, 2 February 1996, 63.

45. McPhee, M. R. "Mental health officials urged to resign." *Boston Globe*, 9 July 1995, 26.

46. Paige, Connie. "Activists ask mental health chiefs to quit." *Boston Herald*, 8 July 1995, 6.

47. Knauss, W. *Advocacy Network News* 44:2 (1996): 3.

48. Nixon, James J., receiver. Letter to Gerald Morrissey, deputy commissioner, DMR, 27 March 1996.

49. Butterworth, John. "BRI receiver endangers freedom of choice." TASH/New England Action alert, 30 April 1996.

50. Chow-Menzer, Margaret. Letter to Hon. James J. Nixon, 2 April 1996.

51. JRC, Inc., Matthew L. Israel; Paul Peterson, Individually and as Parent and Next Friend of David Peterson; Duncan McKnight, Individually and as Parent and Next Friend of David McKnight; and Mari Washington, Individually and as Parent and Next Friend of Jacque Washington; on Behalf of Themselves and All Others Similarly Situated (Plaintiffs v. Philip Campbell, Individually, and Kim Murdock Individually, Defendants. Civil Action No. C96-01146. Superior Court, Bristol, SS. Commonwealth of Massachusetts, 15 August 1996.

52. Judge Rotenberg Educational Center, Inc., & Others v. Commissioner of the Department of Mental Retardation (No. 1), Supreme Judicial Court for the Commonwealth in Case No. SJC-07101, 13 March 1997.

53. Ibid., 57.

54. Armstrong, David. "SJC relieves agency of power over center." *Boston Globe*, 14 March 1997, A1. Estes, Andrea. "SJC supports center on shock therapy use." *Boston Herald*, 14 March 1997.

55. Wong, Doris S., and Vigue, Doreen I. "Campbell quits DMR post. Resignation pleases patients' advocates." *Boston Globe*, 15 March 1997, A1.

56. Estes, A. "SJC supports center on shock therapy use." *Boston Herald*, 14 March 1997.

57. Ibid.

58. Wong, S. D., and Vigue, D. I. "Campbell quits DMR post. Resignation pleases patients' advocates." *Boston Globe*, 15 March 1997, A1.

59. Hammel, Lee. "DMR chief's exit lamented, applauded." *Worcester Telegram and Gazette*, 19 March 1997, A2.

60. Since 2008 Massachusetts has closed six of its eight state-run institutions for people with developmental disabilities; in 2019, according to "Case for Inclusion," 409, people still live in the two remaining state developmental centers.

"Case for Inclusion" sponsored by United Cerebral Palsy, ANCOR Foundation; and Included, Supported Empowered, retrieved 18 April 2021, from http://mediad.publicbroadcasting.net/p/wusf/files/201901/UCP_Case_for_Inclusion_Report_2019_Final_Single_Page.pdf.

61. Hammel, Lee. "Morrissey named acting head of DMR." *Worcester Telegram and Gazette*, 15 April 1997, A2.

62. Markoe, Lauren. "State to pay $1.5M settlement to center for retarded." *Patriot Ledger*, 24 December 1997, 6.

63. Sullivan, Paul, and Heaney, Joe. "Teen injured in fall from moving school bus." *Boston Herald*, 6 May 1998, 16.

64. Heslam, Jessie. "Retarded boy falls from bus on I-95: Teen struggling with counselor." *Patriot Ledger*, 6 May 1998, 13.

65. Wong, Doris. S. "Youth dies after apparent jump from moving bus." *Boston Globe*, 7 May 1998, B10.

11. MORE LEGAL ISSUES, AND ADVOCATES TAKE ACTION

1. Gonnerman, J. "31 shocks later." *New York Magazine*, 31 August 2012.
2. Ibid.
3. Ibid.
4. Ibid.
5. National Alliance of Mental Illness, https://www.nami.org/Learn-More/Treatment/Mental-Health-Medications/Types-of-Medication/Risperidone-(Risperdal).
6. See the following unpublished papers at http://www.effectivetreatment.org/papers.html: Worsham, R., von Heyn, R., and Israel, M. "Medication and behavior modification treatment in cases of schizophrenia, bipolar disorder, and head injury (L.B.M)," 2002; Parrillo, L., Rivera, P., Israel, M., and Boisvert, C. "Effects of positive-only behavioral programming to replace the need for psychotropic medication to control behavior," 2003; von Heyn, R., Israel, M., Paisey, T., Joseph, A., Kelley, M., and Sutherland, H.. "Minimization of the use of psychotropic medication in a large residential facility," 2004.
7. Gonnerman, J. "31 shocks later." *New York Magazine*, 31 August 2012.
8. Ibid.
9. Ibid.
10. Ibid.
11. Ibid.
12. Gonnerman, J. "School of shock." *Mother Jones*, 20 August 2007.
13. Adams, H. "This controversial Massachusetts facility is the last in the country to use electric shock on students." *MassLive*, 22 July 2016, retrieved 24 April 2020 from https://www.masslive.com/news/2016/07/inside_judge_rotenberg_center.html.
14. Gonnerman, J. "31 shocks later." *New York Magazine*, 31 August 2012.
15. Ibid.
16. Adams, H. "This controversial Massachusetts facility is the last in the

country to use electric shock on students." *MassLive*, 22 July 2016, retrieved 24 April 2020 from https://www.masslive.com/news/2016/07/inside_judge _rotenberg_center.html.

17. "Teen is tied down shocked by teachers at 'school' for autistic kids." *Mother Jones*, 11 April 2012.

18. Fox 25 News, 11 April 2012, https://www.driadvocacy.org/video-evidence -of-torture-at-jrc-released-to-public/.

19. Ibid.

20. Ibid.

21. Ibid.

22. Ibid.

23. Neumeier, S. "The Judge Rotenberg Center on trial, part one," 16 April 2012, retrieved 18 April 2020 from https://autisticadvocacy.org/2012/04/the -judge-rotenberg-center-on-trial-part-one/.

24. Ibid.

25. http://www.lubinandmeyer.com/cases/rotenberg-shock.html, retrieved 15 April 2020.

26. https://www.tl4j.com/team/benjamin-r-novotny/, retrieved 15 April 2020.

27. Gonnerman, J. "School of shock." *Mother Jones*, 20 August 2007. Persky, A. "A question of education: For some parents, shock treatment and other aversive interventions are the only hope for helping their kids." *ABA Journal* 99:1 (2013): 13–19, retrieved 21 May 2020 from www.jstor.org/stable/23423832.

28. Fox 25 News, 11 April 2012, https://www.driadvocacy.org/video-evidence -of-torture-at-jrc-released-to-public/

29. New York State Education Department, "JRC Program Visitation Report," 9 June 2006, 14. The full report is at https://autistichoya.net/judge-rotenberg -center/#stategovt. "Video: Jennifer Msumba recounts her experience being at Judge Rotenberg Center," National ADAPT, retrieved 24 April 2020 from https://www.facebook.com/NationalAdapt/videos/1883463555059834/?v= 1883463555059834. Bristol Probate and Family Court, Commonwealth of Massachusetts. Motion to Amend Treatment Plan, February 1989.

30. Reynolds, D. "JRC under three investigations; mom sues state that sent son to facility." *Inclusion Daily Express*, 3 May 2006. Burrell, Chris. "Rotenberg Center under fire in civil lawsuit." *Patriot Ledger*, 14 April 2012.

31. "Deal ends shock-therapy case: Controversial school settles with family of former autistic student from New York state." *Times Union*, 16 September 2010, retrieved 24 April 2020, from https://www.timesunion.com/news/article/Deal -ends-shock-therapy-case-660541.ph.

32. Ibid.

33. Ibid.

34. Salsberg, B. "Suit settled over shock therapy at Mass. school." AP, 15 September 2010, http://archive.boston.com/news/local/massachusetts/articles /2010/09/15/suit_settled_over_shock_therapy_at_mass_school/.

35. Ibid.

36. "TASH resolution opposing the use of aversive and restrictive procedures," adopted November 2001, retrieved 20 April 2020, from www.tash.org.

37. The original steering committee included representatives of the Autism National Committee, the Judge David L. Bazelon Center for Mental Health Law, the Family Alliance to Stop Abuse and Neglect, the Federation of Families for Children's Mental Health, the National Association of Councils on Developmental Disabilities, the National Association of Protection and Advocacy Systems, the National Down Syndrome Congress, the National Association of State Mental Health Program Directors, and the National Down Syndrome Society.

38. Letter to national disability organizations from TASH, 11 March 2004.

39. Current APRAIS member organizations include the American Association of People with Disabilities, the Association of University Centers on Disability, the Autism Society of America, the Autistic Self Advocacy Network, Children and Adults with Attention-Deficit/Hyperactivity Disorder, the Council of Parent Attorneys and Advocates, the Developmental Disabilities Nurses Association, the Disability Rights Education and Defense Fund, the Epilepsy Foundation of America, Families against Restraint and Seclusion, Family Advocacy and Community Training, the Gamaliel Foundation, Inclusion BC, and Keep Students Safe.

40. https://patch.com/massachusetts/canton/letter-to-the-editor-former-teacher-s-aid-at-judge-roea5aecf44e.

41. Miller, G. "I wonder if parents really know what happens to their children at Judge Rotenberg Center," unpublished manuscript, 17 April 2006.

42. Miller, G. Affidavit, 26 April 2007, later published as "A former Judge Rotenberg Center worker speaks out." *Canton Patch*, 13 September 2011.

43. Ibid.

44. Israel, Matthew. "School of shock: Rotenberg Center director Matthew Israel responds." *Mother Jones*, 5 October 2007.

45. Murphy, J. "School that shocks get slapped." *Village Voice*, 20 October 2006.

46. Glorioso, C. "Video of shock therapy shows life inside school for disabled kids." New York, *News Four*. 12 April 2012, https://www.nbcnewyork.com/news/local/skin-shock-therapy-video-judge-rotenberg-educational-center-canton/1976096/.

47. Murphy, J. "School that shocks get slapped." *Village Voice*, 20 October 2006.

48. Ibid.

49. Rothstein, K. "State presses case vs. 'shrinks'; 10 facing charges." *Boston Herald*, 3 May 2006.

50. Rothstein, K. "Center's 'shrinks' legal? State investigates youth facility." *Boston Herald*, 28 April 2006.

51. Murphy, J. "School that shocks get slapped." *Village Voice*, 20 October 2006.

52. Ibid.

53. Correspondence from Marianne Meacham, general counsel, Department of Mental Retardation to Gregory W. Sullivan, Massachusetts inspector general, 1 March 2007.

54. Ibid.

55. Correspondence from Marianne Meacham, general counsel, Massachusetts Department of Developmental Services, to Nancy Weiss, 5 March 2010.

56. Massachusetts Department of Elementary and Secondary Education, Judge Rotenberg Educational Center, Private Special Education School Program Review Report of Findings; Dates of Onsite Visit: January 23–27, 2006; Follow-up Visits: August 2, 10, and 24, 2006; Date of Draft Report: December 20, 2006; Due Date for Comments: January 12, 2007; Date of Final Report: February 26, 2007; Final Report with Additional Finding: March 28, 2007; Action Plan Due: April 10, 2007; Department of Education Onsite Team Members: Kevin Bobetich, Chairperson Suzanne Conrad, Caryn N. Goldberg, Elizabeth Muller; Follow-up Visits Conducted by: Caryn N. Goldberg, Daniel Mosco.

57. Massachusetts Department of Elementary and Secondary Education, Judge Rotenberg Educational Center, Inc.; Private Special Education School Program Review Report of Findings; Dates of Onsite Visit: June 18–22, 2012; Date of Draft Report: July 17, 2012 Date of Final Report: August 7, 2012; Corrective Action Plan Due: Not Applicable; Department of Elementary and Secondary Education Onsite Team Members: Dee Wyatt, Chairperson Caryn Goldberg, Team Member Helen Murgida, Team Member Paul Bottome, Team Member.

58. Weiss, Nancy. Personal communication to the author, 27 October 2020.

59. Vogel, H., and Waldman, A. "New York City sends $30 million a year to school with history of giving kids electric shocks." *ProPublica*, 23 December 2014.

60. Reynolds, D. "JRC under three investigations; mom sues state that sent son to facility." *Inclusion Daily Express*, 3 May 2006.

61. The review took place on April 25 and 26 and May 16–18.

62. Rusty Kindlon, Susan Bandini, and Christopher Suriano, all regional associates, and Paula Tyner-Doyle, a registered dietitian.

63. Caroline Magyar is a "licensed psychologist and a licensed board certified behavior analyst . . . She has held clinical, teaching, administrative, and research positions, including a faculty position in the Neurodevelopmental and Behavioral Pediatrics Division and the University Center of Excellence in Developmental Disabilities at the University of Rochester." Retrieved 8 April 2020 from http://www.magyarpsychservices.com/index.cfm?Page=About. Daniel Crimmins is currently the director of the Center for Leadership in Disability and a professor of public health at Georgia State University. The center's website describes him as having worked to improve the capacity of organizations and individuals to provide evidence-based behavioral and educational interventions for children and adults with neurodevelopmental disabilities. https://publichealth.gsu.edu/profile/daniel-crimmins/. Retrieved 8 April, 2020. David Roll is a professor emeritus at Long Island University. He served as director of clinical training,

and coordinator of the developmental disabilities concentration in the clinical psychology doctoral program. He is a licensed psychologist and a licensed behavior analyst. He was a founder of the New York State Association for Behavior Analysis and served as president of the association and chair or member of the Legislative Committee from 1996 to 2010. https://bipservices.com/our_team/D _Roll.htm. Retrieved 8 April 2020.

64. Massachusetts Department of Developmental Service regulations section 115 CMR 5.14 (Behavioral Modification) defines Level III interventions: "The following shall be deemed Level III Interventions for purposes of 115 CMR 5.14, provided that no such Level III Intervention may be used except in accordance with the standards and procedures set forth in 115 CMR 5.14(4), including without limitation the special certification requirement of 115 CMR 5.14(4)(f) and the general requirement of 115 CMR 5.14(4)(b) that a determination be made that the predictable risks, as weighed against the benefits of the procedure, would not pose an unreasonable degree of intrusion, restriction of movement, physical harm or psychological harm: 1. Any Intervention which involves the contingent application of physical contact aversive stimuli such as spanking, slapping, hitting or contingent skin shock. 2. Time Out wherein an individual is placed in a room alone for a period of time exceeding 15 minutes. 3. Any Intervention not listed in 115 CMR 5.14 as a Level I or Level II Intervention which is highly intrusive and/or highly restrictive of freedom of movement. 4. Any Intervention which alone, in combination with other Interventions, or as a result of multiple applications of the same Intervention poses a significant risk of physical or psychological harm to the individual."

65. New York State Education Department, "JRC Program Visitation Report," 9 June 2006. The report was based on visits on April 25 and 26 and May 16 to May 18. The full report can be found at https://autistichoya.net/judge-rotenberg -center/#stategovt.

66. Israel, Matthew. "School of shock: Rotenberg Center director Matthew Israel responds." *Mother Jones*, 5 October, 2007, 3.

67. Ibid.

68. Seville, L. S., Rappleye, H., Tomassoni, T., and Narizhnaya, K. "New York's boarding school of hard knocks." *219 Magazine*, 24 August 2011, retrieved 17 September 2020 from https://www.219mag.com/controversial-mass-school -depends-on-ny/.

69. Weiss, N. "What kind of people are at JRC now?" Unpublished manuscript, March 2010.

70. Ahern, L., and Rosenthal, E. "Torture Not Treatment: Electric Shock and Long-Term Restraint in the United States on Children and Adults with Disabilities at the Judge Rotenberg Center." Washington, DC: Mental Disability Rights International, 2010, 7.

71. Ibid.

72. Seville, L. S., Rappleye, Tomassoni, T., and Narizhnaya, K. "New York's

boarding school of hard knocks." *219 Magazine* retrieved 17 September 2020 from https://www.219mag.com/controversial-mass-school-depends-on-ny/.

73. Retrieved 18 October from 2020 https://nces.ed.gov/surveys/pss/private schoolsearch/school_detail.asp?Search=1&Zip=02021&Miles=1&ID=A9701991.

74. Massachusetts Department of Early Education and Care. "Investigative report, incident #49037, facility #4904051," 1 November 2007.

75. "Report to the court of the August 26, 2007, incident at the Judge Rotenberg Center, Inc.," submitted by JRC to the probate court, 27 December 2007.

76. Massachusetts Department of Early Education and Care. "Investigative report, incident #49037, facility #4904051," 1 November 2007.

77. Ibid.

78. Ibid.

79. Associated Press. "Staff fired over prank-call shock treatments." 20 December 2007.

80. Pilkington, E. "Founder of electric shock autism treatment school forced to quit." *Guardian*, 25 May 2011.

81. Ibid.

82. Gonnerman, J. "School of shock." *Mother Jones*, 20 August 2007.

83. Ibid.

84. Ibid.

85. Israel, M. "School of shock: Rotenberg Center Director Matthew Israel responds." *Mother Jones*, 5 October 2007, retrieved 22 April 2020 from https://www.motherjones.com/politics/2007/10/school-shock-rotenberg-center-director-matthew-israel-responds/.

86. Ibid.

87. Correspondence from Nancy Weiss and Derrick Jeffries to the American Psychological Association, 10 October 2007.

88. In February 2012, the APA adopted "Guidelines for Ethical Conduct in the Care and Use of Nonhuman Animals for Research," a fourteen-page document describing protections for animals used in experimentation including, "Whenever possible behavioral procedures should be used that minimize discomfort to the nonhuman animal. Psychologists should adjust the parameters of aversive stimulation to the minimal levels compatible with the aims of the research. Consideration should be given to providing the research animals control over the potential aversive stimulation whenever it is consistent with the goals of the research. Whenever reasonable, psychologists are encouraged to first test the painful stimuli to be used on nonhuman animal subjects on themselves." And "Procedures involving more than momentary or slight aversive stimulation, which is not relieved by medication or other acceptable methods, should be undertaken only when the objectives of the research cannot be achieved by other methods."

89. https://autisticadvocacy.org/about-asan/, retrieved April 29, 2020.

90. Ibid.

91. For op-eds, letters to the editor, and editorials, go to https://www

.autistichoya.com. Among them are these: "Past time to ban skin shocks to disabled," by Shain M. Neumeier (*USA Today*, 16 May 2016), and "Why Hasn't Electric Shock Treatment for Autistic People Been Banned?" by Lydia X. Z. Brown (*The Establishment*, 3 August 2016). Blog post and article example: "Autistic Hoya: Level III aversives and the Judge Rotenberg Center," by Lydia X. Z. Brown (22 July 2011). For a summary of my testimony and the JRC's testimony at a 2011 hearing of the Massachusetts Department of Developmental Services regarding new regulations (promulgated) prohibiting the use of the GED shock device on newly admitted students at the JRC, see Shain M. Neumeier, "Silence breaking sound: Tell the FDA: Stop the shock!" 7 May 2016, https://www.autistichoya.com.

92. https://autistichoya.net/judge-rotenberg-center/, retrieved 30 April 2020.

93. Davies, Quentin. "Prisoners of the Apparatus," retrieved 30 April 2020 from https://autisticadvocacy.org/2014/08/prisoners-of-the-apparatus/.

94. https://sites.google.com/site/occupythejudgerotenbergcenter/home, retrieved 30 April 2020.

95. Ari Ne'eman cofounded the Autistic Self Advocacy Network in 2006. He was appointed by President Barack Obama in 2009 to serve on the National Council on Disability. He chaired the council's Policy and Program Evaluation Committee. Diagnosed with Asperger syndrome, he was the first autistic person to serve on the council. In 2019 he was a Ph.D. candidate in health policy at Harvard University.

96. Pilkington, E. "UN calls for investigation of US school's shock treatments of autistic children." *Guardian*, 2 June 2012.

97. In one of President Obama's first acts as president in 2009, he signed an executive order to close the U.S. detention camps at the Abu Ghraib prison and Guantanamo Bay, Cuba. In the first month of his presidency, he signed an order to prohibit the use of harsh interrogation methods beyond those permitted by the U.S. military as waterboarding and other techniques of torture were being discussed regularly in the news and by Americans who either supported or were opposed to Obama's controversial policies. People were referring to Obama as the "anti-torture president."

98. American Association on Intellectual and Developmental Disabilities; Association of University Centers on Disabilities; Arc of the U.S.; the Autism National Committee; Autistic Self Advocacy Network; Center on Human Policy, Law, and Disability Studies, Syracuse University; Disability Rights Education and Defense Fund; Easter Seals; *Exceptional Parent* magazine; National Association of County Behavioral Health and Developmental Disability Directors; National Association of Councils on Developmental Disabilities; National Association for the Dually Diagnosed; National Disability Rights Network; Self Advocates Becoming Empowered; TASH; United Cerebral Palsy; University of Medicine and Dentistry of New Jersey; School of Nursing, University of San Diego; Autism Institute; and others.

99. It was also sent to Office on Disability, U.S. Department of Health and Human Services; secretary of the U.S. Department of Health and Human Ser-

vices; secretary of the U.S. Department of Education; attorney general of the United States; U.S. Department of Justice; House Committee on Education and Labor; and Senate Committee on Health, Education, Labor, and Pensions.

100. Letter: https://autistichoya.files.wordpress.com/2016/04/letter-from -disability-advocates-govt-agencies-and-human-rights-orgs-end-inhumane -practices-sept-09.pdf; addendum: https://autistichoya.files.wordpress .com/2016/04/addendum-to-sept-09-letter-from-disability-advocates-end -inhumane-practices2.pdf. Retrieved 29 April 2020.

101. Duncan, Arne, secretary of education, U.S. Department of Education. Letter to Nancy Weiss, 26 January 2010.

102. Ibid.

103. Wohlenhaus, Renee. Email to Nancy Weiss, complaint about Judge Rotenberg Center, 7 January 2010.

104. Young, Jonathan, chairman, National Council on Disability. Letter to Alison Nichol, chief of the U.S. Department of Justice, Civil Rights Division, Disability Rights Section, 12 April 2012.

105. McKim, J. "FDA misses its deadline to ban shocks at Canton school for students with disabilities." *WGBH News*, 3 January 2020. McKim, Jennifer, investigative reporter, New England Center for Investigative Reporting at WGBH News. Email to Nancy Weiss, 29 April 2020.

106. Gentes-Hunt, Lisa. "Judge Rotenberg Center's founder responds to indictment, allegations." *Patch*, 26 May 2011, retrieved 27 October 2020, from https://patch.com/massachusetts/canton/judge-rotenberg-centers-founder -responds-to-indictment4fce86c98d.

107. Disability Rights International. "Director of Massachusetts 'shock school' resigns after being indicted on criminal charges," 26 May 2011.

108. Pilkington, E. "Founder of electric shock autism treatment school forced to quit." *Guardian*, 25 May 2011.

109. Ibid.

110. Borenstein, I. "Report by Monitor Judge Isaac Borenstein (Ret.) for the Judge Rotenberg Educational Center (JRC)," 22 February 2013, 2.

111. Ibid.

112. Documents reviewed included (as examples) clients' records, human resource records, JRC policies, human rights committee responsibilities and minutes, staff training materials, the JRC employee manual, complaint procedures, staff schedules, resignation summary reports, letters regarding GED spontaneous activations and misapplications, restraint committee policies and minutes, safety committee procedures and minutes, incident review committee minutes, nursing notes, restraint forms, and quarterly progress notes.

113. Borenstein, I. "Report by Monitor Judge Isaac Borenstein (Ret.) for the Judge Rotenberg Educational Center (JRC)," 22 February 2013, 10.

114. Ibid.

115. Ibid., 57.

116. Ibid., 58.

117. Ibid.

118. Ibid. 106.

119. Ibid., 123.

120. Ibid., ii.

121. Ibid., 3.

122. https://canton.wickedlocal.com/x1506808054/Report-criticizes-Canton-school-that-uses-shock-therapy, retrieved 21 May 2020.

123. https://www.driadvocacy.org/, retrieved 11 October 2020.

124. Ahern, L., and Rosenthal, E. "Torture Not Treatment: Electric Shock and Long-Term Restraint in the United States on Children and Adults with Disabilities at the Judge Rotenberg Center, an Urgent Appeal to the United Nations Special Rapporteur on Torture." Washington, DC: Disability Rights International, 2010.

125. Ibid.

126. Hinman, K., and Brown, K. "UN calls shock treatment at Mass. school 'torture': United Nations calls use of skin shocks on students at Mass. school 'torture.'" *ABC News*, 29 June 2010, retrieved 30 April 2020 from https://abcnews.go.com/Nightline/shock-therapy-massachussetts-school/story?id=11047334.

127. Pilkington, E. "Shock tactics: Treatment or torture?" *Guardian*, 11 March 2011.

128. Hinman, K., and Brown, K. "UN calls shock treatment at Mass. school 'torture': United Nations calls use of skin shocks on students at Mass. school 'torture.'" *ABC News*, 29 June 2010, retrieved 30 April 2020, from https://abcnews.go.com/Nightline/shock-therapy-massachussetts-school/story?id=11047334.

129. Méndez, J. E. *Report of the Special Rapporteur on torture and other cruel, inhuman or degrading treatment or punishment.* Human Rights Council Twenty-Second Session Agenda item 3: Promotion and protection of all human rights, civil, political, economic, social and cultural rights, including the right to development, 4 March 2013.

130. Department of Developmental Services. Response to Testimony and Written Comments to Proposed Amendments to Behavior Modification Regulations, 115 CMR 5.14, 14 October 2011.

131. "1. Any Intervention which involves the contingent application of physical contact aversive stimuli such as spanking, slapping, hitting or contingent skin shock. 2. Time Out wherein an individual is placed in a room alone for a period of time exceeding 15 minutes. 3. Any Intervention not listed in 115 CMR 5.14 as a Level I or Level II Intervention which is highly intrusive and/or highly restrictive of freedom of movement. 4. Any Intervention which alone, in combination with other Interventions, or as a result of multiple applications of the same Intervention poses a significant risk of physical or psychological harm to the individual."

132. DeLorenzo, J. P., assistant commissioner, Office of Special Education, New York State Education Department. Letter to Matthew Israel, executive director, 23 March 2009.

133. Ibid.

134. DeLorenzo, J. P, assistant commissioner, Office of Special Education, New York State Education Department. Letter to Glenda Crookes, executive director, JRC, 15 February 2012.

135. Ibid.

136. Seville, L. S., Rappleye, H., Tomassoni, T., and Narizhnaya, K. "New York's boarding school of hard knocks." *219 Magazine*, 24 August 2011, retrieved 17 September 2020 from https://www.219mag.com/controversial-mass-school -depends-on-ny/.

137. Ibid.

138. Ibid.

139. Ibid.

140. Ibid.

141. Ibid.

142. Ibid.

143. Vogel, H., and Waldman, A. "New York City sends $30 million a year to school with history of giving kids electric shocks." *ProPublica*, 23 December 2014.

144. Ibid.

145. New York State Education Department. "JRC Program Visitation Report —6/9/2006." The report was based on visits on April 25 and 26 and May 16 to 18, 2006." The full report is at https://autistichoya.net/judge-rotenberg-center /#stategovt.

146. Ibid.

147. List of past exhibitors: American Probation and Parole Association, 2017; Conference prospectus, Virginia Juvenile Justice Association, 2020; Conference prospectus, National Council of Juvenile and Family Court Judges, 2020; Conference prospectus, New York City Young Child Expo and Conference, 2020. Conference prospectus, National Association of School Psychologists, 2020; National Association of School Psychologists, 2020.

148. Vogel, H., and Waldman, A. "New York City sends $30 million a year to school with history of giving kids electric shocks." *ProPublica*, 23 December 2014.

149. DeLorenzo, James P., New York State Education Department. Letter to Avena Russell, Center for Devices and Radiological Health, FDA, 14 April 2014.

150. Ibid.

151. New York State Education Department. "JRC Program Visitation Report —6/9/2006." The report is based on visits on April 25 and 26 and May 16 to 18, 2006. The full report is at http://boston.com/news/daily/15/school_report.pdf.

152. DeLorenzo, J. P., assistant commissioner, Office of Special Education, New York State Education Department. Letter to Dr. Matthew Israel, executive director, JRC, 23 March 2009.

153. New York State Department of Education and the Office of Mental Retardation and Developmental Disabilities. "Site visit report," January 1979.

154. From http://www.p12.nysed.gov/specialed/privateschools/os.htm, retrieved 14 October 2020.

155. McKim, Jenifer. "Abuse claims persist for Canton-based special needs school." WGBH News/New England Center for Investigative Reporting, 29 October 2018.

156. Ibid. https://www.documentcloud.org/documents/4380424-JRC.html, retrieved 24 September 2020.

157. McKim, Jenifer. "Abuse claims persist for Canton-based special needs school." WGBH News/New England Center for Investigative Reporting, 29 October 2018.

158. The two state agencies that monitor care are the Massachusetts Disabled Persons Protection Commission and the Massachusetts Department of Early Education and Care which licenses residential group care facilities for residents under the age of 22. McKim, J. "Rotenberg Center: Culture of abuse or miracle worker?" *Patriot Ledger*, 29 October 2018. In one incident in June 2010, a thirty-minute brawl erupted in a JRC group home resulting in three teenage residents going to the hospital. Five police officers were sent to control the fight that resulted in injuries including a broken wrist and a broken hip. "Canton police Lieutenant, Patty Sherrill, one of the officers on the scene, said her department may press criminal charges in this altercation which involved students as well as a half-dozen staff members, some of whom had donned helmets." Lieutenant Sherrill said that in her seventeen years with the Canton Police Department, she had "never seen anything like this." She also reported that one of the teenage students turned to her and whispered, "Miss, you have to get me out of here. I fear for my safety." Wen, P. "Three injured in brawl at group home; Canton police may seek charges in altercation." *Boston Globe*, 29 June 2010.

159. Cotter, S. P. "Rotenberg Center employees charged with beating disabled student." *Patriot Ledger*, 13 December 2016.

160. Cotter, S. P. "State finds abuse, seeks changes at Judge Rotenberg Center." *Patriot Ledger*, 22 June 2017.

161. Ibid.

162. Ibid.

163. Ibid.

164. Ibid.

165. Linton, D. "Ex-worker pleads guilty to hitting Attleboro group home resident." *Sun Chronicle*, 18 October 2018.

166. In some of the other incidents, it was residents of the Judge Rotenberg Center who were arrested. In a November 2011 incident, police were called because three group home residents had assaulted staff and had barricaded themselves in a room. All three residents were charged with assault and battery. In August 2016, police arrested a JRC resident for breaking the glass on a framed picture and stabbing another resident. In February 2017, two teenage residents were charged with assaulting staff members during a disturbance at a JRC group home. In August of the same year, police arrested a 20-year-old JRC resident and

charged him with disorderly conduct and resisting arrest. Wen, Patricia. "Three injured in brawl at group home: Canton police may seek charges in altercation." *Boston Globe*, 29 June 2010; Snyder, M. "Three arrested after alleged assault at Rotenberg home." *Wicked Local Stoughton*, 7 November 2011; Shepard, Cody. "Judge Rotenberg Center resident charged with cutting man in Easton," *Enterprise*, 16 August 2016; Shepard, Cody. "Two Rotenberg Center students charged with assaulting Stoughton staff." *Enterprise*, 3 February 2017; Relihan, Tom. "Judge Rotenberg Center resident arrested in Stoughton following fight." *Enterprise*. 18 August 2017.

167. McKim, Jenifer. "Abuse claims persist for Canton-based special needs school." WGBH News/New England Center for Investigative Reporting, 29 October 2018.

168. Ibid.

169. Ibid.

170. Ibid.

171. The self injurious behavior inhibiting system (SIBIS) was cleared by the FDA in 1986 as being substantially equivalent to the Whistle Stop. The FDA described the device's indications for use as being "for the treatment of retarded or autistic clients who exhibit head-banging behavior of sufficient intensity and frequency to cause acute or chronic physical damage. The device should be used only in patients where other forms of therapy have been attempted and failed." A second version of the SIBIS device was cleared by the FDA in 1987 "to treat self-injurious behavior that does not involve blows to the head sufficient to trigger the acceleration sensor," examples being eye gouging, skin pinching, hair pulling, and jaw banging. Finally, the GED was cleared in 1994 "for the treatment of patients, usually diagnosed as retarded or autistic, who exhibit self-injurious behavior of sufficient intensity and frequency to cause serious damage to themselves." It was noted that "the device should be used only on patients where alternate forms of therapy have been attempted and failed." 510(k) #K853178, Clearance date: 2/28/86; FDA Executive Summary prepared for the April 24, 2014 meeting of the Neurological Devices Panel, Electrical Stimulation Devices for Aversive Conditioning, p. 5; 510(k) #K871158, Clearance date: 5/29/87; FDA Executive Summary prepared for the April 24, 2014 meeting of the Neurological Devices Panel, Electrical Stimulation Devices for Aversive Conditioning, p. 5; 510(k) #K911820, Clearance date: 12/5/94; FDA Executive Summary prepared for the April 24, 2014 meeting of the Neurological Devices Panel, Electrical Stimulation Devices for Aversive Conditioning, p. 5.

172. Weiss, N. Letter to Jeffrey Shuren, director, Center for Devices and Radiological Health, FDA, 13 March 2010. The letter identified the multiple places on JRC's website where the center stated or implied that the GED had been approved by the FDA—"The GED is an FDA approved skin shock device used to decelerate inappropriate behaviors"—and also raised concerns about a page on the JRC website that was titled, "Acceptance by the FDA." This page also included the following statement: "GED skin shock device was submitted to FDA

for approval (registration) in 1990. GED device was approved (registered) in 1991."

173. Weiss, N. Letter to Jeffrey Shuren, director, Center for Devices and Radiological Health, FDA, 13 March 2010.

174. Israel, M. L., von Heyn, R. E., and Connolly, D. A. "A remote-controlled electric shock device for behavior modification." JRC pub. no. 92-3r, © Behavior Research Institute, 1992. The article is available at effectivetreatment.org. The website contains dozens of JRC papers, publications, conference presentations, video clips, and other material.

175. Israel, M. L., von Heyn, R. E., and Connolly, D. A. "A remote-controlled electric shock device for behavior modification." JRC pub. no. 92-3r, Behavior Research Institute, 1992. http://www.effectivetreatment.org/remote.html.

176. Ibid.

177. The SIBIS device was submitted for 510(k) premarket notification by John K. Laurie or Oxford Medilog Inc. on July 30, 1985, and received 501(k) clearance on February 26, 1986. It did not have full FDA review and approval but was approved as being substantially equivalent to a previous device. Both it and the substantially equivalent device were cleared under Title 21, Chapter 1, Food and Drug Administration, Part 882 (Neurological Devices), Subpart F (Neurological therapeutic Devices, Sec. 882.5235 (Aversive Conditioning Devices). An aversive conditioning device is defined in the regulations as an instrument used to administer an electric shock or other noxious stimulus to a patient to modify undesirable behavioral characteristics. The SIBIS is considered a preamendments device, a term that refers to devices legally marketed in the United States by a firm before May 28, 1976, that have not been significantly changed or modified since then and for which a regulation requiring a PMA application has not been published by FDA. Devices meeting the criteria are grandfathered in and do not require a 510(k). The device must have the same intended use as that marketed before May 28, 1976. If the device is labeled for a different intended use, it is considered a new device, and a 510(k) must be submitted to FDA for marketing clearance. https://www.fda.gov/medical-devices/premarket-submissions/premarket-notification-510k.

178. Weiss, N. Letter to J. Shuren, M.D., J.D., director, Center for Devices and Radiological Health, FDA, 13 March 2010.

179. A 510(k) is a premarket submission made to the FDA to demonstrate that the device to be marketed is as safe and effective (and therefore substantially equivalent to) as a legally marketed device (section 513(i)(1)(A) FD&C Act) that is not subject to premarket approval. https://www.accessdata.fda.gov/scripts/cdrh/cfdocs/cfpmn/pmn.cfm.

180. The February 2000 FDA letter also established that since modifications had been made to the originally cleared GED device, the new versions of the device, the GED-3A and the GED-4, required FDA clearance and approval. The FDA described the changes that had been made in the GED-3A and the GED-4 that resulted in these two versions of the device now requiring clearance and

approval, including modifications of the intended use by adding "severe behavior problems." In the FDA's view, this added use signified "a new patient population . . . and raises new questions of safety and effectiveness." The letter noted as well that the new devices provided a stronger shock, raising "concerns of tissue heating and burns."

181. From the FDA website: "Each person who wants to market in the U.S., a Class I, II, and III device intended for human use, for which a Premarket Approval application (PMA) is not required, must submit a 510(k) to FDA unless the device is exempt from 510(k) requirements of the Federal Food, Drug, and Cosmetic Act (the FD&C Act) and does not exceed the limitations of exemptions in .9 of the device classification regulation chapters (e.g., 21 CFR 862.9, 21 CFR 864.9). There is no 510(k) form; however, 21 CFR 807 Subpart E describes requirements for a 510(k) submission. Before marketing a device, each submitter must receive an order, in the form of a letter, from FDA which finds the device to be substantially equivalent (SE) and states that the device can be marketed in the U.S. This order 'clears' the device for commercial distribution (see The 510(k) Program Guidance). A 510(k) is a premarket submission made to FDA to demonstrate that the device to be marketed is as safe and effective, that is, substantially equivalent, to a legally marketed device (section 513(i)(1)(A) FD&C Act). Submitters must compare their device to one or more similar legally marketed devices and make and support their substantial equivalence claims. A legally marketed device is a device that was legally marketed prior to May 28, 1976 (pre-amendments device), or a device which has been reclassified from Class III to Class II or I, a device which has been found SE through the 510(k) process, or a device that was granted marketing authorization via the De Novo classification process under section 513(f)(2) of the FD&C Act that is not exempt from premarket notification requirements. The legally marketed device(s) to which equivalence is drawn is commonly known as the 'predicate.' Although devices recently cleared under 510(k) are often selected as the predicate to which equivalence is claimed, any legally marketed device may be used as a predicate. Legally marketed also means that the predicate cannot be one that is in violation of the FD&C Act." Retrieved 9 April 2020 from https://www.fda.gov/medical-devices/premarket-submissions/premarket-notification-510k.

182. FDA. Letter to Matthew Israel of the Judge Rotenberg Center, 23 May 2011.

183. Shamsi, Mutahar S., district director of the New England District, Public Health Service, FDA. Letter to Glenda Crookes, interim executive director, JRC, 29 June 2012.

184. Ahern, L., and Rosenthal, E. "Torture Not Treatment: Electric Shock and Long-Term Restraint in the United States on Children and Adults with Disabilities at the Judge Rotenberg Center, an Urgent Appeal to the United Nations Special Rapporteur on Torture." Washington, DC: Mental Disability Rights International, 2010.

185. Shamsi, Mutahar S., district director of the New England District, Public Health Service, FDA. Letter to Glenda Crookes, interim executive director, JRC,

29 June 2012. A warning letter identifies the violation, such as poor manufacturing practices, problems with claims for what a product can do, or incorrect directions for use. The letter also makes clear that the company must correct the problem and provides directions and a time frame for the company to inform FDA of its plans for correction. FDA then checks to ensure that the company's corrections are adequate. Matters described in FDA warning letters may have been subject to subsequent interaction between FDA and the recipient of the letter that may have changed the regulatory status of the issues discussed in the letter. Retrieved 9 April 2020 from https://www.fda.gov/inspections -compliance-enforcement-and-criminal-investigations/warning-letters/about -warning-and-close-out-letters.

186. Shamsi, Mutahar S., district director of the New England District, Public Health Service, FDA. Letter to Glenda Crookes, interim executive director, JRC, 29 June 2012.

187. Crookes, Glenda, executive director of the Judge Rotenberg Center. Letter to Karen Archdeacon, compliance officer, FDA, 21 December 2012.

188. Joyce, Brian A., senator. Letter to Mutahar S. Shamsi, district director of the New England District, Public Health Service, FDA, 8 January 2013,

189. Centers for independent living are consumer-controlled, community-based, cross-disability, nonresidential, private nonprofit agencies that provide independent living services. At a minimum, centers provide information and referral; skills training; peer counseling; individual and systems advocacy; and services that facilitate transition from nursing homes and other institutions to the community, provide assistance to those at risk of entering institutions, and facilitate transition of youth to postsecondary life. Retrieved 23 April 2020 from https://acl.gov/programs/aging-and-disability-networks/centers-independent -living. Boston Center for Independent Living. Letter to Margaret Hamburg, M.D., commissioner of the FDA, 20 February 2013.

190. Weiss, Nancy, on behalf of the Association of People Supporting Employment First, Center for Self-Determination, Institute for Health Quality and Ethics, Council of Parent Attorneys and Advocates, Griffin-Hammis Associates, National Alliance on Mental Illness, National Association of Councils on Developmental Disabilities, National Disability Rights Network, National Down Syndrome Congress, National Organization of Nurses with Disabilities, Not Dead Yet, Service Employees International Union, TASH, Advocacy Institute, and ARC of the U.S. Letter to Margaret Hamburg, commissioner of the FDA, 29 March 2013.

191. FDA executive summary prepared for the April 24, 2014, meeting of the Neurological Devices Panel, Electrical Stimulation Devices for Aversive Conditioning, 72.

192. Glassman, Richard M., litigation director, and Griffin, Christine, executive director, Massachusetts Disability Law Center. Letter to Steven Silverman, director, Office of Compliance, Center for Devices and Radiological Health, FDA, 22 April 2013.

193. https://www.osha.gov/SLTC/etools/construction/electrical_incidents /mainpage.html, retrieved 26 April 2020.

194. Msumba recently became a member of Mensa, a society that welcomes people who have scored in the top 2 percent on a test that the national Mensa group administers.

195. At first Msumba wanted her letter to be anonymous, but within a few months, she decided that she was safe from the Judge Rotenberg Center (if not from the memories and nightmares of it that still tortured her). She gave permission for her name to be used. Soon after, she began a blog.

196. Disability rights advocates speak to students about institutional abuse and torture in America: https://blog.georgetownvoice.com/2014/10/29/disability -rights-advocates-speak-to-students-about-institutional-abuse-and-torture-in -america/.

197. Msumba, Jennifer. "Letter to FDA," January 2013.

198. The 1915(c) HCBS waiver provides Medicaid funding for home and community-based services to individuals who otherwise would meet the eligibility requirements for Medicaid-funded institutional care. The HCBS waiver permits states to use funds that otherwise would have been used for institutional services to purchase home and community-based services. Retrieved 22 October 2020, from https://www.nasddds.org/resource-library/medicaid-hcbs-authorities /1915c-home-and-community-based-services-hcbs-waiver/.

199. https://www.judgerc.org/admissions.html, retrieved 22 October 2020.

200. In 2017, the Medicaid home and community-based services waiver program funded supports for about 800,000 people with intellectual or developmental disabilities at a cost of nearly $39 billion. Supports cost an average of $44,983 per person. Cost averaged $17,022 per person for people 21 years old and younger. Costs averaged $54,481 per person for people or people 22 years or older. Retrieved 22 October 2020 from https://publications.ici.umn.edu/risp /2017/infographics/medicaid-waiver-recipients-and-expenditures.

201. Case No. 93, 2018C, On appeal from the Superior Court, State of Delaware. v. § C.A. No. N16A-05-010 and No. 94, 2018C, C.A. No. N16A-05-009.

202. Prunckun v. Delaware Department of Health and Social Services., 201 A.3d 525, 528 (Del. 2019).

203. https://casetext.com/case/prunckun-v-del-dept-of-health-soc-servs, retrieved March 29, 2021.

204. *Prunckun v. Delaware Department of Health & Soc. Servs.*, 201 A.3d 525 (Del. 2019)

205. Case No. 93, 2018C, On appeal from the Superior Court, State of Delaware. v. § C.A. No. N16A-05-010 and No. 94, 2018C, C.A. No. N16A-05-009

206. Case No. 93, 2018C, On appeal from the Superior Court, State of Delaware. v. § C.A. No. N16A-05-010 and No. 94, 2018C, C.A. No. N16A-05-009

207. Coakley, Martha, Attorney General. Judge Rotenberg Educational Center, Inc., et al., Plaintiffs v. Commissioners of the Department of Development

Services and the Department of Early Education and Care, Defendants. Defendants' Memorandum of Law in Support of Motion under Probate and Family Court Rule 60 and Mass. R. Civ.P. 60(b)(5) to Vacate Consent Decree. Probate and Family Court Department No. 86E-0018-G1, 14 February 2013.

208. Beaudet, Mike, and Rothstein, Kevin. "State asks judge for ability to ban painful shock treatment for disabled." WCVB, ABC News transcript, 20 October 2016.

209. Ibid.

210. Triunfo, C. "State appeals shock treatment court ruling." State House News Service, 25 July 2018, updated 11 July 2019.

211. Beaudet, Mike. "Judge sides with school that uses electric shocks on its students." WCVB 5 transcript, 28 June 2018.

212. Triunfo, C. "State to appeal decision to allow shock therapy." State House News Service, 24 July 2018, updated 25 July 2018.

12. THE FDA BANS THE ELECTRIC SHOCK DEVICE

1. Announcement of Neurological Devices Panel of the Medical Devices Advisory Committee; Notice of Meeting; Request for Comments; Food and Drug Administration, 21 March 2014.

2. FDA Executive Summary, prepared for the April 24, 2014, meeting of the Neurological Devices Panel, Electrical Stimulation Devices for Aversive Conditioning, 1.

3. Announcement of Neurological Devices Panel of the Medical Devices Advisory Committee; Notice of Meeting; Request for Comments; Food and Drug Administration, 21 March 2014.

4. Retrieved 11 May 2020 from https://www.federalregister.gov/d/2020 -04328/p-45.

5. Ibid.

6. Announcement of Neurological Devices Panel of the Medical Devices Advisory Committee; Notice of Meeting; Request for Comments; Food and Drug Administration, 21 March 2014.

7. Lynda J. Yang, M.D., Ph.D., panel chair; E. Ray Dorsey, M.D., M.B.A., voting member; Jason Connor, Ph.D., voting member; Scott Y. Kim, M.D., Ph.D., nonvoting member; Glenn T. Stebbins, Ph.D., nonvoting member; Guerry M. Peavy, Ph.D., nonvoting member; Erika F. Augustine, M.D., nonvoting member; Steven Miles, M.D. nonvoting member; Donald E. Richardson, M.D., nonvoting member; Karen L. Weigle, Ph.D., nonvoting member; Mark W. Green, M.D., nonvoting member; Brian Iwata, Ph.D., nonvoting member; Wayne K. Goodman, M.D., temporary nonvoting member; Daniel Armstrong, Ph.D., temporary nonvoting member; Warren Bickel, Ph.D., temporary nonvoting member; Norman Fost, M.D., M.P.H., temporary nonvoting member; J. Stephen Mikita, J.D., patient representative; Kristine R. Mattivi, M.S., consumer representative; and John B. Reppas, M.D., Ph.D., industry representative.

8. https://www.federalregister.gov/documents/2020/03/06/2020-04328 /banned-devices-electrical-stimulation-devices-for-self-injurious-or-aggressive -behavior, retrieved 11 May 2020.

9. https://www.federalregister.gov/documents/2020/03/06/2020, retrieved 11 May 2020.

10. https://www.regulations.gov/docketBrowser?rpp=25&so=DESC&sb =commentDueDate&po=1500&dct=PS&D=FDA-2016-N-1111, retrieved 11 May 2020.

11. https://www.federalregister.gov/d/2020-04328/p-49, retrieved 11 May 2020.

12. Ibid.

13. DeLorenzo, James P., New York State Education Department. Letter to Avena Russell, Center for Devices and Radiological Health, FDA, 14 April 2014.

14. https://www.federalregister.gov/d/2020-04328/49, retrieved 11 May 2020.

15. The FDA described comments from JRC and JRC affiliates, including those made during the panel meeting and through submission of comments to the panel meeting docket: "Specifically, these comments were from three former JRC residents, family members of individuals on whom ESDs (electrical stimulation devices) have been used at JRC (one of the parents' association comments included thirty-two letters from family members), a former JRC clinician, a Massachusetts State Representative, and one concerned citizen." Retrieved 11 May 2020 from https://www.federalregister.gov/d/2020-04328/.51.

16. https://www.federalregister.gov/d/2016-09433/p-291, retrieved 11 May 2020.

17. Ibid.

18. Ibid.

19. Glenda P. Crookes, executive director, Judge Rotenberg Educational Center; Nathan Blenkush, Ph.D., BCBA-D director of research, Judge Rotenberg Educational Center; Anthony B. Joseph, M.D., Judge Rotenberg Educational Center; and Edward A. Sassaman, M.D., Judge Rotenberg Educational Center.

20. Margaret Nygren, Ed.D., executive director/CEO American Association on Intellectual and Developmental Disabilities (in support of ban); Barbara Trader, executive director, TASH (in support of ban); Kim Musheno, director, Public Policy Association of University Centers on Disabilities (in support of ban); Ari Ne'eman, president, Autistic Self Advocacy Network (in support of ban); Eric Matthews, Disability Rights International (in support of ban); Rick Glassman, director of Advocacy Disability Law Center (in support of ban); Nancy Thaler, executive director, National Association of State Directors of Developmental Disability Services (in support of ban); Nancy Weiss, M.S.W., director, National Leadership Consortium on Developmental Disabilities at the University of Delaware (in support of ban); Fredda Brown, Ph.D., Queens College Regional Center for Autism Spectrum Disorders (in support of ban); Maureen Fitzgerald, director, disability rights, Arc of the United States (in support of ban); ESME grant director public policy, National Association of Councils on Developmental

Disabilities (in support of ban); Louisa Goldberg BRI Parents & Friends Association (opposed to the ban); Christopher Oliva, Ph.D. Gateways: Educational and Behavioral Consultation Services (in support of ban); Jennifer Bellamy, legislative counsel, American Civil Liberties Union (in support of ban); Lydia Brown, board of directors, TASH: New England (in support of ban); Curtis Decker, J.D., executive director, National Disability Rights Network (in support of ban); Emily Minton Occupy JRC (in support of the ban).

21. Aracelis Sanchez, former JRC student/pro-device use; Brian Avery, former JRC student/pro-device use; James Butler, concerned citizen/against device use; Cheryl McCollins, parent of former JRC student/against device use; Diane Engster, J.D., concerned citizen/against device use; Ian Cook, former JRC student/against device use; Lauren Emmick, parent of JRC student/pro-device use; Marcos Pucha, former JRC student/pro-device use; Ilana Slaff-Galatan, M.D., sister of JRC student/pro-device use; Roger and Sharon Wood, parents of JRC student/pro-device use; Michael J. Cameron, Ph.D., pro-device use; Arthur and Michele Perazzo, parents of JRC student/pro-device use; Gregory Miller, former JRC employee/against device use; Jennifer Msumba (video testimony), former JRC student/against device use; Shain Neumeier, concerned citizen/against device use; Vito Albanese, concerned citizen/against device use.

22. Those who spoke during the public hearing representing organizations were allowed four minutes each, and those who spoke during the general session (not representing an organization) had only three minutes in which to convey their point of view.

23. As of the April 24 meeting, the FDA had received 260 documents that were posted to the docket; 102 of these were not deemed confidential and were available on the FDA website. Documents were posted to docket number FDA-2014-N-0238; 158 of those documents were posted as confidential and not to be made public. Because the panelists were deemed special government employees, all of the 260 documents that were posted to the docket were submitted to the panelists for review. A full transcript of the open public hearing of the Medical Devices Advisory Committee, Neurological Devices Panel; April 24, 2014, is available at https://autistichoya.net/judge-rotenberg-center/#federalgovt.

24. Center for Devices and Radiological Health Medical Devices Advisory Committee Neurological Devices Panel, transcript, 24 April 2014, https://wayback.archive.it.org/7993/20170405192749/https:/www.fda.gov /AdvisoryCommittees/CommitteesMeetingMaterials/MedicalDevices /MedicalDevicesAdvisoryCommittee/NeurologicalDevicesPanel/ucm394252 .htm, 163–164.

25. Kern, R. "FDA panel says no to shock therapy device." *MedPage*, 24 April 2014.

26. Ibid.

27. Ibid.

28. Open Public Hearing of the Medical Devices Advisory Committee, Neuro-

logical Devices Panel, full transcript, 24 April 2014, retrieved 11 May 2020 from https://autistichoya.net/judge-rotenberg-center/#federalgovt.

29. Credentials of James C. Eason as described in his affidavit prepared for the April 24, 2014, open public hearing of the Medical Devices Advisory Committee, Neurological Devices Panel:

1. I am currently an Instructor of Biomedical Engineering at College of Engineering, California Polytechnic State University at San Luis Obispo. My professional address is Biomedical and General Engineering Department, California Polytechnic State University, San Luis Obispo, CA, 93407. 2. I hold the following degrees: a Ph. D. in Biomedical Engineering from Duke University; and a B.S. in Electrical Engineering from North Carolina State University. 3. My career has focused on research in the fields of electrophysiology and cardiac electrophysiology. My particular area of expertise is in the physiological responses of nerve and muscle tissue when exposed to applied electric stimuli. In this capacity, I have completed research projects on defibrillation mechanisms at Duke University, defibrillator electrode design at Tulane University, and microelectrode design at the University of Vermont. 4. My professional practice includes scholarly publications on the interactions and relationships between excitable tissues and electric fields, as described in the attached CV, incorporated herein by reference. 5. For more than ten years, I have taught courses in Bioelectricity at the advanced undergraduate level dealing with the response of nerve and muscle tissue to electric currents. In these courses, I lecture on the physiological mechanisms by which electric currents excite nerve and muscle tissue as well as lecturing on safety requirements of related medical devices. 6. As a result of my training, research, and expertise I have been consulted on several occasions by journalists to discuss and interpret technical data regarding devices that employ an electric shock. In response, I have completed in depth technical reviews of electroshock weapons and electric shock devices used for behavioral modification. 7. Given my extensive experience in studying the interactions between electric currents and the body, I have the knowledge, skill, experience, training and education to render an opinion based on reliable principles and methods as to the technological differences between various electric shock devices and any differences in the effects arising from the use of these devices.

30. Kaufman, Leslie. "Parents defend school's use of shock therapy." *New York Times*, 25 December 2007.

31. https://beta.regulations.gov/docket/FDA-2014-N-0238/document, retrieved 11 May 2020.

32. Ibid.

33. The executive summary of the Proposal to Ban Electrical Stimulation

Devices Used to Treat Self-Injurious or Aggressive Behavior describes Eason's conclusions as follows:

> According to Dr. Eason, when the electrodes are placed on sensitive parts of the body, such as hands, feet, underarms, torso, or neck, all three ESDs are capable of inflicting extreme pain on anyone. Dr. Eason explains that sweating, which may be caused by stress or anxiety about receiving a shock, lowers skin resistance, which in turn may lower one's pain threshold, and that one's pain threshold may also be lowered by repeated shocks. He further concludes all three devices are capable of producing tissue damage due to strong muscle contractions, and all are capable of causing superficial skin burns under certain circumstances. Dr. Eason also concludes that . . . the long-term effects of receiving numerous painful and uncontrollable shocks will be an increased risk for developing ASD or PTSD.

https://www.federalregister.gov/documents/2016/04/25/2016-09433/banned -devices-proposal-to-ban-electrical-stimulation-devices-used-to-treat-self -injurious-or#p-291, retrieved 11 May 2020.

34. Open Public Hearing of the Medical Devices Advisory Committee, Neurological Devices Panel, transcript, 24 April 2014, retrieved 11 May 2020 from https://autistichoya.net/judge-rotenberg-center/#federalgovt. Questions asked of the advisory panel at the at the April 24, 2014, open meeting:

> Question No. 1: In assessing the reasonableness of the risk of illness or injury posed by a device, FDA considers the availability of other treatment options including pharmacological, behavioral, alternative, and experimental therapies for the treatment of SIB and aggressive behavior.
>
> 1a. In general, do you think these other treatments are adequate to address SIB and aggressive behavior?
>
> 1b. Is there a specific subpopulation of patients exhibiting SIB and aggressive behavior for which these options are inadequate?
>
> Question No. 2: When determining whether the risk of illness or injury posed by a device is substantial, FDA will consider whether the risk is important, material, or significant in relation to the device's benefit.
>
> 2a. Please discuss whether available evidence presented at this panel meeting demonstrates that ESDs that are intended to administer a noxious electrical stimulus for the modification of SIB and aggressive behavior provide benefit. If so, please identify any specific population of patients for which effectiveness has been demonstrated. This question was clarified or re-stated as follows: "Do the available evidence presented at the panel meeting show that there is a benefit? that's the yes/no answer. And then if the answer is yes, then what subpopulation, if you can define it.
>
> 2b. FDA has identified the following potential risks related to the use of ESDs that are intended to administer a noxious electrical stimulus for the treatment of Self Injurious Behavior and aggressive behavior: other

negative emotional reactions or behaviors, burns and other tissue damage, anxiety, acute stress/PTSD, fear and aversion/avoidance, pain/discomfort, depression (and possible suicidality), substitution of other negative behaviors (including aggression), psychosis, and neurological symptoms and injury. Please comment on whether this represents a complete list of risks, whether there are any additional risks that you think should be included, and whether any of the risks listed above are not risks posed by ESDs.

Question No. 3: Section 516 of the Food, Drug, and Cosmetic Act (21 U.S.C. § 360f) sets forth the standard for banning devices. Under that provision, FDA is authorized to ban a device if the device presents "an unreasonable and substantial risk of illness or injury" based on all available data and information. Considering the adequacy and availability of alternatives to treat patients exhibiting SIB and aggressive behavior, as well as the benefits ESDs may provide for these patients, please discuss whether ESDs intended to administer a noxious electrical stimulus for the treatment of SIB and aggressive behavior present a substantial and unreasonable risk of illness or injury. In your response, please explain your reasoning.

Question No. 4: If FDA determines that a device does present an unreasonable and substantial risk of illness or injury, the Agency next considers whether this risk may be corrected or eliminated by labeling, and they also consider whether imposing other requirements could correct or eliminate this risk. Please identify potential risk mitigations and discuss how they would address identified risks.

Examples of potential risk mitigation include but are not limited to:
- Restriction on device technology and use (e.g., electrical stimulation output parameters, limitations of number and/or locations of electrodes permitted on an individual).
- Labeling restrictions [e.g., indication only for use in treating only certain populations (e.g., treatment refractory patient populations, patients in certain age groups) or indication for use only when significant injury is being exhibited (e.g., life threatening injuries)].

Question No. 5: If FDA determines that a device presents a substantial and unreasonable risk of illness or injury and proposes to ban it, the Agency must specify whether the ban applies only prospectively or also applies to devices in distribution and/or in use by patients. Please discuss the risks and benefits of applying the ban to devices currently in use by patients and any recommendations regarding how patients should be transitioned to alternative treatments.

Question No. 6: Should the FDA determine not to ban these devices, the Agency may need to determine whether a clinical study could be conducted. Therefore, please discuss what concerns, if any, you may have about conducting a clinical study with these devices in either children or adults.

35. Kern, R. "FDA panel says no to shock therapy device." *MedPage*, 24 April 2014.

36. Ibid.

37. Ibid.

38. Open Public Hearing of the Medical Devices Advisory Committee, Neurological Devices Panel, transcript, 24 April 2014, retrieved 11 May 2020 from https://autistichoya.net/judge-rotenberg-center/#federalgovt.

39. Letter to Stephen Ostroff, commissioner, FDA, 4 June 2014.

National organizations that signed: Access Living, ADAPT, Advocacy Institute, Access Living, Arc of the United States, Association of University Centers on Disabilities, Association of Programs for Rural Independent Living, AutCom, Autistic Self Advocacy Network, Autism Society of America, American Association of People with Disabilities, American Network of Community Options and Resources, Bazelon Center for Mental Health Law, Boston Center for Independent Living, Council of Parent Attorneys and Advocates, Inc., Children and Adults with Attention Deficit Hyperactivity Disorder, Disability & Pride, Disability Rights Center, Disability Rights Education and Defense Fund, Disability Rights International Higher Education, Consortium for Special Education and Teacher Education of the Council for Exceptional Children, Family Alliance to Stop Abuse and Neglect, Family Voices, Lead On, Network Little People of America, Mental Health America, National Association of Councils on Developmental Disabilities, National Association of the Deaf, National Association of State Directors of Special Education, National Autism Association, National Council on Independent Living, National Disability Rights Network, National Down Syndrome Congress, National Down Syndrome Society, National Federation of Families for Children's Mental Health, National Organization of Nurses with Disabilities, Not Dead Yet, Parent to Parent USA, Respect ABILITY Law Center, TASH, United Spinal Association.

State and local organizations that signed: ADAPT Montana, ADAPT New York, AIM Independent Living Center (Corning, NY), Access to Independence of Cortland County, Autistic Self Advocacy Network of Greater Boston, Arc of Illinois, Boston Center for Independent Living, Center for Disability Rights (New York), Directions in Independent Living (Olean, NY), Disability Law Center of Massachusetts, Disability Rights Wisconsin, Easter Seals Massachusetts, Family Voices of New Jersey, Family Voices of Illinois, Family Voices of Tennessee, INCLUDE nyc, Not Dead Yet Montana, PEAK Parent Center, Regional Center for Independent Living (Rochester, NY), Second Thoughts Massachusetts, Self Advocacy Association of New York State, Southern Tier Independence Center (Binghamton, NY), Statewide Parent Advocacy Network (New Jersey), Support for Families (California), TASH New England, Tennessee Disability Coalition, Vermont Family Network, Washington Metro Disabled Students Collective, Westchester Independent Living Center.

40. Ibid.

41. Letter to Dr. Stephen Ostroff, commissioner, U.S. Food and Drug Admin-

istration from Samantha A. Crane, Esq., legal director and director of public policy, Autistic Self Advocacy Network; Christine Griffin, executive director, Disability Law Center of Massachusetts; Jennifer Monthie, director of PADD, PAAT & PATBI Programs, Disability Rights New York; and Nancy R. Weiss, MSW, director, National Leadership Consortium on Developmental Disabilities, University of Delaware, 11 September 2015.

42. Ibid.

43. Department of Health and Human Services, Food and Drug Administration, 21 CFR Parts 882 and 895 [Docket No. FDA-2016-N-1111] Banned Devices; Proposal to Ban Electrical Stimulation Devices Used to Treat Self-Injurious or Aggressive Behavior, Proposed Rule. Retrieved 11 May 2020 from http://federalregister.gov/a/2016-09433.

44. "FDA proposes ban on electrical stimulation devices intended to treat self-injurious or aggressive behavior." FDA news release, 22 April 2016, retrieved 11 May 2020 from https://www.fda.gov/news-events/press-announcements/fda-proposes-ban-electrical-stimulation-devices-intended-treat-self-injurious-or-aggressive-behavior.

45. Ibid.

46. Ibid.

47. Ibid.

48. Letter to Sylvia Burwell, secretary, U.S. Department of Health and Human Services; Robert Califf, M.D., commissioner, FDA; Shaun Donovan, director, Office of Management and Budget; signed by 194 disability organizations, 1 June 2016.

49. Ibid.

50. https://www.hoganlovells.com/en/locations/washington-dc, retrieved 13 May 2020.

51. Kraus,Tom, chief of staff, FDA. Letter to Lina Kontos, counsel, Hogan Lovells US LLP, 3 June 2016.

52. Ibid.

53. https://www.regulations.gov/document?D=FDA-2016-N-1111-1618, retrieved 13 April 2020.

54. Ibid.

55. Ibid.

56. Ibid.

57. Alison Barkoff (Center for Public Representation); David Coulter, M.D., associate professor of neurology, Harvard Medical School, and senior staff neurologist, Boston Children's Hospital; Mary Lee Fay (NASDDDS); Chris Heimerl, M.S.S.W., positive approaches consultant; Ari Ne'eman (ASAN); Maggie Nygren (AAIDD); and Nancy Weiss (NLCDD).

58. Letter to Robert M. Califf, M.D., commissioner, Food and Drug Administration, from the following U.S. senators: Tammy Baldwin, Richard Blumenthal, Cory Booker, Robert Casey, Al Franken, and Christopher Murphy, 22 September 2016.

59. Ibid.

60. Letter to Alex M. Azar II, secretary, HHS, and Scott Gottlieb, M.D., commissioner, FDA. from the following members of Congress: Katherine Clark, Danny K. Davis, Mike Doyle, Jim Langevin, Alan Lowenthal, Sean Patrick Maloney, Seth Moulton, Robert Pittenger, Bill Posey, Jan Schakowsky, David Schweikert, and Christopher H. Smith, 20 September 20.

61. Letter to Robert M. Califf, M.D., commissioner, Food and Drug Administration, from Ari Ne'eman, president, Autistic Self Advocacy Network; Alison Barkoff, J.D., director of Advocacy, Center for Public Representation; and Nancy Weiss, director, National Leadership Consortium on Developmental Disabilities, University of Delaware.

62. Letter to Dr. Robert M. Califf, M.D., MACC commissioner, U.S. Food and Drug Administration, dated 21 December 2016, from Nancy Weiss, signed by: A Better Life, Denver, CO; A Better Way of Living, Albuquerque, NM; Alliance for Person-Centered Accessible Technologies, Tempe, AZ; American Association on Intellectual and Developmental Disabilities (AAIDD), Washington, DC; American Association of People with Disabilities, Washington, DC; American Network of Community Options and Resources (ANCOR), Alexandria, VA; ao Strategies, Palatine, IL; Arc of Massachusetts, Waltham, MA; Arc of the United States, Washington, DC; Arc of New River Valley, Blacksburg, VA; ARC Rutland Area, Rutland, VT; Asperger/Autism Network, Watertown, MA; Association for Autistic Community, Alexandria, VA; Autism Delaware, Newark, DE; Autism Women's Network, Lincoln, NE; Autistic Self Advocacy Network of Greater Boston, Boston, MA; Bazelon Center for Mental Health Law, Washington, DC; Branches of Life, Chester, VA; Capital Recovery Center, Olympia, WA; Center on Disability and Community Inclusion, Burlington, VT; Children's Freedom Initiative, Atlanta, GA; Colorado Bluesky Enterprises, Pueblo, CO; Colorado Developmental Disabilities Council, Denver, CO; Community Haven for Adults and Children with Disabilities, Sarasota, FL; Community Link, Boulder CO; Community Living Victoria, Canada; Council of Parent Attorneys and Advocates, Towson, MD; Council on Quality and Leadership (CQL), Towson, MD; Creative Supports Institute, Boothwyn, PA; Disability Law Center, Boston, MA; Disability Rights Center, Seattle, WA; Disability Rights Vermont, Montpelier, VT; Douglas J. Cartan & Associates, consultants, Brockville, Canada; *Exceptional Parent* magazine, Chattanooga, TN; F I R S T, Asheville, NC; Georgia Advocacy Office, Decatur, GA; Governor's Advisory Council for Exceptional Citizens (GACEC), Dover, DE; Hope House Foundation, Norfolk, VA; Human Services Research Institute, Cambridge, MA; Imagine, Blacksburg, VA; Inclusion Alberta, Edmonton, AB, Canada; Inclusion Press, Toronto, ON, Canada; InclusionWorks!, Victoria, BC, Canada; Institute for Community Inclusion, UMass Boston, Boston, MA; Institute on Disabilities, Philadelphia, PA; International Social Role Valorization Association, Harrisburg, PA; InVision Human Services, Wexford, PA; Jewish Family Service & Children's Center of Clifton/Passaic, Clifton, NJ; Kendrick Consulting International, Holyoke, MA; Key Human Services, Wethersfield, CT; Keystone Institute,

Harrisburg, PA; Keystone Institute India, India; Learning Community for Person Centered Practices, Annapolis, MD; Libraries and Autism: We're Connected, Maplewood, NJ; Linda H. Rammler, consultants, Middlefield, CT; Loveland Center, Venice, FL; Lutheran Services in America Disability Network, Washington, DC; Massachusetts Association for Mental Health, Boston, MA; Massachusetts Developmental Disabilities Council, Quincy, MA; Mental Health Legal Advisors Committee, Boston, MA; Metro Boston Recovery Learning Community, Boston, MA; National Alliance for Direct Support Professionals, Albany NY; National Alliance on Mental Illness–Greater Boston Consumer Advisory Network, Boston, MA; National Alliance on Mental Illness of Massachusetts (NAMI Mass), Boston, MA; National Association of Councils on Developmental Disabilities, Washington, DC; National Council on Independent Living, Washington, DC; Neighbours International, Highland Park, NJ; Northeastern University School of Law Disability Justice Caucus, Boston, MA; Not Dead Yet, Rochester, NY; Occupy the Judge Rotenberg Center, Worcester, MA; OHI, Hermon, ME; Ohio TASH, Westerville, OH; Parent to Parent USA, Washington, DC; Partnership for People with Disabilities at VCU, Richmond, VA; Paul V. Sherlock Center on Disabilities, Providence, RI; People First of Georgia, Lithonia, GA; Port Alberni Association for Community Living, Port Alberni, BC, Canada; Respect ABILITY Law Center, Royal Oak, MI; RISE Services, Mesa, AZ; Self-Advocacy Association of NY State, Schenectady, NY; Self-Advocates Becoming Empowered, Elmhurst, IL.

63. Bruno, D. "An electric shock therapy stops self-harm among the autistic, but at what cost?" *Washington Post Magazine*, 23 November 2016.

64. Ibid.

65. Ibid.

66. Ibid.

67. Ibid.

68. Ibid.

69. https://adapt.org/adapt-demands-the-fda-to-stop-shocking-disabled-people-into-submission/, retrieved 30 April 2020.

70. https://adapt.org/, retrieved 13 May 2020.

71. Adams, H. "ADAPT protests at State House, Judge Rotenberg Center for disability rights; 'I'd rather go to jail than die in Rotenberg!'" *MassLive*, 3 November 2016.

72. https://adapt.org/press-release-pain-and-fear-teach-nothing-an-adapter-reflects-on-the-judge-rotenberg-center/, retrieved 29 April 2020.

73. Ibid.

74. Ibid.

75. Letter to Division of Dockets Management (HFA-305), FDA from Michael P. Flammia, Esq., and attorney with Eckert Seamans, Cherin and Mellott, LLC, Attorneys at Law, on behalf of the Judge Rotenberg Center, dated 7 April 2017; stamped received, 10 April 2017.

76. Letter to Alex M. Azar II, secretary, U.S. Department of Health and Human Services, Scott Gottlieb, commissioner, FDA, and John Michael Mulvaney, di-

rector, Office of Management and Budget, written by the Autistic Self Advocacy Network, signed by 217 disability organizations and advocates, 23 April 2018.

77. Alison Barkoff (Center for Public Representation); Chris Heimerl, M.S.S.W., positive approaches consultant; Nancy Weiss (National Leadership Consortium on Developmental Disabilities, University of Delaware); Julia Bascom (ASAN); David Coulter, M.D. associate professor of neurology, Harvard Medical School, and senior staff neurologist, Boston Children's Hospital; Sam Crane (ASAN); Nicole Jorwic (Arc U.S.); and Maggie Nygren (AAIDD).

78. Represented by Jeffrey Shuren, M.D., J.D., director of the FDA's Center for Devices and Radiological Health and his staff.

79. https://www.change.org/p/fda-ban-torture-of-people-with-disabilities -and-stoptheshock?use_react=false, retrieved 14 May 2020. The petition had 303,843 signatures by this date.

80. Letter to Jeffrey Shuren, M.D., J.D., director, Center for Devices and Radiological Health, FDA, from Julia Bascom, executive director, Autistic Self Advocacy Network; Sam Crane, J.D., director of public policy, Autistic Self Advocacy Network; Margaret A. Nygren, Ed.D., executive director and CEO, American Association on Intellectual and Developmental Disabilities (AAIDD); Nicole Jorwic, J.D., director of Rights Policy Arc of the United States; Brian J. Dion, M.P.A., senior vice president, Innovation and Development Community Options, and board member, TASH; David L. Coulter, M.D., associate professor of neurology, Harvard Medical School, and senior staff neurologist, Boston Children's Hospital; Chris Heimerl, M.S.S.W., positive approaches consultant; and Nancy Weiss, M.S.W., director, National Leadership Consortium on Developmental Disabilities, and director of Disability Initiatives, College of Health Sciences University of Delaware. 29 June 2018.

81. Pilkington, E. "Human rights body calls on U.S. school to ban electric shocks on children." *Guardian*, 18 December 2018.

82. https://www.documentcloud.org/documents/5632074-Resolution-86 -2018-PM-1357-18-US.html, retrieved 14 May 2020.

83. https://www.oas.org/en/iachr/mandate/what.asp, retrieved 14 May 2020.

84. Ibid.

85. https://www.documentcloud.org/documents/5632074-Resolution-86 -2018-PM-1357-18-US.html, retrieved 14 May 2020.

86. Ibid.

87. Pilkington, E. "Human rights body calls on U.S. school to ban electric shocks on children." *Guardian*, 18 December 2018.

88. Ibid.

89. Hanson, Fred. "Under federal investigation, Senator Brian Joyce announces he will not seek re-election." *Patriot Ledger*, 24 February 2016, retrieved 18 May 2020 from https://www.tauntongazette.com/article/20160223 /NEWS/160228501.

90. https://www.mass.gov/service-details/dds-notice-of-public-hearing-and -opportunity-for-public-comment, retrieved 14 May 2020.

91. McKinley, B. "Boston University Statehouse Program. Behavior modification standards under review at Department of Developmental Services." *MetroWest Daily News*, 30 April 2019.

92. Ibid.

93. Ibid.

94. Ibid.

95. Ibid.

96. *Massachusetts Register*, issue 1411, 21 February 2020, 31–79.

97. Pilkington, E. "Founder of electric shock autism treatment school forced to quit." *Guardian*, 25 May 2011. Wen, Patricia, and McGrory, Brian. "Rotenberg founder set to face charges." Boston.com, 25 May 2011.

98. Israel and Weber had cofounded the California Behavior Research Institute in 1977 after Weber visited the BRI in Rhode Island and decided to replicate the program in California to serve her son, Tobin, and other children with disabilities. She hired Israel as the consulting psychologist. In 1979, the board of directors of the North Los Angeles County Regional Center in California halted funding to the California Behavior Research Institute on the basis that the facility had "abused its allegedly 'therapeutic processes', inflicted serious injury to one of its residents, administered non-approved aversives and applied inadequate controls on the use of aversives." As an outcome of a 1982 investigation of the BRI by the California Attorney General's Office, Israel was forbidden to have any involvement in the California-based facility.

99. Adams, J. M. "Controversial psychologist found working at special ed schools." *EdSource*, 27 August 2015.

100. Gafni, M. "Tobinworld special ed campuses suspended by state." *Bay Area News*, 27 August 2015.

101. Ibid.

102. Gafni, M. "Tobinworld schools suspended after shock therapy hire, fudged background checks." *Bay Area News*, 2 September 2015.

103. Gafni, M. "Tobinworld special ed campuses suspended by state." *Bay Area News*, 27 August 2015.

104. Ibid.

105. Coetsee, R. "Tobinworld to close: Antioch special needs school investigated for abuse." *East Bay Times*, 7 July 2016.

106. Janofsky, M. "Tobinworld closing its Antioch school for special education students." *Edsource*, 8 July 2016.

107. Ibid.

108. Smith, K. "Tobinworld special needs school in Glendale to close." *Los Angeles Daily News*, 7 November 2019.

109. http://www.tobinworld.org/#services, retrieved 20 October 2020.

110. Nancy Weiss (NLCDD), Alison Barkoff (Center for Public Representation), Samantha Crane (ASAN), Nicole Jorwic (Arc, U.S.), Maggie Nygren (AAIDD), and Mary Sowers (NASDDDS); meeting held on December 12, 2019, with Danielle Steele representing HHS.

111. Alison Barkoff (Center for Public Representation); David Coulter, M.D., associate professor of neurology, Harvard Medical School, and senior staff neurologist, Boston Children's Hospital; Mary Lee Fay (NASDDDS); Chris Heimerl, M.S.S.W. positive approaches consultant; Ari Ne'eman (ASAN); Maggie Nygren (AAIDD); and Nancy Weiss (NLCDD).

112. Letter to Dr. Stephen M. Hahn, commissioner, FDA, from Senators Patty Murray, Christopher S. Murphy, Bob Casey, Tim Kaine, Maggie Hassan, Doug Jones, Bernie Sanders, and Tina Smith, 10 February 2020.

113. Ibid.

114. Ibid.

115. Murray, P., and Murphy, C. "Democrats urge FDA to immediately ban the use of electrical shock devices on children and adults with disabilities." U.S. Senate Committee Newsroom, 10 February 2020. Retrieved 15 May 2020 from https://www.helsenate.gov/ranking/newsroom/press/murray-murphy -democrats-urge-fda-to-immediately-ban-the-use-of-electrical-shock-devices -on-children-and-adults-with-disabilities-.

116. https://www.federalregister.gov/documents/2020/03/06/2020-04328 /banned-devices-electrical-stimulation-devices-for-self-injurious-or-aggressive -behavior, retrieved 15 May 2020.

117. https://www.regulations.gov/document?D=FDA-2016-N-1111-1743, retrieved 8 October 2020.

118. Ibid.

119. Adams, H. "After FDA bans Judge Rotenberg Center from using electric shock devices, advocates seek public apology, reparations." *MassLive*, 9 March 2020.

120. https://www.federalregister.gov/documents/2020/03/06/2020-04328 /banned-devices-electrical-stimulation-devices-for-self-injurious-or-aggressive -behavior, retrieved 15 May 2020.

121. Ibid.

122. Until 2016, the FDA had banned only one other medical device: prosthetic hair fibers in 1983. The FDA found there was no public health benefit to this device. This device presented a substantial deception to patients or users about the benefits of the device. The prosthetic hair fibers did not stimulate hair growth or conceal baldness and could cause serious infections, illness, and injuries from their implantation. The labeling and advertising materials misrepresented the device as safe, effective, and causing little or no discomfort, among other misleading claims. On December 19, 2016, the FDA published a final rule banning powdered gloves based on the unreasonable and substantial risk of illness or injury to individuals exposed to the gloves. The risks to both patients and health care providers when internal body tissue is exposed to the powder include severe airway inflammation and hypersensitivity reactions. Powder particles may also trigger the body's immune response, causing tissue to form around the particles (granulomas) or scar tissue formation (adhesions) which can lead to surgical complications. Retrieved 15 May 2020 from https://www.fda.gov /medical-devices/medical-device-safety/medical-device-bans.

123. "FDA takes rare step to ban electrical stimulation devices for self-injurious or aggressive behavior." FDA press release, 4 March 2020, retrieved 15 May 2020 from https://www.fda.gov/news-events/press-announcements/fda-takes-rare-step-ban-electrical-stimulation-devices-self-injurious-or-aggressive-behavior.

124. Fortin, Jacey. "F.D.A. bans school electric shock devices." *New York Times*, 6 March 2020, retrieved 18 May 2020 from https://unh.idm.oclc.org/login?url=https://search-proquest-com.unh.idm.oclc.org/docview/2371652303?accountid=14612.

125. Plater, R. "Groups cheer as FDA bans use of electric shock devices used on students." *Healthline*, 11 March 2020.

126. Ibid.

127. Ibid.

128. Ibid.

129. Ibid.

130. U.S. Court of Appeals for the District of Columbia Circuit, The Judge Rotenberg Center, Inc., Petitioner v. United States Food and Drug Administration, et al., Respondents. No. 20-1087, 27 March 2020

131. https://trellis.law/ca/motion-type/motion-to-stay-10, retrieved 15 May 2020.

132. Petition for Stay of Action Pursuant to 21 C.F.R. sec. 10.35, prepared by Eckert Seamans Cherin & Mellott, LLC on behalf of the Judge Rotenberg Center, filed March 20, 2020, 181.

133. Ibid.

134. Ibid.

135. Ibid.

136. Ibid.

137. Ibid.

138. Ibid.

139. Letter to Michael P. Flammia, Eckert, Seamans, Cherin & Mellot, LLC, from Jeffrey E. Shuren, M.D., J.D., director, Center for Devices and Radiological Health, FDA. Re: Petition for Stay of Action, Docket No. FDA-2020-P-1166, 27 March 2020.

140. Letter from Jeffrey Shuren, M.D., J.D. , director, Center for Devices and Radiological Health, FDA to Michael P. Flammia of Eckert, Seamans Cheris & Mellott, LLC, re: Petition for Stay of Action, Docket No. FDA-2020-P-1166, 27 March 2020,

141. Ibid.

142. Ibid.

143. Choma, R. "Schools can no longer use electric shock devices on students says the FDA." *Mother Jones*, 7 March 2020.

1. https://consensus.nih.gov/1989/DestructiveBehaviorsDevelopment075 html.htm, retrieved 29 October 2020.

2. Bambara, L. M., and Kern, L. *Individualized supports for students with problem behaviors: Designing positive behavior plans.* New York: Guilford Press, 2005.

3. Neumeier, S. M., and Brown, L. X. Z. "Torture in the name of treatment: The mission to stop the shocks in the age of deinstitutionalization." In S. K. Kapp (Ed.), *Autistic community and the neurodiversity movement* (195–210). Singapore: Palgrave Macmillan, 2019.

4. Lovett, H. "Empowerment and choices." In L. Meyer, C. Peck, and L. Brown (Eds.), *Critical issues in the lives of people with severe disabilities* (625). Baltimore: Paul H. Brookes, 1989.

5. Foxx, R. M. "Severe aggressive and self-destructive behavior: The myth of the nonaversive treatment of severe behavior." In J. W. Jacobson, R. M. Foxx, and J. A. Mulick (Eds.), *Controversial therapies for developmental disabilities: Fad, fashion and science in professional practice.* Mahwah, NJ: Erlbaum, 2005, 295–310.

6. Mulick, J. A., and Butter, E. M. "Positive behavior support: A paternalistic utopian delusion." In J. W. Jacobson, R. M. Foxx, and J. A. Mulick (Eds.), *Controversial therapies for developmental disabilities: Fad, fashion, and science in professional practice.* Mahwah, NJ: Erlbaum, 2005, 385.

7. Sidman, M. *Coercion and its fallout.* Boston: Authors Cooperative, 1989, vi.

8. Sidman, Murray. Reflection on behavior analysis and coercion. *Behavior and Social Issues* 3:1 & 2 (1993): 78.

9. Brown, F., and Traniello, D. A. (2010). "The path to aversive interventions: Four mothers' perceptions." *Research and Practice for Persons with Severe Disabilities* 35:3–4 (2010), 128–136.

10. Sidman, Murray. "Reflection on behavior analysis and coercion." *Behavior and Social Issues* 3:1 & 2 (1993): 83.

11. Ibid., 81.

12. Msumba, Jennifer. *The fish don't care when it rains.* Easterseals Disability Film Challenge, 13 August 2020.

INDEX

Page numbers in *italics* indicate figures, and those in **bold** indicate tables.

American Association of Mental Deficiency (AAMD), 23, 211, 376n17

American Association on Mental Retardation (AAMR), 147, 163, 165–66, 176, 376n17

American Foundation for Autistic Children, 141, 144

American Foundation for the Blind, 147

American Occupational Therapy Association, 163

American Probation and Parole Association, 282

American Psychological Association (APA), 57, 101, 137, 163, 273, 390n88

Americans with Disabilities Act (ADA), 275

Amnesty International, 199, 274–75

An Act to Protect Disabled Persons, 159, 165, 226

Anderson, Francis, 23

anti-aversive: advocacy, 274; advocates, 56, 100, 124, 153, 157, 159, 162, 164, 166–69, 171, 178–80, 185, 188, 191, 234, 250, 255, 260–61, 273, 296, 300–302; bill, 19, 226, 327; community, 182, 290; legislation/law, 64, 125–26, 157–58, 160, 165, 187, 203–7, 221; vocal activist, 85. *See also* aversives

antipsychotic medications, 17, 84, 256, 258

anxiety, 1; behavioral interventions, 258; life with GEDs, 4; use of aversives, 100, 314

applied behavior: analysis, 12, 29–30, 57, 65; intervention, 50

Applied Physics Laboratory (APL), 136, 138

Arledge, Roone, 126–27

Arterberry, John, 61

Asperger's Syndrome, 6, 273, 298

asphyxia, 17, 97

Association for Behavior Analysis (ABA), 155–56

Association for Persons with Severe Handicaps, The (TASH), 10, 13, 23, 105, 115, 165, 176, 211, 339n13; anti-aversive advocates, 250; board of directors, 262; purpose, 24

Association for Retarded Children, 165

Association for Retarded Citizens (ARC), 13, 23, 28, 105, 131, 147–48, 163, 176–77

Association for Social Design, 25

Association for the Advancement of Behavior Therapy, 29

Association for the Education and Treatment of the Severely and Profoundly Handicapped (AESEPH), 23

Association of Applied Behavioral Analysis, 211

Aswad, Danny, 60–61, 161, 340n18

attention deficit disorder, 268

autism, 9, 26, 33; adults with, 36, 77, 172, 268, 319; children with, 11, 25–26, 41, 44, 68, 77, 90, 109, 132, 137; conference in Boston, 12–13; people with, 12, 23, 36

Autism Research Institute, 65

Autism Society of America (ASA), 11, 65, 147, 176

Autism Society of California, 344n24

autistic children, 26, 41, 44, 68, 77, 90, 109, 132, 137

Autistic Self Advocacy Network (ASAN), 274, 313

automatic vapor spray station (AVS), 89, 117

aversives: approaches, 24; behavior interventions, 52–53, 56–57; conditioning, 81, 397n177; consequences, 28; defined, 14; exceptions to order to cease use of, 109–10; interventions, 8, 10,

Boston Center for Independent Living, 288

Boston Housing Authority, *114*

Bowen, John, 31

Braddock, David, 168

Brady, Joseph, 168

Brandeis Students United, 274

Bricker, Diane, 23

Briggs, Bettina, 234, 236

Brink, Richard, 356n78

Bristol County Probate Court, 114, 119

Brokaw, Tom, 98

Bronston, Bill, 45–46, 49, 52–53

Bronston, Samuel, 39

Bronston, William, 39, 69

Brooklyn, New York, 257

Brown, Edmund "Pat," 55–56

Brown, Gerald "Pat" Sr., 44–45, 50–52

Brown, Jerry, 45, 55

Brown, Lou, 11–12, 23

Brown, Lydia X. Z., 274, 313–14

Bucher, Bradley, 99

Burgess, Anthony, 136

Burns, Arthur, 97–98

Butter, Eric M., 321

Cabral, Donna, 207

Caffersion, Mary B., 85

Calcagno, Phillip, 141

Calderon, Benjamin N., 55

California, 9, 11, 35, 36–64, 68–70, 78, 100; advent of BRI in, 37–38; allegations of physical abuse, 58–59; Aswad, Danny's death, 60–61; attempts to revoke BRI's license, 61–64; BRI's future in, 44–54; disability community in, 37; Northridge, 12

California Advisory Commission on Special Education, 64

California Behavior Research Institute, 412n98

California Board of Education, 44, 64

California Board of Medical Quality Assurance, 42

California Community for Autistic Persons, 343n5

California Department of Developmental Services, 49, 53

California Department of Education, 44, 311

California Department of Health, 37, 39–40, 49, 53

California Department of Social Services (DSS), 48, 53, 54, 62, 68, 347n76

California Department of Social Welfare, 138

California Society for Autistic Children, 37, 47

Campaign Against Violence, 87

Campbell, Magda, 168, 244

Campbell, Philip, 181–82, 192–94, 208–11, 227–28, 234–35, 241–42, 245–47, 249–50, 253–55, 367n31; action against BRI, 196; attack from pro-institution advocates, 222; compliance with state regulations, 217; contempt, 248–53; job loss, 17; against JRC, 11, 224; letter from Israel, 200; MacLeish against, 93

Canton, Massachusetts, 10, 19

Carr, Andrew, 54, 145

Casey, George, 233

Casey, Robert, 304

Casoria, Carlo, 233

Casoria, Janine, 107–10, 119, 122, 356n91

Cataldo, Michael, 167

Cataldo, Paul, 234

Center for Devices and Radiological Health, 145

Center for Public Representation, 189

Centers for Medicare and Medicaid Services (CMS), 291–92, 334

Cerreto, Mary, 17, 163, 208–9, 230–33, 242, 245, 247, 249, 367n31

Eye to Eye with Connie Chung (Rybak), 200–203, 218, 242

Fairbanks, Ronald, 48
Fair Hearing (administration process), 48
Farrell Instrument of Grand Island, Nebraska, 146
Favell, Judith E., 115, 168
Federal Advisory Committee Act, 173
Federal Civil Rights Act of 1983, 253
Federal Communications Commission, 47
Federal Food, Drug, and Cosmetic Act (the FD&C Act), 145, 149, 287, 398n181
Ferleger, David, 124–25, 157, 196, 248
Ferrara, Joseph A., 185
Ferster, Charles B., 21
Field, Katherine, 293
Fine & Ambrogne, 129
Fink, Joan, 90, 96–97, 109–10
Finn, Fred F., 351n46
Finneran, Thomas M., 226
Fischell, Robert E., 144
Fiset, Christopher, 234
Flammia, Michael, 234, 265, 307, 315
Flanagan, Chris, 102
Flanagan, Mary, 92
Flanagan, Robert, 102
Fogerty Center, 25
Food and Drug Administration (FDA), 1, 14, 217; action against BRI, 236; approval to market SIBIS, 166; approved clinical trial, 146; DMR and, 217; electric shock devices, 136, 257, 312–13; failure of JRC to obtain clearance from, 287; graduated electronic decelerator, 284–89, 295–317; minimum standards, 303; premarket notification, 145, 286; withdraw registration of SIBIS, 148. *See also* electric shock on people with disabilities

food deprivation, 15, 31, 89–90, 136, 197, 228, 273, 291
Foxx, Richard, 25, 168, 321
Franken, Al, 304
Franklin N. Flaschner Award, 186, 356n78
Frazier, Shervert, 131
Fredericks, Robert W., 37, 40
Freedom of Information Act 121; Request, 14
French, Joseph, 168
Froemming, Roy, 214

Gallant, Joseph, 254
Garrahy, J. Joseph, 30–33
Gately, Peter M., 244
Gerry, Martin H., 178
Gibson, Abigail, 161
Gibson, Paul, 144
Gillis, Larry, 255
Glassman, Rick, 299
Glavin Regional Center, 16
Gleich, James, 157
Gold, Mark, 23
Goldman, Mari, 44, 53–54
Goldman, Stan, 187
Gonnerman, Jennifer, 272, 339n1, 356n91
Gonzalez, Silverio, 255–56, 322
Goodman, Walter, 202–3
Gottlieb, Scott, 305
government, 208–33; court, 230–34; experimental treatment, 217–18; former employees and parents, 218–20; human rights, 223–26; Judge Rotenberg Center, 220–23, *221*; LaStaiti, Elizabeth, 229–30; legislate against aversives, 226; Rivendell Team of Minnesota, 210–17; showdown, 227–29; Tuesday Morning Group, 208–9
graduated electronic decelerator (GED), 136, 149–50; approval for, 5; cause of behavior problems, 4;

64–65, 67–70, 77, 182, 266–68;
attempts to change behavior
modification regulations, 309–10;
attempts to regulate JRC, 293–94;
aversive interventions, 53; BRI in,
12; JRC, 20; judges in, 15; lawmak-
ers, 16; litigation in, 29; permitting
and regulating aversives, 157–61
Massachusetts Appeals Court, 106,
111, 114
Massachusetts Association for
Retarded Citizens, 165
Massachusetts Attorney General's
Office, 277
Massachusetts Board of Bar Over-
seers, 101
Massachusetts Board of Education,
116
Massachusetts Civil Liberties Union,
92, 105
Massachusetts Civil Rights Act, 253
Massachusetts Coalition for the Legal
Rights of People with Disabilities,
215
Massachusetts Department of
Developmental Disabilities, 265
Massachusetts Department of
Developmental Services (DDS), 62,
279–80, 293, 309–10, 388n64
Massachusetts Department of Early
Education and Care, 270, 283,
395n158
Massachusetts Department of
Education (DOE), 28, 46, 52, 67–70,
72, 75, 88, 159, 266
Massachusetts Department of Mental
Health, 106, 117–18, 157–58
Massachusetts Department of Mental
Retardation, 140, 157–58, 165, 203,
225, 279
Massachusetts Department of
Professional Licensure, 264
Massachusetts Department of Social
Services, 271

Massachusetts Disability Law Center,
85, 244, 288, 308
Massachusetts Disabled Persons
Protection Commission, 225, 283,
395n158
Massachusetts Division of Special
Education, 68
Massachusetts Executive Office
of Health and Human Services
(EOHHS), 291, 349n8
Massachusetts Federation for
Children, 87, 92
Massachusetts Office for Children
(OFC), 61, 69, 71–72, 88–89, 129,
132, 155, 189, 349n8, 352n14; BRI's
request for variances of, 115–17;
denying BRI's variance requests to
use aversives, 118–19; OFC *versus*
probate court, 110–112; regula-
tions, 110–11
Massachusetts Office of Handicapped
Affairs (OHA), 124, 379n58
Massachusetts Office on Disability,
233, 379n58
Massachusetts Psychological
Association, 76, 105, 115
Massachusetts Society for Autism, 87
Massachusetts State Review Board,
69–70, 72
Massachusetts Supreme Judicial
Court (SJC), 183–85, 227
Matson, Johnny L., 119, 131, 165,
359n134
Maurer, Adam, 57
McCarthy, Mary, 181–82
McClure, Betty, 89–90, 98, 121
McCollins, Andre, 63, 257–61, 290
McCollins, Cheryl, 257–58, 260
McConnell, John, 46
McKnight, Arthur Duncan, 183
McKnight, Christopher David, 183–84
McKnight, David, 184
McKnight, Duncan, 219, 233
McVeigh, Billy, 7–8, 31–32

McVeigh, Sheila, 78

McVeigh, William, 7, 78

Meacham, Marianne, 265

Medicaid, 249, 254, 291–92, 400n198, 400n200

Méndez, Juan, 279, 309

Mental Disability Rights International, 20, 278

Mental Health, Retardation, and Hospitals (MHRH), 34

Mental Health Law Project, 147, 176

Mental Health Legal Advisors Committee, 308

Mesa, Deacon Ricardo, 13

Meyer, Lisa, 98

Meyer, Luanna, 100, 105, 115, 156, 167

Michigan State Protection and Advocacy, 165

Mikulski, Barbara, 179

Miles, Steven, 300

Millard, Anne Marie, 204, 218

Miller, Greg, 263–64

Milletich, Eric, 112, 118–19

Milletich, Mary Ann, 87, 127

Milletich, Vincent, 17, 61, 84–135, 161, 181, 207; admitted to BRI, 84; anti-aversive, 124–26; "biased" experts, 106–7; BRI civil lawsuit, 126–27; BRI seeking preliminary injunction, 119–21; BRI's request for variances of OFC regulations, 115–17; BRI *versus* Leonard, 113–15; closure of residences, 89–92; exceptions to the order to cease use of aversives, 109–10; inquest into death of, 85, 127–29, *128*, 133–35; legal fees, 129–30; Leonard, Mary Kay, 121–24; MacLeish, Roderick (Eric) Jr., 93–95, *94*; Massachusetts Office for Children (OFC) attempt to decertify BRI, 88–9; OFC, 130–32; OFC *versus* probate court, 110–12; phenylketonuria (PKU), 84–85; plan to remove students

from BRI, 117–18; research on use of aversives, 98–100; Rotenberg, Ernest, 107–9; settlement decree, 135; substituted judgment, 133; Tourette syndrome, 84

Mintz, Jim, 126

Misilo, Fred, 194, 208

Mizner, Susan, 305

Mollins, Ken, 261, 264

Montgomery, Cal, 307

Montpelier, Vermont, 118

Morris, Edward, 155

Morrissey, Gerald J., 250, 254

Morse, Thomas, 123

Moser, Hugo W., 141

Moss, John, 32

Msumba, Jennifer, 1–6, 190, 289–90, *289*, 296, 298, 319, 323, 400n194–95

Mulick, James A., 321

Murdock, Kim, 61, 121, 181, 192, 196, 208, 213, 252, 254, 382n60

Murphy, Christopher, 304, 312

Murray, Patty, 312

muscle squeezes, 49, 75, 89–90, 121, 225

Nadeau, Gilbert "Gil," 247–48

Nader, Moss, 45, 54

Nader, Ralph, 106

National Aeronautics and Space Administration (NASA), 143

National Association for Retarded Citizens (NARC), 69

National Association of Developmental Disabilities Councils, 176

National Association of Protection and Advocacy Services (NAPAS), 13, 176

National Association of Rehabilitation Facilities, 176

National Association of School Psychologists, 282

National Association of Social Workers, 163

BRANDEIS SERIES IN LAW AND SOCIETY

Rosalind Kabrhel, J.D., and Daniel Breen, J.D., Editors

Justice Louis D. Brandeis once said that "if we desire respect for the law, we must first make the law respectable." For Justice Brandeis, making the law "respectable" meant making it work in the interests of humankind, as a help rather than a hindrance in the manifold struggles of persons of all backgrounds to achieve justice. In that spirit, the Law and Society Series publishes works that take interdisciplinary approaches to law, drawing richly from the social sciences, and humanities, with a view towards shedding critical light upon the variety of ways in which legal rules, and the institutions that enforce them, affect our lives. Intended for practitioners, academics, students, and the interested general public, this series will feature titles that contribute robustly to contemporary debates about law and legal reform, all with a view towards adding to efforts of all sorts to make the law "respectable."

For a complete list of books
that are available in the series, visit
brandeisuniversitypress.com

ABOUT THE AUTHORS

Jan Nisbet is professor emeritus at the University of New Hampshire (UNH). Prior to retiring in 2020, she served for ten years as the senior vice provost for research. Before assuming that position, she was the founding director of the Institute on Disability and a tenured professor in the Department of Education at UNH. She received her Ph.D. from the University of Wisconsin in 1982. She has published extensively in the field of disabilities; served on several organizational, editorial, and advisory boards; and has presented nationally and internationally. She has been a principal investigator on many state and nationally funded projects related to children and adults with disabilities. She is the recipient of UNH's Excellence in Research Award, its Alumni Association's Award for Excellence in Public Service, and the Charles Holmes Pettee Medal awarded in recognition of outstanding accomplishment or distinguished service to the state, nation, or the world. She has written numerous articles and edited several books, including *Part of the Community: Strategies for Community Membership* (2000) and *Natural Supports in School, at Work, and in the Community for People with Severe Disabilities* (1992).

Nancy R. Weiss is a faculty member and the director of the National Leadership Consortium on Developmental Disabilities at the University of Delaware. The National Leadership Consortium is a partnership of eighteen national disability organizations focused on ensuring the quality and commitment of the next generation of disability leaders. She is also the director of disability initiatives for the College of Health Sciences at the University of Delaware and directs the university's master's program in leadership in disability services.

Weiss has more than forty years of experience in the field of intellectual and developmental disabilities. She has worked extensively providing community living and positive behavioral supports. She was the former executive director of TASH, an international advocacy association committed to the full inclusion of people with disabilities, and was the director of the Department for Community Services at the Kennedy Krieger Institute in Baltimore. She also served as the executive director of Community Systems, an agency providing progressive supports for adults with intellectual and developmental disabilities.

She is the recipient of the 2007 Presidential Award of the American Association on Intellectual and Developmental Disabilities "for career-long commitment to lives of independence, satisfaction and meaning for people with disabilities; exemplary leadership, and unflinching advocacy," the 2015 American Association on Intellectual and Developmental Disabilities' Dybwad Humanitarian Award, and the 2015 TASH Positive Behavior Support Award.